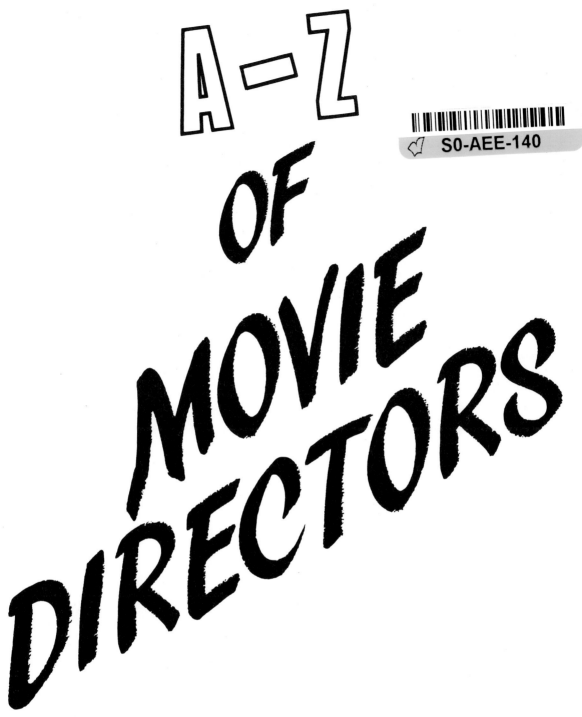

A-Z OF MOVIE DIRECTORS

RONALD BERGAN

PROTEUS
LONDON & NEW YORK

PROTEUS BOOKS is an imprint of
The Proteus Publishing Group.

United States
PROTEUS PUBLISHING CO INC
9 West 57th Street, Suite 4504
New York, NY 10019

distributed by
THE SCRIBNER BOOK COMPANIES, INC
597 Fifth Avenue
New York, NY 10017

United Kingdom
PROTEUS (PUBLISHING) LTD
Bremar House
Sale Place
London W2 1PT

ISBN 0 86276 066 6 (paperback)
0 86276 067 4 (hardback)

First published in UK 1982
First published in US 1983

Editor: Chris Goodwin
Design: Dave Fudger
Typeset by SX Composing Ltd
Printed and bound in Spain by Printer Industria Grafica sa, Barcelona
D.L.B. 29277 – 1982

Photo credits:
Joel Finler
The Kobal Collection
The National Film Archive
Flashback Archive

Author's Note

The only good director is a dead director, at least in a book that strives to be as up-to-date as possible. As I write, there are directors emerging from obscurity, renowned ones adding to their filmographies and new wunderkinder being discovered. Nevertheless, this *A-Z of Movie Directors* does include the young and the old, the quick and the dead, the significant and not so significant, international independent geniuses, Hollywood greats, studio hacks, cult figures, Third World film-makers, 'underground' and experimental directors and the more well-known animators. My main criterion has been to include those directors whose work has been widely shown (whether in commercial cinemas or 'art houses') in the English-speaking world.

I have not attempted to suppress my personal likes and dislikes, prejudices, blind-spots or enthusiasms. Often I'm in agreement with the critical consensus on a director but at times find myself out on a limb. And, although I haven't opted for a bland, dry-as-dust approach, I hope to have given the reader enough objective information to be able to assess the type, quality, content and style of each director's work.

Filmographies

It would have been misleading in a book of this nature to list full filmographies; as some studio-contract directors made literally hundreds of movies, this would have meant, say, George Archainbaud having a far longer entry than Antonioni, and Lloyd Bacon taking up more space than Bunuel. In general, every significant title or those most representative of the director are mentioned. The 'Also' list is neither exhaustive nor qualitative, but acts as a general guide to the reader.

Titles

Foreign films are given the English title only when it is a direct translation from the original. eg. Truffaut's *Shoot the Pianist* for *Tirez sur le Pianiste*, but both titles are given for *Day for Night* (*La Nuit Americaine*). Films such as *L'Avventura*, *La Dolce Vita*, *Pather Panchali* and *Le Million* remain untranslated, because this is how they are generally referred to in English. The differences between US and British titles are only given where there might be confusion. eg. *The Longest Yard* (*The Mean Machine* – GB), but not *Hallelujah, I'm a Bum* (*Hallelujah, I'm a Tramp* – GB).

Ronald Bergan

ABRAHAMS Jim

American. Born 1944. Part of the triumvirate that directed *Airplane* (1980). The others were brothers Jerry and David ZUCKER. All three attended Wisconsin U. and in 1971 opened the Kentucky Fried Theater, later devising *Kentucky Fried Movie* (1977). They wrote, directed and produced *Airplane* for Paramount at a cost of 3.5 million dollars. A big money-maker, it was an outrageous and undisciplined spoof on the *Airport* cycle of movies. Most of the humour belies the age of the directors.

AKERMAN Chantal

Belgian. Born 1950. Certain feminists place Akerman's minimalist films rather high. Her camera generally remains fixed, recording what little happens in front of it. Her best known and most characteristic film is *Jeanne Dielman, 23 quai du Commerce, 1080 Bruxelles* (1975) which shows the minutiae of three days (225 mins of film time) in the life of a Belgian housewife and part-time prostitute (Delphine Seyrig) where the act of peeling potatoes is given as much importance as anything else. **Others:** *News from Home* (76), *Les Rendezvous d'Anna* (78).

ALBICOCCO Jean-Gabriel

French. Born 1937. Worked as assistant to Jules DASSIN before making his first film, *La Fille aux yeux d'or* (1968), an adaptation of a Balzac story, starring his wife, Marie Laforet. His only film to make any impact outside France was *Le Grand Meaulnes (The Wanderer* 1969), a flashy attempt to recreate the fairy-tale atmosphere of the adolescent's classic novel.

ALDA Alan

American. Born 1936. Son of actor Robert Alda. 'Hawkeye' in M*A*S*H TV series. Wrote and directed many episodes, always trying to extend the limitations of the genre. The same can't be said for his first feature as director, *The Four Seasons* (1981), a well-observed but complacent tale of middle-aged friends.

ALDRICH Robert

American. Born 1918. First job in films as production clerk for RKO. Worked as first assistant to RENOIR, MILESTONE, LOSEY, etc. Directed TV series (The Doctor, China Smith) until MGM offered him his first feature, *The Big Leaguer* (1953). Something of a maverick in Hollywood terms, he has struggled long for creative independence. To this end he became his own producer in 1955 with *Kiss Me Deadly,* a multi-layered film noir that uses a Mickey Spillane story to make an anti-McCarthy statement. It is still considered by many critics to be his best film. His career since has had more downs that ups. Aldrich's bludgeoning style can be described by the titles of three of his films – *Attack!* (1956), *The Big Knife* (1955) and *Hustle* (1975). His characters tend toward the hysterical and his direction often matches them. Overhead shots, vast close-ups, shock cuts and angles leave little to the spectator's imagination. In the Gothic extravagances of *What Ever Happened to Baby Jane?* (1962), the Hollywood histrionics of *The Big Knife* (1955) and *The Legend of Lylah Claire* (1968), and the grotesque dykeries of *The Killing of Sister George* (1968), the performers are like opera singers trying to be heard over a loud orchestra, in this case the over-the-top direction. Given his virile, unsubtle approach, Aldrich's most successful movies have been those with all-male subjects, demonstrating his central theme of 'man's efforts to prevail against impossible odds'. *Attack* (1956) and *The Dirty Dozen* (1966) are powerful but chillingly ambiguous war pictures. *Ulzana's Raid* (1972) with its 'Vietcong' Apaches and the *violently* funny *The Longest Yard* (1974; *The Mean Machine* GB) help one forget recent aberrations such as *The Choirboys* (1977) and *The Frisco Kid* (1979). **Others:** *Apache* (54), *Vera Cruz* (54), *Autumn Leaves* (56), *The Garment Jungle* (57), *10 Seconds to Hell* (58), *The Angry Hills* (59), *The Last Sunset* (61), *Sodom and Gomorrah* (with Sergio LEONE, 62), *4 For Texas* (63), *Hush, Hush, Sweet Char-* lotte (64), *The Flight of the Phoenix* (65), *Too Late the Hero* (69), *The Grissom Gang* (71), *Emperor of the North* (73), *Twilight's Last Gleaming* (77), *All the Marbles (California Dolls* – GB 1981).

ALEA Tomas Gutierrez

Cuban. Born 1928. Studied in Rome. Although he made a documentary about coal miners in 1955, it was only after the 1959 revolution that he could begin to make feature films. Castro's revitalization of the film industry, allowed creative scope to film-makers. *Death of a Bureaucrat* (1966) is an amusing satire on Red red-tape and *Memories of Underdevelopment* (1968) subtly and ironically examines the role of the intellectual in the new Cuba. In *The Last Supper* (1976), Alea used colour for the first time with excellent results.

ALEXANDROV Grigori

Russian. Born 1903. Worked as stage-manager in Meyerhold's Moscow theatre before becoming EISENSTEIN's assistant at the age of twenty-one. He collaborated on and acted in *Strike* (1924), *Battleship Potemkin* (1925) and *October* (1928), but left Eisenstein after a clash of ideas on the ill-fated *Que Viva Mexico*. Started his career as director of four pleasant Hollywood-style musicals, *Internationale* (1932), *Jazz Comedy* (1934), *Circus* (1936), and *Volga-Volga* (1938). After becoming artistic director of Mosfilm in 1944, his meagre output tended towards 'socialist realism' and academicism with *Glinka* (1952), *Lenin in Poland* (1961) and *Star and Lyra* (1973).

ALLÉGRET Marc

French. 1900-1973. In 1925 accompanied his patron André Gide on a trip to the Congo, bringing back a full-length documentary, *Voyage au Congo*. Gide encouraged him to devote himself to the cinema. His best films, made in the 30's, show a delicacy of touch and a sense of fantasy. He directed Raimu in more than five films, Louis Jouvet, Charles Boyer and Michele Morgan, as well as giving many future stars their first breaks (Simone Simon, Jean-Pierre Aumont, Jeanne Moreau). He is most widely known outside France for *Fanny* (1932), the second and best part of the PAGNOL trilogy. His work declined considerably in the 50's as younger directors emerged. **Others:** *Lac Aux Dames* (34),

A–Z

OF

MOVIE

DIRECTORS

Tony Roberts, Woody Allen and Diane Keaton in *Annie Hall* (1977)

Gribouille (37), *Orage* (38), *Entreé des Artistes* (38), *Blanche Fury* (GB 47), *Lady Chatterley's Lover* (55), *Le Bal du Comte d'Orgel* (69).

ALLÉGRET Yves

French. Born 1907. Brother of Marc ALLÉGRET. As different from his brother as *craie et fromage*. Marc was 30's gay, Yves was 40's gloom. He was married to Simone Signoret from 1944-1949 with whom he made three doom-laden films: *Dédée d'Anvers* (1947), *Une Si Jolie Petite Plage* (1948) and *Manèges* (1949). His kind of poetic-realism faded in the 50's and 60's and so did his career.

ALLEN Irwin

American. Born 1916. Writer/producer with a taste for science fiction, fantasy and one of the main perpetrators of the disaster-movie craze of the 70's. Directed many of his own productions including *The Lost World* (1960), *5 Weeks in a Balloon* (1962), *Towering Inferno* (with John

GUILLERMIN 1974), *The Swarm* (1978) and *Beyond the Poseidon Adventure* (1979).

ALLEN Lewis

British. Born 1905. Former stage director who went to Hollywood in 1942. After a good debut with *The Uninvited* (1944), a ghost story, he made a string of workmanlike movies for Paramount until 1949. As a freelance, he made a plodding biopic *Valentino* (1951), an undistinguished thriller with Sinatra *Suddenly* (1954) and two formula movies with Edward G. Robinson *A Bullet for Joey* (1955), *Illegal* (1956). Returned to England to make *Another Time, Another Place* (1958), a ludicrous melodrama with Lana Turner.

ALLEN Woody

American. Born 1935 (in Flatbush NY as Allen Stewart Konigsberg). Before directing, he was a writer and stand-up comic who took his own obsessions, mainly his relationship with women, his analyst and Death,

as his subject matter. He extended and elaborated on this material when he began to make his own films. As a performer he combines the chutzpah of Groucho Marx with the wise-cracking cowardice of Bob Hope, using humour to deflate or make bearable serious situations. Not the romantic type physically, being short, freckled and bespectacled, he beds the most beautiful women in the name of the average male spectator. His first five films were constructed as closely-linked revue sketches, although in *Love and Death* (1976), a witty pastiche of 19th century Russian literature, more attention was paid to form. *Annie Hall* (1977) was a breakthrough. One of the most successful pictures of a relationship (based on his own with Diane Keaton), it also manages to be satiric about California, TV pap, media people, WASPS and his own Jewish identity. *Manhattan* (1979) is a paean to the city he loves, although his view of himself comes a close second. It contains stunning black and white photography counterpointed by the music of Gershwin. *Interiors* (1978), the first movie he made without his presence in front of the camera, sometimes verges on parody. Expertly made, it dissects a cold goy family who are figuratively and literally given the kiss of life by a warm outsider. Despite its faults, *Interiors* is a worthy homage to Ingmar BERGMAN. *Stardust Memories* (1980) merely filched FELLINI's stylistic devices to make a hollow statement. Few films have so subjectively portrayed how the famous see the fans and bores that pester them. However, the point is hammered home relentlessly, and where his other films are astringent, this is merely sour. But it is consistent with the rest of his oeuvre, being a necessary catharsis. Self-absorbed as he is, he has managed to speak to a whole generation of intelligent New Yorkers, and communicate to those outside his own age group and city. **Others:** *Take the Money and Run* (69), *Bananas* (71), *Everything you always wanted to know about Sex* (72), *Sleeper* (73), *A Midsummer Night's Sex Comedy* (82).

ALLIO Rene
French. Born 1924. Made his name as costume and set designer in the theatre in France and England. His first film is also his best known. *The Shameless Old Lady (La Vieille Dame Indigne* 1966), based on a story by Brecht, laid on both the charm and the message rather thickly. Politically committed to the Left, he uses traditional forms. His largest enterprise to date is a costume drama, *Les Camisards* (1970).

ALTMAN Robert
American. Born 1925. German-Catholic family. Raised in Kansas City, Missouri. Left the church in 1943. A B.54 bomber pilot during the war. Made industrial films and worked in TV for seven years (Bonanza, etc.). After directing four forgettable movies, Altman was offered *M*A*S*H* because 'fourteen more acceptable directors turned it down'. It grossed 41 million dollars and won the Cannes Grand Prix. Its iconoclasm struck a responsive chord in a disenchanted nation who saw its Korean War setting as a reference to Vietnam. Only two of his subsequent movies *Nashville* (1975) and *Popeye* (1981), did well at the box-office. Altman's individualism gained him the reputation for being a difficult

man for producers to work with. (He was fired from *Ragtime* (1981). Unusual by American standards, he has refused to make formula pictures, trying to do something different with each film. Nevertheless, they are all shot in the rectangular-shaped Panavision. He also likes to use the same actors and technicians from film to film, often getting his performers to write or improvise their own dialogue. His experimental use of sound is an important feature. The simultaneous conversations and loudspeaker announcements in *M*A*S*H* (1970), the 8-track sound system in *California Split* (1974) and the 16 tracks in *Nashville,* produce sounds heard, overheard, misheard and garbled. There is no music score in *Thieves Like Us* (1973) except the constant music from the radio. Altman adeptly maps out imaginary areas where a group of people are brought together for a particular purpose. Innovative is his manipulation of twenty-four characters in *Nashville* and forty in *A Wedding* (1978), requiring expert editing. However, despite the admirable aspects of his films, they are interestingly wrapped packages with nothing much inside. The two boorish sexist heroes of *M*A*S*H*, riding rough-shod over everybody are accepted at face-value. *Brewster McCloud* (1971) is a whimsical satire as dated as the flower-child philosophy it presents. *McCabe and Mrs Miller* (1971) is over-burdened with contemporary allusions. *Images* (1972) is a tricksily shot view of mental illness. *The Long Goodbye* (1972) reduces Chandler to a Hollywood party game. *Three Women* (1977) and *Quintet* (1979) are as deadly as listening to a stranger's dreams. *Health* (1980) and *Nashville* are glib and confused political allegories. As Altman himself admits, 'I have nothing to say . . . I have no philosophy'. **Others:** *The James Dean Story* (with George W. George 57), *Countdown* (68), *That Cold Day in the Park* (68), *Buffalo Bill and the Indians* (76), *A Perfect Couple* (79), *Come Back to the Five and Dime, Jimmy Dean, Jimmy Dean* (82).

ALVAREZ Santiago
Cuban. Born 1919. Joined Cuban Communist Party in 1942. Imprisoned more than once by Batista's regime. After the revolution in 1959, started to make weekly newsreels. In the 60's, using newsreel footage, stills, cartoons and various other devices, he made a name as a leading

exponent of agit-prop documentaries. 'Cinema is not an extension of revolutionary action. Cinema is and must be revolutionary action in itself,' he believes. The Vietnam war provided him with material for many of his best short films, *Hanoi, Tuesday 13* (1967), *LBJ* (1968), *79 Springs* (1969).

ANDERSON Lindsay
British. Born 1923 in India. Son of an army officer. Educated at Cheltenham public school and Oxford. Gained attention as a harsh critic in *Sequence,* an influential quarterly film magazine (1946-1952). Became part of the movement called Free Cinema (with Tony RICHARDSON and Karel REISZ) which moved from the middle-class dominated British films towards more naturalistic movies about the working classes. His first feature, *This Sporting Life* (1963) is an over-directed but powerful story set in the industrial north; *If* (1968) (a virtual remake of VIGO's *Zero de Conduit*) is an eclectic but cogent view of the public school ethos, *O Lucky Man* (1972) and *Brittania Hospital* (1982) over-ambitious and long-winded satires on the State of the Nation. Somehow, despite or because of a handful of films, Anderson has gained the reputation as the keeper of the British cinema's conscience. Unlike most of his contemporaries, he has not gone in for Transatlantic blockbusters but has remained British to the core. There is still something touchingly 60's about his films, relics of the satire boom of the period, made by an 'Angry Old Man'. As an in-joke, he was cast as a stuffy member of the Establishment in *Chariots of Fire* (1981).

ANDERSON Michael
British. Born 1920. Entered the film business at 15 as an office boy at Elstree Studios. After a series of jobs in the studio and assisting Peter USTINOV on two films, he directed his first feature in 1950. He alternates between Hollywood and Britain, making fairly competent commercial pictures with big stars. His first big pay-day came with Mike Todd's star-studded but unscintillating *Around the World in 80 Days* (1956).**Others:** *The Dam Busters* (1955), *1984* (1955), *Yangtse Incident* (1956), *Operation Crossbow* (1965), *The Quiller Memorandum* (1966), *The Shoes of the Fisherman* (1968), *Orca* (1977).

ANGELOPOULIS Theo

Greek. Born 1936. Only recently emerged on to the international scene after the seven years of military dictatorship in Greece. The main body of his work is the impressive triptych of *Days of 36* (1972), *The Travelling Players* (1975) and *The Huntsmen* (1977). The films are long (often over three hours), slow moving, rather impenetrable but ultimately rewarding allegories of Greek history and politics of this century. Using pauses, slow pans, long sequence shots, he attempts to give the spectator time to assess the films rationally.

ANGER Kenneth

American. Born 1929. At six played the Indian changeling in the 1935 film of *A Midsummer Night's Dream*. At seventeen made *Fireworks* (1947), a surrealist movie heavily influenced by Jean COCTEAU. Using dynamic montage, most of his films are ritualistic happenings awash with Satanic and homoerotic imagery which, to the uninitiated, are protracted, meaningless and self-indulgent. *Scorpio Rising* (1964) with its leather bike-boys orgy juxtaposed with clips from DE MILLE's *King of Kings* (1927) could be said to be a seminal force in the U.S. Underground cinema.

ANNAKIN Ken

British. Born 1914. Worked as a journalist, actor and theatre director before embarking on the lucrative career of directing about 35 'entertainment' movies in 35 years including block-busters for Zanuck and Disney. His only 'non-commercial' film, *Across the Bridge* (1957) with Rod Steiger was also his most interesting. **Others:** *The Planter's Wife* (1952), *Three Men in a Boat* (1956), *The Swiss Family Robinson* (1960), *The Longest Day* (1962), *Those Magnificent Men in Their Flying Machines* (1964), *The Battle of the Bulge* (1965).

ANNAUD Jean-Jacques

French. Born 1943. Former TV commercial director whose first feature, *Black and White in Color* (1977), an amusing but strained satire on colonialism shot in the Ivory Coast, surprised everyone by winning the Oscar for the best foreign film. (It wasn't.) *The Quest for Fire* (1981), set in the Stone Age against beautifully shot landscapes with an invented language (by Anthony Burgess), seems to be aimed at the world market as no dub-

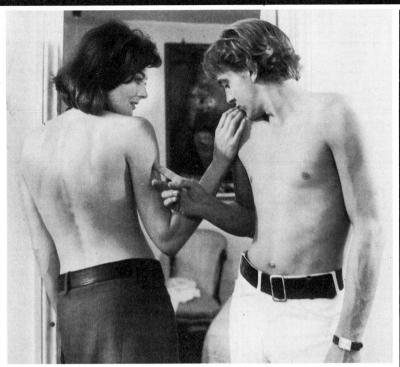

Vanessa Redgrave and David Hemmings in Antonioni's *Blow-up* (1967).

bing or subtitles are needed.

ANTHONY Joseph

American. Born 1912. Former dancer and actor. Directed on stage and TV. Has made a number of stagey films from stage comedies such as *The Rainmaker* (1956), *The Matchmaker* (1958) and *Career* (1959). Best film to date is *Tomorrow* (1972), an adaptation from Faulkner starring Robert Duvall.

ANTONIONI Michelangelo

Italian. Born 1912. Former film critic who only started making his own films in his mid-thirties. Worked as assistant to ROSSELLINI and CARNÉ before directing his first feature, *Cronaca di un Amore* (1950). Already a personal stamp was noticeable, but it was four films and ten years later that his style reached its maturity with *L'Avventura* (1960), one of the few masterpieces of the last two decades. It realigned our views of time and space in the cinema. The long tracking shots, the set-pieces, the limited dialogue, the jettisoning of conventional dramatic construction, the attention to decor and architecture and the relationship between the characters and their environment were to become the hallmarks of an Antonioni film. In *L'Avventura* (as in *Blow-up* – 1967 and *The Passenger* – 1975) he creates an unsolved mystery story. The long search for the missing Anna on the Sicilian island, is merely a catalyst for bringing the two leading characters together. *La Notte* (1960) and *The Eclipse* (1962) make up what is now seen as a trilogy of alienation. At the end of the latter (a series of about fifty-two shots of 'things'), all that remains is a modern city empty of living creatures. Adding meticulous colour to *The Red Desert* (1964), did not disguise the fact that Antonioni was at a dead end. It told of a housewife being driven mad by the industrial landscape around her, although it was of the most soothing reds and greens. Leaving Italy his style underwent a sea-change. Although *Blow-up* was commercially and, on the whole, critically successful, it couldn't help echoing the shallowness of its trendy photographer hero at the centre of the 'swinging London' of the 60's. Like *Blow-up*, *Zabriskie Point* (1970) has plenty of surface appeal, but Antonioni is far too fascinated by the American landscape to bother about the vapid adolescent love story taking place in front of it. The spectacular ending of a materialistic society blowing up would be just as telling out of context. *The Passenger* (1975), his first movie for five years (excepting *Chung Kuo* (1974), a documentary on China), while seeming to be making a significant statement about

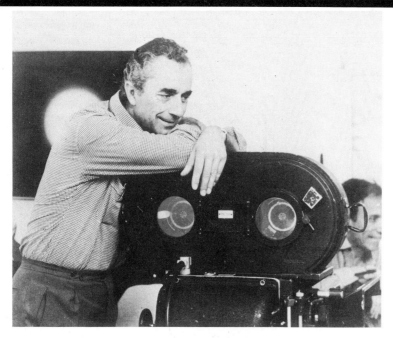

Michelangelo Antonioni

identity, is as arid as its N. African setting. What one remembers is the stunning final seven minute single-shot sequence. Returning to Italy and a reunion with Monica Vitti (with whom he had made four films and cohabited), he shot *Il Mistero di Oberwald* (1981), a flawed but interesting experiment in making a film in video. **Others:** *I Vinti* (1952), *La Signora Senza Camelie* (1953), *Le Amiche* (1955), *Il Grido* (1957), *Identification of a Woman* (1982).

APTED Michael

British. Born 1941. Worked for nine years in British TV directing plays and documentaries. His first feature, *Triple Echo* (1972), a TV-sized drama, sensitively handled a cross-dressing theme. After a few bungled ventures such as *Agatha* (1979) and an abortive movie with Bianca Jagger, Apted made it big in America with the impressive *Coal Miner's Daughter* (1981), nominated for seven Academy Awards. **Others:** *Stardust* (1974), *The Squeeze* (1977), *Continental Divide* (1981).

ARCHAINBAUD George

American. French born. 1890-1959. In Hollywood from 1917 making hundreds of staple movies. From the 40's onwards, mostly B westerns. A few of his bigger budget movies were *Broadway Scandals* (1929), *Thrill of a Lifetime* (1937), *Her Jungle Love* (1938) and *Thanks for the Memory* (1938).

ARLISS Leslie

British. Born 1901. Son of the actor, George Arliss. Wrote screenplays in the 30's. Although Gainsborough Pictures produced comedies and thrillers, their most characteristic films were wickedly enjoyable costume melodramas, the two most popular being Arliss's *The Man in Grey* (1943) and *The Wicked Lady* (1945) both with James Mason and Margaret Lockwood relishing the roles as sadistic lover and sexy villainess. In the early 50's, after the 'Gainsborough Lady' stopped nodding to the audience at the beginning of each film, Arliss had fewer successes and moved into TV. **Also:** *The Night Has Eyes* (42), *Love Story* (44), *A Man About The House* (47), *See How They Run* (55).

ARMSTRONG Gillian

Australian. Born 1951. Graduate of the Sydney film school. After some praiseworthy shorts, she directed the prize-winning picturesque period piece, *My Brilliant Career* (1979). **Also:** *14's Good, 18's Better* (1981).

ARNOLD Jack

American. Born 1916. Former Broadway actor. During World War II, worked on training films under Robert FLAHERTY. Documentary film-maker before joining Universal in 1950. Reputation rests on the sf/horror movies made between 1953 and 1958 for that studio: *It Came From Outer Space* (1953) and *The Creature from the Black Lagoon* (1954), (both flat made-in-3D movies), *Tarantula* (1955) and *The Incredible Shrinking Man* (1957). The rest of his output should be sent into space including *The Mouse that Roared* (1959).

ARZNER Dorothy

American. 1900-1980. Virtually the only woman director working in Hollywood in the 20's and 30's. Daughter of a Hollywood restauranteur. Began as editor. Edited *Blood and Sand* (1922) and *The Covered Wagon* (1923). Her own films are mostly romantic dramas with strong female characters in the leads. *Honor Among Lovers* (1931) with Claudette Colbert, *Merrily We Go To Hell* 1932 with Sylvia Sidney, *Christopher Strong* 1932 with Katharine Hepburn, *Craig's Wife* 1936 with Rosalind Russell, *The Bride Wore Red* 1937 with Joan Crawford. Many of these soapers show the strain of a 'feminist' working within Hollywood conventions. Even in a minor musical, *Dance, Girl, Dance* (1940), the heroine submits unwillingly to the role forced upon her. Arzner gave up directing in 1943 to work for the American Department of Education and to lecture at U.S.C.

ASHBY Hal

American. Born 1936. First job at the age of 17 in the RKO mailroom. Became a distinguished editor, winning recognition for his work on four Norman JEWISON movies. (Won an Oscar for *In the Heat of the Night* – 1967.) Jewison produced Ashby's first movie, *The Landlord* (1970) which, like many of his films, is flabbily radical. *Harold and Maud* (1971), a black comedy covered by a syrupy idealism about youth and the 'young at heart', gained college-kid cult status. *The Last Detail* (1973), *Shampoo* (1975) and *Bound for Glory* (1976), all basically subjects requiring a tough-minded approach, are flawed by a sugaring of the pill. *Coming Home* (1978), which shows a dangerously sentimental attitude to Vietnam vets, is discreetly more about 'coming' than home or the war. Despite lapses, Ashby's best film is *Being There* (1980), mainly because of the script and Peter Sellers' haunting performance.

ASQUITH Anthony

British. 1902-1968. Son of British Liberal Prime Minister (1908-1915). At his best in the 40's and early 50's directing well-made, literate films told with a slightly quivering stiff upper-lip, but later made tired and passé entertainments. Collaborated with playwright Terence Rattigan on over half-a-dozen splendid adaptations of his plays (including *The Winslow Boy* – 1948, *The Browning Version* – 1950) and original scripts such as the moving R.A.F. drama *The Way to the Stars* (1945), the lamentable *V.I.P.'s* (1963) and *The Yellow Rolls Royce* (1964). Of his four Shaw adaptations, *Pygmalion* (1937) and *The Importance of Being Earnest* (1951) are delightful, *The Doctor's Dilemma* (1959) and *The Millionairess* (1961) are the opposite. **Others:** *Tell England* (1931), *French Without Tears* (1939), *Quiet Wedding* (1940), *The Demi-Paradise* (1943), *Fanny by Gaslight* (1944), *Orders to Kill* (1958), *Libel* (1960).

ASTRUC Alexandre
French. Born 1923. Studied law and literature. Novelist and film critic. In an article in L'Ecran Francais in 1948, he invented the phrase 'camera-stylo' and wrote of the cinema becoming 'a means of writing as supple and as subtle as that of written language'. He was unable to practise what he preached in his own pretty turgid films. **Some titles:** *The Crimson Curtain* (a short – 1951), *Une Vie* (1958), *La Proie pour L'Ombre* (1961), *L'Education Sentimentale* (1961), *Sartre par Lui-Meme* (three hour documentary on the writer – 1976).

ATTENBOROUGH Richard
Born 1923. Became a film actor at the age of 19. For years played mainly whining cockney cowards, but with age became a useful character actor. Started producing low-key films in 1959. As a director, he's an excellent actor. His first film, *Oh What a Lovely War!* (1969) transformed what in the theatre was a scabrous and lively satire on the Great War into an over-blown, grossly unsubtle epic. His other films have plodded along the same path, i.e. *Young Winston* (1972), *A Bridge Too Far* (1977), *Magic* (1978). **Also:** *Ghandi* (83).

AUDRY Jacqueline
French. 1908-1977. Started as script girl and then assistant to Max OPHULS and G. W. PABST. Her first features were three films based on stories by Colette, including *Gigi* – 1949 starring Danielle Delorme. Best known for *Huis Clos (No Exit* – 1954) an adaptation from the Sartre play.

Her aim in her work was 'to see women's struggle in different epochs'. This she did with only minor success. She was killed in a car accident.

AUER John H.
American. Hungarian born. 1906-1975. In America since 1929. Wrote, produced and directed a string of programme fillers for Republic and RKO before going over to TV in 1957. The movies' loss was a gain. *City That Never Sleeps* (1953), *The Eternal Sea* (1955) and *Johnny Trouble* (1957) are three of his better movies.

AUTANT-LARA Claude
French. Born 1903. Former set-designer. Experimented with early wide-screen techniques in 1927. Worked as assistant to René CLAIR. His output is variable, but was an essential part of French mainstream cinema from 1933-1960, with stylish farces *Occupe-Toi d'Amélie* (1949), a delightful fantasy, *Sylvie et le Fantome* (1945, with Jacques TATI as a ghost); 'risqué' comedies *The Red Inn* (1951) and *The Green Mare's Nest* (1959); an excellent comedy-drama, *La Traversée de Paris* (1956) and two rather academic adaptations from classic novels, *Le Rouge et le Noir* (1954), and *The Gambler* (1958) both with Gerard Philipe.) He courted controversy with *Le Diable au Corps* (1946) with Philipe as the adolescent lover of an older married woman and two heavy, didactic films, *Thou Shalt Not Kill* (1962) about conscientious objectors and *Journal d'une Femme en Blanc* (1965) about abortion.

AVERBACK Hy
American. Born 1925. Worked as an announcer-writer on radio for many years. Long career in TV, directing mostly comedy shows. Lacking canned laughter, his not-very-funny movies include *Where Were You When The Lights Went Out?* (1968). Answer – Heading for the Exits, *I Love You Alice B. Toklas* (1968) and *Suppose They Gave a War and Nobody Came* (1970).

AVERY Tex
American. Born 1907. The most screwball and imaginative animator of them all. Started work with Walter Lantz in 1928. He created Daffy Duck and Bugs Bunny for the Warners cartoon unit. It was with MGM that his anarchism was given free rein in a series of crazy cartoons

that exploded the boundaries of the genre. Among his best are *Screwball Squirrel* (1944), *King-Sized Canary* (1947), *Half-Pint Pigmy* (1948) and *Symphony in Slang* (1951).

AVILDSEN John G.
American. Born 1937. Worked on commercials and sexploitation movies before making *Joe* (1970). This story of a hardhat, made on a shoe-string, turned out to be a 'sleeper'. His pictures are naïve, overstated, and implausible. 'My films are about people who have dreams, because I'm prone to fairy tales,' he says. *Rocky* (1976) was an ideal subject for Avildsen and won him an Oscar for best direction. **Others:** *Cry Uncle* (1971), *Save the Tiger* (1972), *W.W. and the Dixie Dance Kings* (1976), *Slow Dancing in the Big City* (1978), *Neighbours* (1981).

AXELROD George
American. Born 1922. A New Yorker. Playwright (The Seven Year Itch, etc) and screen writer whose first film as director, *Lord Love a Duck* (1966) was a mostly funny black comedy that unfortunately flopped. *The Secret Life of an American Wife* (1968) is disappointingly conventional in its attempt at bad taste.

BACON Lloyd
American. 1890-1955. An actor in many Mack SENNETT and early CHAPLIN silent shorts. Seventeen years (1926-1943) at Warner Bros. for whom he made an average of four movies a year, making him one of the most prolific of all Hollywood directors. He was the ideal Warner's director of the 30's. Whether a musical – *Gold Diggers of 1937* (1936), prison drama – *San Quentin* (1937), gangster drama – *Marked Woman* (1937),

comedy thriller – *A Slight Case of Murder* (1938) or screwball comedy – *Boy meets Girl* 1938), they were all economical, fast-paced, and down-to-earth with a feeling for the social setting. His vivid contribution to the landmark musicals, *42nd Street* (1933) and *Footlight Parade* (1933) has been over-shadowed by Busby BERKELEY's dance direction. After leaving Warners, his style changed to suit the more genteel demands of Fox. **Others:** *The Singing Fool* (28), *Wonder Bar* (34), *In Caliente* (35), *The Oklahoma Kid* (39), *Brother Orchid* (40), *Knute Rockne* (40), *I Wonder Who's Kissing Her Now* (47), *Give My Regards to Broadway* (48), *Call Me Mister* (51), *Golden Girl* (51), *The I Don't Care Girl* (53), *The French Line* (54).

BADHAM John

American. Son of English actress Mary Hewitt. Left Yale Drama School to work in Universal Pictures mail-room. Began directing on TV where he made his name with *The Law* (1974), a tough (for TV) crime drama. Impressive film debut with the funky *The Bingo Long Traveling All-Stars and Motor Kings* (1976). Hit the jackpot with the discoital Travoltage of *Saturday Night Fever* (1977). His handsomely mounted but bloodless *Dracula* (1979) was needed like a hole in the neck, and the "opening out" of the moving little play, *Whose Life is it Anyway?* (1982) was more of a disembowelment.

BAKER Roy Ward

British. Born 1916. Worked his way up from tea-boy to assistant director at Gainsborough Studios before joining the army in 1940. Had a short spell in Hollywood after making the claustrophobic submarine drama *Morning Departure (Operation Disaster – USA* 1950). A quirky independence occasionally emerges from his films, such as in the eerie *Don't Bother to Knock* (1952) with a pre-*Niagra* Marilyn Monroe and *The Singer not the Song* (1960), a British Western with homosexual undertones. *A Night to Remember* (1958) about the Titanic disaster is full of solid virtues with its stiff upper deck. In the late 60's, he embarked on a series of lousy Hammer horrors including *Dr. Jekyll and Sister Hyde* (1971). **Others:** *The October Man* (47), *I'll Never Forget You* (51), *Inferno* (52), *Passage Home* (54), *The One That Got Away* (57), *The Anniversary* (68), *Asylum* (72).

BAKSHI Ralph

American. Born 1939. Worked as animator for Terrytoons (Mighty Mouse etc). His *Fritz the Cat* (1971), based on an "underground" strip and *Heavy Traffic* (1973), mixing animation with live-action, were the first X-rated cartoon features, thus depriving the audience they were obviously meant for – smutty-minded kids – from seeing them. *Wizards* (1977) and *The Lord of the Rings* (1978) prove that Disney's heir is yet to be found.

BARDEM Juan-Antonio.

Spanish. Born 1922. Studied at the Madrid Film School. In 1951 made his first film, *This Happy Couple* co-directed by Luis BERLANGA. *Death of a Cyclist* (1957) was a decent attempt to make a socially critical film in Franco's Spain. It won the Cannes Grand Prix and remains his most famous work. Greatly influenced by the Italian neo-realists, he never developed much beyond the naturalism of his earlier films. He was imprisoned in 1956, but was released after two weeks because of public opinion. He also bravely produced BUNUEL's controversial *Viridiana* (1961).

BARNET Boris

Russian. 1902-1965. Former boxer and film actor. Appeared in films by KULESHOV and PUDOVKIN. Made a number of delightfully fresh satirical comedies such as *Girl with the Hatbox* (1927) and *House on Trubnaya Square* (1928). Although he continued to direct into the 50's, his films never recaptured the spontaneity of those of the 20's and early 30's (almost a parallel with Soviet art in general). He committed suicide.

BARTON Charles

American. 1902-1981. Spent ten years at Universal making mostly second-feature comedies. The favourite director of Abbott and Costello with whom he made eight movies including their best, *The Time of Their Lives* (1946) and their last, *Dance with Me, Henry* (1956). Also directed Disney's first live-action comedy, *The Shaggy Dog* (1959). Worked a great deal in TV.

BAVA Mario

Italian. Born 1914. Former cameraman who often photographs and writes his own films which are mainly ludicrous tongue-in-the-neck horror movies starring fading British and American stars. However, they are sometimes redeemed by a startling pictorial quality. **A few titles:** *Black Sunday* (60), *Black Sabbath* (63), *Blood and Black Lace* (64), *Planet of the Vampires* (65), *Dr. Goldfoot and the Girl Bombs* (66), *Diabolik* (68).

BAXTER John

British. Born 1896. Maker of a number of interesting proletarian comedies and dramas in the 30's and 40's, the titles of which speak for themselves; *Doss House* (1932), *Song of the Plough* (1932), *Love on the Dole* (1940), *The Common Touch* (1941). Later, still with the common touch, he made weak, unexportable British slapstick comedies.

BEATTY Warren

American. Born 1937. Younger brother of Shirley MacLaine. Star footballer at High School. A dropout of Northwestern U. after a year of speech and drama. With the help of playwright William Inge, got the part of the randy adolescent in *Splendor in the Grass* (1961) and has been playing, more or less, the same role ever since. Not just a pretty face, he produced and starred in *Bonnie and Clyde* (1967) and *Shampoo* (1975). His first venture into directing (with Buck Henry) was the feeble football fantasy, *Heaven Can Wait* (1978) which he also starred in, produced and co-wrote. *Reds* (1981) was an ambitious project, beautifully photographed by Vittorio Storaro, but directed with little pace. Diane Keaton's radical chick is too modern and Beatty too bland in the role of American Communist John Reed. Images of the Russian Revolution have been done better elsewhere and the presence of 'actual witnesses' makes one long for a documentary instead of the romantic Reds-on-the-bed guff that is passed off as truth.

BEAUDINE William

American. 1892-1970. Routine director of countless low-budget movies, quite a few for Poverty Row Monogram Studios. Booth Tarkington's *Penrod and Sam* (1923 and 1931), and one of W. C. Fields' best movies, *The Old Fashioned Way* (1934) were standouts in his career.

BEAUMONT Harry

American. 1893-1966. The high point of Beaumont's career was as director of the first all-talking, all-singing, all-dancing, *The Broadway Melody* (1929). It was the first sound movie to win an Oscar (Best Picture) and Beaumont was nominated for Best Direction. The first 'backstage' musical, it had original songs (by Arthur Freed and Nacio Brown) and a ballet sequence in Technicolor. Previously he had directed the most famous of all Jazz Age silents, *Our Dancing Daughters* (1928) with Joan Crawford as a flapper.

BECKER Jacques
French. 1906-1960. Son of a wealthy industrialist. After seeing *La Chienne* (1931), he begged Jean RENOIR to take him on as an assistant. Worked with Renoir for eight years before World War II separated them. Renoir's influence can be seen in all his work, although Becker's is the slighter talent. His love for modern Paris shone through three delicate social comedies: *Antoine et Antoinette* (1947), *Rendezvous de Juillet* (1949) and *Edouard et Caroline* (1951). *Casque d'Or* (1952) was set in a lovingly recreated Paris at the turn of the century and, despite the *crime passionnel* plot, it almost equals the radiance of Renoir *pere et fils*. In his last film, *Le Trou* (*The Hole* 1960), which meticulously details a prison escape, he seemed to be taking a new direction by using non-professional actors and a more austere camera style. **Others:** *Falbalas* (42), *Touchez pas au Grisbi* (54), *Ali Baba* (55), *The Adventures of Arsène Lupin* (56), *Montparnasse 19* (57).

BELL Monta
American. 1891-1958. His films of the 20's seem to show the influence of Ernst LUBITSCH. Edited CHAPLIN's *A Woman of Paris* (1923). Had the task of directing Garbo in her first Hollywood movie, *The Torrent* (1926) despite kibitzing from her mentor Mauritz STILLER.

BELLOCCHIO Marco
Italian. Born 1939. Studied philosophy, acting and directing in Italy before taking a year's film course at the Slade School in London in 1964 under Thorold DICKINSON. Raised around 50,000 dollars to make his first film, *Fists in the Pocket* (1966), an overt critique of the Italian bourgeois family. It tells of a blind widow with four children, three of whom are epileptics. Soon after joining the Italian Communist Party, he continued the theme with *China is Near* (1968) which dealt with state repression through family repression. *In the Name of the Father* (1971), set in a harsh Catholic boys' school, is a powerful allegory of Italian political life. His metaphors became rather muddied in his later films, i.e. *Marcia Trionfale* (1976) and *Leap into the Void* (1980). **Also:** *The Eyes and the Mouth* (82).

BENEDEK Laslo
Hungarian. Born 1907. Writer, editor and cameraman in Germany in the 30's. Went to Hollywood in 1937 and joined MGM's montage department. Has made about a dozen films in over 30 years, although his small output doesn't necessarily denote fastidiousness. Only *The Wild One* (1954) stands out. The Tame One by today's standards, it was the first movie in which the motor-cycle and Marlon BRANDO emerged fully as sex-symbols and it spawned a whole series of bike movies. He was unable in *Death of a Salesman* (1952) to find a filmic solution to Elia KAZAN's stage production. **Others:** *The Kissing Bandit* (48), *Bengal Brigade* (54), *Affair in Havana* (57), *Malaga* (62), *The Night Visitor* (71).

BENNETT Compton
British. 1900-1974. Former editor. *The Seventh Veil* (1945), his first and best film, was one of the most successful British melodramas. His expertise seemed to promise more good films. The two movies he made for MGM were travesties of English popular classics: *That Forsyte Woman* (1949) – from The Forsyte Saga – a film as vulgar as its title, and the reasonably enjoyable, *King Solomon's Mines* (1950).

BENTON Robert.
American. Born 1932. Former painter and illustrator. Worked as art director for Esquire magazine before entering films as a screenwriter. Co-wrote the screenplays of *Bonnie and Clyde* (1967) and *What's Up, Doc?* (1972). After the success of *Bad Company* (1972), an arty and artful Western, Robert ALTMAN produced *The Late Show* (1977), an amusing and controlled Chandler pastiche unlike Altman's own *The Long Goodbye* (1972). Five Oscars and box-office records for *Kramer vs Kramer* (1979) betoken an appeal for well-made, middle-class domestic dramas with a soupçon of feminism. **Also:** *Stab* (82).

BERESFORD Bruce
Australian. Born 1940. After Sydney University, spent two years in Nigeria as film editor. In England, he became Head of Production of the British Film Institute's experimental film fund. Made the first film to be funded by the Australian government, the ghastly *The Adventures of Barry McKenzie* (1971). A curiously crude start to a now flourishing industry in which Beresford has played a major part. *Don's Party* (1976), *The Getting of Wisdom* (1977), *The Club* (1978) *Breaker Morant* (1979) and *Puberty Blues* (1982). all show a vigorous if undisciplined talent.

BERGMAN Ingmar
Swedish. Born 1918. Son of a severe Lutheran pastor, his films are full of religious imagery, paradoxically expressing a God-less, love-less universe. The entire oeuvre can be seen as the autobiography of his psyche. Started directing in the theatre in 1944 and continued to divide his year between the stage (Winter) and films (Summer). He drew his famous repertory company mostly from the Royal Dramatic Theatre in Stockholm, forming a closely-knit group with Bergman as pater familias. He has been married six times and has nine children, one by Liv Ullmann the actress whose doleful face has filled his films since *Persona* (1966). Players and the theatre exist throughout his work, underlining the constant theme of the duality of personality in a closed world of illusions. Bergman lives on the lonely island of Faro, and at least five of his films take place on an island, a circumscribed area like the stage. The subject of his early work is of adolescents struggling against an unfeeling adult world. Gunnar Fischer, his photographer until 1960, captured brilliantly the transient sun-soaked summer days, the only period of happiness before the encroachment of Autumn and reality. The operetta-like comedy of manners, *Smiles of a Summer Night* (1955) was the culmination of this first period. *The Seventh Seal* (1957) established his international reputation. Shot in only thirty-five days, it is a medieval morality with luminous images derived from early church paintings. *Wild Strawberries* (1957) is a modern morality of an old professor (Victor SJÖSTRÖM) seeking some meaning to his life, the action shifting skilfully between past and present, dream and reality. The trilogy, *Through a Glass Darkly* (1961), *Winter Light* (1963) and *The Silence* (1963) showed him moving into an angst-ridden and

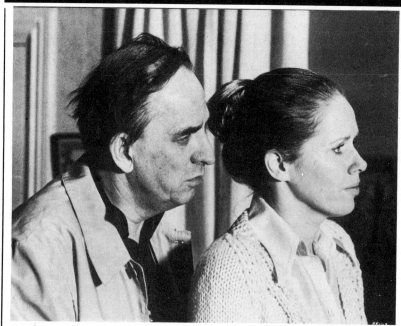

Bergman directs Liv Ullmann in *Face to Face* (1975).

more intimist world. (Sven Nykvist was now his constant cameraman.) With *Persona* (1966), the female face in closeup became his field of vision. Women had always been central in his films, not only because of his sexual and psychological interest in them, but perhaps he sees them as more passive, more imprisoned biologically and socially than men. A succession of obsessive and airless psycho-dramas followed including *Cries and Whispers* (1972), which has four women suffering exquisitely in emotionally-charged colour. In *Autumn Sonata* (1978), Bergman points an accusing finger at parental neglect (his own parents? himself?). His namesake Ingrid Bergman gives a remarkable performance in this long night's journey into day. Night gives way to light and joy in *The Magic Flute* (1975), despite the Coca-Cola-ad overture and some perverse liberties with the text. **Others:** *Summer Interlude* (50), *Waiting Women, Summer with Monika* (52), *Sawdust and Tinsel* (53), *A Lesson in Love* (54), *Journey into Autumn* (55), *So Close to Life, The Face* (58), *The Virgin Spring* (59), *The Devil's Eye* (60), *Now About These Women* (64), *Hour of the Wolf, The Shame* (68), *The Rite* (69), *A Passion* (70), *The Touch* (71), *Scenes from a Marriage* (73), *Face to Face* (75), *The Serpent's Egg* (78), *From the Life of the Marionettes* (81), *Fanny and Alexander* (82).

BERKELEY Busby

American. 1895-1976. Broadway director brought to Hollywood by Samuel Goldwyn to stage the production numbers for the Eddie Cantor musical, *Whoopee* (1930). He immediately eliminated three of the four camera crews and began to experiment with ways of freeing the musical from its stagey confines. His most characteristic work was done at Warner Bros. from 1933 to 1937. There he was able to create musical numbers purely in terms of his one dancing camera by dollying in erotically on the lines of identically dressed dream girls, and forming those famous kaleidoscopic effects with high overhead shots from a mobile crane. Close-ups of the chorines humanized the abstract, Art-Deco and *trompe l'oeil* patterns. Girls shaped as an enormous neon-lit violin, girls at 56 pianos, multitudes of girls forming themselves into Ruby Keeler's face or into the American Eagle. There were also the great narrative numbers such as My Forgotten Man *(Gold Diggers of 1933)*, Shanghai Lil *(Footlight Parade – 1933)* and Lullaby of Broadway *(Gold Diggers of 1935)* in which the contours of Winnie Shaw's face appear as the shape of the Manhattan skyline. In his first film in colour, *The Gang's All Here* (Fox 1943), sixty girls did suggestive things with sixty giant bananas. At MGM, Berkeley adapted to the sexless house style, bringing out the best in Mickey Rooney and Judy Garland and creating spectacular aqua-ballets for Esther Williams. **Others:** (as Director) *Hollywood Hotel* (37), *They Made Me a Criminal* (39), *Babes in Arms* (39), *Strike Up The Band* (40), *Babes on Broadway* (41), *For Me and My Girl* (42), *Take Me Out to the Ball Game* (49). (**As Dance Director**) *42nd Street* (33), *Roman Scandals* (33), *Wonder Bar* (34), *Dames* (34), *Gold Diggers of 1937, Ziegfeld Girl* (41), *Girl Crazy* (43), *Two Weeks with Love* (50), *Million Dollar Mermaid* (52), *Small Town Girl* (53), *Easy to Love* (53), *Rose Marie* (54), *Jumbo* (62).

BERLANGA Luis

Spanish. Born 1921. Studied at the Madrid Film School where he met Juan-Antonio BARDEM. They co-directed *This Happy Couple* (1951), an American-style comedy. While his colleague went on to make rather grim dramas, Berlanga's taste was for satire. *Welcome Mr. Marshall* (1953) is a sardonic look at the effect on a

Bengt Ekerot as Death and Max von Sydow in Bergman's *The Seventh Seal* (1957).

up "gonzesses", without condemnation or praise although the "charm" of the performances incline to the latter. *Get Out Your Handkerchiefs* (1978), gentler and funnier, has a 13-year-old boy getting a woman in her 20's pregnant. It won the Oscar for the Best Foreign Film. **Also:** *Buffet Froid* (79), *Stepfather* (81).

BLYSTONE John G.
American. 1892-1938. Former actor. Happened, among the dross, to direct one of Buster KEATON's best comedies, *Seven Chances* (1928), and a couple of good Laurel and Hardy features, *Swiss Miss* (1938) and *Blockheads* (1938).

BOETTICHER Budd
American. Born 1916. Former professional matador. Adviser on *Blood and Sand* (1941). Made three bull-fighting movies, two of which, *The Bull-Fighter and the Lady* (1951) and *The Magnificent Matador* (1955) had more bull outside the ring than inside. More is said about dignity and courage in the series of seven B Westerns (all around 70 mins.) starring Randolph Scott. Made in twelve to eighteen days, they were as taut and laconic as their hero, had a classic plot told with an unselfconscious narrative force that makes them models of the genre. They were *Seven Men from Now* (1956), *Decision at Sundown* (1957), *The Tall T* (1957), *Buchanan Rides Alone* (1958), *Ride Lonesome* (1959), *Westbound* (1959) and *Comanche Station* (1960). He spent from 1963-1968, working independently on a documentary of the great Mexican bull-fighter, Carlos Arruza. Entitled simply *Arruza*, it's strictly for afficianados. **Also:** *The Killer is Loose* (55), *The Rise and Fall of Legs Diamond* (60), *A Time for Dying* (69).

BOGART Paul
American. Born 1919. Recruit from TV. His first movie, *Halls of Anger* (1968), set in a black Blackboard Jungle is, like many a teleplay, well-meaning and reassuring. The rest of his work ranges from so-so (an anachronistic "liberal" Western, *The Skin Game* – 1971, and *Class of '44* – 1973) to abysmal (*Cancel My Reservation* – 1971 with Bob Hope).

BOGDANOVICH Peter
American. Born 1939. A former film critic (with books on DWAN, FORD and LANG) who made an impressive debut with *Targets* (1968) featuring Boris Karloff. In a way, he continued his criticism into his films, which are really movies of movies. Sometimes they are more than just *exercises de style*. Both *The Last Picture Show* (1972) and *Paper Moon* (1974) lovingly invoke, in black and white, the spirit of Ford, WELLMAN, WYLER, RENOIR and the cameraman Gregg Toland. Despite their allusiveness, they appeal to the non film-buff. *What's Up, Doc?* (1972), however, was a heavy homage to hectic HAWKSian humour. Suffering from necro-cinephilia, and like a child let loose in a science lab, he produced such bombs as *Daisy Miller* (1974), Henry James without the Prose, *At Long Last Love* (1975), a flat-footed and off-key musical, and the slapdash slapstick *Nickelodeon* (1976). *Saint Jack* (1979) was a sincere attempt to get away from Hollywood in both senses. It has a splendid sense of location (the red-light district of Singapore), but it is reminiscent of *The World of Suzy Wong* (1960) and *Tokyo Joe* (1949). He just can't win. In his film documentary on John Ford, he disarmingly allows himself to be put down by the great man.

BOLESLAWSKI Richard
Polish. 1889-1937. In Hollywood from 1930. Actor at the Moscow Arts Theatre for 10 years before World War I. Wrote books on Stanislavsky. Not a trace of the master of 'Method' is to be found in his glossy entertainments. He was privileged to direct the only film in which all three Barrymores appeared together, *Rasputin and the Empress* (1932), Garbo in *The Painted Veil* (1934) and the first picture produced by the newly-formed Twentieth Century-Fox Company, *Metropolitan* (1935), an amusing satire on the opera. His one venture into glorious Technicolor was the exotic *The Garden of Allah* (1936) with Marlene Dietrich and Charles Boyer thickly spreading their accents in the desert. **Also:** *Clive of India* (35), *Les Miserables* (35), *Theodora Goes Wild* (36).

BOLOGNINI Mauro
Italian. Born 1923. Studied architecture. Worked as assistant to Yves ALLÉGRET and Jean DELANNOY in France. Directed for TV. Four of his early films were scripted by PASOLINI, *La Notte Brava* (*Night Heat* – 1959) and *I Bell' Antonio* (1960) being the best. They have a spontaneity lacking in his subsequent films, many of them staid and studied adaptations from 19th century literature. *Mademoiselle de Maupin* (1966), although still pictorially self-conscious, was less of a drag than usual with Claudia Cardinale in drag.

BONDARCHUK Sergei
Russian. Born 1920. Acted with the Theatre of the Soviet Army during the war. Appeared in many films, including *Othello* (1956) and DOVZHENKO's last film, *Michurin* (1948). His four-part *War and Peace* (1966-1967) in eight hours, is a remarkable achievement. Never just content to use the vast resources at his disposal to illustrate the masterpiece, he attempts to find visual equivalents of Tolstoy's prose. Extensive use of a subjective camera and his own affecting performance as Pierre, make it almost a personal history. The Battle of Borodino, is not only a breathtaking spectacle, but Pierre becomes the spectator's surrogate in the midst of the horror. Its frequent lapses into grandiloquence and its reliance on the dissolve, don't detract from the stunning use of overhead tracking shots, split-screen technique or the constant shifting from the epic to the intimate. *Waterloo* (1970) fell into most of the traps of the screen spectacle that *War and Peace* managed to avoid. **Also:** *Mexico in Flames (82)*.

BOORMAN John
British. Born 1933. Directed documentaries for BBC TV from 1962-1965. His first film, *Catch Us If You Can* (*Having a Wild Weekend* – U.S. 1965), had a fresh approach despite being a vehicle for the extinct pop group, The Dave Clark Five. In the USA, he cast his private eye on the world of organized crime in *Point Blank* (1967). Set in a hyper-realist L.A., it was a powerful, rather turbid, parable of man in the jungle of the cities. Urban man is caught in the real jungle in *Deliverance* (1972). The first half is a tightly controlled crescendo of violence, as the four businessman on a canoeing trip are shot at, terrorized and sodomized by mountain men. The film, however, gets into shallow and muddy waters as they escape to safety and The Message is propounded. The rest of Boorman's work also demonstrates his taste for the allegorical. This is pushed to risible lengths in the stoneage sci-fi, *Zardoz* (1974), the desperate visuals of *Exorcist II – The*

Heretic (1977), and *Excalibur* (1981), that lengthy razor-blade commercial. **Also:** *Leo the Last* (1970), *Hell in the Pacific* (1968).

BOROWCZYK Walerian
Polish. Born 1923. Started as an animator in Poland. Experimented with various techniques such as painting directly on film. Has lived in France since 1959. His animated films are bitterly ironic creations of cruel surrealistic worlds. His first live-action feature, *Goto, Island of Love* (1969) continued in this vein. With *Blanche* (1971) he turned to a series of erotic and decorative period pieces. **Others:** *Immoral Tales* (1974), *The Story of Sin* (1975), *Behind Convent Walls* (1977).

BORZAGE Frank
American. 1893-1962. Having been on the stage in his teens, he entered the movies as an actor. In 1916, he started directing dozens of two-reelers for Thomas INCE. *Seventh Heaven* (1927), a beautifully photographed gooey love-story, was the very first film to win an Oscar. (Best Direction. Best Actress – Janet Gaynor.) He went on to direct Gaynor (and the ineffectual Charles Farrell) again in *Street Angel* (1928) and *Lucky Star* (1929). Borzage's forté was clearly for bitter-sweet romances with lovers fighting against adversity. Hemingway's tough *A Farewell to Arms* (1933) was turned out in the same soft mould. The sentimental urban poetry of *Man's Castle* (1933),

about a young couple looking for a ray of hope in the Depression, suited his gentle gifts more. His best work came in the four movies he made with the delicate and tragic actress, Margaret Sullavan, *Little Man, What Now?* (1934), *Three Comrades* (1938), *The Shining Hour* (1939) and *The Mortal Storm* (1940). The first and best being a poignant and prescient love story set against the growing threat of Nazism. In 1948 the "blacklist" forced him out of work for ten years. **Others:** *Desire* (36), *History is Made at Night* (37), *Mannequin* (38), *Smilin' Through* (41), *His Butler's Sister* (44), *The Spanish Main* (46), *Moonrise* (48), *The Big Fisherman* (59).

BOULTING John and Roy
British. Born 1913. Interchanged as producer and director, although Roy has directed more pictures than John. Their best films were war-time documentaries and low-key atmospheric dramas in the 40's. *Thunder Rock* (1942 – Roy), set on a lighthouse, *Brighton Rock* (1947 – John), an excellent adaptation from Graham Greene, and *Seven Days to Noon* (1950 – John) a suspenseful thriller about a scientist threatening to blow up London. After a lean period, they hit upon a successful series of broad satirical comedies which looked at British Institutions such as the army (*Private's Progress* 1956 – John), industrial relations (*I'm All Right Jack* 1959 – John), the law (*Brothers in Law* 1956 – Roy) and the church

(*Heaven's Above* 1963 – John).

BOURGUIGNON Serge
French. Born 1928. His very first feature, *Sundays and Cybele* (1962) won the Oscar for the Best Foreign movie, a simple story of the relationship between a shell-shocked German and a little girl. Nothing he has done since merits much attention e.g. *The Reward* (65), *Two Weeks in September* (67), *The Picasso Summer* (69).

BOX Muriel
British. Born 1905. Writer/Producer/ Director. Wrote the screenplay for *The Seventh Veil* (1946) and less successful British pictures. Her films as director are flat and without personality. The best is *The Beachcomber* (1954), based on a Maugham story and the worst is *The Truth About Women* (1957), a feeble farrago with Laurence Harvey.

BRABIN Charles
British. 1883-1957. Worked in Hollywood in the 20's and 30's then disappeared. He directed the first of three versions of the Edna Ferber weepie, *So Big* (1923), a taut crime-thriller with Jean Harlow called *The Beast of the City* (1932), but *The Mask of Fu Manchu* (1923) with Boris Karloff as the evil oriental, will remain Brabin's dubious legacy to the world.

BRANDO Marlon
American. Born 1924. Brando was allegedly so wasteful with Paramount's time and money, that *One-Eyed Jacks* (1960) remains the only movie he has directed. Stanley KUBRICK was originally to make it, and Sam PECKINPAH directed one sequence. It is a long, rambling, self-indulgent revenge Western, with superb photography by Charles Lang Jr. and a brooding Byronic performance from its star and director.

BRAHM John
German. Born 1898. In Hollywood from 1937. Worked in the theatre in Germany before coming to England in 1934 where he co-directed a couple of films. His best work was done at Fox with two atmospheric chillers set in a foggy Victorian London, *The Lodger* (1944) and *Hangover Square* (1945) both featuring the heavy Laird Cregar. *Guest in the House* (1944) and *The Locket* (1946) are other murky melodramas containing psychopaths. His career faded, ending ignominiously with a teen bike-movie

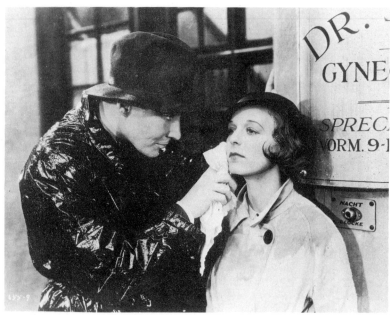

Douglass Montgomery and Margaret Sullavan in Borzage's *Little Man, What Now?* (1934).

Claude Laydu in Bresson's *Diary of a Country Priest* (1951).

called *Hot Rods to Hell* (1957).

BREIEN Anja

Norwegian. Born 1940. Studied at the IDHEC film school in Paris from 1962-1964. *Wives* (1975), the only Norwegian film to get world-wide distribution, was an enjoyable feminist romp, a reaction to John CASSAVETES' *Husbands* (1970). Her other films continue along the line of a non-conformist view of women in society: *Games of Love and Loneliness* (76), *Arven* (79), *Witch Hunt* (81).

BRESSON Robert

French. Born 1907. Studied literature, philosophy and painting. Came late to cinema. Has made only twelve films in 39 years. His extreme scrupulousness, his avoidance of publicity, his Catholic stoicism, his austere, uncompromising, elliptical films have built his reputation as a saintly figure, a Trappist film-maker who has only "spoken" twelve times in the last four decades. Like all gurus, he is open to accusations of phoneyness. It could be said that his very simplicity is a kind of dandyism, his insistence on using non-actors (or "virgins") only results in bad performances and that his Jansenist beliefs are reactionary

and anathema to modern thought. Saint or charlatan? Whatever one's views, there is no doubt that Bresson has created a mythology and an impressively consistent oeuvre over the years. During the war, he spent eighteen months in a German prison. (Four of his films have prison settings.) As for his rejection of professional actors he says, "Art is transformation. Acting can only get in the way.". The actors are blank sheets on which his rites are written. His first two films, *Les Anges du Péché* (1943) and *Les Dames du Bois de Boulogne* (1945) use professional performers, have "literary" texts and were shot in a studio. The former set in a nunnery tells of the redemption of a female criminal by a sacrificial nun, and the second, set among the *haute bourgeoisie* shows the redemption of a woman of "easy virtue" through the love of a man. The cold artificiality of the images and the transposition of an 18th century story to a 20th century setting with few plot changes lays bare the ethical issues of the fable. He used non-actors, natural sound and locations for the first time in *The Diary of a Country Priest* (1951). The consciously pleonastic literary device of a narration is used over shots of the isolated and dying priest's diary. The

title of *A Man Escaped* (1956) immediately eliminates any suspense which might interfere with the spectator's contemplation of a prisoner gaining grace and liberty. In *Pickpocket* (1961), the representational "sinner" of the title (there is no article) also finds divine grace, this time through the love of a woman. The style of heightened flatness continues in *The Trial of Joan of Arc* (1962) which follows the exact transcript of Joan's trial, using a practically immobile camera at eye-level. In *Balthazar* (1966) the suffering victim this time is a donkey who, it is not too frivolous to note, gives one of the best Bressonian performances. In *Mouchette* (1967), the suffering victim is a fourteen-year-old peasant girl who, after being raped, commits suicide to Monteverdi's Magnificat. Like the use of Mozart's Requiem in *A Man Escaped*, the music is like lipstick on a corpse and only overstresses the spirituality that is supposed to be inherent in Bresson's economical method. In 1969 with *A Gentle Creature* (1969), he began to use colour for the first time and a more overt sensuality was noticeable. Colour also gave the works a different intensity and "modernity", although the intrusion of hippies in

Quatre Nuits d'un Reveur (*Four Nights of a Dreamer* – 1971) seems curiously false. *The Devil, Probably* (1977) manages to integrate a modern theme (i.e. pollution – literal and figurative) more convincingly. Away from modern civilisation, *Lancelot du Lac* (1974) is a series of chivalric ceremonies ending in death and destruction. In more than one sense, Bresson is the grey eminence of the cinema.

BRIDGES Alan
British. Born 1927. TV and film director. *The Hireling* (1973), a tasteful version of L. P. Hartley's novel, won the Grand Prix at Cannes in what must have been a bad year. ALSO: *Phobia* (1979), *The Return of the Soldier* (1982).

BRIDGES James
American. Worked in theatre and TV as an actor and writer. Wrote eighteen *Alfred Hitchcock Presents* for TV. Writes his own scripts. Seems to go for commercially controversial subjects. *The Baby Maker* (1970), *The Paper Chase* (1973), the tendentious *The China Syndrome* (1979) and *Urban Cowboy* (1980), as mechanical and wooden as the automatic rodeo bull that John Travolta rides.

BROOK Peter
British. Born 1925. A distinguished experimental theatre director, whose films are undistinguished and mildly experimental. At 19, while at university, made a film version of Sterne's *A Sentimental Journey*. His first feature, *The Beggar's Opera* (1953) was conventional. The three films adapted from Royal Shakespeare Company productions, *The Marat/Sade* (1966), *Tell Me Lies* (1967) and *King Lear* (1970) prove that the most successful theatrical effects can go for nothing on the screen. He also failed to bring to life two transpositions of novels, *Moderato Cantabile* (1960) and *Lord of the Flies* (1963). The first being too deliberate, the second being too loose. His attempt to put Gurdjieff's philosophy onto film in *Meetings with Remarkable Men* (1979) demonstrates that what is indigestible in print is even more so on film.

BROOKS Albert
American. Writer/Director/Comedian. Made comic shorts before his first feature, *Real Life* (1979) showed him as a director and performer in the Woody ALLEN mould,

Basil Rathbone and Greta Garbo in Clarence Brown's *Anna Karenina* (1935).

without the intimations of mortality and immortality. *Modern Romance* (1981) is even funnier with Brooks, playing an obnoxious film editor, struggling to save a B sci-fi movie and his relationship with his girl-friend.

BROOKS Mel
American. Born in Brooklyn in 1926 as Melvin Kaminsky. TV gag writer for many years (such as Sid Caesar's *Show of Shows*.) His first film, *The Producers* (1968) plays fast and loose with the concept of "bad taste" and the idea of a producer hoping to make more money out of a flop than a hit. The wonderfully camp "Springtime for Hitler" number is believable enough to shock the New York audience. Unfortunately, once the number has made its point, Brooks loses the effect by continuing with a corny vaudeville routine. *Blazing Saddles* (1974), *Young Frankenstein* (1975) and *Silent Movie* (1976), despite bad TV-fodder jokes and excesses, have enough belly laughs and are well enough made to display some feeling for the genres parodied. *High Anxiety* (1977) has virtually no feeling or understanding for HITCHCOCK's work which is used as the basis for low comedy. *The History of the World Part 1* (1981) is a tatty ragbag in which Brooks regresses to his early TV days and beyond to infancy. He is undoubtedly a very funny man who has yet to learn how far to go too far.

BROOKS Richard
American. Born 1912. A former sports reporter and radio commentator. Wrote screenplays for eight years (e.g. *Brute Force* – 1947, *Key Largo* – 1948) before directing his first movie, *Crisis* (1950), a thriller set in S. America. Already perceptible were

the writer/director's liberal views expressed in a heavy, literal style, overstating the obvious. Worthy ventures such as *Blackboard Jungle* (1955) and *Something of Value* (1957) demonstrate this. Of his three Westerns, *The Last Hunt* (1956) has the edge on spectacle, but the polarization of the liberal and fascist buffalo hunters is too predictable. *The Professionals* (1966) is an ochre-coloured Western in which cynicism gives way too easily to romance and *Bite the Bullet* (1975) takes a long time to follow its stereotypes on a 600-mile horse race to reach its flabby anti-competitive conclusion. His two Tennessee Williams adaptations (*Cat on a Hot Tin Roof* – 1958, *Sweet Bird of Youth* – 1962), though castrated, contain interesting performances, but his best film remains *Elmer Gantry* (1960) which is considerably helped by Burt Lancaster in the title role and John Alton's colour photography. **Others:** *The Last Time I saw Paris* (54), *A Catered Affair* (56), *The Brothers*

Karamazov (58), *Lord Jim* (65), *In Cold Blood* (67), *Looking for Mr. Goodbar* (77).

BROWN Clarence

American. Born 1890. Obtained an engineering degree before entering films as assistant to Maurice TOURNEUR. Worked with the French silent film director for 7 years. Brown carried over the pictorial qualities he had learnt in the silent cinema into his sound films. Perhaps more than any other director, typifies the MGM style of the '30's. Glossy, mellow dramas set in plush surroundings, elegant without being sophisticated, well-mannered without being mannered, photographed with soft-focus effects and high-key lighting. He directed seven of Garbo's pictures, getting her to talk for the first time in *Anna Christie* (1930) and even to act in *Anna Karenina* (1935). Away from that posturing profile, he was able to make idealistic, warm-hearted examples of Americana for the studio that more than any other cosily reinforced middle-class values. *Ah Wilderness!* (1935), *The Human Comedy* (1943) and *National Velvet* (1944), all with Mickey Rooney, and *The Yearling* (1946) and *Intruder in the Dust* (1949), both with lanky boy-actor Claude Jarman Jr., are splendid family entertainments staying the right side of sentimentality.

BROWNING Tod

American. 1882-1962. At 16 ran away from home and joined a circus. A meeting with D. W. GRIFFITH brought him into films. Was assistant director on *Intolerance* (1916). In 1918, signed with Universal and made seventeen films in five years for them, including two in which Lon Chaney had small roles. After Chaney became a big star, he persuaded MGM to hire Browning and it was the start of a hideous friendship. They made eight horror movies together from 1925-1929. All enveloped with an eerie atmosphere, they were excellent vehicles for "the man of a 1000 faces", such as his old woman in *The Unholy Three* (1925) and the armless knife-thrower in *The Unknown* (1927). After Chaney's death in 1930, Browning moved back to Universal to make *Dracula* (1931) setting the style for a whole cycle of horror films from that studio. Helped enormously by Karl FREUND's camerawork and Bela Lugosi's lurid performance, it is one of Browning's best films. In the same genre is the

campy, *The Mark of the Vampire* (1935) and the inventive, *Devil Doll* (1936), brilliantly using the miniaturization of humans to the size of insects. In a way, *Freaks* (1932) is an anti-horror movie. It urges the spectator not to be repulsed by the parade of monsters, a trunkless man, a dwarf, pinheads, and Siamese twins. They are never sentimentalized and they wreak a terrible revenge on the two "normal" people who crossed them. This compelling masterpiece was hardly seen for 30 years. Only a few weeks before his death (of throat cancer like Chaney), the film was rehabilitated at the Venice Film Festival.

BROWNLOW Kevin

British. Born 1938. Filmologist, film collector and expert on the silent era. Took years to reconstruct Abel GANCE's masterpiece *Napoleon* (1927). His book "The Parade's Gone By" is dedicated to Gance. The TV series *Hollywood* (1979) was a treasure trove of sequences from the silent cinema, beautifully put together. While still in his teens, Brownlow, with Andrew Mollo, started seven years shooting, with limited finances, *It Happened Here* (1966), an effectively realistic portrayal of a Nazi-occupied Britain. *Winstanley* (1975) is a trenchant reconstruction of a real historical event, the failed attempt to establish a peasant's commune in 17th century England.

BRUCKMAN Clyde

American. 1895-1955. Comedy screen writer and director. Co-directed one of Buster KEATON's most beautifully made films, *The General* (1927). Made three pictures for Harold Lloyd including his best talkie, *Movie Crazy* (1932) and a vintage W. C. Fields comedy, *The Man on the Flying Trapeze* (1935).

BRUNEL Adrian

British. 1892-1958. Made a reputation in the 20's with competent dramas such as *The Constant Nymph* (1927). Co-directed *Elstree Calling* (1930) with Alfred HITCHCOCK.

BUCQUET Harold S.

British. 1891-1946. Spent most of his time at MGM churning out Dr Kildare movies from 1939-1947. Co-directed *Dragon Seed* (1944) with Americans vainly trying to be convincing as Chinese.

Luis Buñuel and Jeanne Moreau on the set of *Diary of a Chambermaid* (1964).

BUÑUEL Luis

Spanish. Born 1900. Appropriately born with the century. Came from a cultured bourgeois family and was educated at a Jesuit school. His background and education turned him into the most consistently anti-middle class and anti-clerical of directors. At the University of Madrid he met Salvador Dali who wrote the screenplay of his first two films. In Paris, under the influence of André Breton's Surrealist Manifesto, he embarked on his career with one of the most startling images in all cinema, an open eye being slashed in half, the opening shot of *Un Chien Andalou* (1928), a 25 minute film which was the equivalent of the surrealists' automatic writing. *L'Age d'Or* (1930) contained all the themes that would reappear in his future films; with the logic of a dream, a couple's sexual desires are constantly being thwarted by a bourgeois society. After *Land Without Bread* (1932) a stark documentary on the contrast between the poverty of the peasants and the wealth of the church, Buñuel left Spain and didn't make a film for fifteen years, an incredibly long silence for a major film-maker. In 1947, he emigrated to Mexico and after making commercial trash, he was able to return to serious film-making with *Los Olvidados* (*The Young and the Damned* – 1950), a powerful and yet detached view of the cruel world of juvenile delinquents. In Mexico until 1955, he made about a dozen cheap films for the home market still managing to throw up gems such as *El* (1952), which continues the theme of l'amour fou in *L'Age d'Or*, and curiosities like *Robinson Crusoe* (1952), in which he subverts Defoe's Christian message, and *Wuthering Heights* (1953), a favourite novel of the surrealists. *Viridiana* (1961) was the first film he made in his native land for twenty-nine years, and as it is a savage comedy on the Catholic mentality and rituals, he made damn sure it was his last. *The Exterminating Angel* (1962), made in Mexico, is an extremely effective parable in which guests at a sumptuous party find it physically impossible to leave. In *The Discreet Charm of the Bourgeoisie* (1972), the wealthy middle-class characters find it impossible to get anything to eat. This was the best of four later films which have loose anecdotal structures, sometimes betraying a certain laziness, but Buñuel has never wavered in his ideas and vision from the very beginning. He is perhaps the most mordantly comic and subversive of all the great directors. **Also:** *The Criminal Life of Archibaldo de la Cruz* (55), *Nazarin* (58), *The Young One* (60), *Diary of a Chambermaid* (64), *Belle de Jour* (67), *The Milky Way* (68), *Tristana* (70), *That Obscure Object of Desire* (77).

BUTLER David

American. 1894-1979. Started as a film actor, then became a producer (*Seventh Heaven* 1927). An expert purveyor of fluff, he directed four Shirley Temple vehicles and five movies with Doris Day. He started as he meant to continue with *Sunny Side Up* (1929), a pioneering musical set among the tenements of a section of New York, in which the camera moved more than previously in talkies. **Some titles:** *Bright Eyes* (34), *The Little Colonel* (35), *The Littlest Rebel* (35), *Captain January* (36), *Caught in the Draft* (41), *Road to Morocco* (42), *Thank Your Lucky Stars* (43), *Tea for Two* (50), *Calamity Jane* (53).

A surrealistic scene from Buñuel's *Los Olvidados* (1950).

BUZZELL Edward

American. Born 1897. Former musical-comedy actor who directed two of the Marx Brothers least good movies, *At the Circus* (1939) and *Go West* (1940), the last and least of the Thin Man series, *Song of the Thin Man* (1947) and one of the weakest MGM colour musicals, *Best Foot Forward* (1943), but one of the best Esther Williams musicals, *Neptune's Daughter* (1949). You can't lose 'em all.

BYRUM John

American. Former screen writer. His first film *Inserts* (1976) was generally reviled. It's an interesting attempt to make a film about filming using theatrical conventions. *Heart Beat* (1980) about Jack Kerouac and friend, never gets to the heart of the Beats.

CACOYANNIS Michael

Greek. Born 1922. Spent the war years in London with the BBC Greek service. Returned home in 1953. Gave Melina Mercouri her first screen role in *Stella* (1955), set in Athens. Put Greek cinema on the map with two penetrating studies of modern life in Greece, *The Girl in Black* (1955) and *A Matter of Dignity* (1957), both revolving around the beauty and talent of Ellie Lambetti, with keen-edged black and white photography from Walter Lassally. Because of political and financial pressures, he turned from modern to Ancient Greece with his uninspiring Euripedes trilogy, *Elektra* (1961), *The Trojan Women* (1971), and *Iphegenia* (1976), all featuring Irene Papas chewing the scenery. *Zorba the Greek* (1965), his biggest international success, imposes itself, as its "life-force" hero, like a drunk at a party insisting you drink and dance with him.

CAMERINI Mario

Italian. 1895-1981. Leading director, with BLASETTI, in the Italian cinema of the 30's. An expert at charming romantic comedies, seven of which starred Vittorio DE SICA. *Men Are Such Rascals* (1932) was the first Italian film to be shot entirely on location and greatly influenced younger film-makers. In the 50's he directed galumphing spectacles, such as *Ulysses* (1955) with Kirk Douglas.

CAMUS Marcel

French. 1912-1981. Painter and sculptor. Assisted on films by BUÑUEL and others in the 40's. His second film, *Black Orpheus* (1960), won the Grand Prix at Cannes and gained world-wide distribution. A crude transposition of the Orpheus myth to modern Rio during the Carnival, its appeal lies in its exoticism, vigorous dancing and music. His other films made little impact.

CAPRA Frank

American. Born 1897. Emigrated with his parents from Sicily when he was 6. Came to worship and propagandize the "land of opportunity". A land where an honest, patriotic, clean-living American boy can overcome all corruption, proving the power of the individual over the mob and those who do not conform to the best traditions of American democracy. He realized the American Dream by working his way through college. Joined Columbia Studios where he directed Harry Langdon in *The Strong Man* (1926) and *Long Pants* (1927), two of the "wonderful baby"'s best films. In the following seven years, Capra provided rapid, hard-edged, mad-cap comedies such as *Rain and Shine* (1930), *Platinum Blonde* (1931), *American Madness*

Frank Capra

(1932) and the Oscar-winning *It Happened One Night* (1934). While Josef von STERNBERG was playing Svengali to Marlene Dietrich at Paramount, he was making Barbara Stanwyck into a star at Columbia with four movies, trying to outdo Sternberg in erotic exoticism with *The Bitter Tea of General Yen* (1932). (The other three were *Ladies of Leisure* – 1930, *The Miracle Woman* – 1931, *Forbidden* – 1932). It happened one night in 1935 that, according to Capra's autobiography, an unknown man came to him and told him to use his God-given gifts for His purpose. The suggestiveness, sensuality and anarchy of his films disappeared. Women no longer occupied the centre, being replaced by idealistic boy-scout heroes (Gary Cooper, James Stewart). This resulted in the sequence of sanctimonious, sentimental social comedies which gained the adjective Capraesque, often referred to as Capracorn. *Mr Deeds Goes to Town* (1936), *You Can't Take*

Gary Cooper (left) and Jean Arthur in Capra's *Mr. Deeds Goes to Town* (1936).

It With You (1938), *Mr Smith Goes to Washington* (1939), *Meet John Doe* (1941) glorify the "little man" fighting for what's right and decent and losing the battle until the hectic rush to achieve the happy ending. Politically naive and demagogic as they are, they have comic pace and invention and terrific performances, particularly from Jean Arthur as the sexless heroine, and Edward Arnold as the bloated plutocrat. Script-writer Robert Riskin and cameraman Joe Walker worked on most of his films. **Others:** *Dirigible* (31), *Lost Horizon* (37), *Arsenic and Old Lace* (44), *It's a Wonderful Life* (47), *State of the Union* (50), *Here Comes the Groom* (51), *A Hole in the Head* (59), *Pocketful of Miracles* (61).

CARDIFF Jack
British. Born 1914. Brilliant photographer, known mostly for his dramatic use of colour in three Michael POWELL films, he mistakenly turned to directing in 1958. He made decent enough jobs of *Sons and Lovers* (1960) and *Young Cassidy* (1965). He directed the first film in *ODORAMA, Scent of Mystery* (1960), while *My Geisha* (1962), *The Lion* (1962) and *The Girl on the Motorcycle* (1968) all stink in a more figurative sense.

CARNÉ Marcel
French. Born in Montmartre in 1909. Entered films as a cameraman. Assistant to Jacques FEYDER on four films, before getting a chance to direct Feyder's wife, Francoise Rosay in *Jenny* (1936), co-scripted by the poet Jacques Prévert. The following six films he made with Prévert in the next decade, established Carné as a major director. Filmed against the studio-sets of Alexander Trauner, they created a melancholy poetic realism, often artificial and theatrical, but beautifully crafted, written and played. *Drôle de Drame* (1937), a bizarre comedy-thriller set in an imaginary Victorian London, was followed by *Quai des Brumes* (1938) and *Le Jour Se Lève* (1939) both with the brooding magnificence of Jean Gabin. The Occupation forced them to make "escapist" films, so *Les Enfants du Paradis* (1944) was conceived. Still on many people's lists as one of the greatest films ever made, it is certainly a richly entertaining evocation of 19th century Paris and the theatre of the day. After the war, Carné made a few attempts to recapture that old rapture, also resorting to making some "with-it" youth films. He was without it. **Also:** *Hôtel Du Nord* (1938), *Les Visiteurs Du Soir* (42), *Les Portes de la Nuit* (46), *La Marie du Port* (50), *Juliette ou la Clé des Songes* (51), *Thérèse Raquin* (53).

CARPENTER John
American. Born 1948. Studied at the University of S. California. One of the generation of movie-crazy "movie brats", steeped in the films made under the studio system, especially the low-budget thrillers, serials and space-movies of the 40's and 50's, and the work of HITCHCOCK and HAWKS. It's a case of the young devouring their elders. For Carpenter there is nothing outside movies, no life after The End. *Dark Star* (1974) is a domestic science-fiction movie, launched on a shoestring, an antidote to KUBRICK's *2001; Assault on Precinct 13* (1976), a modern *Rio Bravo* made with bravura, and *Escape from New York* (1981), set in 1997, a patchwork of ciné-borrowings. *Halloween* (1978) showed Carpenter suffering from *Psycho*-sis. Janet Leigh's daughter, Jamie Lee Curtis, as the intended victim of a mad killer, is pursued relentlessly by a subjective camera and a Bernard Herrmann-like theme (written by Carpenter). Both *Halloween II* (1981) and *Halloween III* (1982), which he only wrote and produced, contain more tricks than treats. **Also:** *The Fog* (79), *The Thing* (82).

CARRERAS Michael
British. Born 1927. Son of James Carreras, one of the founders of Hammer Films, the profitable and horrible horror studio. Produced and directed much of their ordinary blood-curdling fare such as *Maniac* (1962) and *The Curse of The Mummy's Tomb* (1964).

CARSTAIRS John Paddy
British. 1912-1970. Wrote thirty books and had paintings exhibited at the Royal Academy. Made about forty-five films, the majority being the most gawd-awful British rubbish some starring Norman Wisdom, Tommy Steele and Charlie Drake (!!). **Best film:** *Sleeping Car to Trieste* (1948), a Hitchcock and bull espionage tale.

CASS Henry
British. Born 1902. Featherweight director of non-consequential British romantic dramas, the most famous being the unintentionally funny, *The Glass Mountain* (1948). **Best film:** *Last Holiday* (1950), mainly due to Alec Guinness's subtle performance of a man living it up because he thinks he's dying.

CASSAVETES John
American. Born 1929. Brought up in the Bronx. Son of a Greek-born businessman. Made it as an actor on TV in the early 50's. Johnny Staccato, the private eye he played, is an apt nickname for him as actor and director. With money earned from acting, he made his first film, *Shadows* (1959), shot on 16mm on location in New York with a crew of four and a script based on the actors' improvisations. It had a raw vitality and inspired other young film-makers to make independent movies outside the studio system. His next two movies, *Too Late Blues* (1961) and *A Child is Waiting* (1963), made within the system, were not happy experiences. From 1968, he was able to make films his own way with a group

Jean-Louis Barrault in Carnés *Les Enfants du Paradis* (1944).

of technicians, actor-friends (Peter Falk, Ben Gazzara, Seymour Cassel) and his wife, Gena Rowlands. Like jazz, which often accompanies the films, they are made in an improvisational manner with the actors given a fairly free rein. Using cinema verité techniques with vast close-ups, the characters/actors are revealed to the camera/psychoanalyst, generally depicting menopausal (male and female) emotional crises. The result is something between a home movie, est, and Arthur Miller drama. Cassavetes seems to be aware that such a method does not so easily determine Truth, and acting itself becomes a theme, whether acting out one's social roles in *Faces* (1968), the inability to identify any longer with the role of wife and mother, in *A Woman Under the Influence* (1974), or in actual stage acting in *Opening Night* (1977). **Others:** *Husbands* (70), *Minnie and Moskowitz* (71), *The Killing of a Chinese Bookie* (76), *Gloria* (80).

CASTELLANI Renato
Italian. Born 1913. Worked as scriptwriter in 30's. A minor figure in the neo-realist movement. Best known for *Romeo and Juliet* (1954), his first film in colour, which won the Golden Lion at Venice. Freely adapted by the director, it has a certain visual style, but the coldly enunciating Laurence Harvey and the inexperienced Susan Shentall make it more of a disaster than a tragedy.

CASTLE William
American. Born 1914. Made dozens of second-rate second features from 1943-1957 before producing and directing a sequence of laughter-inducing spooky movies, often accompanied by gimmicks such as skeletons on wires dangling over the audience, seats that give electric shocks, and "fright breaks" so that cowards could leave. **Some titles:** *Macabre* (58), *House on Haunted Hill* (59), *The Tingler* (59), *Homicidal* (61).

CAVALCANTI Alberto
Brazilian. Born 1897-1982. A strange cosmopolitan figure whose best work was done at Ealing Studios in England from 1942-1949. Studied architecture in Geneva. Entered films as a set designer in Paris. In 1934 joined the GPO film unit in England. Worked as sound engineer on the Auden-Britten film-poem, *Night Mail* (1936). Joined Ealing where he made his first feature, *Went the Day Well?* (1942), an interesting but far-fetched piece about Nazi paratroopers arriving in an English village, the likeable Victorian musical *Champagne Charlie* (1945), two of the longest episodes in the eerie *Dead of Night* (1945), and the splendid *Nicholas Nickleby* (1947). After leaving England he made films in Brazil, taught in America, filmed documentaries on Israel, made dramas for French TV and worked with Brecht on a film version of *Puntila and his Servant Matti* (1955).

CAVANI Liliana
Italian. Born 1937. Made documentaries and dramas for Italian TV. Gained international fame with *The Night Porter* (1974), a pernicious and titillating tale of the sado-masochistic relationship between an ex-Nazi officer and his former concentration camp rape victim. Her sensationalism is also evident in *The Cannibals* (1969), a modern reworking of "Antigone", and *Beyond Good and Evil* (1977) about the relationship between Nietzche and Lou Salome. Beyond belief.

CAYATTE André
French. Born 1909. Journalist and lawyer. His flat, didactic films deal mostly with French legal situations. Made his name with a modern-day Romeo and Juliet story, *Les Amants de Verone* (1948), written by Jacques Prévert and needing Marcel CARNÉ. *The Crossing of the Rhine* (1960), a plodding war-time escape story, gathered a few awards.

CHABROL Claude
French. Born 1930. One of the group of young critics in the 50's on the magazine 'Cahiers du Cinema', who would later make films themselves. In 1957 (with Eric ROHMER) he published a book on HITCHCOCK, which saw the director as a Catholic moralist. It is easier to see in retrospect that in describing Hitchcock, the writers were describing themselves. Murder is at the heart of all his films, seen as an inevitable act, often a necessity to restore the status quo of bourgeois life. Chabrol likes to present himself as a well-fed, happily married man who, in his films, mocks the complacency of bourgeois marriage with the added spice of his wife, Stephane Audran (generally called Hélene), as the victim or cause of murder. Whatever is seething under the surface of his characters – guilt, jealousy or crime, the niceties of life go on. Large meals at home or in a restaurant have become his signature. Unlike some of his former colleagues on Cahiers (GODARD, RIVETTE, TRUFFAUT) he has always been happier in the mainstream, although it is his *Le Beau Serge* (1958), made on location in his own village, that is considered the first film of the *Nouvelle Vague*. He followed it with *Les Cousins* (1959) which is more associated with the aesthetics of the movement, being shot in the cafés and streets of Paris. After the ironic comedy, *Les Bonnes Femmes* (1960), his tendency towards the grotesque and an eye on the commercial, led him into seven years of paltry stuff. He re-established his reputation in 1968 with *Les Biches*, an elegantly enacted bi-sexual menage á trois, and began the "Hélene cycle". *La Femme Infidele* (1968), *La Rupture* (1970), *Juste Avant La Nuit* (1971), *Les Noces Rouges* (1972) are all variations on the theme of infidelity leading to murder. Added to this, *Killer!* (1969) and *Le Boucher* (1970) it is an impressive, if rather limited oeuvre.

CHAFFEY Don
British. Born 1917. Worked at Gainsborough Studios art department. Directed a hodge-podge of commercial movies including spectacles such as *Jason and the Argonauts* (1963) and *One Million Years B.C.* (1966) of which the raison d'être is Ray Harryhausen's special effects. **Others:** *The Man Upstairs* (59), *Greyfriars Bobby* (60), *The Prince and the Pauper* (62), *Viking Queen* (67), *Creatures the World Forgot* (71).

CHAPLIN Charles
British. 1889-1977. Born in the slums of Lambeth in London. Died in Switzerland as the wealthy Sir Charles. Became one of the most famous men in the world on the strength of over sixty silent shorts made before 1920 and only a handful of features. Son of music-hall performers, he joined Fred Karno's Company as a child. In 1913 went to Mack SENNETT's Keystone Studios in Hollywood where he appeared in dozens of short slapstick comedies. He was soon directing and writing all his own vehicles and the Little Tramp was created for *Kid Auto Races* (1914), a character he was to play until 1936 *(Modern Times)*. Gradually he broke away from the mechanical and crude techniques of the Sen-

Chaplin directs Chaplin

---

nett comedies and introduced pathos and a detailed social background into more structured and ambitious farces such as *Easy Street* (1917) and *The Immigrant* (1917), which, within the comic limitations, include social comment and autobiographical touches. He took nearly a year to make his first feature, *The Kid* (1920), set in the London slums, with the remarkable six-year-old Jackie Coogan. After forming United Artists with Mary Pickford, Douglas Fairbanks and D. W. GRIFFITH, he made *Woman of Paris* (1923) with Edna Purviance, his leading ladÿ in almost thirty comedies, playing a high-class prostitute. Although its subtle handling of a rather dated melodrama was a critical success and an influence on Ernst LUBITSCH, it failed at the box-office and Chaplin didn't allow it to be shown for over fifty years. The public was obviously more interested

in Charlie the Tramp than Edna the Tramp. His next three films were his greatest. *The Gold Rush* (1925), *The Circus* (1928) and *City Lights* (1931), all manage in a Dickensian manner to shift from satire to pathos to broad comedy to didacticism. Feeling that the "talkies" would limit his world-wide appeal, he resisted using spoken dialogue for thirteen years. In *Modern Times* (1936) the tramp is heard for the first and last time singing in gibberish so that he was still communicating in a universal language. *The Great Dictator* (1940) was his first film to use sound fully and despite the naive and embarrassing six-minute oration in the end, it contains wonderful comic set-pieces. In 1947, he shocked the public by playing a multiple wife-murderer in *Monsieur Verdoux*. His performance is an elegant masterpiece, but his direction had not really evolved very far from the 30's. He courageously played an old-fashioned comic who no longer makes people laugh in *Limelight* (1952). Although verbose, over-

sentimental and clumsily made, the material is transcended by his presence and the memorable music-hall sequence with Buster KEATON, with Chaplin hogging the limelight. *A King in New York* (1957 – made in Britain) is a sour, intermittently funny attack on the USA's shabby treatment of him. His last film, *The Countess from Hong Kong* (1967) was a crude, unfunny and sad ending to an indispensable career.

CHRISTENSEN Benjamin
Danish. 1879-1959. Former opera singer, writer and actor. Started directing in 1913. One of the earliest exponents of the horror genre, he was greatly admired by Carl DREYER. His most famous film, *Witchcraft Through the Ages* (1922), took three years to make. With himself as the devil, he conducts us through a semi-documentary made up of a series of tableaux inspired by Bosch and Bruegel. In Hollywood from 1926, he made a couple of comedy-thrillers with Chester Conklin and *Mockery*

(1927) with Lon Chaney. The last sixteen years of his life were spent in obscurity in Denmark.

CHRISTIAN-JAQUE
French. Born 1904. Studied music and architecture. Married to Martine Carol whose blonde buxomness he exploited in costume romances such as *Lucrezia Borgia* (1952) and *Nana* (1954). Attracted to French 19th century Romantics, he had Jean-Louis Barrault as Berlioz composing during a thunderstorm in *La Symphonie Fantastique* (1941), Gerard Philipe swashing his buckle in *La Chartreuse de Parme* (1947) and *Fanfan La Tulipe* (1951), and in Dumas' *The Black Tulip* (1963) Alain Delon had the classic line (in the dubbed version), "The horse tossed me off."

CHUKRAI Grigori
Russian. Born 1921. Assistant to Mikhail ROMM. Mainly known in the West for *Ballad of a Soldier* (1959), prize winner at Cannes. It's a simple, sentimental, quite effective view of people's suffering in war as seen through the eyes of a young soldier. ALSO: *The Forty First* (56), *Clear Sky* (61), *Life is Wonderful* (82).

CHYTILOVÁ Vera
Czech. Born 1929. Studied philosophy and architecture. Former fashion model. Attended Prague Film School and was part of a lively movement in Czechoslovakia in the 60's, which included Milos FORMAN and Ivan PASSER. Her first films were influenced by GODARD, using non-actors and improvisation. *Daisies* (1966) is the most adventurous and anarchic Czech film of the period. Two bored girls decide by a series of outrageous practical jokes to destroy the conventions around them. With a bold use of colour, double exposure and fragmentation, it is the cinema of the absurd. *The Fruits of Paradise* (1969), produced by a Belgian company, carried on her experiments in visual metaphors. She has since made bright but undemanding comedies, e.g. *Calamity* (1980).

CIMINO Michael
American. Born 1939. Graduated with an MFA from Yale in 1963. Military service as a medic with the Green Beret Training Unit in Texas. Wrote screenplays before Clint EASTWOOD gave him a chance to direct *Thunderbolt and Lightfoot* (1974), an

Christopher Walken held captive in Cimino's *The Deer Hunter* (1978).

overblown macho heist movie with Eastwood and Jeff Bridges as buddy-buddies. His second film, *The Deer Hunter* (1978) won five Academy Awards and exactly caught the mood of the time – the need for America to find some justification for the war in Vietnam. The set-pieces such as the wedding (almost a production number) and the hunt are epically conceived. The war itself is no more convincing than Errol Flynn or John WAYNE's heroics against the Japs, and the Russian roulette metaphor doesn't ring true. The homecoming works hard on the emotions but patriotism, like temptation, is difficult to resist. Despite its Adventure Magazine story attitudes, the three hour structure is impressive, whereas *Heaven's Gate* (1981), already famous as the most expensive floperoo of all time (36 million dollars) has a sprawling, confused narrative. As the characters are never focused, the intimate scenes suffer in comparison with the virtuoso sweep of the panoramic ensembles. This monumental Western on the Johnson County War between the cattlemen and the immigrant farmers, has only suffered more by being cut to a ninety minute version.

CLAIR René
French. 1898-1981. Born René Chomette in Paris. His films have the same reputation for gaiety as that city and his pseudonym means clear, limpid. There are few clouds in Clair's world. In his silent films he lifted his beret to his idol CHAPLIN. *Entr'acte* (1924) is a twenty-minute Dada joke, shot in Parisian locations and featuring members of the avant-garde such as Picabia, Man Ray and Marcel Duchamp. Far funnier is his adaptation of Labiche's 19th century farce, *The Italian Straw Hat* (1927), made with clockwork precision. Clair felt that the preparation for a film was more important than the filming, which accounts for a certain theatricality, but they still retain a freshness. His first sound film, *Sous Les Toits de Paris* (1930) uses songs and street noises with a minimum of dialogue. The two musical comedies, *Le Million* (1931) and *À Nous La Liberté* (1931) are dominated by songs and movement, filmed against the sly, artificial sets of Lazare Meerson. They were both great influences on the development of the Hollywood Musical in the use of related action and songs, while the latter inspired

René Clair

Chaplin's *Modern Times* (1936). Just before the war, he left France to work abroad. Whether in England (*The Ghost Goes West* – 1935) or in America (*I Married a Witch* – 1942) he continued on his carefree way. His post-war films were a little darker and less successful, but his gentle irony is still evident in *Summer Manoeuvres* (1955), his first film in colour. **Others:** *The Flame of New Orleans* (41), *It Happened Tomorrow* (44), *Le Silence est d'Or* (47), *La Beauté du Diable* (50), *Porte des Lilas* (57).

CLARKE Shirley
American. Born 1925. Trained in Modern Dance with Martha Graham. She became part of the growing counter-cultural movement in American cinema with her "poetic" documentaries (1953-1958). Her first feature, *The Connection* (1961) is a powerful cinema-in-the round translation of the Living Theater's play about junkies. *The Cool World* (1963), a view of ghetto life in Harlem, fails to bring together coherently documentary and fiction techniques, while *Portrait of Jason* (1967) is an intrusive and embarrassing monologue by a black homosexual getting more and more stoned. She works mostly in video now.

CLAYTON Jack
British. Born 1921. Worked as assistant to John HUSTON in 1952-1953. His short, *The Bespoke Overcoat* (1955) won a prize at Venice. *Room at the Top* (1958), his first feature, had a realism and "sexiness" not often seen hitherto in British cinema but was soon surpassed by the early films of REISZ, RICHARDSON, SCHLESINGER and TV drama. Abandoned realism for *The Innocents* (1961), a pale version of "The Turn of the Screw", and *The Pumpkin Eater* (1964) both of which suffer from a clash of styles. As director, he takes the main blame for the glossy vacuities of *The Great Gatsby* (1974).

CLEMENT René
French. Born 1913. Studied architecture. Entered films as a cameraman. Assistant on COCTEAU's *Beauty and the Beast* (1946). His first feature, *La Bataille du Rail* (1946), contains the stark realism of his documentary shorts. It tells of the work of the French railway workers in the Resistance, with the men themselves re-enacting their roles. The direct and simple style of *Forbidden Games* (1952) on the effects of war on children, is very moving. His sensitivity is used in a different way in the charming comedy, *Knave of Hearts* (1954) set in a real London as seen by Gallic philanderer, Gerard Philipe. Since then the only ray of warming light in his career came with *Plein Soleil* (*Purple Noon* – 1959), a perverse tale beautifully photographed by Henri Decae around the Mediterranean. **Others:** *Gervaise* (55), *This Angry Age* (58), *Is Paris Burning?* (66), *The Deadly Trap* (71).

CLINE Edward
American. 1892-1961. Very active comedy director who started with Mack SENNETT and continued into the 40's. Co-directed over a dozen Buster KEATON shorts. His best feature-length sound movies were four W. C. Fields vehicles: *Million Dollar Legs* (1932), *My Little Chickadee* (1940), *The Bank Dick* (1940), *Never Give a Sucker an Even Break* (1941). The rest were mostly programmers for Universal including five Andrews Sisters musicals e.g. *Moonlight and Cactus* (1944).

CLOUZOT Henri-Georges
French. 1907-1977. Wrote scripts from 1932-1942. Worked in Berlin in the early 30's, directing French versions of German films. Mainly because of ill-health, he only made eleven films after 1942, most of them exceptionally dark in character, and in the case of *The Spies* (1958) downright obscure. His second film, *Le Corbeau* (1943), about the effect poison-pen letters have on the inhabitants of a French village, is a bleak view of provincial life and he was accused of making anti-French Nazi propaganda. (The film was produced by Germans but not shown in Germany. It was remade by Otto PREMINGER as *The 13th Letter* – 1951). He was not able to make another film until after the war. In 1953, he made one of the most successful French films ever, *The Wages of Fear*, an extraordinary suspenseful story of four truck drivers transporting nitro-glycerine for three hundred miles. Pretty chilling too is *Diabolique* (1955), a tale of murder set in a gruesome private school. Among the gloom is a surprisingly bright operetta, *Miquette et Sa Mere* (1950) and the intriguing documentary of Picasso at work, *The Picasso Mystery* (1956). He ended his days televising symphony concerts. ALSO: *Quai des Orfèvres* (47), *Manon* (48).

COCTEAU Jean
French. 1889-1963. Poet/novelist/playwright/film director/designer/painter/stage director/ballet producer/patron/myth-maker/friend of the great/raconteur/wit. Jacques of all trades and master of all. It is difficult to isolate the six films he directed and those he wrote and inspired from his work in other art forms. Films were another form of poetry, and the poet is at the centre of his oeuvre i.e. himself. Made his first film when he was forty-one and already famous. *The Blood of a Poet* (*Le Sang d'un Poete* – 1930) contains all the signs and symbols of personal mythology evident from his novels, poems and drawings. The death and resurrection of a poet (Orpheus), the link between death and youth (beautiful young men), the bull-fight, the living statues, opium, the passing to the other side of the mirror. Although surrealist in manner, it is too calculated and conscious to have been accepted as such, but was a great influence on the American avant-garde. The second of his Orphic trilogy, *Orpheus* (1950) is his finest work. A perfect marriage between Greek myth and Cocteau's own and although it uses reverse slow-motion and negative images to suggest the Underworld (reached through the looking glass), the modern-day

domestic life of Mr and Mrs Orpheus is filmed "realistically". Also in *Beauty and the Beast* (1945), a fairy tale for children and intelligent adults, he tried to show unreality in terms of reality. The beast is played touchingly by Cocteau's monstre-sacré, Jean Marais and in the end Beauty is slightly disappointed when he turns into the romantic Jean Marais. *The Testament of Orpheus*, his valedictory film, is a self-indulgent, self-mocking, self-portrait, meaningless without previous knowledge of his films, writings and life. He himself wanders through the film, his feet hardly touching the ground, explaining his art with the help of friends (Marais, Picasso, Yul Brynner etc). *The Eagle has Two Heads* (1947) and *Les Parents Terribles* (1948), clever transpositions of his plays to the screen, are wordy and over-ripe melodramas, happier behind a proscenium arch. Although directed by others, his presence is strongly felt in *L'Eternal Retour* (1943) and *Les Enfants Terribles* (1950).

COLLINSON Peter
British. 1938-1980. His first film, *The Penthouse* (1967) is a nasty little shocker. After the strained naturalism of *Up the Junction* (1968) and the car-chase caper movie, *The Italian Job* (1969), he returned to making nasty little shockers.

COMENCINI Luigi
Italian. Born 1916. Studied architecture. Film critic and photographer during the war. Made a promising start as director of the prize-winning short, *Bambini in Citta* (1946) about children in post-war Milan, but his main output has been conventional Italian fare of which *Bread, Love and Dreams* (1953) and *Bread, Love and Jealousy* (1954) with Gina Lollobrigida are his best known abroad. His talent for working with children emerged occasionally, especially in the made-for-TV, *The Adventures of Pinocchio* (1971).

CONWAY Jack
American. 1887-1952. Former actor with D. W. GRIFFITH's company. Started directing in 1912 and continued into his sixties. Close friend of Irving Thalberg, head of MGM production, he became an MGM stalwart. With all the best people working for him all he had to do was shout, "Action!" and action was what he liked most. Of his five movies with

Clark Gable, *Too Hot to Handle* (1938), a fast and furious comedy about globe-trotting newsreel cameramen, is the best. He skilfully recreated the Mexican Revolution (*Viva Villa* – 1934) and the French Revolution (*A Tale of Two Cities* – 1935) on the MGM backlot. **Others:** *New Moon* (30), *Arsene Lupin* (32), *A Yank at Oxford* (38), *Boom Town* (40), *Honky Tonk* (40), *The Hucksters* (47), *Julia Misbehaves* (48).

COOPER Merian C.
American. 1893-1973. Journalist, explorer, pilot in World War I. Together with the cameraman, Ernest B. SCHOEDSACK, he produced and directed two documentary features, the first sound version of *The Four Feathers* (1929) and *King Kong* (1933). The latter, filmed in a studio with ingenious use of back projection and models by Willis O'Brien, has seldom been equalled in the monster genre. Cooper and Schoedsack can be seen for a few seconds as the pilots of the plane trying to shoot Kong on the Empire State Building. He became a producer of many John FORD pictures.

COPPOLA Francis Ford
American. Born 1939. Son of Italian immigrant parents. Film graduate of UCLA where he studied with Dorothy ARZNER. Worked as writer and assistant director to Roger CORMAN, who enabled him to direct his first movie, a gruesome cheapie called *Dementia 13* (1963). *You're a Big Boy Now* (1966) is a lively comedy, set in New York, about a young man's sexual education. Very much a movie by a 26-year-old of the mid-60's, with techniques derived from Richard

LESTER's Beatles films, it was shot on a limited budget in under a month, proving to Warner Bros. that he was a man to watch. His second film for them wasn't worth watching. *Finian's Rainbow* (1968) is indigestible Irish whimsy interspersed with songs and platitudes. In 1969, emulating Corman, he opened his own studio, American Zoetrope, in an office in San Francisco, with George LUCAS. *Rain People* (1969) was shot on location across America from New York to L.A., but wasn't very sure where it was going. This well-acted view of an alienated America, is weighed down by flashbacks and a playing on the emotions. *The Conversation* (1974), made for Zoetrope, is an initially fascinating post-Watergate thriller of a professional eavesdropper being bugged himself, that moves spuriously from the physical to the metaphysical. *The Godfather* (1971) made the public an offer they couldn't refuse. This long (175 mins) and leisurely apotheosis of The Mafia and The Family builds up a rich pattern of relationships, detailing meticulously the rituals of an enclosed group. The film, only tenuously linking the Mafia with American society as a whole, is laudatory and romantic. *Godfather II* (1975) has a more complex structure and its attitudes are similarly more complex, even vainly attempting to establish (through the outsider played by Diane Keaton) an objective viewpoint. Pulp fiction is often made into fine films but, despite the impressive control of the diffuse material, both *Godfathers* remain pulp cinema. *Apocalypse Now* (1979) assaults the senses and numbs the mind with some extraordinary set pieces. Coppola wanted to "give its audience a sense of the horror, the madness, the sensuousness and the moral dilemma of the Vietnam war". But the quest to find Marlon BRANDO in "the heart of darkness" (it is loosely based on Conrad's story) by river, is like a nightmarish Disneyland ride. Unfortunately, at the end of the ride, we are forced to listen to the muddled mumblings of the crazed Brando. *One From The Heart* (1982) is a 25 million dollar musical romance filmed in a huge set of Las Vegas. **Also:** *The Outsiders* and *Rumblefish* (1983).

CORMAN Roger
American. Born 1926. Entered the movies as an errand boy at Fox in 1948. Set up Roger Corman Productions in 1953 and for the next five

Their credo is violence...Their God is hate...The most terrifying film of our time!

JOINT... the fuzz-hater show him a badge and he sees red!

BULL... swinging a cycle chain in each hand and lusting for "action"

DEAR JOHN... the "hog stomper" whose God is speed... he had a bath once but didn't like it.

AMERICAN INTERNATIONAL PRESENTS

PETER FONDA · NANCY SINATRA
STARRING IN
THE WILD ANGELS
IN PANAVISION® AND PATHECOLOR

CO STARRING BRUCE DERN AND DIANE LADD PRODUCED AND DIRECTED BY ROGER CORMAN · WRITTEN BY CHARLES GRIFFITH WITH

MEMBERS OF HELL'S ANGELS OF VENICE, CALIFORNIA

Corman's *The Wild Angels* (1966).

years, on a tiny budget and in rented studios, he produced and directed such Z movies as *She-Gods of Shark Reef* (1956), and *Teenage Caveman* (1958). In the early 60's, for American International, he went more up-market with a series of adaptations from Edgar Allan Poe. Using the team of designer Daniel Haller and cameraman Floyd Crosby, he created garish, *frightfully* amusing shockers, taking their tone from Vincent Price's sibilant, ghoulish hamming. Nothing amusing in the blood-splattered *St Valentine's Day Massacre* (1967) nor *Bloody Mama* (1970) nor in the dire youth-oriented movies, *Wild Angels* (1966) and *The Trip* (1967). Gave up directing in 1971 after the nose-dive of *Von Richthofen and Brown* (*The Red Baron* – GB). In 1974, he set up his own company called New World and continued to produce cheap formula pictures for the youth market as well as putting his money into pres-

tige films from Europe. He gave, among others, Peter BOGDANO-VICH, Francis Ford COPPOLA and Monte HELLMAN their first chances to direct. **The Poe titles:** *House of Usher* (60), *The Pit and the Pendulum* (61), *The Premature Burial* (61), *Tales of Terror* (61), *The Raven* (62), *The Masque of the Red Death* (64), *The Tomb of Ligeia* (64).

CORNELIUS Henry
British. 1913-1958. S. African born. Studied and worked in Germany with Max Reinhardt. Came to Britain in the mid-30's. Started as film editor. Directed the first "Ealing Comedy", *Passport to Pimlico* (1948) which is typically about ordinary people in a small community to which extra-ordinary events happen. *Genevieve* (1954) delightfully perpetuates the myth of English quaintness with its view of two couples on the London-Brighton vintage car run. *I am a Camera* (1955) is nearer to the spirit of the original Isherwood novel ("Goodbye to Berlin") than *Cabaret* (1972), the musical version. **Also:** *The*

Galloping Major (51), *Next to No Time* (57).

COSTA-GAVRAS Constantine
French. Born 1933 in Greece. Came to France at 18 to study at the Sorbonne. Drawn to political subjects, not so much to the ideas but the effect those ideas have on people. Because of the success of *Z* (1968), a very slick and effective condemnation of the Colonels' regime in Greece, he was able to continue to make uncomplicated, dramatic movies with a political theme. Yves Montand is assassinated in *Z*, tortured by the Czech police in *The Confession* (1970) and kidnapped in Uraguay in *State of Siege* (1972). Turned down *The Godfather* as he felt it glorified The Mafia. His first American film *Missing* (1982), tells of a father's (Jack Lemmon) anguish when his son is arrested by the military junta in Chile. The camera work (Ricardo Aronovich) chillingly captures the atmosphere of a Police state and the message is unequivocal, but politics is more complex than his political

thrillers suggest.

COTTAFAVI Vittorio

Italian. Born 1914. Assistant to Vittorio DE SICA. Directed much on Italian TV. His B movie spectacles (a contradiction in terms), almost parodies of the genre, are made bearable by his often striking visual sense. Stopped directing beefcake films in 1965 when the "Spaghetti" Westerns took over the market. **Some titles:** *Hercules Conquers Atlantis* (61), *The Vengeance of Hercules* (60), *The Hundred Horsemen* (64).

CRABTREE Arthur

British. Born 1900. Former cameraman. In an uneven career, the highlights were two romantic Romany melodramas, *Madonna of the Seven Moons* (1944) and *Caravan* (1946), both starring the dashing Stewart Granger. **Also:** *Lilli Marlene* (50), *Hindle Wakes* (52), *Horrors of the Black Museum* (59).

CRICHTON Charles

British. Born 1910. Former film editor. Joined Ealing Studios in its heyday. Contributed to the episode film of the supernatural, *Dead of Night* (1945). His light touch is evident in "The Golfing Story". Went on to direct two of the funniest and most typical "Ealing Comedies" *The Lavender Hill Mob* (1951) and *The Titfield Thunderbolt* (1953). With British comedy becoming harsher and broader, he continued in the Ealing tradition with *The Battle of the Sexes* (1959) in which Peter Sellers gives one of his most nicely judged character performances. **Also:** *Hue and Cry* (46), *Hunted* (52), *The Love Lottery* (54), *The Divided Heart* (54).

CROMWELL John

American. 1888-1979. Stage actor and director who, after making films for over twenty years, returned to the stage. Directed most scripts that were given to him by his studio bosses as professionally as possible, encouraging the performers to give of their best. Mostly at RKO in the 30's, it was he who gave Bette Davis her first meaty part in *Of Human Bondage* (1934). Such smoothly-made hits as *The Prisoner of Zenda* (1937), *Anna and the King of Siam* (1946) and *Since You Went Away* (1944) added to his prestige. After seven years away from Hollywood, he returned to make *The Goddess* (1958), a rambling, over-written, over-acted tale of an anguished film star (Kim Stanley).

He appeared in a few films, most recently in Robert ALTMAN's *Three Women* (1977) and *A Wedding* (1978). **Others:** *Little Lord Fauntleroy* (36), *Algiers* (38), *Made for Each Other* (39), *Abe Lincoln in Illinois* (39), *The Enchanted Cottage* (45), *Dead Reckoning* (47), *Caged* (50).

CROSLAND Alan

American. 1894-1936. Earns his place in movie history as director of two epoch-making films. *Don Juan* (1926), with a leaping, kissing Douglas Fairbanks, was the first full-length feature to use sound effects and synchronized music, and the schmaltzy *The Jazz Singer* (1927), the first film with spoken dialogue, in which Al Jolson speaks the prophetic words, "You ain't heard nothin' yet!" Crosland continued to make minor, old-fashioned movies before being killed in an auto accident on Sunset Boulevard at the age of forty-one.

CUKOR George

American. Born 1899. Originally a director on Broadway, came to Hollywood, when movies first spoke, as dialogue director. The name of Cukor on the titles conjures up the image of a sophisticated and affable host at a dinner party where one will meet elegant and beautiful women, witty men and where the conversation will be pitched at just the right level, neither vulgar nor too highbrow. His long career started shakily when Ernst LUBITSCH gradually took over the direction of the Maurice Chevalier-Jeanette MacDonald musical, *One Hour with You*

(1932). He sued Paramount and got credited as sole director. Seven years later, he was taken off *Gone with the Wind*, which he had begun. At MGM he was soon directing glossy, literate prestige productions such as *Dinner at Eight* (1933), *Little Women* (1933), *David Copperfield* (1934), and *Romeo and Juliet* (1936) and gained the reputation, which stuck with him all his life, of being a "woman's director". It is not unjustified. *Little Women*, big women in the all-woman cast of *The Women* (1939) (even the dog was a bitch), fallen women (Garbo languishing in *Camille* – 1936), *Two-Faced Woman* (1941 – Garbo's last role), *A Woman's Face* (1941) with Joan Crawford, *Les Girls* (1957) and *My Fair Lady* (1964). His favourite actress Katharine Hepburn was at her most radiant in *Holiday* (1938), her wittiest in *Philadelphia Story* (1940) and her most affecting as a boy in *Sylvia Scarlett* (1935). He moved into the 50's with a harder-edged type of comedy, generally working with the Garson KANIN-Ruth Gordon writing team, on two Tracy-Hepburn vehicles, *Adam's Rib* (1949) and *Pat and Mike* (1952), and three Judy Holliday movies, *Born Yesterday* (1950), *The Marrying Kind* (1952) and *It Should Happen to You* (1954). He reached his peak with *A Star is Born* (1954) in which Judy Garland gives the performance of her life. Cukor's use of CinemaScope, lighting, colour and costumes surpassed all other attempts at a musical on the wide screen. Nothing he has done since touches it. **Others:** *A Bill of Divorcement* (32), *What Price Hollywood?* (32), *Gaslight* (44), *A Double Life* (48), *Edward My Son* (48), *The Actress* (53), *Bhowani Junction* (56), *Heller in Pink Tights* (59), *Let's Make Love* (60), *The Chapman Report* (62), *Justine* (69), *Travels with My Aunt* (72), *The Blue-Bird* (76), *Rich and Famous* (81).

CUMMINGS Irving

American. 1888-1959. Former silent film actor. Spent most of his career at Fox, directing sweet, colourful musicals without much content, starring their top blondes, Shirley Temple (four films), Alice Faye (two films) and Betty Grable (four films). **Some titles:** *Curly Top* (35), *Little Miss Broadway* (38), *Lillian Russell* (40), *Down Argentine Way* (40), *That Night in Rio* (41), *My Gal Sal* (42), *Springtime in the Rockies* (42), *Sweet Rosy O'Grady* (43), *The Dolly Sisters* (45).

R to L: Ingrid Bergman, Humphrey Bogart, Paul Henreid and Claude Rains in Curtiz's *Casablanca* (1943).

CURTIZ Michael

Hungarian. 1888-1962. Actor and producer in the Budapest theatre. Worked with STILLER and SJOSTROM in Sweden before coming to Hollywood in 1926. At Warner Bros. for twenty-seven years, turning out over a hundred films for them. His English was notoriously bad and obviously he couldn't say "No". His main output was adventure movies told with economy, fluency and pace. He made over a dozen pictures with Errol Flynn, directed James Cagney screaming on his way to the electric chair in *Angels with Dirty Faces* (1938) and tap-dancing zippily to his only Oscar in *Yankee Doodle Dandy* (1942) and the first serious boxing drama, *Kid Galahad* (1937). His Midas touch was most evident in *Casablanca* (1943). Although nobody on the set knew what was happening, Curtiz brought together plot, piquant dialogue, cherishable performances, emotional music, atmospheric photography to create the epitome of 40's Hollywood romance. As time goes by, it looks even better. **Some titles:** *20,000 Years in Sing Sing* (32), *The Mystery of the Wax Museum* (33), *Jimmy the Gent* (34), *Captain Blood* (35), *The Charge of the Light Brigade* (36), *The Adventures of Robin Hood* (38), *The Private Lives of Elizabeth and Essex* (39), *The Sea Hawk* (40), *The Sea Wolf* (41), *Passage to Marseilles* (44), *Mildred Pierce* (45), *Night and Day* (46), *Life with Father* (47), *Young Man with a Horn* (50), *The Breaking Point* (50), *Trouble Along the Way* (53), *The Egyptian* (54), *White Christmas* (54), *We're No Angels* (55), *The Vagabond King* (56), *The Best Things in Life are Free* (56), *King Creole* (58), *The Comancheros* (61).

CZINNER Paul

Hungarian. 1890-1972. Came to England in 1930 as a political exile, after making several films in Germany. All his story-feature films star his wife, German actress Elizabeth Bergner, and are vehicles for her syrupy charms, including *As You Like It* (1936) with Laurence OLIVIER's Orlando being pushed out by close-ups of Mrs Czinner's Rosalind. In the 50's, he concentrated on filming great opera and ballet. Using a multiple camera technique, his transpositions of stage productions to the screen are now done much better on TV. **Some titles:** *Catherine the Great* (34), *Escape Me Never* (36), *Don Giovanni* (55), *Der Rosenkavalier* (61).

D

DA COSTA Morton

American. Born 1914. Director on Broadway, he brought pazazz from The Great White Way into two big Warners movies, *Auntie Mame* (1958) and *The Music Man* (1962), both of which he had directed on stage. ALSO: *Island of Love* (1963).

DASSIN Jules

American. Born 1911. Actor with the Yiddish theatre and the left-wing Group Theatre in the 30's. Started directing shorts at MGM, before graduating to second features. It was with *Brute Force* (1947), a tough prison drama, that he discovered his real talent lay in films noirs. *Naked City* (1948) won acclaim for its dramatic use of New York locations and was followed by *Thieves' Highway* (1949) and *Night and the City* (1950), in which he used a sleazy London milieu as effectively as he had used New York. After being forced out of Hollywood in 1950 by the McCarthy blacklistings, he settled in France where he made *Rififi* (1956), a clever heist movie with a 30-minute robbery sequence without dialogue. On these five crime thrillers, Dassin's reputation must rest. Artistically, his marriage to Melina Mercouri did more damage to his career than Senator McCarthy. Her ouzo-soaked voice croaked passionately to best effect as prostitutes in *He Who Must Die* (1958) and *Never on Sunday* (1959), remembered more for its bouzouki music than its contrived meeting between the intellectual (ineffectively played by the director) and the life-enhancing whore. He updated the Greek classics, *Phaedra* (1962) and *A Dream of Passion* (Medea – 1978) with ludicrous results and the tear-stained *Promise at Dawn* (1970) with his missus as a "wonderful" mother would cure anyone of an Oedipus complex. **Also:** *Topkapi* (64), *10.30pm Summer* (66), *Uptight* (68).

DAVES Delmer

American. 1904-1977. Lived with Red Indians for a short time in his youth which might account for *Broken Arrow* (1950), with Jeff Chandler as Cochise, one of the first really sympathetic portrayals of a Red Indian. He is known mainly for half-a-dozen brooding, slightly didactic Westerns with psychological undertones. Three with Glenn Ford, *Jubal* (1956), *3.10 to Juma* (1957) and *Cowboy* (1958) are sturdy examples. A screenwriter in the 30's, he continued to write his own scripts as director. His most interesting films are *Pride of the Marines* (1945), a harrowing story of a soldier (John Garfield) blinded in the war in the Pacific, and *Dark Passage* (1947) in which the first forty minutes are seen entirely through the eyes of the hero (Humphrey Bogart). His last seven movies were soggy soap-operas, four of them featuring Warner Bros. bland, blond young star, Troy Donahue. *Youngblood Hawke* (1964), about the literary world(!!), is hilariously silly. **Some titles:** *Destination Tokyo* (43), *Hollywood Canteen* (45), *The Red House* (47), *Demetrius and the Gladiators* (54), *The Last Wagon* (56), *Kings Go Forth* (58), *A Summer Place* (60), *Parrish* (61), *Susan Slade* (61), *Rome Adventure* (62), *Spencer's Mountain* (63), *The Battle of the Villa Fiorita* (65).

DAY Robert

British. Born 1922. Former cameraman. Director of five Tarzan movies featuring three different Tarzans between 1960-1968, plus a few amiable British comedies. Married to Dorothy Provine. **Some titles:** *The Green Man* (57), *Two-Way Stretch* (60), *The Rebel* (61), *She* (65).

DEARDEN Basil

British. 1911-1971. Started at Ealing Studios co-directing three deliciously wacky Will Hay comedies (1941-1943). His own films, generally produced and sometimes co-directed by Michael Relph, are ponderous, well-intentioned dramas with a social message, apart from a couple of minor comedies, *The Smallest Show on Earth* (1957) and *The League of Gentlemen* (1960). In *Frieda* (1947), a German bride bravely copes with anti-German feeling in an English town and in *Pool of London* (1951) a black takes a smuggling rap for his white buddy. The messages in *Sapphire* (1959) and *Victim* (1961) are wrapped inside lousy melodramatic B-movie plots. The former tries to tackle racial prejudice and the latter makes a plea for tolerance of homosexuals. The same strained seriousness was brought to bear on *Khartoum* (1966), the biggest budget movie he ever directed. Dearden was killed in a road accident. **Others:** *The Bells Go Down* (43), *The Captive Heart* (46), *Saraband for Dead Lovers* (48), *The Blue Lamp* (49), *The Square Ring* (53), *The Rainbow Jacket* (54), *Woman of Straw* (63),

Melina Mercouri in Dassin's *10.30 p.m. Summer* (1966).

Masquerade (64).

DE BROCA Philippe

French. Born 1933. Assistant director on Claude CHABROL's first three films. His own first three films are effervescent sex comedies *Playing at Love* (1959), *The Joker* (1960), and *Infidelity* (1961) featuring a bouncing Jean-Pierre Cassel (a De Broca look-alike). The next three films with Jean-Pierre Belmondo, although equally frivolous, are weighed down by larger production values. *King of Hearts* (1966) has an interesting idea: lunatics from an asylum seem sane during World War I, but it is rammed into the ground. The rest of his output are modest, well-made, French main-stream films. **Some titles:** *Cartouche* (62), *That Man From Rio* (63), *Dear Inspector* (77).

DE CORDOVA Frederick

American. Born 1910. Directed on stage and TV. His movies are mainly second-feature light comedies including *Bedtime for Bonzo* (1951), in which a talented chimp acted the pants off Ronald Reagan, and the sequel, sans Reagan, *Bonzo Goes to College* (1952). **Also:** *The Countess of Monte Cristo* (48), *The Gal Who Took the West* (49), *I'll Take Sweden* (65), *Frankie and Johnnie* (66).

DELANNOY Jean

French. Born 1908. Former journalist and film editor. Started his career promisingly with Jean COCTEAU's modern version of the Tristan and Isolde legend, *L'Eternal Retour* (1943), made during the Occupation with its Aryan lovers pleasing to the occupiers. After the war, Michele Morgan chose him to direct her first film on her return to France as the blind, peasant girl in André Gide's *La Symphonie Pastorale* (1949). The rest of his work was steady and unexceptional, save for the rather touching *Les Amities Particulaires* (*This Special Friendship* – 1964), set in a Catholic boys' school. His *Hunchback of Notre Dame* (1956), with Anthony Quinn, couldn't hold a candle to the first two versions (1923, 1939). **Also:** *Marie Antoinette* (56), *Maigret Sets a Trap* (57).

DELLUC Louis

French. 1892-1924. One of the first critics to consider film as an art form and work out a film theory. Coined the word "cineaste", meaning a film-maker. His films, of which only a few remain, explore the past and present by extensive use of flashback. The Prix Louis Delluc is awarded annually to the best French film of the year. **Titles:** *Fievre* (21), *La Femme de Nulle Part* (22), *L'Innondation* (24).

DEL RUTH Roy

American. 1895-1961. Gag writer and director for Mack SENNETT in the early days of Hollywood. Typical characterless studio director who ably marshalled the forces at his disposal. Out of fifty sound films almost half were musicals, the best being the delightful *Born to Dance* (1936) with Eleanor Powell. His very last movie was called *Why Must I Die?* (1960). **Others:** *The Desert Song* (29), *Kid Millions* (34), *Folies Bergere* (35), *Broadway Melody of 1936* (35), *On the Avenue* (37), *Broadway Melody of 1938* (37), *Du Barry Was a Lady* (43), *The Babe Ruth Story* (48), *The West Point Story* (50), *On Moonlight Bay* (51), *Phantom of the Rue Morgue* (54).

DELVAUX André

Belgian. Born 1926. Former teacher, TV documentary film-maker and once cinema pianist for silent pictures like the central character in *Rendezvous at Bray* (1971). A slightly precious director, an image-maker as a writer can be a phrase-maker, his preoccupation with the merging of dream and reality puts him in the tradition of other Flemish artists from Bosch to Magritte. *Women in Twilight* (1978) is more concerned with reality than his previous films. Set during the German Occupation of Flanders, it tells of a woman torn between a resistance fighter and her collaborator husband. His ninety minute documentary on Woody ALLEN, *Woody Allen, from Europe with Love* (1980) came as a surprise, but they are both interested in surrealism and beautiful, unobtainable women. **Also:** *The Man Who Had His Hair Cut Short* (66), *Un soir. Un Train* (69), *Belle* (73).

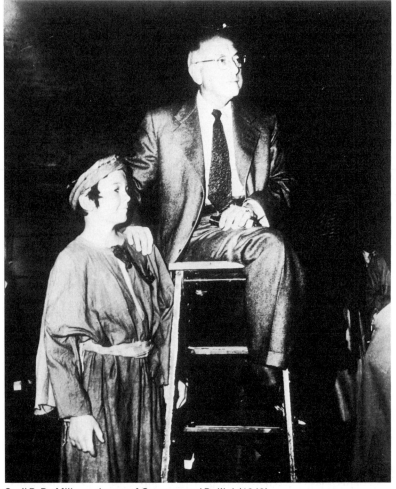

Cecil B. De Mille on the set of *Samson and Delilah* (1949).

DE MILLE Cecil B (Blount)

American. 1881-1959. Attended military college and the American Academy of Dramatic Arts. Wrote plays, acted and produced operas. The aesthetics of 19th century Grand Opera and Victorian theatre inform most of his pictures. In 1913, with Jesse Lasky and Samuel Goldfish (later Goldwyn), started the Lasky Feature Play Company in the village of Hollywood. *The Squaw Man* (1913) was one of the first major films produced there. After a few more Westerns, he brought out Met soprano, Geraldine Farrar for a silent *Carmen* (1915). She gestured through five other films including *Joan the Woman* (1917), the sort of spectacle that was to be associated with De Mille's name. In 1918 he discovered sex in a series of risque domestic comedies, six of them with Gloria Swanson, with titles such as *Don't Change Your Husband* (1919), *Male and Female* (1919) and *Why Change Your Wife?*(1920). In 1923 he discovered The Bible. *The Ten Commandments* which parallels the Biblical story with a modern story of the wages of sin, still looks pretty spectacular. The Good Book provided material for bad movies such as *King of Kings* (1927), H. B. Warner as Christ first seen through the eyes of a blind girl regaining her sight, *The Sign of the Cross* (1932), Claudette Colbert as a vampy Poppeia, and *The Crusades* (1935), sex and religion being bedfellows in all of them. De Mille's obsession with bath-tub scenes reached its peak with the milk bath in *Cleopatra* (1934) with Claudette Colbert, an enjoyably Shavian film. Wedged between the pious prurient epics and the opulent peep-shows, is De Mille's best period from 1937 to 1947. *The Plainsman* (1937), *Union Pacific* (1939), *North West Mounted Police* (1940) and *Unconquered* (1947) are energetic, colourful, unsubtle, patriotic celebrations of the frontiersmen of America, extolling strength, perseverance and forthright manliness. De Mille saw himself as a pioneer and he would introduce and narrate the stories in a grandiloquent manner. After the war, he returned to the Bible with *Samson and Delilah* (1949), told with flamboyance, and three hours forty minutes of *The Ten Commandments* (1956) in which De Mille outdid God. As the Barnum of Hollywood, he was naturally attracted to the circus, and *The Greatest Show on Earth* (1952) is in the same line as his Biblical movies. When he took ill during the making of *The Buccaneer* (1958), his son-in-law Anthony Quinn took over the direction. He had been planning an epic story of the Boy Scout movement to be called *Be Prepared*. **Also:** *Madam Satan* (30), *Reap the Wild Wind* (42), *The Story of Doctor Wassal* (44).

DEMME Jonathon

American. Another Roger CORMAN protégé. A sales rep until meeting Corman in England in 1969. Directed low budget exploitation movies such as *Crazed Heat* (1974), *Crazy Mama* (1975) and *Fighting Mad* (1977). His first film to get wide distribution and attention was *Citizens Band (Handle with Care* – 1977), a rhythmic social comedy set in a small Southwestern town where the characters communicate by CB. *Melvin and Howard* (1981) substantiated the promise of *Citizens Band*, being a good-humoured, understated study of the friendship between one of the richest men in America (Howard Hughes) and a gas-station attendant. **Also:** *Last Embrace* (78).

DEMY Jacques

French. Born 1931. Brought up on the Atlantic coast of France, the setting for three of his films. An admirer of American movies, especially musicals, COCTEAU and OPHULS, he's an erratic purveyor of modern fairy tales. Made a number of shorts including *Le Bel Indifferent* (1957) based on Cocteau. His first feature *Lola* (1960) was dedicated to Ophuls, and although the circular construction, frothiness and long tracking shots remind one of the dedicatee, it owes as much to *On The Town* (1949) with its sailors on leave, chance meetings and fleeting love. *The Young Girls of Rochefort* (1967) was a direct homage to the MGM musical with Gene KELLY'S presence making the comparison work to the film's detriment. Instead of painting the town red like the American sailors, Demy literally painted the houses of Rochefort in pastel shades as a backdrop to the insubstantial songs by Michel Legrand and the uninventive dancing. In his previous attempt at a musical, *The Umbrellas of Cherbourg* (1964), all the dialogue is "sung" to Legrand's tinkly music, less enchanting than chanting, against a background of more prettified houses. *Donkey Skin* (1970), an airy-fairy story is tolerable enough matinee fare, but suffers when likened to Cocteau's *Beauty and the Beast* (1945) to which it pays tribute, and *The Pied Piper* (1972) tries dismally to mix dark with light and is hampered by the ineffectual Donovan in the title rôle. Before whimsy soaked Demy's tissue-thin talent, he made *La Baie des Anges* (1962). A love story set on the Cote d'Azur with a roulette wheel as the motif and motive, it is one of the most vivid and poetic evocations of gambling fever on film. Demy is married to Agnes VARDA. **Others:** *Model Shop* (69), *The Slightly Pregnant Man* (73), *Lady Oscar* (79), *La Naissance du Jour* (81).

DE PALMA Brian

American. Born 1940. Son of a surgeon. Majored in Physics at Columbia U., where he began making movies. Had ambitions to become the American GODARD, but became yet another American HITCHCOCK. *Sisters* (*Blood Sisters* – GB 1973) shows a mature command of manipulative cinema, particularly cross-cutting and split-screen techniques. A reporter sees a murder from his Rear Window and tracks down the Psychotic killer. In the rock-horror movie, *Phantom of the Paradise* (1974) the gaudy imagery matches the music and the Faustian story which ends in a blood-bath. Blood is also the dominant image in *Carrie* (1976), linked here with menstruation. Carrie is a high-school girl with telekinetic powers who goes berserk when a bucket of pig's blood is poured over her after she has worried about her periods. The Curse becomes The Omen in this repulsively compulsive movie. *Obsession* (1976) is another empty exercise in Hitchcockiana, more likely to create dizziness than Vertigo. *The Fury* (1978) is more Psychokinetic trash while *Dressed to Kill* (1980) reaches the peak of the director as voyeur, using his camera to rape and mutilate women. The opening of *Blow Out* (1981) is a sly, defensive joke on the director's obsession with girls in showers, but this technically brilliant "political thriller" has little politics and fewer thrills.

DE SANTIS Giuseppi

Italian. Born 1917. Started as film critic then wrote scripts for the neorealist films of VISCONTI and ROSSELLINI. *Bitter Rice* (1949) about city women working in the rice crops is his best-known film. It suffers from a tendency towards melodrama and sentimentality, but Silvana Mangano, in short shorts emoting in the rice, became an international name.

DE SETA Vittorio

Italian. Born 1923. Studied architecture. Gained awards for his colour documentaries on Sicily and Sardinia. His first feature, *The Bandits of Orgosolo* (1961) is played entirely by Sardinian peasants. It is impressive in its honesty and splendid photography.

DE SICA Vittorio

Italian. 1902-1974. Studied accountancy. In 1922 became a stage actor and then a very successful film actor. Throughout the 30's he appeared in light comedies until, in 1940, he began to direct. *The Children Are Watching Us* (1942), his first important collaboration with the writer Cesare Zavattini who worked on virtually all his films, was one of the first neo-realist films. (The term was first applied to VISCONTI's *Ossessione* of the same year.) *Shoeshine* (1946) is set in Rome during the Allied Occupation and dealt with the main theme of the neo-realists – poverty in post-war Italy. Using non-actors in real locations, it created a sensation internationally. De Sica had to raise the money himself for *Bicycle Thieves* (1948). David O Selznick offered to produce it with a star like Cary Grant, but De Sica refused and continued his policy of working with non-actors. Filmed in the working-class districts of Rome, it tells the simple story of an unemployed man who is offered a job only if he has a bike. On the first day of work the bike is stolen and he spends a day with his small son looking for it. At the time it must have seemed fragmentary and naturalistic, but today we see it as a highly organized script, rather romantically filmed, which still has the power to move. *Miracle in Milan* (1951) prefigures the work of FELLINI and PASOLINI and shows that neo-realism can be used in a fantasy. In a shanty town, the poor get all they desire by a series of miracles. *Umberto D* (1952) was probably the last neo-realist film and the end of De Sica's great period. Dedicated to his father, it traces the struggles and humiliations of an old-age pensioner's attempts to subsist. Affecting as these films are, there is something a little too easy and calculated about De Sica's choice of characters. Children in *Shoeshine* and *Bicycle Thieves* and a dignified old man and his dog in *Umberto D* cannot fail to elicit sympathy, but the four films do show, in De Sica's words, "the indifference of society towards suffering. They are a word in favour of the poor and unhappy." A more rigorous political philosophy has made De Sica's humanism seem quaint. His work declined, the sentimentality incipient in his earlier films took over and any social message that remained was wrapped in a glossy package. **Others:** *Indiscretion of an American Wife* (53), *Gold of Naples* (54), *The Roof* (56), *Two Women* (61), *The Condemned of Altona* (70), *Yesterday, Today and Tomorrow* (64), *Marriage Italian Style* (64), *After the Fox* (66), *Woman Times Seven* (67), *Sunflower* (69), *The Garden of the Finzi-Contini* (70), *The Journey* (74).

DE TOTH Andre

Hungarian. Born 1913. In Hollywood from 1943. Actor and scriptwriter in Hungary and Germany in the 30's. Assistant to Alexander KORDA in England. Most of his films are incisive, small-scale Westerns, including six with Randolph Scott, less classical but more variable than those Scott made with BOETTICHER. Among the best of his work was a chilling Western, *The Day of the Outlaw* (1959), *Crime Wave* (1954), a realistic story of an ex-con's problems and *Monkey on my Back* (1957) on drug addiction. He directed one of the first horror films in 3D, *House of Wax* (1953) but as De Toth had only one eye he couldn't possibly have seen its effects. Curiously he was married to Veronica Lake whose "peek-a-boo" hair-style gave the impression of having one eye. He directed her in *Ramrod* (1947) and *Slattery's Hurricane* (1949). **Also:** *Man in the Saddle* (51), *Carson City* (52), *Springfield Rifle* (52), *The Stranger Wore a Gun* (53), *Thunder over the Plains* (53), *Riding Shotgun* (54), *The Bounty Hunter* (54), *The Indian Fighter* (55), *Play Dirty* (69).

DICKINSON Thorold

British. Born 1903. Started as sound editor. After making a handful of films, he retired to teach film theory at the Slade School in London. His best films have an aesthetic sensibility, creating a tension between the characters and the settings, and fluid camerawork. *Gaslight* (1940) has

L to R: Enzo Staiola and Lamberto Maggiorani in De Sica's *Bicycle Thieves* (1948).

much more atmosphere than the lavish 1944 CUKOR remake. *The Queen of Spades* (1948), based on Pushkin's story, photographed by Otto Heller in Oliver Messel's spacious sets with Edith Evans as the ancient Countess, shows Dickinson at his best with more than a nod towards EISENSTEIN. During the war, he lent his skills to propaganda films. **Also:** *The Arsenal Stadium Mystery* (39), *The Prime Minister* (42), *Secret People* (52), *Hill 24 Doesn't Answer* (54).

DIETERLE William

German. 1893-1972. Former actor and student of Max Reinhardt in Germany. Went to Hollywood in 1929 to direct German-language versions of American films. His first film in America was *The Last Flight* (1931), an interesting drama of the "lost generation". In 1935 he collaborated with his old master, Reinhardt, on Warner Bros. curious cultural concoction, *A Midsummer Night's Dream* with James Cagney, Mickey Rooney, Dick Powell and other Warner contract players. From then his main work consists of a number of solemn biopics with Paul Muni grimacing behind heavy make-up as Pasteur (*The Story of Louis Pasteur* – 1935), Zola (*The Life of Emile Zola* – 1937) and *Juarez* (1939) and with Edward G. Robinson in *Dr. Ehrlich's Magic Bullet* (1940) about the man who found a cure for VD, and *A Dispatch from Reuters* (1940) about the news-service man. Other Hollywooden biopics from Dieterle were *Madame Du Barry* (1934 with Dolores Del Rio), *The White Angel* (1936 with Kay Francis as Florence Nightingale) and the laughable *Magic Fire* (1956 with Alan Badel as Richard Wagner). More distinguished were *The Hunchback of Notre Dame* (1939) which gave full rein to his rich pictorial sense (vast sets by Van Nest Polglase, brilliant characterisation by Charles LAUGHTON), and the gentle poetry of *Love Letters* (1945) and *Portrait of Jennie* (1948) both with Jennifer Jones and Joseph Cotten in the leads. **Others:** *Satan Met a Lady* (36), *Kismet* (44), *Salome* (53), *Elephant Walk* (54), *Omar Khayyam* (57).

DMYTRYK Edward

American. Born 1908 in Canada. Got a job at Paramount at the age of fifteen. Film editor in the 30's. Made nineteen B-movies at Columbia and RKO for ten years before *Murder My*

The barn dance from Donen's *Seven Brides for Seven Brothers* (1954).

Sweet (*Farewell My Lovely* – G.B. 1944) proved his ability to handle down-beat thrillers and changed Dick Powell's image from soft tenor to hard-boiled private-eye. *Crossfire* (1947), one of the few post-war films to deal with anti-semitism, is a tense film noir dominated by Robert Ryan's sneer. In the same year he fell foul of the House of UnAmerican Activities, left the States and made three pictures in England before returning home to six months' imprisonment. He finally recanted and started directing low-budget movies for Stanley KRAMER, including *The Sniper* (1952), the sort of tight suspenser he did best. Fortunately for his bank balance and unfortunately for us, he suddenly switched to directing big, bad movies. **Others:** *Till the End of Time* (46), *The Juggler* (53), *The Caine Mutiny* (54), *Broken Lance* (54), *The End of the Affair* (54), *Soldier of Fortune* (55), *The Left Hand of God* (55), *The Mountain* (56), *Raintree County* (57), *The Young Lions* (58), *Warlock* (59), *The Blue Angel* (59), *Walk on the Wild Side* (62), *The Carpetbaggers* (64), *Where Love Has Gone* (64), *Alvarez Kelly* (66), *The Battle of Anzio* (68), *Bluebeard* (72).

DONEN Stanley

American. Born 1924. Dancer and choreographer on Broadway, he came to Hollywood to stage the numbers for *Best Foot Forward* (1943). His career as director can be described as "tripping the light fantastic". After choreographing a number of MGM musicals (working with Gene KELLY on four films), Arthur Freed, the most creative producer of musicals in Hollywood, gave Donen and Kelly the chance to direct their own film together. The result was the joyous and innovative *On the Town* (1949). Conceived balletically, it follows three sailors on a 24-hour leave in New York. The opening number, "New York, New York", was actually filmed on location in that "wonderful town". The partnership then came up with the apogee of MGM musicals, *Singin' in the Rain* (1952). One can but assume that Kelly was too busy dancing to have also been responsible for the camera-work in the title number, including a breathtaking crane shot. There was an effective and amusing use of split-screen technique in *It's Always Fair Weather* (1955), the last and least good of their collaborations, but still one of the better musicals at the end of a great era. Donen's first solo job as director had been *Royal Wedding* (*Wedding Bells* – G.B. 1951) whose silly plot was forgotten amidst the spectacular numbers performed by Fred Astaire. It is, however, with *Seven Brides for Seven Brothers* (1954), making exuberant use of the wide screen to dance across, that he can feel most pride. *The Pajama Game* (1957) and *Damn Yankees* (1958), both co-directed by George Abbott, have some of the same style, expertly breaking away from their theatrical origins. *Funny Face* (1957) is notable for its visuals, supervised by Richard Avedon; pastel colours, filters, soft-focus. Set in the haute couture world of Paris, it gives the erroneous impression of sophistication. With the demise of the Hollywood musical, Donen's career faltered with a number of leaden comedies, but revived for a short while with two flashy Hitchcock-type thrillers, *Charade* (1963) and *Arabesque* (1966). His one return to the musical was the disastrously twee, *The Little Prince* (1974). *Movie Movie* (1978) is an affectionate pastiche of Hollywood films of the past, a past where Donen was happiest. **Others:** *Give a Girl a Break* (53), *Deep in My Heart* (54), *Kiss Them for Me* (57), *Indiscreet* (58), *Once More with Feeling* (59), *Surprise Package* (60), *The Grass is Greener* (60), *Two for the Road* (67), *Bedazzled* (68), *Staircase* (69), *Lucky Lady* (75), *Saturn 3* (1980).

DONNER Clive

British. Born 1926. Film editor for over ten years. After five modest movies, he gained respect with *The Caretaker* (1963), a low-budget, televisual film of the Pinter play. His best film, *Nothing But the Best* (1964) started as a wicked satire on the British class structure, but succumbed to the "swinging London" image so detrimental to British films of the sixties, the same malaise that effected the achingly unfunny, *What's New Pussycat?* (1965) and *Here We Go Round the Mulberry Bush* (1968). The calamitously expensive failure of *Alfred the Great* (1969) stopped the sixties from swinging. **Also:** *Luv* (67), *Vampira* (74), *Rogue Male* (76), *The Thief of Baghdad* (78), *Oliver Twist* (83).

DONNER Jorn

Finnish. Born 1933. Lived in Sweden in the 60's where he made a name for himself as a film critic, being especially severe on Ingmar BERGMAN. He has since made a number of filmed interviews with Bergman. His wife Harriet Andersson, one of Bergman's favourite actresses, starred in his first four films. All of them, written by himself, are concerned with sexuality and the means of expressing it on film. *Portraits of Women* (1970) is about a film director of erotic movies, played by himself. He also takes the leading roles in *69* (1969), the year and sexual position, and *Black on White* (1968). **Also:** *A Sunday in September* (63), *To Love* (64), *Adventure Starts Here* (65), *Anna* (70), *Men Can't Be Raped* (78).

DONNER Richard

American. Born 1931. Former actor and TV director. Made the first ever *Kojak*. Film career started inauspiciously until *The Omen* (1976) put him into the big time. That sensationalistic cashing in on the occult fad, led to his directing the 70mm super comic strip, *Superman* (1978). The special effects and the leading man (Christopher Reeve), make it an enjoyable load of tripe. When taken off *Superman II* (1981), Donner moved to the intimacies of *Inside Moves* (1981), a sentimental story of basket-ball and basket cases. **Also:** *X-15* (62), *Salt and Pepper* (68).

DONSKOI Mark

Russian. 1901-1981. Imprisoned during the Civil War. Studied at the Moscow Film School. A disciple of the Marxist proletarian writer Maxim Gorky, his fame rests on the three films he made on Gorky's autobiography, *The Childhood of Maxim Gorky* (1938), *My Apprenticeship* (1939), *My Universities* (1940). They are rich in incident, character and period detail, shot through with Gorky's humanism and patriotism. *The Childhood*, in particular stands out, with Varvara Massilitinova memorable as the old grandmother. There is a slight falling off towards the end, but it is one of the masterpieces of Socialist Realism, that strait-jacket of Soviet cinema under Stalin. After making patriotic films during the war, he returned to Gorky with the remake of PUDOVKIN's *Mother* (1956). Two films on Lenin's mother, *Heart of a Mother* (1967) and *A Mother's Devotion* (1967), despite their Victorian ballad titles, vividly portray people caught up in vast social changes.

DOUGLAS Bill

Scottish. Born 1937. Brought up in a bleak mining village in Scotland. Went down the pit at 14. During his national service, his hut-mate introduced him to the world of art and ideas. After various odd jobs, he was given £3,500 to shoot his trilogy, *My Childhood* (1971), *My Ain Folk* (1972), and *My Way Home* (1979). It is an intensely personal (90% autobiographical), unsentimental view of a deprived childhood, many of the images reminiscent of DONSKOI's Gorky trilogy. The same boy (Stephen Archibald) plays the lead from the age of 14 to 21. Douglas had to wait for him to grow up before shooting the (slightly self-conscious) last part.

DOUGLAS Gordon

American. Born 1909. Started as gag writer for Hal Roach and as director of Our Gang shorts. His long career contains little that is not impersonal and routine. There is not much to distinguish his many B movies in the 40's from the main features later, apart from Technicolor, bigger budgets and bigger stars. Musicals with Doris Day, Virginia Mayo and Elvis Presley, Westerns with Alan

A scene from Donskoi's *The Childhood of Maxim Gorky* (1938).

38

Ladd and three Tony Rome thrillers with Frank Sinatra are all middle-brow, middle of the road and re-actionary. **Some titles:** *Come Fill the Cup* (51), *The Iron Mistress* (52), *She's Back on Broadway* (53), *The Charge at Feather River* (53), *Them* (54), *Young at Heart* (55), *Santiago* (56), *Rachel Cade* (61), *Follow That Dream* (62), *Robin and the 7 Hoods* (64), *Harlow* (65), *Stagecoach* (66), *In Like Flint* (67), *Tony Rome* (67), *The Detective* (68), *Lady in Cement* (68), *Viva Knievel* (77).

DOVZHENKO Alexander

Russian. 1894-1956. Brought up on a farm in the Ukraine. Worked in the Diplomatic service. Studied painting and became a newspaper cartoonist. Most of his films are lyrical pane-gyrics to the life and history of the Ukraine. *Zvenigora* (1927), an experimental allegorical film, chang-ing from dream to reality, past to present, was the last flowering of the exciting avant-garde Russian cinema, the product of a young revolutionary society. His next three films were political poems dedicated to the Ukraine. *Earth* (1930), a pastoral symphony, lingers lovingly on the land and its people, creating the in-delible vision of a rural paradise gained by the blood of the peasants. *Ivan* (1932), his first sound film, brought the same lyricism to the building of a hydroelectric project. These two films and *Arsenal* (1929) on collectivisation, greatly influenced documentary movements in other countries. Despite bureaucratic interference, his later films still retain a brisk pace and luminous photo-graphy. The vast Ukranian trilogy he was planning was filmed by his widow Yulia SOLNTSEVA, who had al-ready co-directed three of his films. **Others:** *Aerograd* (35), *Shchors* (39), *Michurin* (48).

DREYER Carl

Danish. 1889-1968. Orphaned as a child, he was adopted by a Lutheran couple. As screenwriter, wrote over twenty films. His early films were greatly influenced by D. W. GRIF-FITH. The first works of his maturity such as *Mikael* (1924) are closer to German Expressionism while *Master of the House* (1925) is more natural-istic, yet they all reveal a formality and restrained emotional intensity. These qualities were most in evidence in *The Passion of Joan of Arc* (1928) made in France. Based on the actual transcripts of the trial, Joan's twenty-

Falconetti as Dreyer's *Joan of Arc* (1928).

nine examinations are telescoped into one day. Its most memorable aspects are the long held closeups of faces wearing no make-up, and par-ticularly the agonized face of Falco-netti in her only film. *Vampyr* (1932) makes most other horror films pale into insignificance. Photographed by Rudolph MATÉ (as was *Joan of Arc*), the natural settings, the cross-cutting, the atmospheric lighting, the terse dialogue take it beyond the purely Gothic. Neither masterpiece was a financial success and Dreyer was forced into ten years silence. This was broken by *Day of Wrath* (1943), set in 17th century Denmark, about a witch hunt. Told at a measured pace, and more academic than his two previous films, it was taken as an allegory for occupied Denmark and

Carl Dreyer

Dreyer had to take refuge in Sweden until after the war. *Ordet* (1954) also has a religious subject. Its story of the death of a woman in child birth and her miraculous resurrection brought about by human love, is an extra-ordinary expression of spiritual opti-mism. The miracle is how Dreyer, with deceptively simple means, achieves the powerful effects. *Gertrud* (1964), made after a ten year gap, was Dreyer's final film. It tells of a woman's search for the perfect love and takes place in a series of duo-logues as she rejects the proposals of three men in succession. With an al-most immobile camera, immensely long takes, it obtains a serenity achieved in the best of chamber music.

DUPONT E. A. (Ewald André)

German. 1891-1956. Former film critic and script-writer, he is known mainly for *Variety* (1925), a story of passion and jealousy among trapeze artists, notable for the spectacular camera effects (Karl FREUND) and the impressionistic use of swirling light and movement. He also made Europe's first all-talkie, *Atlantic* (1929). This respected European director found himself making the cheapest B movie trash in Hollywood and when he fell out with the Dead End Kids on *Hell's Kitchen* (1939), he gave up directing for twelve years be-fore returning to make more trash. **Also:** *Moulin Rouge* (28), *Piccadilly* (28), *The Scarf* (51), *Return to Treasure Island* (54).

DURAS Marguerite

French. Born 1914 in Indo-China. Came to Paris at 18 where she studied science and law. First novel published in 1943. In the 50's and 60's was one of the authors of *le nouveau roman*. Several of her novels were filmed unsatisfactorily. Her first work in the cinema was the original script for Alain RESNAIS' *Hiroshima Mon Amour* (1959). Started directing her own films when in her 50's, and almost immediately established a filmic equivalent of her writing style. Disjointed narrative, the merging of past and present, the concern with one crucial moment in her women characters' lives and a penchant for exotic names, titles and locations. *India Song* (1975), set at a French embassy party in the India of the 30's, was filmed in a house in Paris, the sounds as much as the camerawork giving the impression of India, and yet an India remembered from Paris. In her films, sound and image are often at variance, a narrator comments on a place and time other than what the camera perceives, generally in long, slow tracking shots. As there is often more to hear than to see, the images take on a separate significance. Her thwarting of the spectator's expectations have made her a "difficult" but ultimately rewarding director. **Others:** *La Musica* (66), *Destroy, She Says* (69), *Jaune le Soleil* (71), *Nathalie Granger* (72), *The Woman of the Ganges* (74), *Vera Baxter ou les Plages de L'Atlantique* (76), *The Truck* (77), *Aurelia Steiner-Melbourne-Vancouver* (81), *Agatha* (81).

DUVIVIER Julien

French. 1896-1967. Former stage actor. Directed his first film in 1919 and continued to make smooth, tasteful, decorative, undemanding films right up to his death. His five films with Jean Gabin in the 30's were his best work, especially *Pepe-Le-Moko* (1937) set in the teeming studio-constructed Casbah of Algiers. It established Gabin as a star and its influence can be seen in films like *Casablanca. Un Carnet de Bal* (1937) elegantly links several stories around the memories aroused by a dance programme. It was so successful that he virtually remade it in Britain as *Lydia* (1941) and continued the episodic formula with *Tales of Manhattan* (1942) and *Flesh and Fantasy* (1943). His first film in America was *The Great Waltz* (1938), a schmaltzy but tuneful biopic of Johann Strauss.

Returning to Europe after the war, he made the pallid and pretty *Anna Karenina* (1948) with a disappointing Vivien Leigh. Back in France, he revived Fernandel's popularity with two Don Camillo films, *The Small World of . . .* (1951) and *The Return of . . .* (1953). **Also:** *Poil de Carotte* (32), *Maria Chapdelaine* (34), *Golgotha* (35), *La Belle Equipe* (36), *Le Golem* (36), *Pot-Bouille* (57), *Marie-Octobre* (58).

DWAN Allan

American. 1885-1981. Born in Canada. Typifies the best of the workmanlike Hollywood directors who turned their hand to anything offered them, making bricks out of straw. Dwan's career stretches over five decades and literally hundreds of movies. Probably happiest in the silent era where action spoke louder than inter-titles. Directed the leaping Douglas Fairbanks in ten movies, the best being the spectacular *Robin Hood* (1922) with some of the biggest sets yet constructed. He also brought out the actress in Gloria Swanson in the eight films he made with her, including *Zaza* (1923) and *Manhandled* (1924). Spent the 30's at Fox making mainly second features of little interest, three Shirley Temples and the big-budget *Suez* (1939) with Tyrone Power as the canal-builder. In the 40's he made a number of skilful little comedies and the archetypal Jap-killing movie, *Sands of Iwo Jima* (1949) with John WAYNE. The best of his late films were small-scale, unpretentious, extrovert Westerns, including two with strong women leads, *Montana Belle* (1952 – Jane Russell) and *Cattle Queen of Montana* (1954 – Barbara Stanwyck). **Others:** *The Iron Mask* (29), *Heidi* (37), *Rebecca of Sunnybrook Farm* (38), *Tennessee's Partner* (55), *Slightly Scarlet* (56).

EASTWOOD Clint

American. Born 1930. After various jobs (including lumberjack) and a spell in the army, he was signed up as an actor by Universal in 1954. Appeared in small roles in ten films before moving to CBS TV for the lead in *Rawhide* which ran seven years. Picked up his film career in Italy in the mid-sixties in three Sergio LEONE Spaghetti Westerns. In America made five films for Don SIEGEL in which he continued to

play the impassive, laconic loner. There are elements of Leone and Siegel in his own films. His first, *Play Misty for Me* (1971) is a chilling, misogynistic thriller with a castration complex. All his other movies set out to prove that the director/star has balls, the director looking at the star with increasing admiration. An implicit vein of self-mockery sets out to disarm criticism of the hollowness of the central character (himself) and of the reactionary and macho codes he represents. In *High Plains Drifter* (1973) he protects a town from outlaws in a cold, vicious and plodding manner. He goes over the top on a mountain in *The Eiger Sanction* (1975) after bedding a bevy of beauties, disposing of a wicked homosexual, and throwing someone out of a window. In *The Outlaw Josey Wales* (1976) he violently wreaks revenge on the renegades that killed his family. The special effects in *The Gauntlet* (1977) cost one million dollars alone, not enough to cover up the holes in the plot of a dumb cop and a hooker being chased across the country. By parodying his persona even more in *Bronco Billy* (1980) he gains in likeability what he loses in conviction. **Also:** *Firefox* (82), *Honkeytonk Man* (83).

EDWARDS Blake
American. Born 1922. Wrote for radio, TV and acted in five films in the 40's. Wrote the screenplay for six

The Odessa steps sequence from Eisenstein's *Battleship Potemkin* (1925).

Richard QUINE movies from 1952-1957. First directed a Frankie Laine musical, *Bring Your Smile Along* (1955) (Quine had directed two of the same). Almost indistinguishable from Quine's efforts, were three Tony Curtis pictures, but it was *Breakfast at Tiffany's* (1961), a sugary version of the Capote story, that made his name in the charm school of cinema of which Quine was a member. *Days of Wine and Roses* (1963), however, is a surprisingly black, realistic portrayal of alcoholism with Jack Lemmon (a favourite of Quine and Billy WILDER) getting his meatiest role so far. It was compared to Wilder's *Lost Weekend* (1945). Then Edwards' development was arrested by Inspector Clouseau, in the shape of Peter Sellers, whose endless battle with inanimate objects continued from *The Pink Panther* (1964) through *A Shot in the Dark* (1964), *The Return of the Pink Panther* (1974), *The Pink Panther Strikes Again* (1976), and *The Revenge of the Pink Panther* (1978). While Sellers fell about (and many in the audience), Edwards took a couple of pratfalls himself with two movies starring his wife, Julie Andrews, *Darling Lili* (1969) and *The Tamarind Seed* (1974). His fidelity to his wife continued to better

effect in three of his more recent films, although she doesn't have much to do in *10* (1979) except wait around for Dudley Moore to have scruples about Bo Derek and return to her for the soppy, happy ending. It's a mellow Californian movie – a Tanned Panther; Billy Wilder without the edge. Comparisons with Wilder continued with *S.O.B.* (1981), a bile-filled satire on Hollywood featuring William Holden, star of Wilder's Hollywood-on-Hollywood pictures, *Sunset Boulevard* (1950) and *Fedora* (78), giving it a resonance it might not have had. Playing with his wife's Mary Poppins image revealed more of Edwards' sour grapes than her slightly larger breasts. Back in Wilder country again, *Victor-Victoria* (1982) has Miss Andrews playing a woman pretending to be a man playing a woman. Despite the expected timid ending and unnecessary slapstick, it is one of the best gay comedies, in both senses of the word. **Also:** *Operation Pettycoat* (59), *High Time* (59), *The Great Race* (65), *The Party* (68), *Wild Rovers* (71), *The Trail of the Pink Panther* (82), *The Curse of the Pink Panther* (82).

EISENSTEIN Sergei
Russian. 1898-1948. Son of a German-Jewish architect and Russian mother. Studied architecture in Petrograd. In 1918 enlisted in the Red Army for which he designed propaganda posters. After the civil war, joined the Proletkult theatre as designer. Made his first film, *Strike* (1925) with members of the company. Many of his agit-prop stylistic devices were already in evidence. Caricature, visual metaphors and shock cutting – a factory boss uses a lemon squeezer as police move in on striking workers and shots

of a slaughter house are cut in as the police mow them down. *Battleship Potemkin* (1925) concentrates on the mutiny on a battleship of the Black Sea Fleet during the 1905 Revolution with the massacre on the Odessa steps (an invention of Eisenstein's) one of the most memorable and exciting sequences in all cinema. Down a seemingly endless flight of steps march soldiers advancing on the fleeing citizens. A nurse is shot and the baby-carriage and baby bounce down the steps to destruction. Some shots last less than ten seconds. Edvard Tissé, Eisenstein's constant cameraman, devised effects by using a camera trolley and a camera strapped to the waist of an acrobat. Dynamic montage was also used in *October* (1927) based on John Reed's "10 Days That Shook the World", but its constantly contrasting images and ambiguous attitude to religious relics, disoriented audiences and the powers that were. The emotional and rhythmic composition shows the storming of the Winter Palace, the dismemberment of the Tsar's statue, and a dead horse caught at the top of an opening draw-bridge. Eisenstein tried to toe the Party line with *The General Line* (1928 – aka *Old and New*), a more approachable film about a peasant woman's fight to keep collective farming in her community, but because of the slightly satirical approach to the peasantry he was accused of "formalism". The left-wing novelist Upton Sinclair agreed to finance *Que Viva Mexico* (1931-32), which was intended to be a four-part documentary on the contradictions of Mexican life, but Eisenstein over-ran the time and the budget, so money was withdrawn. Today it exists in various truncated, re-edited forms and its moments of baroque images tinged with eroticism make one regret the loss. Charged again with "formalism" on the unfinished *Bezhin Meadow* (1936), of which only stills remain, he recanted by making the patriotic spectacle, *Alexander Nevsky* (1938). Far more conventional stylistically than his previous work, it is still a richly enjoyable epic, with stirring images and a dramatic use of Prokofiev's music, especially in the famous Battle on the Ice sequence. Taking his imagery from Grand Opera, the Japanese Kabuki Theatre and Russian icons, he embarked on the three parts (only two were completed) of *Ivan the Terrible* (1942-1945). Stalin approved part I, but as Ivan's character became more complex he turned against it. Part II was not released until 1958. It is a slow-moving (the rapid montage of his early films has disappeared), absorbing, opulent work with a brooding central performance by Nikolai Cherkassov (the hero of *Nevsky*) in the title role.

ELVEY Maurice
British. 1887-1967. A competent and extremely prolific director whose career spanned more than forty years and over three hundred features. Not much can be salvaged for posterity, but his best work was done in the 30's and 40's. *The Clairvoyant* (1935) is an excellent atmospheric thriller with Claude Rains as a fake mindreader who discovers he can really predict the future. When England was up against it, he made *The Gentle Sex* (1943 co-directed by Leslie Howard) as a tribute to soldier girls and *The Lamp Still Burns* (1943) as a tribute to nurses. **Also:** *The Hound of the Baskervilles* (21), *Sally in our Alley* (31), *Potipher's Wife* (31), *Salute John Citizen* (42), *Beware of Pity* (46), *Dry Rot* (56).

ENDFIELD Cy
American. Born 1914 in S. Africa. Studied drama at Yale. Became producer and drama teacher. After the war, entered movies as writer and director of a series of second features. Forced to leave the USA during the McCarthy period he settled in England. After a few minor films in a minor key, he made *Mysterious Island* (1961) based on Jules Verne relying on Ray Harryhausen's special effects to liven it up. Formed a production company with the actor Stanley Baker with whom he made two African adventures, *Zulu* (1964) and *Sands of the Kalahari* (1965). The first is a successful and colourful story of brave British colonials defending themselves against hordes of black warriors between clipped exchanges of dialogue. **Also:** *The Underworld Story* (50), *Tarzan's Savage Fury* (52), *Hell Drivers* (57), *De Sade* (69), *Universal Soldier* (71).

ENRIGHT Ray
American. 1896-1965. Former gag-writer for Mack SENNETT. At Warners from 1927-1941 turned out routine stuff, including thirteen musicals (six with Dick Powell) of which the best was *Dames* (1934) mainly due to Busby BERKELEY's stunning production numbers. When he moved to Universal, he concentrated on low-budget Westerns (most of them with Randolph Scott), including *The Spoilers* (1942) which has the necessary bonus of Marlene Dietrich as a bar-room gal. **Also:** *Alibi Ike* (35), *Ready, Willing and Able* (37), *Gold Diggers in Paris* (37), *On Your Toes* (39), *The Wagons Roll at Night* (41), *Gung Ho!* (43), *China Sky* (45), *Flaming Feather* (51).

EPSTEIN Jean
French. 1897-1953. Born in Poland. Settled in France in 1908. Studied medicine at Lyons. Author of an influential book on film theory, "Bonjour Cinema" (1921) and others. His first films were part of the avant-garde movement. He recreated the eery poetry of the Poe story, *The Fall of the House of Usher* (1928) in which slow-motion was used probably for the first time in a fictional film. Then followed a cycle of films set in Brittany of which the most renowned is *Finis Terrae* (1929) shot on the islands with fishermen as actors, making it a precursor of neo-realism. **Also:** *Coeur Fidele* (23), *La Grace à Trois Faces* (27).

ETAIX Pierre
French. Born 1928. Music-hall clown and mime. Assistant to Jacques TATI on *Mon Oncle* (1958). Appeared in a few films including BRESSON's *Pickpocket* (1959). Directed a few short comic films before his first full-length feature, *The Suitor* (1962). His films rely almost exclusively on physical humour, constructed around a series of comic set-pieces featuring himself, and reminiscent of the work of Buster KEATON and Max Linder. He is often amusing but never very original, sometimes pinching shamelessly from dead comedians. **Others:** *Yoyo* (65), *Tant qu'on à la santé* (66), *Le Grand Amour* (69), *Pays de Cocagne* (71).

EUSTACHE Jean
French. 1938-1981. Made some interesting medium-length films in the 60's but it was with *The Mother and the Whore* (1973) that he achieved international recognition. This 3½ hour series of conversations and monologues is the summation of the French Wave then reaching the shore. Funny, irritating, obsessive, verbose, witty, provocative and erotic, it deals with Jean-Pierre Léaud's confrontations with three different women. *Mes Petites*

Amoureuses (1975) also has a sexual subject, the sexual awakening of an adolescent boy, but is less dense and intense than the previous film and too long for the subject. It was not a success. Eustache committed suicide in 1981.

FANCK Arnold

German. 1889-1974. Worked as ski-instructor. Created the "mountain film", symbolic and didactic melo-dramas made under difficult condi-tions in natural Alpine settings, the best being *The White Hell of Pitz Palu* (1929 – co-directed by G. W. PABST) starring Leni RIEFEN-STAHL. During the war, he made Nazi propaganda films and docu-mentaries on German art. **Also:** *The White Frenzy* (31), *S.O.S. Eisberg* (33).

FARROW John

Australian. 1904-1963. In Hollywood from the mid-thirties. Wrote stage plays and scripts. A Catholic convert, he wrote books on Thomas Moore and the papacy. One is hard put to it to find much of his seriousness or preoccupations in his films, few of which stand out. *The Big Clock* (1948) with Ray Milland closing in on newspaper-editor murderer Charles LAUGHTON, shows a talent for tense, well-acted thrillers not often exploited. *Alias Nick Beal* (1949) also has a sense of menace, but is an un-even allegory with Ray Milland as the Devil corrupting an honest politician. A few good Westerns, including *Hondo* (1954) with John WAYNE, a couple of atmospheric melos with Robert Mitchum (*Where Danger Lives* – 1950, *His Kind of Woman* – 1951) just about outweigh stinkers such as *The Sea Chase* (1955) and *John Paul Jones* (1959). While writ-ing the screenplay for *Tarzan Escapes* (1936) he met and married Maureen O'Sullivan (Jane) of whom Mia Farrow was the issue. **Also:** *A Bill of Divorcement* (40), *The Hitler Gang* (44), *Two Years Before the Mast* (46), *The Night has a 1000 Eyes* (48), *Copper Canyon* (50), *Submarine Command* (51), *Ride Vaquero* (53), *Botany Bay* (53).

FASSBINDER Rainer Werner

German. 1946-1982. Almost a one-man film industry, he made over thirty films in twelve years. It is a surprisingly consistent, entertaining, probing and lively output. Studied acting and joined the Munich Action Theatre in 1967. With friends from the group, he began making films in 1969, rapidly becoming part of the new generation of young German directors who put German cinema back on the map after thirty years. He revealed, with his team of stock players, a heartless, avaricious, materialistic New Germany. Most of his characters are repressed and frustrated by the barrenness of urban existence, sometimes turning to violence. In *Why Does Herr R. Run Amok?* (1969) and *The Merchant of 4 Seasons* (1972), the leading charac-ters are so oppressed by modern life that they kill themselves. Using Douglas SIRK's Hollywood melo-dramas of the 40's and 50's as his prime model, *Fear Eats the Soul* (1974) and *Mother Kusters Goes to Heaven* (1975) show ageing, lonely women liberating themselves by, in the former, having an affair with a younger man, an Arab and, in the latter, becoming a left-wing urban guerilla. Women are generally at the centre of his films and *The Marriage of Maria Braun* (1978), *Veronika Voss* (1979) and *Lola* (1981) present them trying to survive in the harshly and ironically evoked post-war Germany. A more flamboyant style is used in these recreations of an era than the static camera set-ups of his earlier contemporary films. Sexuality as a means for the strong to control and manipulate the weak runs through most of the pictures whether heterosexual or, as in *The Bitter Tears of Petra von Kant* (1972), *Fox* (1974) and *In the Year with 13 Moons* (1978), homosexual. **Also:** *The American Soldier* (70), *Martha* (73), *Effie Briest* (74), *Satan's Brew* (76), *Chinese Roulette* (76), *Despair* (78), *The Third Generation* (79), *Lilli Marlene* (80), *Querelle* (82).

FELLINI Federico

Italian. Born 1920. "If the cinema didn't exist, I might well have become a circus director," said Fellini. It could also be said that if the circus didn't exist, he might not have be-come a film director. The circus as metaphor (and reality) plays an im-portant role in his films with positive and negative results. Fellini sees him-self as a ringmaster with the world as a rather rundown circus, humanity as grotesque or innocent clowns, and where the music is by Nino Rota. He was born in the seaside town of Rimini (remembered beach scenes are sprinkled throughout the films). Like Moraldo in *I Vitelloni* (1953), he left his layabout friends and went to Rome to become a journalist. There the young man is drawn into the cor-rupt, big city life like the leading

Rainer Werner Fassbinder

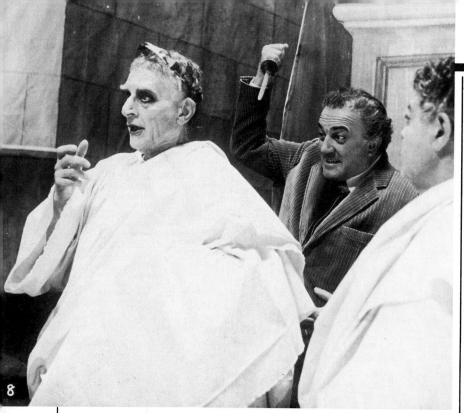

Federico Fellini demonstrating a scene in *Roma* (1972).

character in *La Dolce Vita* (1959) and *Roma* (1972) but he (or rather his alter ego) remains uncorrupted. He worked as a caricaturist (he is a great picker of unusual faces and bodies), and also wrote songs and sketches for the music-hall. (There are wonderfully bad music-hall turns in *Lights of Variety* – 1950, his first film, codirected by Alberto LATTUADA, and in *Roma*.) For twelve years he wrote film scripts, many for Roberto ROSSELLINI. He was never a neorealist and almost immediately established his own mythology. *La Strada* (1954) made his wife, Giulietta Masina, and himself internationally known. She is the innocent whitefaced clown, brutally mistreated by the travelling strongman, Anthony Quinn. Only at her death does he realise he loves her. The sentimentality is offset by the realistic settings – desolate provincial towns and night scenes. Masina's waif-like persona was less successful as the "innocent" prostitute in *Nights of Cabiria* (1956) which had the kind of sweet charity perfect for a Broadway musical. *La Dolce Vita* is an impressive three-hour wide-screen prude's eye view of Roman high society. We follow the gossip columnist hero (Marcello Mastroianni) through seven nights and seven days leading an unsatisfactory, shallow existence until he glimpses innocence in the form of a young girl on the beach at dawn. Mastroianni is the film director

in *8½* (1963), the number of Fellini's films by then, a calculated self-portrait which on first viewing is visually stunning and surprising, but on further viewings becomes too self-indulgent, the satire superficial. His wife comes under scrutiny in *Julietta of the Spirits* (1965), his first full-length colour feature. A middle-aged housewife experiences dreams and fantasies (closely allied to Fellini's own) while her husband philanders. The brilliant photography (Gianni di Venanzo, his usual cameraman) and designs by Piero Gheradi, can't detract from the Vogueish silliness of the story. Although it contains one or two moments of Fellini at his best, *Fellini's Satyricon* (1969) is La Dolce Vita in Ancient Rome with the director looking ponderously and with assumed disapproval at the goings-on of a pre-Christian society, and the "spiritual" episode is not far from Cecil B. DE MILLE. He renewed his inspiration in his next three films by going back to his youth and early manhood with *The Clowns* (1970), *Roma* and the magical and nostalgic *Amarcord* (1974), in which the pleasure principle is utmost. *Casanova* (1976), however, is a cold, empty, repetitive film, following the hero (Donald Sutherland) going to bed mechanically with one girl after the other until he has sex with an automaton. With *Orchestra Rehearsal* (1978) and *City of Women* (1981) he seems to be trapped in

simple-minded allegories with the danger that he is no longer the ringmaster but the clown. **Others:** *The White Sheikh* (52), *Il Bidone* (55), Episodes in *Boccaccio '70* (62) and *Histoires Extraordinaires* (67).

FERRER José
American. Born 1912 in Puerto Rico. Well-known stage and screen actor who directed seven films between 1955 and 1962, starring in five of them. *The Shrike* (1955) and *The Great Man* (1956) were the best of a so-so bunch. The former has the audacity to cast sweet June Allyson as a nagging wife, and the latter is an astringent look at the Great Enemy of the 50's, not Communism, but TV. **Others:** *Cockleshell Heroes* (56), *I Accuse* (57), *The High Cost of Loving* (58), *Return to Peyton Place* (61), *State Fair* (62).

FERRERI Marco
Italian. Born 1928. Former journalist. Lived in Spain for a while where he made three films, the best known being *The Wheelchair* (1960), a black comedy in the BUÑUEL vein. His attraction for the grotesque continued with *The Conjugal Bed* (1963) and *The Ape Woman* (1964), misogynistic and heartless comedies. *Dillinger is Dead* (1969), a more controlled piece, gained critical acclaim as a bleak study of a man at home surrounded by significant objects. Shock tactics, excrementary, schoolboy humour made *Blow-Out* (1972 – *La Grande Bouffe*) a wearisome, excessive movie about excess. In *The Last Woman* (1976) the hero castrates himself with an electric carving knife, another example of Ferreri's crude symbolism. **Also:** *Touchez pas la Femme Blanche* (74), *Bye, Bye, Monkey* (78).

FEUILLADE Louis
French. 1873-1925. Started as scriptwriter for Gaumont in 1905 and was soon directing thrillers and sentimental dramas. He filmed five of the *Fantomas* series about a diabolical criminal. After the success in France of the American serial, *The Perils of Pauline* (1914), he made the popular serial, *Les Vampires* (1915-1916) in ten episodes. Without much camera movement or dynamic montage and set in realistic surroundings, they have a dreamlike quality that the surrealists as well as the general public admired. He concentrated on serials till the end of his career, most of them shot on location and derived from

19th century melodrama, yet with a sense of 20th century evils. **Others:** *Judex* (16), *Tin Minh* (19), *Barabas* (19).

FEYDER Jacques

Belgian. 1887-1948. Stage actor who appeared in films by FEUILLADE and MÉLIÈS. After directing a number of shorts, he made the exotic *L'Atlantide* (1921) and Garbo's last silent movie, *The Kiss* (1929), but it is for the three films he made in 1934 and 1935 starring his wife Françoise Rosay that his name survives. *Le Grand Jeu* (1934), set in the desert with a Foreign Legion hero, concentrates on the inhabitants of a cafe, eschewing romanticism for poetic realism. *Pension Mimosas* (1935) also centres on a small community, the hotel of the title. *The Carnival of Flanders* (1935 – *La Kermesse Heroique*) is a farce set in 17th century Flanders where Spanish troops enter a small town. Lazare Meerson's sets and costumes conjure up the period with the eye of Brueghel (a character in the film) and the witty script and performances have made it a continual favourite, although its attitude to collaboration was liked by the Nazis. Another opulent but less stylish production was *Knight without Armour* (1936), made in England for KORDA, had Robert Donat rescuing Marlene Dietrich from the Russian Revolution.

FISHER Terence

British. Born 1904. Former seaman, he worked as film editor before and after World War II. From 1957, he was the principal director of Hammer Film's neo-Gothic horrors, making twenty-four of them in sixteen years. Sometimes stylish, they were mostly garish and predictable. Before being caught in the Hammerlock, he made a far scarier film *So Long at the Fair* (co-directed by Anthony Darnborough 1950) with Jean Simmons searching for her brother who mysteriously disappears during the 1889 Paris Exposition. **Some titles:** *The Curse of Frankenstein* (56), *Dracula* (57), *The Hound of the Baskervilles* (58), *Brides of Dracula* (59).

FITZMAURICE George

American. French-born. 1885-1941. A director who even looked old-fashioned in the 20's with *Son of the Sheik* (1926) starring Valentino attempting to repeat his triumph in

Nanook the Eskimo in Flaherty's *Nanook of the North* (1922).

The Sheik five years earlier. Also made two of the most plodding of Garbo films, *Mata Hari* (1932) and *As You Desire Me* (1932), a creaky adaptation from Pirandello.

FLAHERTY Robert

American. 1884-1951. Considered by many to be the "Father of the documentary film". Brought up and educated in Canada, he explored and mined with his father. On an expedition to the North, he took along a movie-camera and a cineaste was born. Spent sixteen months living with the Eskimos in order to capture their way of life for *Nanook of the North* (1922), an extraordinary document of endurance and hardship, with an unprecedented rapport between the people and the man behind the camera. Ethnologically it is too romantic and slightly dubious (Flaherty got them to hunt a walrus, something they had ceased doing), but its tone had a great effect on the evolution of the documentary film. Because of its success, Paramount asked him to make a "Nanook" of the South Seas, and he spent two years in the Samoan Islands making *Moana* (1926). Unlike the cold hell of the North, Flaherty pictured an Eden where noble savages hunt, fish and cook. It was after seeing *Moana* that John Grierson was said to have invented the word "documentary". He left both *White Shadows of the South Seas* (1928) and *Tabu* (1931) because of disagreements with its co-directors, W. S. VAN DYKE and F. W. MURNAU respectively. However, Gainsborough Studios gave him a free hand on *Man of Aran* (1934). Again he spent two years living with the Aran islanders, detailing their daily lives. It expresses his constant view of the importance of primitive societies and the natural environment, but here he seems more concerned with the sea-scape than the people. He went to India to do location shooting for *Elephant Boy* (1936) where he discovered the 11-year-old Sabu for the title role. Unfortunately, most of his work on this film was scrapped and much of the footage was directed in the studio by Zoltan KORDA. During the war, he worked for the War Department Film Division with Frank CAPRA. *Louisiana Story* (1948), his last film, was commissioned by Standard Oil, and Flaherty and the film accepts the invasion of the machine into unspoiled territory. It describes the drilling for oil in the swamplands of Louisiana as seen through the eyes of a young boy. Richard LEACOCK's camerawork and Virgil Thomson's music help to make it into a poetic slice of Americana.

FLEISHER Dave and Max
American. Both were newspaper cartoonists who went into animated films. Max (1889-1972) was artistic and technical director and Dave (born 1894) was producer and overall director. Their first cartoons were *Out of the Inkwell* (1921) with Koko the Clown. They also created Betty Boop and Popeye. Betty Boop was stopped by the Hayes Office for being immoral, but Popeye, adapted from a comic strip, was very popular from 1933 to 1947. They tried to rival Disney's full-length cartoons with *Gulliver's Travels* (1939) and *Hoppity Goes to Town* (1941), which were perhaps too sophisticated for kids to have been commercial successes.

FLEISHER Richard
American. Born 1916. Son of Max FLEISHER. During World War II made shorts and newsreels and, from 1946-1952, B movies for RKO. Out of the blue, he was offered *20,000 Leagues under the Sea* (1954), the enjoyable Jules Verne fantasy-adventure. Other big-budget movies that he handled with pace and precision were *The Vikings* (1958), *Fantastic Voyage* (1966) about a journey through the human body, and *Tora! Tora! Tora!* (1970), on the

events from both sides in the attack on Pearl Harbour. They all had their ridiculous side, but they do not explain turkeys such as *Dr. Doolittle* (1967), *Che* (1969), *Mandingo* (1975), *The Incredible Sarah* (1976), and *Ashanti* (1979) to name but a few. He is happiest when dealing with his favourite subject, famous murder cases, in a slick manner, e.g. *Compulsion* (1959 – Leopold-Loeb case), *Girl in the Red Velvet Swing* (1955 – Stanford White murder), *The Boston Strangler* (1968 – Tony Curtis with a false nose) and *10 Rillington Place* (1970). **Also:** *Violent Saturday* (55), *Bandido* (56), *The New Centurians* (72), *Soylent Green* (73), *Mr. Majestyk* (74).

FLEMING Victor
American. 1883-1949. *Gone with the Wind* (1939) and *The Wizard of Oz* (1939) are not bad titles to have in one's filmography. If truth be told, Fleming was nothing more than a good craftsman, part of an expert team, who happened to be at MGM at the right time. Much of *Gone with the Wind,* that over-ripe, over-long, over-praised historical romance, was conceived by producer David O. Selznick. George CUKOR shot at least three long sequences and Sam WOOD completed it when Fleming took ill during shooting. It was again Cukor who first established Judy Garland's character in *The Wizard of Oz* and King VIDOR directed the black and white sequences, but Fleming made an excellent job of the rest. He began directing in 1919 after working as a cameraman for D. W. GRIFFITH and Douglas Fairbanks. Actors liked working with him and he got good performances from Clara Bow in *Mantrap* (1926), Gary Cooper in his first sound picture, *The Virginian* (1929), Gable and Harlow in *Red Dust* (1932) and Spencer Tracy in *Captain's Courageous* (1937) and *Dr. Jekyll and Mr. Hyde* (1941). *Treasure Island* (1934) is a cracklingly good studio version of the children's classic, but his last three films are best buried, i.e. *A Guy Named Joe* (1943), *Adventure* (1946) and *Joan of Arc* (1948). **Also:** *Bombshell* (33), *Reckless* (35), *The Farmer Takes a Wife* (35), *Test Pilot* (38), *Tortilla Flat* (42).

FLOREY Robert
French. 1900-1979. Former child actor. Went to Hollywood in 1921 as journalist and publicity man for Douglas Fairbanks. Started directing

experimental shorts. In twenty years in Hollywood, for various studios, he made mostly fast-moving, economical B movies. His best work was three effective horror movies influenced by early German cinema: *Murders in the Rue Morgue* (1932) with Bela Lugosi, *The Face Behind the Mask* (1941) and *The Beast with Five Fingers* (1946), both with Peter Lorre. He had the distinction of directing The Marx Bros. in their very first movie, *Cocoanuts* (1928) and Johnny Weissmuller in his last Tarzan role, *Tarzan and the Mermaids* (1948). **Also:** *The Woman in Red* (35), *The Magnificent Fraud* (39), *The Desert Song* (43).

FORBES Bryan
British. Born 1926. Studied drama. Appeared in about eighteen films as supporting actor between 1948 and 1959. Began writing scripts which led to direction. Most of his films are suitable for bored, superficial suburban housewives with nothing better to do on a wet afternoon. The "realism" of *The L-Shaped Room* (1962) is terribly dated and *The Wrong Box* (1966) and *The Madwoman of Chaillot* (1969), originally charming light classics, are ruined by leaden and insensitive direction. Occasionally some style emerges as in the over-long *The Slipper and the Rose* (1976). **Also:** *Whistle Down the Wind* (61), *Seance on a Wet Afternoon* (64), *King Rat* (66), *The Whisperers* (67), *The Stepford Wives* (75), *International Velvet* (78).

FORD John
American. 1895-1973. Real name Sean Aloysius O'Feeny. Youngest child of Irish immigrant parents. After high-school, he joined his brother Francis, an actor at Universal, in Hollywood. His first film was a Western (*The Tornado* 1917) and it remained his favourite genre; it was he who gave it epic stature. A series of two-reelers followed featuring cowboy star, Harry Carey. His first major film was *The Iron Horse* (1924), a 2¾ hour saga on the building of the first trans-continental railway, shot entirely on location in Nevada, which evokes the spirit of the pioneers in a down-to-earth manner. He continued along the same lines with *3 Bad Men* (1926) and *4 Sons* (1928). John WAYNE appears for a moment in *Hangman's House* (1928), the first of over fifteen films they were to make together. *Dr. Bull* (1933), *Judge Priest* (1934), and

FOSTER Norman
American. 1900-1976. Screen actor in the 20's and 30's. Directed a series of cheapies until Orson WELLES was taken off *Journey into Fear* (1943) and Foster took over. There are enough Wellesian touches in this spy-drama to feel that Welles was at Foster's shoulder throughout. Only two other Foster movies are worth a mention, *Kiss the Blood off my Hands* (1948), a rather nasty thriller with Burt Lancaster, set in England, and the likeable romantic-comedy, *Rachel and the Stranger* (1948). **Also:** *Sombrero* (53), *Davy Crockett* (56), *The Sign of Zorro* (60).

FRANJU Georges
French. Born 1912. Founder of the French Cinematheque with Henri Langlois in 1936. As an archivist, he was drawn to early French and German cinema, a taste apparent in his own films. First made a reputation with his short documentaries (often considered the best part of his oeuvre). *Le Sang des Bêtes* (1949 – *The Blood of Animals*) shows with a cold eye and vivid detail, the daily slaughter of animals in an abattoir, juxtaposed with images of everyday life in Paris not long after the carnage of World War II. Those who have managed to keep their eyes on the screen find it a powerful and moving statement. His other shorts continue to find poetry in horror. Much of his first feature, *La Tete Contre Les Murs* (1958 – *The Keepers*) was filmed in an actual mental hospital, the frightening reality of which does not sit well with the fictional story of an apparently sane young man committed to the brutal institution. *Les Yeux Sans Visage* (1959 – *Eyes without a Face*) is a Gothic melodrama in which a surgeon kidnaps young girls in order to graft their features onto the disfigured face of his daughter. Unlike a Hollywood version of the same material, Franju tries to film this surreal fantasy in a realistic manner. It is, however, too conscious of its efforts to elevate the subject and of its debts to Jean COCTEAU and German cinema. FEUILLADE is the conscious reference for *Judex* (1963), a remake of the 1916 serial, full of magical and playful images that conjure up a lost era. He has continued to make films, but they have little of the cold beauty and resonance of his early work. Franju is like the troupe of actors in *The Last Melodrama* (1978), regretting the passing of an audience for melo-drama. **Also:** *Thérèse Desqueroux* (62), *Thomas L'Imposteur* (65), *La Faute de L'Abbé Mouret* (70), *L'Homme sans Visage* (74).

FRANK Melvin
American. Born 1917. Began as comedy script-writer. Produced a number of comedies in the 40's with Norman PANAMA, mostly starring Bob Hope. They co-directed three later Hope features, *That Certain Feeling* (1956), *The Facts of Life* (1961), and the dismal end to the Road series, *Road to Hong Kong* (1962). Frank's solo efforts were Hopeless. *Buona Sera Mrs. Campbell* (1968), a frantically unfunny farce on paternity, and tedious "comedies" featuring the desperately mugging George Segal i.e. *A Touch of Class* (1972), *The Duchess and the Dirtwater Fox* (1976) and *Lost and Found* (1979). **Also:** *Strange Bedfellows* (64), *The Prisoner of Second Avenue* (75).

FRANKENHEIMER John
American. Born 1930. Former actor. TV director mostly with CBS. One of the first generation of TV directors to make it on the big screen. Brought to the cinema a surface realism (many of his films are in black and white) and a liking for strong plots and situations. His first two features dealt with juvenile delinquency, a popular subject in the late 50's and early 60's. *The Young Stranger* (1957) and *The Young Savages* (1961) offer pat "solutions" to the problem. A greater maturity is evident in *All Fall Down* (1961) which also deals with youth, this time in steamy William Inge country. Most of *Birdman of Alcatraz* (1962) takes place in a

Angela Lansbury in Frankenheimer's *The Manchurian Candidate* (1962).

prison cell, but the intensity of the direction and Burt Lancaster's mesmeric performance brilliantly sustains it over 2½ hours. *The Manchurian Candidate* (1962) is an enjoyable, but over-febrile piece of political hokum. *7 Days to May* (1964) enters similar territory, but its seven day structure moving towards a military take-over of the US Government and ending in platitudes about freedom, needed far more rigorous direction. *Seconds* (1966) has some of the mixture of parody and drama that makes it, with *The Manchurian Candidate*, his best film. *Grand Prix* (1966) has some spectacular visuals, but the plot is a drag. **Others:** *The Fixer* (68), *I Walk the Line* (70), *The Horsemen* (70), *French Connection II* (75), *Black Sunday* (77), *Prophesy* (79), *The Challenge* (82).

FRANKLIN Sidney
American. 1893-1972. Co-directed many silent comedies with his brother Chester from 1914. Between 1919 and 1927, he made a sequence of insipid romances featuring the ringleted Mary Pickford, Norma Talmadge (*Smilin' Through* – 1922) and eight pictures with Constance Talmadge. At MGM from 1928, he was producer on some of their biggest wartime hits, generally starring middle-class English lady Greer Garson smiling through her tears as the bombs fell. He directed five tasteful tearjerkers with Norma Shearer including the remake of *Smilin' Through* (1932) and *The Barretts of Wimpole Street* (1934). Gave up directing in 1937 after being one of five directors on *The Good Earth*, only to return to remake a dreary *Barretts of Wimpole Street* (1957) twenty-three years after his first effort. **Also:** *The Actress* (28), *Wild Orchids* (29), *The Last of Mrs. Cheyney* (29), *The Guardsman* (31), *Reunion in Vienna* (33), *Dark Angel* (35).

FREELAND Thornton
American. Born 1898. Former cameraman. In his two most famous Hollywood movies, *Whoopee* (1930) and *Flying Down to Rio* (1933) his contribution is completely overshadowed by others. The former made Eddie Cantor a star and introduced dance director Busby BERKELEY to the screen. The latter brought Fred Astaire and Ginger Rogers together for the first time. Made light films of little merit in Britain from 1935.

FREGONESE Hugo

Argentinian. Born 1908. Former journalist. After making three films in Argentina, went to Hollywood in 1950 where he directed turgid Westerns, ponderous adventures and a couple of awesome misfires: *Decameron Nights* (1953) without sex and *Marco Polo* (1961) without spectacle. *My Six Convicts* (1952) is an unusual prison-comedy and *Man in the Attic* (1953) had Jack Palance at his menacing best as Jack the Ripper. **Others:** *Saddle Tramp* (50), *One Way Street* (50), *Mark of the Renegade* (51), *Untamed Frontier* (52), *Blowing Wild* (53), *The Raid* (54), *Black Tuesday* (54), *Harry Black and the Tiger* (58), *Savage Pampas* (66).

FREND Charles

British. Born 1909. Former film editor. Built his reputation on several realistic wartime dramas for Ealing Studios such as *The Foreman Went to France* (1942), *San Demetrio, London* (1943) and *Johnny Frenchman* (1945). After the war, he continued to praise British pluck with worthy ventures like *Scott of the Antarctic* (1948) and *The Cruel Sea* (1952). *The Magnet* (1949) is an imaginative comedy told from a child's point of view with a delightful twelve-year-old William (later James) Fox. **Others:** *Lease of Life* (55), *Barnacle Bill* (57), *Cone of Silence* (60).

FREUND Karl

German. 1890-1969. The distinguished cinematographer closely associated with the German expressionistic movement. In Germany he shot films by F. W. MURNAU, Fritz LANG and Carl DREYER. In Hollywood he was responsible for some superbly lit films including BROWNING's *Dracula* (1931). Of the eight pictures he directed, only two are of any interest: his first, *The Mummy* (1932) and last, *Mad Love* (1935). The former is a spine-chilling horror movie in the Germanic tradition with Boris Karloff in the title role awakening after centuries and finally crumbling to dust. The latter is a remake of the silent German classic, *The Hands of Orlac* (1924), the story of a concert pianist who loses his hands in an accident and has those of a murderer grafted on to him by a crazed doctor, played by Peter Lorre in his first American film.

FRIEDKIN William

American. Born 1939. Began direct-

Friedkin's *Exorcist* (1973)

ing TV shows in his teens. After ten years in the medium, he directed his first film, the forgettable *Good Times* (1967), featuring the forgettable husband-wife pop team, Sonny and Cher. This was followed by the showy, *The Night They Raided Minsky's* (1968), a dull version of Pinter's *Birthday Party* (1968) and the stereotyped homosexual birthday party in *Boys in the Band* (1970), the best part of which was the pre-credit sequence. *The French Connection* (1971) is a coolly manipulative cops-and-robbers thriller; the good performances and New York locations give it a certain authenticity, and it ends with an exciting chase. Shock-tactics are used splashily enough in *The Exorcist* (1973) to retain the box-office momentum, but *Sorcerer* (1977) – a meaningless title to cash in on *The Exorcist* – is a completely needless remake of CLOUZOT's *Wages of Fear* (1953) and flopped. *Cruising* (1980), a tawdry piece of film-making delving into the gay underworld, is a movie Friedkin needs to exorcise from his soul, preferably in the way it was done to Linda Blair in his own demon opus. Married briefly to Jeanne Moreau. **Also:** *The Brinks Job* (78).

FULLER Samuel

American. Born 1911. Former journalist, crime reporter. Wrote pulp fiction before becoming a scriptwriter in the 30's. Served in N. Africa and Europe as an infantryman during the war. His anti-intellectual movies, mostly written by himself, reflect his experience in tabloid journalism and in the US Army with graphic use of a moving camera, often as a blunt instrument. In GODARD's *Pierrot-le-Fou* (1965) he says, "the film is like a battleground, love, hate, action, violence, death . . . in one word, Emotion." After the war, he returned to Hollywood and produced, wrote and directed his first picture, *I Shot Jesse James* (1948). *The Steel Helmet* (1950) and *Fixed Bayonets* (1951) were the first of his taut, tough, simplistic war films which follow a group of multiracial Americans fighting the dirty commies to keep America free. *China Gate* (1957) sees the soldiers helping the French counteract Red influence in Indo-China and in *Merrill's Marauders* (1961) the relentless action pictures them wiping out Japs in Burma in a "war is hell" manner. The war in Europe is reduced to its essentials in the stylised *The Big Red One* (1980). His crime movies are like sensationalist newspaper articles with banner headlines. In *Pickup on South Street* (1952) pickpocket Richard Widmark cracks a 'commie' spy ring, *The House of Bamboo* (1955) and *Underworld USA* (1961) all reveal corruption and brutality among cons and cops alike. *Shock Corridor* (1963) and *The Naked Kiss* (1964) are both lurid, high-pitched melodramas that pack a punch. Fuller's directness, unselfconsciousness, and rawness matched with superb travelling shots have appealed to European directors such as Godard and Wim WENDERS, but he remains the epitome of the Ugly American. **Also:** *Park Row* (52), *Hell and High Water* (54), *Run of the Arrow* (57), *40 Guns* (57), *Verboten!* (58), *The Crimson Kimono* (59), *Dead Pigeon on Beethoven Street* (72), *White Dog* (82).

FURIE Sidney J

Canadian. Born 1933. Worked on Canadian TV. In Britain from 1960 where he made a couple of teenage dramas, *The Boys* (1962) and *The Leather Boys* (1963) containing an outspokenness prevalent in British films of the period. Also made two youth oriented musicals starring Britain's lame answer to Elvis Presley, Cliff Richard: *The Young Ones* (1961), *Wonderful Life* (1964). It was with *The Ipcress File* (1965), the best of the Michael Caine/Harry Palmer movies, that Furie made a splash. It is a well-told spy story despite the arty camera angles. These became almost a tic in the drawling Marlon BRANDO Western, *Appaloosa* (1966) and the complex spy drama, *The Naked Runner* (1967) with Furie not making things easier by infuriatingly shooting through whiskey glasses and from behind obstacles. *Little Fauss and Big Halsy* (1970) is a lively bike movie, although it echoed past successes, but biopics *Lady Sings the Blues* (1972), supposedly about Billie Holliday, and *Gable and Lombard* (1976) are mediocre and rotten respectively. **Also:** *The Lawyer* (69), *Sheila Levine is Dead and Living in New York* (75), *The Boys from Company C* (77).

GALEEN Henrik

Dutch. 1882-1949. Actor/scriptwriter/director whose main body of work was done in Germany from 1910 to 1928. Co-directed (with Paul WEGENER) the first screen version of the old Jewish legend, *The Golem* (1914). His directorial contribution to the horror strain of German expressionism was the second version of *The Student from Prague* (1926) with Conrad Veidt as the student who sells his reflection. The studio sets and lighting created a supernatural atmosphere, making it one of the last German "Caligarism" films i.e. those influenced by Robert WIENE's *The Cabinet of Dr. Caligari* (1919). His sound films are of little interest. Emigrated to the US in 1933.

GANCE Abel

French. 1889-1981. Wrote poems and plays. Acted in films from 1909. Began directing after World War I. At the start he experimented with various techniques. In *La Folie du Docteur Tube* (1915) he uses a subjective camera and distorting mirrors for effect. *J'Accuse* (1919) is a 2½ hour pacifist statement actually shot during the war. It begins with soldiers forming the letters of the title and ends with dead soldiers rising from their graves contrasted, in a split-screen sequence, with a victory parade to the Arc de Triumph. (Gance remade it in 1938.) The rest of the film is mainly taken up by an over-melodramatic love-story. The interest of *La Roue* (1922 – *The Wheel*) is not in the plot of a father and son in love with the same girl, but in the rapid montage techniques, the location work in a railway yard and on a train. His innovations reached their apogee in *Napoleon* (1927), originally shown at the Paris Opera in a five hour version. After its first showing, it was released in various truncated forms until Kevin BROWNLOW pieced together as much of the original as possible and in 1980 it was shown at the London Film Festival with a 43-piece orchestra. It is a pyrotechnical display of almost every device of the silent screen and beyond; hand-held cameras (one strapped to a horse's back), wide-angle lenses, superimposition, rapid cutting and a triple screen (Polyvision), anticipating Cinerama by 30 years, but like its hero, the film is demagogic. Gance's Romantic visual imagination was constrained with the coming of sound. He became a

Gance's *Napoleon* (1927).

Prometheus bound. Many of his later films are routine, although he sometimes used the same ideas and sequences from his silent films. Often they are badly structured, badly acted and badly scripted. Poignant and paradoxical is the sequence in *Un Grand Amour de Beethoven* (1937) when the hero loses his hearing, revealed by silent shots of violins, birds and bells. The loss of sound for Beethoven and the coming of sound for Gance were equally agonizing. **Others:** *The Tenth Symphony* (18), *Lucrece Borgia* (35), *Paradis Perdu* (39), *La Venus Aveugle* (40), *La Tour de Nesle* (54), *Austerlitz* (60), *Cyrano et d'Artagnan* (63).

GARNETT Tay

American. 1894-1977. Flying instructor in World War I. Entered films as stuntman. Scriptwriter from 1925-1928. Working for various studios, he made forty-two films in forty-two years (not a lot for an artisan director) of which about fourteen have quality (quite a lot for an artisan director). His best films have a gentle humanity and humour as well as a feeling for exotic locations. Both *Her Man* (1930), set in Havana and starring the wonderfully named pair, Phillips Holmes and Helen Twelvetrees, and *One Way Passage* (1932) with William Powell and Kay Francis on board ship, are about doomed love. Ships and ports are the settings for *China Seas* (1935 – Gable-Harlow), *Slave Ship* (1937), *Trade Winds* (1938) and *Seven Sinners* (1940 – Dietrich vamping John WAYNE) – all highly enjoyable. The two sagas he made for MGM with Greer Garson, *Mrs. Parkington* (1944) and *Valley of Decision* (1945) are models of their kind. *The Postman Always Rings Twice* (1946), the third version of James. M. Cain's downbeat murder story, has a surprising amount of electricity, despite the softened ending, and excellent performances from John Garfield and Lana Turner as the passionate lovers who bump off Lana's husband. **Others:** *Love is News* (37), *Stand-in* (37), *Joy of Living* (38), *Eternally Yours* (39), *Slightly Honourable* (40), *Bataan* (43), *The Cross of Lorraine* (43), *A Connecticut Yankee in King Arthur's Court* (48), *The Black Knight* (54), *Cattle King* (63), *The Delta Factor* (70).

GASNIER Louis

French. 1882-1962. Directed some of the first films of dapper French comic Max Linder. In America from 1912 he made serials until 1920. *The Perils of Pauline* (1914) starring Pearl White, created a sensation in France and influenced Louis FEUILLARD. Miss White continued to be rescued from incredible situations in each episode of *The Exploits of Elaine* (1914). Gasnier made a few routine adventure features until 1941. **Also:** *Topaz* (33), *The Last Outpost* (35).

GERASIMOV Sergei

Russian. Born 1906. Director/Actor/Scriptwriter. Known mainly for *And Quiet Flows The Don* (1958), based on the Sholokov novel about the events in and around a small village during World War I, told in a quietly flowing lyrical but academic manner. He is Head of the Soviet Institute of Cinematography.

GERMI Pietro

Italian. 1914-1974. Started directing serious, realistic features on post-war Italy (e.g. *The Road to Hope* – 1950). He himself played the railway engineer in the solemn *Man of Iron* (1956). In the 60's he changed to broad, satirical sex comedies, the best being *Divorce Italian Style* (1961). ALSO: *Seduced and Abandoned* (63), *Serafino* (68), *Alfredo, Alfredo* (73).

GILBERT Lewis

British. Born 1920. Former child actor. First feature, *The Little Ballerina* (1947) was made for children. Almost all his other films are for adolescents or overgrown schoolboys. A competant director, his forté is for uplifting war movies such as *Albert R. N.* (1953), *The Sea Shall Not Have Them* (1954), *Carve Her Name with Pride* (1958), *Sink the Bismark!* (1960) and *Operation Daybreak* (1976). *Reach for the Sky* (1956), the story of legless pilot Douglas Bader overcoming all obstacles to walk and even fly again, is one of the best of the disease/affliction pictures. In between the rhetoric of war, he made a calm study of a young girl's blossoming in *The Greengage Summer* (1961 *Loss of Innocence* – US). His three James Bond movies, *You Only Live Twice* (1967), *The Spy Who Loved Me* (1977) and *Moonraker* (1979) are entertainingly done within the tired and tested formula. **Others:** *The Admirable Crichton* (57), *Ferry to Hong Kong* (59), *HMS Defiant* (62), *Alfie* (66), *The Adventurers* (69), *Friends* (71), *Paul and Michelle* (74), *Educating Rita* (83).

GILLIAT Sidney

British. Born 1908. Screenwriter for many years with Frank LAUNDER, notably on Alfred HITCHCOCK's *The Lady Vanishes* (1938). His early films have an unerring feeling for time, place and character, especially in a Blitzed London, a realistic treatment often disguises rather far-fetched plots. **Some titles:** *Waterloo Road* (44), *The Rake's Progress* (46 *The Notorious Gentleman* – US), *Green for Danger* (46), *London Belongs to Me* (48), *The Story of Gilbert and Sullivan* (53), *The Constant Husband* (55), *Only Two Can Play* (62), *The Great St. Trinian's Bank Robbery* (65), *Wild Cats of St. Trinian's* (80).

GILLIAM Terry

American. Born 1940. Resident in

England since 1967. Animator on the madcap Monty Python series on TV in 70's. Co-directed (with Terry Jones) the 2nd Python movie, *Monty Python and the Holy Grail* (1974), battling to sustain the humour over ninety minutes. Less funny but less uneven is his cartoonist's eye view of medieval England, *Jabberwocky* (1977). Six dwarfs capture a small boy and whizz him through the history of the world in *Time Bandits* (1981) with excellent special effects and effective special guest stars, including Ralph Richardson as God.

GLENVILLE Peter

British. Born 1913. Stage director whose seven films are heavy-going despite distinguished casts. Jack Hawkins persecutes Alec Guinness in *The Prisoner* (1954), Curt Jurgens persecutes Danny Kaye in *Me and the Colonel* (1958), Peter O'Toole persecutes Richard Burton in *Becket* (1964) and Glenville persecutes Tennessee Williams, Feydeau and Graham Greene in *Summer and Smoke* (1960), *Hotel Paradiso* (1966) and *The Comedians* (1967) respectively. Laurence OLIVIER is the persecuted teacher in *Term of Trial* (1961).

GODARD Jean-Luc

Swiss. Born 1930. In 1950 acted in short films by friends Jacques RIVETTE and Eric ROHMER with whom he founded a film magazine. Wrote articles for 'Cahiers du Cinema'. His first feature, *Breathless*

Jean-Paul Belmondo and Jean Seberg in Godard's *Breathless* (1960).

(1960), dedicated to Monogram Pictures (the all-B movie studio), attempted to recapture the directness and economy of the American gangster movie. The story of a young car-thief on the run from the police was shot entirely on location using a hand-held camera, often with the cameraman (Raoul Coutard) in a wheelchair. In order to achieve an immediacy in the performances, Godard cued the actors (who weren't allowed to learn their lines) during the takes. Jump-cutting eliminated the usual establishing shots so that the film lives up to its title. *Le Petit Soldat* (1960) wasn't released until 1963 because of its ambivalent attitude to the Algerian war, affronting both Left and Right with its reflection of brutality on both sides, filmed in a matter-of-fact way. It was the first film of Anna Karina whom Godard married in 1961. They separated five years and eight films later. *Vivre Sa Vie* (1962 – *My Life to Live*) is a probing examination of a prostitute (Karina), using the Brechtian device of episodes with texts, quotations and interviews, the long takes and direct sound giving it a documentary tone. *Les Carabiniers* (1963 – *The Riflemen*) also uses Brechtian distancing from the subject (a war in a fictional kingdom), shot in the grainy images of old newsreels. Colour and a wide screen is used for *Le Mépris* (1963 *Contempt*), a sharp comment on international film-making with a multi-lingual cast including Fritz LANG playing himself. Colour is used dramatically and symbolically in *Pierrot-le-Fou* (1965), a stunning study of violence (there are references to Angola, Vietnam etc) and the transience of a relationship, (Belmondo/Karina. Godard/Karina?). Godard's style was becoming more elliptical in films such as *Made in USA* (1966) and *Two or Three Things I Know About Her* (1966), but they have a spontaneity, topicality and pop-artistic brilliance. With *La Chinoise* (1967) he moved towards a Maoist commitment which only crystallised with the Events of May 1968. Always concerned with the complexities of communication, he explored it even further in *Le Gai Savoir* (1968 – *The Joyful Wisdom*) a discussion on images and sound in an empty film studio. Godard was plainly trying to formulate a true Left-wing language freed from the dominant bourgeois culture. This resulted in his break from all commercial film-making, starting to shoot a series of cine-tracts in 16mm and later video. *British Sounds* (1969) starts with a quote adapted from Marx: "The bourgeoisie created the world in its own image, comrades we must destroy that image." He has been attempting to destroy that image ever since. From 1968 to 1972, his films were co-directed by Jean-Pierre Gorin with whom he formed the Group Dziga VERTOV. In an attempt to get their ideas across to a wider public, they made *Tout Va Bien* (1972) with Jane Fonda and Yves Montand. The message is radical, but the medium is conservative and, despite the stars, audiences stayed away. After a serious motor-cycle accident and a break with Gorin, he returned with *Ici et Ailleurs* (1975) which wrestles with ways of presenting the Palestinian problem on film, and *Numero Deux* (1975) which uses only part of the screen until the end. *Sauve qui peut* (1980) – *Slow Motion*) explores the role of sexuality in the consumer society. His didactic aim is not only political, but a challenge to the audience to re-educate themselves to see differently. Godard's influence has been extensive and he is one of the great dialectical directors. **Also:** *Bande à Part* (64), *Une Femme est une Femme* (61), *Une Femme Mariée* (64), *Alphaville* (65), *Masculin-Feminin* (66), *Weekend* (67), *One Plus One* (68), *Pravda* (69), *Vent d'Est* (69), *Passion* (82).

GOLD Jack
British. Born 1930. Works mostly on TV. His first films were unexciting adaptations from stage plays, *The Bofors Gun* (1968), *The National Health* (1973), whereas *Aces High* (1976) is a complete revamping of 'Journey's End' to include many spectacular World War I aerial sequences, and *Man Friday* (1975) clumsily tries to impose current liberal racial attitudes on Defoe's classic. **Also:** *The Reckoning* (69), *Little Lord Fauntleroy* (80).

GORDON Michael
American. Born 1909. Directed on stage. Entered films as editor. Made ten movies between 1943 and 1951 before the McCarthy blacklist forced him out of the USA for eight years. *The Web* (1947), *An Act of Murder* (1948) and *Woman in Hiding* (1949) are taut little murder melodramas and *Another Part of the Forest* (1948) is a well-acted version of Lillian Hellman's family drama. *Cyrano de Bergerac* (1950) is a stagey but effective showcase for Jose FERRER's Oscar-winning performance. In the second phase of his career, he made sleek, hollow, coquetish romantic comedies for glossy producer Ross Hunter, including two Doris Day hits, *Pillow Talk* (1959) and *Move Over, Darling* (1963). **Also:** *The Lady Gambles* (49), *I Can Get It For You Wholesale* (51), *Portrait in Black* (60), *Boy's Night Out* (62), *For Love or Money* (63), *A Very Special Favour* (65), *Texas Across the River* (66), *The Impossible Years* (68), *How do I Love Thee?* (70).

GORETTA Claude
Swiss. Born 1929. Beneficiary of the 1962 Swiss Government's provision of cash for the film industry. His films are quietly observant, undemonstrative 'serious' comedies which, like his own country, are beautiful and uneventful. *The Invitation* (1972) wryly watches the behaviour of people at a

garden party and *Pas si merchant que ca* (1975 – *The Wonderful Crook*), gently tells the story of a young man who robs banks in order to pay the employees of his furniture factory. *The Lacemaker* (1977), a discreet, slightly loaded, study of an intellectual student's relationship with a sensitive but uneducated girl, became an 'art-cinema' success. **Also:** *The Girl from Lorraine* (81).

GOULDING Edmond
British. 1891-1959. Former child actor. Went to America after serving in World War I. Wrote a successful play which got him invited to Hollywood as scriptwriter. Mainly directed classy soap-operas with taste and intelligence. At Warners he provided Bette Davis with four of her best and most typical melodramas, *That Certain Woman* (1937), *Dark Victory* (1939), *The Old Maid* (1939), *The Great Lie* (1941). At Fox (where he remained from 1943 to his death), he smoothly handled two Somerset Maugham adaptations, *Of Human Bondage* (1946) with Eleanor Parker, and *The Razor's Edge* (1946) which gives the mistaken impression that it might be a good novel. In 1927, he made the grotesque, *Love,* the silent version of 'Anna Karenina' with Garbo. He directed Garbo again to even less effect in *Grand Hotel* (1932), but showed his sense of humour by allowing a take-off of Garbo and John Barrymore in the above film by Marion Davies and Jimmy Durante in the bouncy backstage musical, *Blondie of the Follies* (1932). **Also:** *Reaching for the Moon* (31), *Riptide* (34), *The Dawn Patrol* (38), *The Constant Nymph* (43), *Claudia* (43), *Nightmare Alley* (47), *We're Not Married* (52), *Mardi Gras* (58).

GREEN Alfred E
American. 1889-1960. Hollywood hack director from 1912 to 1954 who made one of the biggest box-office hits of the 40's, *The Jolson Story* (1946), which saved Columbia Studios from disaster, made Larry Parks a star (before McCarthy destroyed him), and revived Jolson's popularity (Parks mimed to Jolson's voice). It is a well-put-together package of songs and clichés. An attempt to follow up this bonanza biopic with *The Fabulous Dorseys* (1947) and *The Eddie Cantor Story* (1953) failed miserably. Now *The Alfred E. Green Story* would be something. **Also:** *Thoroughbreds Don't Cry* (37), *A*

Thousand and One Nights (44), *Copacabana* (47), *Invasion USA* (52), *Top Banana* (54).

GREEN Guy
British. Born 1913. Former cinematographer of merit. A few of his films have serious intent, while the rest are trashy soap-operas. *The Angry Silence* (1960) is a shamly realistic anti-Trade Union tract, as rabble-rousing as the unions it attacks; *The Mark* (1961) deals superficially with a sex-killer while *Light in the Piazza* (1962) sugars a potentially interesting subject. **Others:** *House of Secrets* (56), *Diamond Head* (62), *Patch of Blue* (65), *The Magus* (68), *A Walk in the Spring Rain* (69), *Luther* (74), *Jacqueline Susan's Once is Not Enough* (74).

GREENAWAY Peter
British. Born 1942. Experimental film-maker. Trained at art school. His films are full of haunting images of strange worlds akin to those of Lewis Carroll, Borges, Kafka and RESNAIS' *Last Year in Marienbad.* He has a fascination with maps, the English landscape and birds. TITLES: *A Walk Through H* (78), *Vertical Features Remake* (78), *The Falls* (81), *The Draughtsman's Contract* (82).

GREMILLON Jean
French. 1901-1959. A native of Normandy. Former musician. Wrote the music for many of his films. After documentaries and experimental shorts, he entered the commercial cinema with two populist pictures starring Jean Gabin, *Gueule D'Amour* (1937) and *Remorques* (1941). Under the restrictions of Vichy France, he made the melancholy, *Lumiere D'Été* (1943). One or two of his bleakly naturalistic films deserve to be better known outside France. After the war he concentrated on documentaries of his native province.

GRIES Tom
American. 1922-1977. Producer/writer/director. Worked in TV. Most of his work consists of slam-bang macho movies featuring the likes of Charlton Heston, Burt REYNOLDS and Charles Bronson. The best is *Will Penny* (1968) with Heston as a loner cowboy. Gries died of a heart attack after completing the tame Muhammed Ali movie, *The Greatest* (1977). **Also:** *100 Rifles* (69), *Number One* (69), *The Hawaiians* (70), *Lady Ice*

(73), *Breakout* (75), *Breakheart Pass* (76).

GRIFFITH D. W. (David Wark)
American. 1875-1948. Born in Kentucky. His father, a Confederate officer, was killed when Griffith was 10. Left home to join a travelling theatre company. Wrote plays and sold a script to the Biograph Company in 1917. Offered a film to direct and, with the help of cameraman Billy Bitzer (the photographer on nearly all his films), made *The Adventures of Dolly* (1908), the first of hundreds of one and two reelers he turned out, learning his craft and inventing a technical grammar for the silent screen. By 1911, he had used close-ups, changed the camera setups within one scene and developed cross-cutting. The Biblical spectacle, *Judith of Bethulia* (1914) was the first American 4-reeler, and *Birth of a Nation* (1915) was its first master-

Griffith's *Birth of a Nation* (1915).

54

piece. In 2¼ hours, it interweaves the story of two families on either side of the Civil War. After the defeat of the South, the negroes gain equality and when a white girl is raped by a black soldier, the hero forms the Ku Klux Klan. This grotesque distortion of history was, even in 1915, extremely offensive and the film was picketed and boycotted. Despite its reactionary attitudes, it remains a remarkable work in which all the technical innovations of his earlier films reach maturity. Griffith wrote no script, but carried the complex structure in his head. In order to answer his critics to some extent, his next film was a 3¼ hour epic called *Intolerance* (1916), containing four separate stories to illustrate his theme. A modern story, the Crucifixion, the massacre of the Protestants in Paris in 1572, and the Fall of Babylon, with the image of a woman (Lillian Gish) rocking a cradle between episodes. Although a great achievement, its episodic nature and length were not tolerated by the public. Today, *Birth of a Nation* and especially *Intolerance* are sat through more out of duty and historical interest than enjoyment. Far more endearing are Griffith's smaller movies starring the waif-like Lillian Gish. *Hearts of the World* (1918) uses documentary material of World War I and a studio reconstruction of a French village under German occupation; *Broken Blossoms* (1919) a poignant love story set in a fog-shrouded Limehouse; and *Way Down East* (1920) with Gish as the orphan girl turned out into the cold, but rescued from drowning in an ice-filled river – the most memorable sequence of the trite story. The touching performances, the exciting cross-cutting (usually to build suspense during a last-minute rescue)

and the interaction between long shot and close-ups, make many of these creaky Victorian melodramas watchable. Gradually, his narrow view of the world, the advances of younger directors and the coming of sound made Griffith, one of the most important figures in the history of film, seem one of the most old-fashioned. For seventeen years until his death, he led an obscure existence in Hollywood, almost a forgotten man. **Also:** *True-Heart Susie* (19), *Orphans of the Storm* (21), *America* (24), *Isn't Life Wonderful?* (24), *Sally of the Sawdust* (25), *Abraham Lincoln* (30).

GUEST Val
British. Born 1911. Former journalist. Wrote screenplays for 30's comedies. A long and undistinguished career in British pictures from trite comedies (*Mr Drake's Duck* – 1950) through tame sci-fi (*The Day the Earth Caught Fire* – 1962) and tiresome spy spoofs (*Where the Spies Are* – 1965) to tedious sex farces (*Confessions of a Window Cleaner* – 1974). **Also:** *The Runaway Bus* (54), *Quatermass II* (56), *When Dinosaurs Ruled the Earth* (69).

GUILLERMIN John
British. Born 1925 in London to French-born parents. Studied at Cambridge. After a spell in the R.A.F., made documentaries. Since his first feature in 1949, he has made over thirty, mostly workmanlike, movies. *The Blue Max* (1966), *The Bridge at Remagen* (1969), *The Towering Inferno* (1974) and *King Kong* (1976) showed that he was good at handling large forces in an undemanding Saturday-night-at-the-movies manner. **Also:** *I Was Monty's Double* (58), *Tarzan's Greatest Adventure* (59), *Never Let Go* (60), *Waltz of the Toreadors* (62), *Tarzan goes to India* (62), *Guns at Batasi* (64), *House of Cards* (68), *El Condor* (70), *Skyjacked* (72), *Shaft in Africa* (73), *Death on the Nile* (78).

GUITRY Sacha
French. 1885-1957. Director/actor/playwright/wit. On stage from an early age. His light, boulevard comedies were mostly vehicles for his own portly theatrical presence and his various actress wives. He made a documentary film as early as 1915, *Ceux de Chez Nous*, showing a number of cultural figures (Sarah Bernhardt, Monet, Rodin, Degas and his father, the actor Lucien Guitry), but resisted the cinema for a

further twenty years before deciding to record his own plays for posterity. Some of them are straight adaptations from the theatre, but *Le Roman d'un Tricheur* (1936 – *The Story of a Cheat*), *Les Perles de la Couronne* (1937 – *The Pearls of the Crown*) and *Nine Bachelors* (1939) are full of inventive and amusing cinematic devices. At the end of his life, he made a series of stagey historical 'comedies' in colour: *Si Versailles M'était Conté* (1953), *Napoleon* (1955) and *Paris Nous Etait Conté* (1956) with himself and numerous guest stars cropping up. His reputation suffered in France after the war, because of accusations of collaboration during the German Occupation.

GUNEY Yilmaz
Turkish. Born 1931. Born into a peasant family, he worked his way through high-school and took an economics degree. Became a star in the Turkish cinema in action roles. Imprisoned various times for his left-wing activities and for supposedly killing a judge. He conceived *The Herd* (1978) and *The Way* (1981) in prison, sending detailed instructions to friends who directed these poetic, passionate panoramas of Turkish society.

HALL Alexander
American. 1894-1968. Former Broadway director. Made mostly romantic comedies with a surface sophistication for twenty-four years from 1932. He worked very often with Melvyn Douglas, the type of smooth actor that perfectly suited his films. Directed Shirley Temple's first starring vehicle, *Little Miss Marker* (1934), making her into the world's biggest and smallest star, and the other curly-headed blonde, Mae West in *Going to Town* (1935), in which she sings an aria from the opera

'Samson and Delilah'. His greatest success was *Here Comes Mr Jordan* (1941), about a prizefighter taken to heaven in error. This amusing whimsy was welcomed in the dark days of 1941. Continued in the same comedy-fantasy vein with *Once Upon a Time* (1944), Cary Grant and a dancing caterpillar, and *Down to Earth* (1947) with gorgeous Rita Hayworth in glorious Technicolor as the goddess of dance plus Mr Jordan and other characters from the earlier and better movie. **Others:** *The Doctor Takes a Wife* (40), *My Sister Eileen* (42), *She Wouldn't Say Yes* (45), *The Great Lover* (49), *Louisa* (50), *Let's Do It Again* (53), *Forever Darling* (56).

HALPERIN Victor
American. Born 1895. Murder Legendre (Bela Lugosi), a sugar-mill owner, has zombies working for him in *White Zombie* (1932), a chilling example of Hollywood horror in the 30's. It is the only one of his films that remains alive. *Supernatural* (1933), *Revolt of the Zombies* (1936), *Torture Ship* (1939) and *Buried Alive* (1940) are best left undisturbed.

HAMER Robert
British. 1911-1963. Former film-editor and script-writer. Became part of the regular team of Ealing Studio directors after making 'The Haunted Mirror' episode in *Dead of Night* (1945). It was a stylish debut and he went on to make a series of elegant, imaginative comedies and dramas, generally avoiding a realistic approach. Even *It Always Rains on Sundays* (1947), about a man on the run in a drab suburb of London, stresses the use of studio locations. The Brighton of the Victorian era is pointedly evoked in the murder story, *Pink String and Ceiling Wax* (1945). Murder is uppermost in *Kind Hearts and Coronets* (1949), committed with finesse by the amoral hero (Dennis Price) in order to inherit the family fortune. Considered to be the first British black comedy, it is rendered by Hamer, helped by beautifully judged performances, into more of a comedy of manners. Alec Guinness played twelve roles in four of Hamer's films, including all eight victims in *Kind Hearts*, G. K. Chesterton's priest-detective in *Father Brown* (1954), and a dual role in *The Scapegoat* (1959). Hamer's style is frustratingly swamped in the latter by Hollywood studio imperatives. His last film, *School for Scoun-*

drels* (1960) was the kind of modest comedy the British did best. Sadly, he was taken off the film before completion. He died three years later – an alcoholic.

HAMILTON Guy
British. Born 1922 in Paris. Came to England at the age of 18. Served in the navy. After the war, became assistant on many films including three by Carol REED. His first pictures (*The Ringer* – 1952, *An Inspector Calls* – 1954) have some of Reed's personality, soon to be replaced by no personality. A good technician, he followed in other people's footage with four James Bond movies (*Goldfinger* 1964, *Diamonds are Forever* 1971, *Live and Let Die* 1973, *The Man with the Golden Gun* 1974), the second Harry Palmer (Michael Caine) movie, the slow *Funeral in Berlin* (1966), the damp squib, *Force 10 from Navarone* (1978) and two all-star Agatha Christie who-cares-who-dunnits, *The Mirror Crack'd* (1981) and *Evil under the Sun* (1982). **Also:** *The Colditz Story* (54), *Manuela* (57), *A Touch of Larceny* (59), *The Devil's Disciple* (59), *The Battle of Britain* (69).

HARLAN Veit
German. 1899-1964. Notorious director of *Jew Süss* (1940), the anti-semitic Nazi propaganda film, who was charged with war crimes by the Allies. The case was dropped. Harlan, with Goebbels' encouragement, made a number of historical epics and a remake of MURNAU's *Sunrise, Journey to Tilsit* (1939), his best film.

HARVEY Anthony
British. Born 1931. Child actor (played the boy Ptolemy in *Caesar and Cleopatra* – 1946). Former editor. Jumped from a modest, impressive first feature, *Dutchman* (1966), set in the N.Y. subway and shot in five days with two speaking roles, to long-winded, theatrical history-dramas, *A Lion in Winter* (1968) and *The Abdication* (1974). His reputation was slightly redeemed by *Eagle's Wing* (1978), a symbolic pre-Western, splendidly photographed in New Mexico, but *Players* (1979) has the bounce of an old, wet tennis ball. **Also:** *They Might be Giants* (71), *Richard's Things* (80).

HAS Wojciech
Polish. Born 1925. Best known work is *The Saragossa Manuscript* (1964) based on an 18th century Polish novel

written in French. Probably its Chinese-box effect (a story within a story etc) worked better in print, but its use of the wide-screen and Zbigniew Cybulski's comic performance made it popular.

HASKIN Byron
American. Born 1889. Famous cinematographer in the 20's. His sci-fi movies for producer George Pal have amusing and lively special effects without the high-tec showing-off of *Star Wars* etc. *The War of the Worlds* (1953), *Conquest of Space* (1955), *From the Earth to the Moon* (1958) and *Robinson Crusoe on Mars* (1964) are nearer the comic book or cartoon than a space-invaders machine, and more enjoyable for that. **Also:** *Treasure Island* (50), *His Majesty O'Keefe* (53), *The Naked Jungle* (54), *Long John Silver* (55), *Captain Sinbad* (63).

HATHAWAY Henry
American. Born 1898. Former child actor. A reliable director of action films, he was under contract to Fox for twenty years (1940-1960). Inside Hathaway, there often seems a John FORD or Howard HAWKS struggling vainly to get out. Among his best films are the uncharacteristic *Peter Ibbotson* (1935), retaining some of the quality of the Du Maurier novel in

which a prisoner (Gary Cooper) leaves his cell each night in a dream to meet his sweetheart; two neat thrillers, *The Dark Corner* (1946) and *Kiss of Death* (1947), the latter introducing Richard Widmark to the screen as a giggling psychopath killer; and *Niagra* (1953), the splashy melodrama that made Marilyn Monroe into a sex goddess. In the 40's, he introduced the semi-documentary thriller (*The House on 92nd Street* – 1945, *13 Rue Madeleine* – 1947, *Call Northside 777* – 1948) which treated the subjects (now out-dated) as if they were newsreel reports by the F.B.I. In 1969, 71-year-old Hathaway helped 62-year-old John WAYNE win his first Oscar for *True Grit*, which made Wayne, with his black eye-patch, look like John Ford and Hathaway look like Hathaway, alas. **Also:** *Lives of a Bengal Lancer* (35), *Home in Indiana* (44), *Nob Hill*

Lauren Bacall and Humphrey Bogart in Hawks' *The Big Sleep* (1946).

Smith (66), *Five Card Stud* (68), *Raid on Rommel* (71).

HAWKS Howard

American. 1896-1977. Pilot in World War I, he brought authenticity to his four flying films, *The Dawn Patrol* (1930), *Ceiling Zero* (1936), *Only Angels Have Wings* (1939) and *Air-Force* (1943). A former designer and driver of racing cars, he recreated the excitement of the track in *The Crowd Roars* (1932) and *Red Line 7000* (1965). A huntin', shootin' and fishin' sportsman attracted to the subjects of *Hatari!* (1962) and *Man's Favorite Sport?* (1964). Started in films as property man, assistant editor and scriptwriter. Head of Paramount's story department from 1924 to 1926. The title of his first film, *The Road to Glory* (1926), a maudlin story of a blind girl, was significant. 'One of the greatest directors Hollywood has known' – Richard Roud. 'The greatest optimist the cinema has produced'

Marilyn Monroe (far right) in Hathaway's *Niagra* (1953).

(45), *The Black Rose* (50), *Rawhide* (51), *The Desert Fox* (51), *White Witch Doctor* (53), *Prince Valiant* (54), *Garden of Evil* (54), *The Racers* (55), *Legend of the Lost* (57), *7 Thieves* (60), *North to Alaska* (60), *The Sons of Katie Elder* (65), *Nevada*

– David Thomson. 'The greatest American artist' – Jean Luc GODARD (over 20 years ago). Comparisons have been made with Shakespeare, Mozart, Whitman. The case has been made for Hawks, a case that needed to be made in the 50's when, according to Andrew Sarris, he was 'the least known and least appreciated giant in the American cinema'. His assured narrative style and handling of most genres was less immediately obvious as 'art' than, say, John FORD or Orson WELLES. Now the battle has been won, there is a tendency to go too far the opposite way. His constant themes of the camaraderie of men who risk their lives, or the battle of the sexes and gender role-swapping may be examples of repressed homosexuality and gynophobia, but it doesn't make the often naive and sentimental view of masculine friendship any deeper nor the predatory female funnier or less hackneyed. *Bringing up Baby* (1938) is a raucous screwball comedy of ill-manners with Katharine Hepburn at her bleating worst and Cary Grant double-takingly backing away from her, without one jot of flesh and blood in any of the characters. The same applies to the juvenile high-jinks of *Monkey Business* (1952), *Hatari!* (John WAYNE trapping animals and Elsa Martinelli trapping him), and *Man's Favorite Sport?* in which Rock Hudson catches his tie in a girl's zipper, hops around in a sleeping bag he is unable to unzip, and catches a fish with the help of a bear among other even more inane gags. The pathetic attempt to remake *Ball of Fire* (1941), his own dimwitted farce about intellectuals as *A Song is Born* (1946) with Danny Kaye in the Barbara Stanwyck role, the jingoism and sanctimoniousness of *Sergeant York* (1941) – pacifist Gary Cooper learning to kill Germans and liking it – 'Fried Jap coming down' in *Air Force*, the fake Egyptology of *Land of the Pharoahs* (1955), and the witless, plotless solemnities of *Red Line 7000*. But . . . the superlatives are justified by the dazzling machinegun fire dialogue and delivery in *Twentieth Century* (1934) and *His Girl Friday* (1940), containing recognizable human beings beneath the comic surface; Cary Grant telling Jean Arthur that there is no room for sorrow among fliers in *Only Angels Have Wings*, the sublime sexual interplay between Humphrey Bogart and Lauren Bacall in *To Have and Have Not* (1944) and *The Big Sleep* (1946). 'The Look' of Bacall in the former, the clarity of direction of a complex script in the latter. The stunning opening number and other moments from *Gentlemen Prefer Blondes* (1953) and the dual character studies, deeper than anything in John Ford, of John Wayne with Montgomery Clift in *Red River* (1948), with Dean Martin in *Rio Bravo* (1959), with Robert Mitchum in *El Dorado* (1967); the brilliant pace and atmosphere of *Scarface* (1932) all make Hawks a candidate for Hollywood immortality, whatever that's worth in the stakes of greatness. **Also:** *A Girl in Every Port* (28), *The Criminal Code* (31), *Tiger Shark* (32), *Barbary Coast* (35), *I was a Male War-Bride* (49), *The Big Sky* (52), *Rio Lobo* (70).

HEIFITS Josif

Russian. Born 1906. His sensitive direction of *The Lady with the Little Dog* (1959), based on a Chekhov story, set in a subtly-evoked Yalta in summer and Moscow in winter in the 90's, won international acclaim. He returned to Chekhov for *In the Town of S.* (1966).

HEISLER Stuart

American. 1894-1979. Former film editor. An extremely modest output with some areas of interest. *The Glass Key* (1942), starring Alan Ladd and Veronica Lake, is a punchy version of Dashiell Hammett's story and Heisler's best movie. *Storm Warning* (1951), a curious film about a Ku Klux Klan murder, has Ginger Rogers and Doris Day in dramatic roles and Ronald Reagan as a good cop. He managed to make the Irving Berlin musical, *Blue Skies* (1946), with Bing Crosby and Fred Astaire, tedious, and two humdrum Humphrey Bogart pictures, *Tokyo Joe* (1949) and *Chained Lightning* (1950). **Also:** *Along Came Jones* (45), *Smash-up* (47), *Tulsa* (49), *Dallas* (50), *The Star* (53), *Beach-head* (54), *I Died a 1000 Times* (55), *The Burning Hills* (56), *Hitler* (61).

HELLMAN Monte

American. Born 1932. Studied drama at Stanford U. and film at UCLA. Got his first chance to direct under the aegis of Roger CORMAN. Made a couple of poverty-row adventures in the Philippines with the unknown Jack NICHOLSON in 1964. In 1966, on a shoe-string budget, took off with a crew of ten to the Utah desert to make two Westerns, *The Shooting* and *Ride the Whirlwind* at the same time in three weeks, both featuring Jack Nicholson, who scripted the latter. *The Shooting* was the better and, despite or because of the rough edges, became an emblematic, enigmatic and realistic revenge tale. *Two-Lane Blacktop* (1970) raised Hellman to cult status, although it flopped at the box-office. About two car-freaks who race across America, challenging others along the way, its structure is as linear as the road it follows, although its allegorical pretentions are inclined to side-track it. However, Hellman captures beautifully the two-lane back-drop to this American sub-culture. *The Cockfighter* (1974) also strives for the mythic but seems to lean too far in order to please his followers. Nevertheless, he has, with very few films, retained his reputation as a maverick like his favourite actors, Jack Nicholson and Warren Oates.

HERZOG Werner

German. Born 1942. A singular figure drawn to bizarre characters and situations in strange surroundings. His background is equally colourful. He studied literature, theatre and history in Munich and Pittsburgh. Travelled extensively, had various jobs including rodeo rider, made films for NASA and worked on American TV. *Signs of Life* (1967), his first feature, takes place on a Greek island during the 2nd World War, where a German soldier recovering from a wound, refuses to obey further orders. An effective parable it foreshadows later preoccupations with outsiders refus-ing or unable to conform to a limited social structure. *Even Dwarfs Started Small* (1970), set on a bleak island entirely populated by dwarfs, seems too systematic and forced as a distorted mirror-image of society, while *Fata Morgana* (1970), filmed in the Sahara, tells an Indian legend of creation, the desert standing for pre and post civilisation. *The Enigma of Kaspar Hauser* (1974), about the wild boy who appeared from nowhere in the early 19th century, depends almost entirely on the disturbing and remarkable presence of Bruno S., a man who spent twenty-two years in institutions, in the title role. In *Stroszek* (1977) he plays a simple German trying to adapt to life in Middle America, an obvious outsider's view of the barrenness of American life. Herzog's greatest success has been *Aguirre, Wrath of God* (1972). Shot in the Peruvian Andes about a conquistador's search for El Dorado, it is a ponderous morality, the fascination deriving from the jungle atmosphere and pictorial flair. Returning to home ground, he made hollow but stylish renderings of two German classics, *Nosferatu, The Vampire* (1978) and *Woyzeck* (1979) both with the hammy Klaus Kinski (Aguirre). Back to the exotic climes of Peru for *Fitzcarraldo* (1982), about a man (Kinski) who wishes to bring opera to the primitive tribes. **Also:** *Heart of Glass* (76).

Bruno S. in Herzog's *The Enigma of Kaspar Hauser* (1974).

HILL George Roy

American. Born 1922. Served in World War 2. Studied in Dublin and acted at the Abbey theatre. Returned to the USA where he directed for the theatre and TV for many years. His first two movies were tame adaptations from minor stage plays by Tennessee Williams (*Period of Adjustment* – 1962) and Lillian Hellman (*Toys in the Attic* – 1963). His next three pictures were *The World of Henry Orient* (1964), a light hors d'oeuvre of a comedy with Peter Sellers as a mediocre concert pianist, *Hawaii* (1966), a stodgy unappetising 3-hour main course and *Thoroughly Modern Millie* (1967), a charmingly frothy musical dessert lampooning the 20's. The romanticized version of the true story of *Butch Cassidy and the Sundance Kid* (1969), borrowing from *Jules and Jim* and *Bonnie and Clyde*, and *The Sting* (1973) were two of the biggest box-office hits of all time. Slick, sentimental, brash and devoid of any real sense of period (despite arty art-work and ragtime music), buddy-buddies, Paul NEWMAN and Robert REDFORD, are contemporary men in fancy dress. Redford does a flying-ace number in *The Great Waldo Pepper* (1975) and Newman tries ineffectually to convince as an ageing, infantile jock in *Slap-Shot* (1977), a film about ice-hockey that expounds the theory, 'Speak dirty and carry a big stick.' The director drops his pants half-way and then gets cold feet. To show his eclecticism (or lack of personality), he moved away from his half-cocked macho movies to the yukkiness of *A Little Romance* (1979). **Also:** *Slaughterhouse Five* (72). *The World According to Garp* (82).

HILL James

British. Born 1919. Former documentary film-maker. Made a prize-winning short, *Giuseppina* (1961) then graduated to making a film with a lion (*Born Free* – 1966), a horse (*Black Beauty* – 1971) and a fox (*The Belstone Fox* – 1973) for kiddie matinees. **Others:** *The Dock Brief* (62), *A Study in Terror* (65), *Captain Nemo and the Underwater City* (69).

HILL Walter

American. Born 1942. Studied history and English literature at Michigan U. Spent ten years writing screenplays (the only one he is proud of is *The Getaway* – 1972). His five movies have already established him as one of the most forceful and

Robert Redford in George Roy Hill's *The Great Waldo Pepper* (1975).

interesting personalities in mainstream American cinema. Influenced by action-directors such as Raoul WALSH, he has a striking visual sense with narrative and dialogue reduced to essentials. However, too much reliance on locale, and a tendency to simplification and undercharacterization mar his work. In his first film, *Hard Times* (*The Streetfighter* – UK – 1975), Charles Bronson is the archetypal movie loner, surviving during the Depression by taking on all-comers in bare-knuckle fights. Hill tries too hard for mythic qualities against a background cluttered with period detail. An American parable-maker is evident in *The Driver* (1978) as Ryan O'Neal's loner is pursued across a film-noir landscape by the law. Set mostly in the N.Y. subways *The Warriors* (1979) tells of one night's odyssey of a street gang, avoiding and battling with other gangs, on their way back to their own territory. Nobody in the movie being over twenty (the cops are shadowy figures), it is one of the few teenage sub-culture movies that do not have middle-class, middle-aged perceptions imposed upon it, although there are unconvincing sections when the deprived characters become self-aware. *The Long Riders* (1980), yet another Western on the James brothers, injects new life into old material with its symbolic treatment of the outlaws' existence, and by casting four sets of real brothers in the main roles (two Guests, three

Carradines, two Quaids, two Keaches). In *Southern Comfort* (1981), the handling of allegorical material is even more assured, echoing the war in Vietnam. The Louisiana bayou becomes, like the New York streets in *Warriors,* a hostile territory through which a platoon of National Guardsmen must find their way.

HILLER Arthur

Canadian. Born 1923. Only shines with a good script, preferably a caustic comedy such as Paddy Chayevsky's *The Americanization of Emily* (1964) and *The Hospital* (1971), Neil Simon's *The Out-of-Towners* (1966) and *Plaza Suite* (1970), *Silver Streak* (1976) and *The In-Laws* (1979). *Love Story* (1970) has a happy ending when the insufferable Ali McGraw dies of an incurable disease, while *Making Love* (1982) suggests the characters have to live with an incurable disease, namely homosexuality. *Man of La Mancha* (1972) was a slow-Quixotic-slow caterwauling musical to be avoided like the plague. **Others:** *Penelope* (66), *Tobruk* (67), *Popi* (69), *W. C. Fields and Me* (76), *Nightwing* (79).

HILLYER Lambert

American. Born 1889. Director and writer of almost all of William S. Hart's movies from 1919 to 1922, the first cowboy screen hero. Later he made *The Invisible Ray* (1936), a proficient Boris Karloff-Bela Lugosi frightener and *Dracula's Daughter* (1936). Also responsible for the *Batman* serials in the 40's.

HITCHCOCK Alfred

British. 1899-1980. The only director whose name is as famous as a film star's. Educated at a Jesuit school. Entered films in 1920 as designer of silent film titles, soon becoming art-director, scriptwriter and assistant director. After nine silent movies, including *The Lodger* (1926) and *The Ring* (1927), he made the first British sound film, *Blackmail* (1929) fol-lowed by a number of superb thril-lers: *The Man Who Knew Too Much* (1934), *The 39 Steps* (1935), *Young and Innocent* (1937), *The Lady Vanishes* (1938). In 1940, he went to America to make *Rebecca* (1940) and stayed for most of his life. Hitchcock has variously been considered 1) A moralist. CHABROL and ROH-MER in 1957 saw him as a Catholic artist whose 'transference of guilt' was the key to his work. 2) A Freudian. His films being perfect manifestations of the unconscious, dreams and infant phobias. 3) An ex-ponent of 'pure cinema' who has said he doesn't care about the morality, the subject, the acting or the message but only the technique of film to stir the audience. 4) A great director who squandered his extraordinary talent on empty commercial thrillers. 5) A

as an entertainer who uses the suspense story to play upon his audience's expectations and attack their complacency. The theological, psychological and metaphysical side is incidental. The more obvious Catholicism in films such as *I Confess* (1952) and *The Wrong Man* (1957) are no more than elements in the plot. The surface psychology of *Spellbound* (1945), *Psycho* (1960) and *Marnie* (1964) is extremely half-baked and facile. Hitchcock's politics are even more shallow, generally reduced to a fear of fifth columnists, usually in the guise of upper-class gentlemen (Otto Kruger in *Saboteur* – 1942, Herbert Marshall in *Foreign Correspondent* – 1940, James Mason in *North by Northwest* – 1959), and his sorties into 'enemy territory' (East Germany in *Torn Curtain* – 1966, Cuba in *Topaz* – 1969) were inept. The pleasure of his films lies elsewhere. The picaresque pursuit (an innocent bystander is involved in a crime and must prove his innocence while being chased by both police and criminals), the underlying sense of menace in the most unexpected places and from apparently innocuous sources, the aesthetics of murder mixed with romantic comedy and self-parody. The extravagant sense of location: the struggle on the top of The Statue of Liberty *(Saboteur)*, the shooting planned to co-incide with a clash of cymbals during a symphony at The Albert Hall (*The Man Who Knew Too Much* – 1934 and 1955), the killing at the UN building in New York and the climax on Mount Rushmore (*North by Northwest*), strangulation in Covent Garden Market (*Frenzy* – 1971). The element of surprise in the 'crop-dusting' sequence in *North by Northwest* where nothing on the empty plain in which Cary Grant finds himself could threaten him, the murder of the leading lady (Janet Leigh) half-way through *Psycho*, and the gradual transformation of the mundane into the nightmarish in *The Birds* (1963). Hitchcock's sadistic enjoyment in seeing 'the cool blonde' rattled and his own ritual appearances (usually early in the film so audiences will not be watching out for him). The pulsating music of Bernard Herrmann (since 1956) and the camerawork of Robert Burks (since 1951). A murder seen through the victim's fallen spectacles in *Strangers on a Train* (1951), the "poisoned" glass of milk (lit from within) in *Suspicion* (1941), the cut from the plug-hole of the shower to the dead Janet Leigh's eye in *Psycho*, the tracking shot at the end of *Young and Innocent* which reveals a closeup of the murderer, the assassin fleeing through a sea of umbrellas in *Foreign Correspondent*, the extraordinary composite set in *Rear Window* (1954) and so on and so on . . . **Others:** *Murder* (30), *Sabotage* (36), *Shadow of a Doubt* (43), *Notorious* (46), *Rope* (48), *Under Capricorn* (49), *Stage Fright* (50), *Dial M for Murder* (54), *To Catch a Thief* (55), *The Trouble with Harry* (56), *Vertigo* (58), *Family Plot* (76).

great entertainer with a supreme mastery of the medium and nothing to say, whose only desire is to put 'his audiences through it'. Although points 1-4 are valid, 5 seems nearest the truth. Hitchcock's sly humour mocks those who see him other than

Cary Grant in Hitchcock's *Suspicion* (1941).

HODGES Mike

British. Born 1932. Former TV director. His first feature, *Get Carter* (1971), about gangster Michael Caine investigating the death of his brother in Newcastle, has a toughness and feeling for seedy locations unusual in British films of the time. A promising start to a career that continued with a lightweight thriller, *Pulp* (1972), a violent, down-beat sci-fi movie, *The Terminal Man* (1974), and the campy, *Flash Gordon* (1980).

HOLT Seth

British. 1923-1971. Started in films as editor in 1942. Made five gripping melodramas before dying of alcoholism like his brother-in-law, Robert HAMER. **Filmography:** *Nowhere to Go* (58), *A Taste of Fear* (*A Scream of Fear* – US 61), *Station Six Sahara* (64), *The Nanny* (65), *Danger Route* (67), *Blood from the Mummy's Tomb* (71 – finished by Michael CARRERAS).

HONDA Inoshiro

Japanese. Born 1911. Specialized in monster movies which were great box-office successes in Japan and abroad. Many of the threatening creatures are mutants as a result of the radio-activity caused by nuclear bombs. The dubbing in the West was atrocious, but the special effects were fun. **Some titles:** *Half-Human* (55), *Godzilla* (56), *Rodan* (56), *Gorath* (62), *King Kong vs Godzilla* (63), *Godzilla vs The Thing* (64), *Godzilla's Revenge* (69).

HOOPER Tobe

American. Born 1943 in Texas. Made TV commercials and documentaries. His second feature, *The Texas Chain Saw Massacre* (1974), made for less than 200,000 dollars in 16mm, brought in a lot of cash, mainly from the midnight circuit where dating teenage couples can cling to each other in fear in the darkness. This sickeningly gory story is full of startling images. In the same vein (or spurting artery) are *Death Trap* (1976), *Salem's Lot* (1979), *The Funhouse* (1980) and *Poltergeist* (1982– produced and partly directed by Steven SPIELBERG), ideal for the growing home-video market.

HOPPER Dennis

American. Born 1935. Young 'method' actor in the 50's who appeared with his idol, James Dean in *Rebel without a Cause* (1955) and *Giant* (1956). Played Napoleon in *The Story of Mankind* (1957) and with something of the Bonaparte in him, managed to make his first feature, *Easy Rider* (1969) independently for less than 400,000 dollars, starring himself and the producer, Peter Fonda. The film was a 'sleeper' whose combination of drugs, rock music, violence, counter-culture stance, and motor cycles as ultimate freedom machines, caught the imagination of the young and led to a string of imitations. It is self-pitying, masochistic, sentimental, naive and simple-minded and these 'children of the sixties' now seem as dated as the "bright, young things" of the 20's. *The Last Movie* (1971), shot in Peru, made for the stoned by the stoned, was stoned by the critics. After ten years came *Out of the Blue* (1981), a wild piece of post-Hippy American Gothic centreing on a 15-year-old punk girl (Linda Manz) trying to survive in a world of drunks, junkies, dykes and rapists.

HORNE James V

American. 1880-1942. As Laurel and Hardy's jaunty signature tune fades out, his is the last name seen at the opening of many of their two-reelers. Directed them again in three of their best features, *Bonnie Scotland* (1935), *The Bohemian Girl* (1936) and *Way Out West* (1937), the latter containing two classic song and dance numbers performed by the irresistible duo. *College* (1927) is one of the best examples of Buster KEATON's physical grace even when, in this case, he is meant to be incompetent at sports.

HOWARD William K

American. 1899-1954. From 1921 made a number of lively action pictures which contained spectacular sequences such as the buffalo stampede in *Thundering Herd* (1925) and the volcanic eruption in *Volcano* (1926). His most interesting sound film was *The Power and the Glory* (1933), a precurser of *Citizen Kane* with its story of a millionaire (Spencer Tracy) who commits suicide, told in a series of unchronological flashbacks. Other capable products were the Kern-Hammerstein operetta, *The Cat and the Fiddle* (1934), *Sherlock Holmes* (1932) with Clive Brook and Reginald Owen and *Johnny-come-lately* (1943) with James Cagney. *Fire Over England* (1937), made in England, is a dull Elizabethan epic, despite the presence of Flora Robson, Laurence OLIVIER and Vivien Leigh.

HUDSON Hugh

British. Born 1936. Many TV commercials, some of them winning awards. His Oscar-winning first feature, *Chariots of Fire* (1981) is a whopping great dose of good old-fashioned patriotism and nostalgia for Empire, drowning any mild jibes at the Establishment it contains. All the manipulative devices of prize-winning commercials are stunningly pulled out for the final triumph of the British athletes at the 1924 Paris Olympics. A film with legs, it will run and run.

HUGHES Ken

British. Born 1922. After the war, made documentaries and shorts, including The Scotland Yard series. His films are a mixed bag, without much personality emerging. *The Trials of Oscar Wilde* (1960) was done with taste, sensitivity and luxury with a winning Oscar performance from Peter Finch. Hughes is as sympathetic to Wilde's hedonism as he is to the puritanism of *Cromwell* (1970), a wordy but handsome epic. Back to hedonism with *Sextette* (1978), 86-year-old Mae West's last fling flung at the public in this horrendous Wilde West freak-show. His biggest success was the 2½ hour pedestrian musical about a flying car, *Chitty, Chitty, Bang, Bang* (1968). **Also:** *Joe Macbeth* (56), *The Small World of Sammy Lee* (63), *The Internecine Project* (74).

HUMBERSTONE H. Bruce

American. Born 1903. An adept contract director whose best movies were fluffy forties musical vehicles for Fox blondes such as Sonja Henie in *Sun Valley Serenade* (1941) and *Iceland* (1942), Alice Faye in *Hello, Frisco, Hello* (1943) and Betty Grable in *Pin-Up Girl* (1944). **Others:** *Wonder Man* (45), *3 Little Girls in Blue* (46), *East of Java* (49), *Happy Go Lovely* (51), *She's Working Her Way Through College* (52), *The Desert Song* (53).

HURST Brian Desmond

Irish. Born 1900. Most famous film was the well-made melodrama, *Dangerous Moonlight* (1941) starring Anton Walbrook as the Polish concert pianist who joins the RAF during World War II through which "The Warsaw Concerto" is played. **Others:** *Scrooge* (51), *The Malta Story* (53), *Simba* (55), *The Black Tent* (56), *Dangerous Exile* (57).

HURWITZ Leo

American. Born 1909. Committed left-wing documentary film-maker. Made films about The Spanish Civil War (*Heart of Spain* – 1937), The Chinese Revolution (*China Strikes Back* – 1938) and racism in the USA (*Strange Victory* – 1948). *Native Land* (1941), narrated by Paul Robeson, attacked anti-Union terrorism in America. He has continued to go his own way, making forceful, personal film essays including a four-hour autobiographical picture dedicated to his late wife called *Dialogue with a Woman Departed* (1980).

HUSTON John

American. Born 1906. Son of the actor Walter Huston. He has led a diversified existence as painter, boxer, horseman, hunter, actor, gambler, drinker, raconteur and writer who doesn't discourage tales of his hell-raising. His films reflect his wide interests but, like his favourite actor Humphrey Bogart, they reveal a tenderness and romantic idealism beneath their rough exterior. Most of his heroes are fiercely independent and/or misfits (women are peripheral in his masculine world) such as Toulouse Lautrec (*Moulin Rouge* – 1953), Captain Ahab (*Moby Dick* – 1956), *Freud* (1962), the boxers in *Fat City* (1971) and the preacher in *Wise Blood* (1979). Fatalism and irony pervade his best films which are rich in character and plot, told in a decisive narrative style. After writing screenplays for a number of successful Warner Bros. dramas, he made an astonishingly assured debut with *The Maltese Falcon* (1941), the strong cast (headed by Bogart's Sam Spade) and sharp script rendering Dashiell Hammett's prose style into film terms. Huston met the approval of the mysterious B. Traven, author of *The Treasure of the Sierra Madre* (1947), directing his father and Bogart in a great yarn of human greed. Greed is also the theme of *Key Largo* (1948). The continuously changing dramatic set-ups and powerful performances from Edward G. Robinson, Lionel Barrymore and Bogart, never allow the enclosed setting to become static. Strangely, *Beat the Devil* (1954), one of his most perfect movies, is his only true comedy. It parodies *The Maltese Falcon*, Bogart's persona, Huston's style, and yet remains a good story in itself. Much of Huston's other work is of interest: the expert crime-thriller, *The Asphalt Jungle* (1950), made in a semi-documentary style, but ending

John Huston

mythically; his two excursions into the African Jungles *The African Queen* (1952), an amusing and unlikely duologue, and *The Roots of Heaven* (1958), a heavily symbolic tale whose image of doomed elephants in a real African landscape comes across strongly; *Reflections in a Golden Eye* (1967), an absorbing movie based closely on Carson McCullers' short novel; and *Fat City* and *Wise Blood*, despite a self-consciousness and surface pessimism, are accomplished films. There have been a number of slap-dash movies that seriously blot his reputation, namely *The Bible* (1966), *Sinful Davey* (1969), *A Walk with Love and Death* (1969), *The Life and Times of Judge Roy Bean* (1972), *The Mackintosh*

Man (1973) and the abysmal *Escape to Victory* (1981). **Also:** *Across the Pacific* (42), *We Were Strangers* (49), *The Red Badge of Courage* (51), *Heaven Knows, Mr. Allison* (57), *The Barbarian and the Geisha* (58), *The Unforgiven* (60), *The Misfits* (60), *The List of Adrian Messenger* (63), *Night of the Iguana* (64), *The Kremlin Letter* (70), *The Man Who Would Be King* (75), *Annie* (82).

HUTTON Brian G.

American. Born 1935. Highlights in Hutton's action-packed career were *Where Eagles Dare* (1968) and *Kelly's Heroes* (1970), two action-packed World War II movies starring a wooden Clint EASTWOOD, and *Zee and Company* (1971) and *Night Watch* (1973), two inaction-packed melodramas starring an all-enveloping Elizabeth Taylor. **Others:** *The Pad* (66), *Sol Madrid* (67).

ICHIKAWA Kon

Japanese. Born 1915. Started as a cartoonist. Made cartoons and puppet films. His first features were mostly satirical comedies, earning him the nickname of 'the Japanese CAPRA'. Nothing Capraesque about the films that made his reputation in the West. War, the memory and threat of war are dominant themes. Both *The Burmese Harp* (1956) and *Fires on the Plain* (1959) are concerned with the effect of the defeat of the Japanese army, the anguish and degradation that resulted from it, depicted in visionary black and white images. In *Conflagration* (1958), based on Mishima's novel, a young man sets fire to a holy temple because he feels it has been contaminated by the people of post-war Japan. As in all his major films, it is a study of a man pushed to extremes. Using the wide screen to magnificent effect in *Alone in the Pacific* (1963), he tells the true story of a young yachtsman who sailed from Osaka to San Francisco, a dangerous three month voyage on a nineteen foot craft. One of his most fascinating, complex and ambiguous films is *An Actor's Revenge* (1963). The revenge is that of an actor of female roles in the Kabuki Theatre against three men responsible for the death of his parents. The DaieiScope screen is used to give the impression of Japanese prints, the theatre stage and comic strips at the centre of which is the prodigious performance of Kazuo Hasegawa as the hero/heroine. For *Tokyo Olympiad* (1965) he 'attempted to capture the solemnity of the moment when man defies his limits.' To achieve his aims, he employed 164 cameramen who used 232 different lenses. The result was a triumph of Japanese technical wizardry and creative genius. Sadly, nothing he has made since has had much impact. **Others:** *The Key* (59), *Her Brother* (60), *The Wanderers* (73).

Shoji Yasui in Ichikawa's *The Burmese Harp* (1956).

IMAMURA Shohei

Japanese. Born 1926. Assistant to Yasujiro OZU. Part of the Japanese New Wave of the 60's, influenced by the French New Wave and moving away from traditional Japanese subjects. His films are mostly concerned with social outcasts and/or sexual deviants. His best known work is *The Pornographer* (1966), a tragi-comic view of the world of blue movies. **Others:** *The Insect Woman* (63), *Intentions of Murder* (64), *The Profound Desire of the Gods* (68), *Vengeance is Mine* (79).

INCE Thomas

American. 1882-1924. First Hollywood tycoon. Entered the film industry from the theatre. Directed hundreds of one and two reelers, mostly Westerns, between 1911 and 1914, before producing and 'supervising' other people's movies. One of the few feature-length pictures he directed was *Civilisation* (1916) in which Christ returns as a submarine engineer to preach pacifism. Died in mysterious circumstances aboard one of William Hearst's yachts.

INGRAM Rex

American. 1893-1950. Born in Ireland. Went to America at eighteen. Studied sculpture at Yale. Began in films as actor, designer and screenwriter in 1915. *The Four Horsemen of the Apocalypse* (1921) made Valentino into a super star. The Aryan beauty of Ingram's wife, Alice Terry, sets off Valentino's dark good-looks in this and in *The Conquering Power* (1921). He also made two spectacular swashbucklers, *The Prisoner of Zenda* (1922) and *Scaramouche* (1923) with the other Hollywood Latin lover, Ramon Novarro. His films are superbly lit with a particular feeling for sets, costumes and locations. Disappointed at not being given *Ben Hur* (1927) to direct, he and his wife left Hollywood for Nice where he set up his own studio. He shot a great deal on location, making *The Garden of Allah* (1927) and *Baroud* (1933), his only sound film, in Morocco. He later became a Muslim, gave up the cinema and returned to sculpture and writing. **Others:** *Where the Pavement Ends* (23), *The Arab* (24), *Mare Nostrum* (26).

IVENS Joris

Dutch. Born 1898. Writer and director of left-wing documentaries. Father sold photographic equipment. Began making films in 1928 and continued to shoot all over the world for over five decades, proving that 'a documentary is deeper and more personal than newsreel truth.' *Borinage* (1933) shows the misery inflicted on the miners during a strike in Belgium. *Spanish Earth* (1937) has an effectively understated commentary written and spoken by Ernest Hemingway supporting the Republican cause in the Spanish Civil War. He attacked Dutch colonialism in *Indonesia Calling* (1946) and made many films on the Chinese Revolution. (He was a personal friend of Chou-en-Lai.) His remarkable documentary, *How Yukong Replaced the Mountains* (1976) reveals parts of everyday life in China unseen before in the West. All his films, sometimes prosaic, sometimes lyrical, are shot through with sincerity and passion and concern for the people he is filming.

IVORY James

American. Born 1930. Film graduate of the University of Southern California. Fewer than half his films are set in America. Made by his own company, set up with producer Ismail

Merchant and written by the novelist Ruth Prawar Jhabvala, they are literate, ironic, subtly intellectual, slightly precious and over-refined. The major themes are the Jamesian ones of the encounter between two cultures and the corruption or attempted corruption of innocence. His first four features were made in India, showing the influence of Henry James, Satyajit RAY, E. M. Forster and Jean RENOIR's *The River*. *Shakespeare Wallah* (1965), following an English travelling theatre company around India, is gently satirical about the cultural pretentions of both the British and the Indians. *The Guru* (1968), dealing with the clash between western pop culture and eastern mysticism, is far more obvious, straying too far from Ivory's mentors. Returning to India for *Hullabaloo over Georgie and Bonnie's Pictures* (1978), the Ivory-Merchant-Jhabvala team came up with a witty divertisement on the attempts of a Scots lady and an American art-dealer to obtain pictures from a Rajah's collection. It was inevitable that Ivory should go directly to Henry James for inspiration and *The Europeans* (1979) comes nearer the novelist's style than any other attempt on film. Of the truly American movies, *The Wild Party* (1975), based on a poem about the Fatty Arbuckle murder-scandal, and *Roseland* (1977), three bitter-sweet stories set in the New York Dance Hall, achieve a certain verisimilitude of place and tone completely missing from *Jane Austen in Manhattan* (1980). **Others:** *The Householder* (63), *Bombay Talkie* (70), *The Autobiography of a Princess* (75), *Quartet* (81).

Jancsó's *The Round-up* (1965).

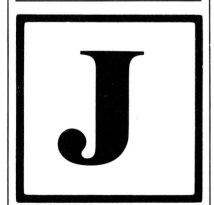

J

JAEKIN Just
French. Born 1940. Former TV director of commercials, variety programmes, sport etc. Purveyor of erotic chic. His films are packaged like glossy girlie magazines. *Emmanuelle* (1974), *The Story of O* (1975) and *Lady Chatterley's Lover* (1981) are pornography dressed up (or undressed) as art with Sylvia Kristel on display. He has been compared to Roger VADIM, a comparison he takes as a compliment.

JAGLOM Henry
American. Born 1943. Attended The Actor's Studio in New York. Acted on stage and TV for 5 years. Joint film editor (with Jack NICHOLSON) on cutting *Easy Rider* (1969) from over 5 hours to 95 mins. Neither *A Safe Place* (1971), an unruly piece of psychedelic symbolism, nor *Tracks* (1976) had much success. The latter was shot on a train when the guard wasn't looking and starred a hallucinating Dennis HOPPER taking a coffin with the body of his friend, who had been killed in Vietnam, back home to be buried. The film, like the coffin, turns out to be empty. *Sitting Ducks* (1981), however, won plaudits as a crazy comedy road movie, a homage to those earlier Road movies with Bing Crosby and Bob Hope.

JANCSÓ Miklós
Hungarian. Born 1921. There are few directors so akin to a choreographer. His films are elaborate ballets, emblematically tracing the movements in the fight for Hungarian independence and socialism. Ritual dances of life and death which take place on a bleak Hungarian plain where power continually shifts hands. Horsemen drive the people to and fro. The Whites defeat the Reds. The Reds defeat the Whites. Tyranny is everywhere and men and women stripped of their clothes are vulnerable and humiliated, nudes in a landscape. People survive in groups, singing and dancing. Sometimes the groups split up and realign, moving in different directions. The camera weaves in and out like an invisible observer, sometimes dancing with the people, sometimes following them across the plains, tracking them down, shooting them. A tracking shot takes on new meaning in Jancsó's films. After studying law, ethnography and art, he entered the Film Academy in Budapest. His very personal style blossomed in *The Round-Up* (1965) set in 1868, when Austro-Hungarian troops tried to break the unity of the Hungarian partisans by torture, interrogations and killings. There is little dialogue, the characters are depersonalized, the setting is timeless. Colour is used symbolically in *The Confrontation* (1969), young revolutionaries follow a boy in a red shirt, chanting slogans and singing. *Agnus Dei* (1970) and *Red Psalm* (71) are hymns of despair and celebration, orchestrated by the laterally-tracking camera and long takes. There are said to be only thirteen takes in the whole of *Winter Sirocco* (1969). However, the style was becoming an affectation, the nudity arbitrary, the subjects mere excuses for abstract patterns. Away from Hungary, Jancsó let his hair down, often obscuring his vision. In Italy he made the playful *Private Vices and Public Virtues* (1976) where

the nudity of most of the protagonists is essential in this representation of the Mayerling story in terms of an orgy. The Hungarian plains were abandoned except at the end of *The Tyrant's Heart* (1981), based on Boccaccio. The set of a castle, in which strange cavortings take place, is raised to reveal horsemen riding over the plain reminding us of Jancsó's better days. **Others:** *The Red and the White* (67), *Silence and Cry* (68), *Elektra* (75), *Hungarian Rhapsody* (78).

JARMAN Derek

British. Born 1942. Studied art. Former set designer and art director. Made a series of Super 8 films. His first feature, *Sebastiane* (1975) retells the story of the martyr and saint in Latin dialogue (with sub-titles and no subleties) and homosexual imagery. Jarman waggishly explained that the budget didn't allow for authentic costumes, hence the nudity. What the silly *Sebastiane* is to gay, the juvenile *Jubilee* (1978) is to punk. This futuristic tale of girl gangs running wild in a lawless Britain which Elizabeth I comes back to observe, is brazenly spunky punky for those on the same wavelength. *The Tempest* (1979) is best when it stops doing The Bard and goes in for a version of Stormy Weather sung by Elizabeth Welch and a chorus of sailors.

JARROTT Charles

British. Born 1927. Worked on TV before making big, dull, interminable, expensive, prestige movies. Costume soapers, *Anne of a Thousand Days* (1970) and *Mary, Queen of Scots* (1972) at least had strong performances from Genevieve Bujold (Anne Boleyn), Vanessa Redgrave (Mary), Glenda Jackson (Elizabeth I), but the 'musical' *Lost Horizon* (1973) made Shangri-la into 2½ hours of purgatory. Unfortunately, *The Other Side of Midnight* (1977) was the same side of Jarrott. **Also:** *The Dove* (74), *The Littlest Horse Thieves* (77).

JEFFRIES Lionel

British. Born 1926. Bald character actor who often blows his top, showed an extremely delicate touch in his handling of children's stories, *The Railway Children* (1970), *The Amazing Mr Blunden* (1972) and *The Water Babies* (1977).

JENNINGS Humphrey

British. 1907–1950. Poet/critic/ painter/photographer. Studied at Cambridge. Joined the GPO film unit in 1934 where he directed a few short documentaries. It is, however, for the documentaries he made during wartime that he will be remembered. Films about the effect of war on the ordinary people of Britain. *The First Days* (1939), *London Can Take It* (1940) and *Listen to Britain* (1942) all gave a picture of the unity, courage and humour of the British people in adversity, doing much to influence public opinion in America and which still forms part of the image, myth and reality, of the Tight Little Island during the war. *Words for Battle* (1941) used well-known poetry and prose as a commentary, but generally there was no commentary at all, the sights and sounds were allowed to speak for themselves. News from the radio, popular music, concerts at the National Gallery, people at a dance while the Home Guard scan the heavens for German planes, overheard conversations, women working in factories. *Fires Were Started* (1943), his only full-length film, described 24 hours in the life of firemen during the Blitz. His visual sensibility and ability to select meaningful moments of civilian life prompted Lindsay ANDERSON to call him 'The only real poet the British cinema has yet produced'. He was not at ease in post-war Britain, making only a few minor documentaries. He was killed in Greece, falling from a cliff

while filming. **Others:** *Heart of Britain* (41), *The 80 Days* (44), *A Diary for Timothy* (45), *Dim Little Island* (49).

JESSUA Alain

French. Born 1932. Assistant to OPHULS, BECKER and CARNÉ. His first feature, *Life Upside Down* (1964) about a man who retreats into his own inner world, was very promising. His few films since have not fulfilled that promise, although they are far from contemptible. **Some titles:** *Jeu de Massacre (Comic Strip Hero* – 67), *Shock Treatment* (73), *Armageddon* (76), *The Dogs* (78).

JEWISON Norman

Canadian. Born 1926. Graduate of Toronto U. Wrote scripts and acted for the BBC in London. Directed TV in USA, including spectaculars with Judy Garland and Danny Kaye. His films are a mixture of the good, the bad and the ugly. (Not in that order.) *The Cincinnati Kid* (1965) was a good card-game rerun of *The Hustler* (1961) played between Steve McQueen as The Kid and wily, old Edward G. Robinson. *In the Heat of the Night* (1967) contains an entertaining but equally artificial game played between black Sidney POITIER and redneck Rod Steiger. The game of *Rollerball* (1975), a cross between Roller Derby, football and motor-cycling, is the apogee of violence in sport. Directed glossily, it wallows in the violence it pretends to be condemning. 'Life is a game of

A scene from Humphrey Jennings' *Fires were Started* (1943).

Rollerball', is the salutary message. *The Thomas Crown Affair* (1968) is not helped by a multi-screen technique; *F*I*S*T** (1978) and *And Justice for All* (1979) drained all interest from the subjects (Union power and the judicial system respectively) by a shallow approach, weak scripts and bad acting. Any vitality that existed on stage was lost in the location-filmed *Fiddler on the Roof* (1971) and *Jesus Christ Superstar* (1973), both God-filled God-awful musicals. **Others:** *The Thrill of it all* (63), *Send Me No Flowers* (64), *The Russians are Coming, the Russians are Coming* (66) *Gaily, Gaily* (69).

JOHNSON Lamont
American. Born 1920. Directed in the New York theatre and TV. Two movies with a sports subject are a cut above the rest of his output. The portentous title of *The Last American Hero* (1973), about stock car racing, promises more than it delivers and *One on One* (1977), about college basketball, is the stuff (and nonsense) that dreams are made of. *Lipstick* (1976) was a smudgy exploitation movie posing as a serious film about rape. **Others:** *The MacKenzie Break* (70), *A Gunfight* (71), *The Ground-Star Conspiracy* (72), *You'll Like My Mother* (72), *Somebody Killed Her Husband* (78).

JOHNSON Nunnally
American. 1897–1977. Scriptwriter/ Producer/Director. Renowned more for his many screenplays (*The Grapes of Wrath*–1940, *The Woman in the Window*–1944) than the eight efficient movies he made for Fox between 1954 and 1960. Joanne Woodward only gained one Oscar for her three brilliant performances as the woman with three identities in *The 3 Faces of Eve* (1957). *Oh, Men! Oh Women!*, a zippy comedy about psychiatry, was made in the same year. **Others:** *Night People* (54), *Black Widow* (54), *How to be very, very, popular* (55), *The Man in the Gray Flannel Suit* (56), *The Man who Understood Women* (59), *The Angel Wore Red* (60).

JONES Chuck
American. Born 1915. Attended art school. Worked his way up in the early animation studios, directing his first cartoon in 1938. At Warner Bros., he reached the acme of his profession making hundreds of Looney Tunes cartoons featuring Bugs Bunny, Porky Pig, Daffy Duck and Tweety Pie, with titles like *What's Up, Opera?* (All of Wagner in six minutes), *Claws for Alarm, Ah, Sweet Mouse–story of Life, Louvre Come Back To Me, To Beep or not to Beep*. *The Road Runner* series was a more recent creation, using the desert landscape to devastating effect. Less anarchic than Tex AVERY, he tried to work within the cartoon's own crazy logic. His full-length features (which he co-directed), *Gay Puree* (1962) and *The Phantom Tollbooth* (1969), had similarities with his own skunk character, Pepe le Pew.

JULIAN Rupert
American. 1886–1943. Made a number of films in the 20's of which only two are worth remembering. Erich von STROHEIM's extravagance caused him to be taken off *Merry-Go-Round* (1922) as director to be replaced by Julian. Not much of his original footage remains, but the lavish setting (19th Century Europe) and the story of lovers from different classes, are very much Stroheim's. *The Phantom of the Opera* (1925), filmed in 2-tone colour, is a splendidly eerie melodrama starring Lon Chaney with sumptuous sets of the Paris Opera in which all the action takes place.

KADÁR Jan
Czechoslovakian. Born 1918. Studied law. Worked in Nazi labour camps during the war. In 1947, he met the writer Elmar Klos with whom he directed most of his Czech films. *Shop on the High Street* (1965. *Shop on Main Street*–US) was the first Czech film to win an Oscar. It tells of the relationship between an old Jewish woman (Ida Kaminska) and a carpenter (Josef Kroner) who protects her in a small Slovak town under the Nazis. The period atmosphere and the acting of the two leads make it a moving drama. Kadar left for the USA after the Soviet invasion of his country. In America, he continued with Jewish themes, but the underlying sentimentality of *Shop on the High Street* is more evident in *The Angel Levine* (1970) and *Lies My Father Told Me* (1975).

KALATOZOV Mikhail
Russian. 1903–1973. His best known work is *The Cranes are Flying* (1957), one of the first films after 'the thaw' which seemed to usher in a new liberty in Soviet cinema. A touching love story set during World War II, it benefits from the performance of Tatiana Samoilova and some sweeping camerawork.

KANE Joseph
American. 1894–1975. Considering he worked at Republic Studios and had to direct 'Wild Bill' Elliot, Rod Cameron, Forrest Tucker and especially Vera (Hruba) Ralston, the studio boss's wife, Kane did a good job. He got to direct their biggest star John WAYNE in a civilised comedy–Western, *Flame of the Barbary Coast* (1944), but was generally stuck with Miss Ralston crooning to stoical cowboys. **Some titles:** *The Cheaters* (45), *The Plainsman and the Lady* (46), *The Plunderers* (48), *Jubilee Trial* (53), *Fair Wind to Java* (53), *Timberjack* (55).

KANIN Garson
American. Born 1912. Former jazz musician and stage actor. Known mainly for the many smart comedies he wrote with his wife Ruth Gordon, especially screenplays directed by George CUKOR. Apart from his two post-War aberrations, *Where It's At* (1969) and *Some Kind of Nut* (1969), all his seven features were made between 1938 and 1941. They give the impression they would have been better directed by, say, Preston STURGES, HAWKS or Mc-CAREY. Nevertheless, *The Great Man Votes* (1939) is an entertaining tragicomedy with John Barrymore as a drunken professor. Ginger Rogers enlivens the puerile plots of *Bachelor Mother* (1939) and *Tom, Dick and Harry* (41), Cary Grant double-takes between two spouses in *My Favorite Wife* (1940) to an irritating degree, and neither Charles LAUGHTON nor Carole Lombard are especially comfortable in *They Knew What They Wanted* (1940).

KARLSON Phil

American. Born 1908. After years as assistant director and then director of 2nd features of little distinction in the 40's, he gained a reputation for a few tight-knit, tough low-budget crime movies in the 50's, the best being *The Phenix City Story* (1955) about a crusading lawyer cleansing a small town of crime. Eighteen years later, he returned to the same theme in the far more violent, *Walking Tall* (1973) concerning Sheriff Buford Pusser (Joe Don Baker) forcing law and order with a vicious baseball bat. Also made *The Silencers* (1966), the first of the facetious Matt Helm series with Dean Martin, and the last, *The Wrecking Crew* (1968). **Others:** *Lorna Doone* (51), *Scandal Sheet* (52), *99 River Street* (53), *Tight Spot* (55), *Five Against the House* (55), *The Brothers Rico* (57), *Gunman's Walk* (58), *The Scarface Mob* (59), *Key Witness* (60), *The Young Doctors* (61), *Kid Galahad* (62), *Hornet's Nest* (70), *Ben* (72).

KAUFMAN Philip

American. Born 1936. His first feature, *The Great Northfield Minnesota Raid* (1971) shows a certain flair for making a genre movie such as this much-filmed story of the Younger and James Brothers. *The White Dawn* (1974), took him and his splendid cameraman Michael Chapman to Baffin Island for a non-genre film about the rescue of three whalers in 1896 by Eskimoes. To remake a classic generally requires courage and/or stupidity; Kaufman's *Invasion of the Body Snatchers* (1978) did not suffer the studio restrictions of Don SIEGEL's 1956 film, but with big screen, colour and Dolby sound, it can't touch the earlier movie. Set in San Francisco, every image strains towards a bizarre effect. The script of *The Wanderers* (1979), even in the monosyllabic tradition of street-gang movies, is moronic. The mixture between expressionism and naturalism fails to reconstruct life in the Bronx in 1963.

KAZAN Elia

American. Born 1909 in Istanbul of Armenian parents who emigrated to the USA in 1913. In 1932 joined the radical Group Theatre run by Lee Strasburg. A member of the Communist Party from 1934–1936. Set up the Actors' Studio in 1948. In 1952, testified before the Un-American Activities House Committee where he named names. These biographical

Elia Kazan

Marlon Brando and Vivien Leigh in Kazan's *Streetcar Named Desire* (1951).

details are relevant to his work. When he comes too close to his own experiences as in his screenplays for *America, America* (1964), an initially affecting story of his uncle's (and by proxy his own) emigration to the USA, or *The Arrangement* (1969), from his novel about a writer's breakdown, his subjectivity falls into self-pity and theatricality. A justification for his role as a 'friendly witness' in the McCarthy hearings mars the ending of *On the Waterfront* (1954) which caricatures the problem of union corruption and unconvincingly transforms the BRANDO character into a Hollywood hero dedicated to the 'virtues of American democracy'. A strong contempt for 'the mob' is also evident in *A Face in the Crowd* (1957), a biting satire on the manipulation of the masses by TV, but ending as an 'it's lonely at the top' melodrama. After a couple of bland liberal films, *Gentleman's Agreement* (1947) on anti-semitism and *Pinky* (1949) on racism, he soon lost any 'pinky' image he might have had. All his films, however, have strong social themes and a keen sense of location, as with the New York of *On the Waterfront* and the Southern settings of *Panic in the Streets* (1950), *Baby Doll* (1956) and *Wild River* (1960). His sympathy with actors from his work in the theatre and the 'Studio', allowing them to develop their roles during shooting, has produced some of the finest modern screen acting. Marlon Brando and Vivien Leigh in *Streetcar Named Desire* (1951), James Dean in *East of Eden* (1955), Karl Malden, Carroll Baker and Eli Wallach in *Baby Doll*, Jo Van Fleet and Lee Remick in *Wild River*, and Natalie Wood in *Splendor in the Grass* (1961). It was Kazan who first built Brando into a star, 'discovered' James Dean and gave Jack Palance, Zero Mostel, Lee Remick and Warren BEATTY their first screen roles. He worked well with the writers Tennessee Williams (*Streetcar* and *Baby Doll*), John Steinbeck (*Viva Zapata*–1952) and Paul Osborne (*East of Eden* and *Wild River*). His collaboration with Harold Pinter on Scott Fitzgerald's *The Last Tycoon* (1976) was an incompatible marriage that produced a dead child. Kazan's own son wrote the script for *The Visitors* (1972), shot on a low-budget in his house in Connecticut, a torpid post-Vietnam parable that is concerned with the ethics of informing on one's friends. **Others:** *A Tree Grows in Brooklyn* (45), *Sea of Grass*

(47), *Boomerang* (47), *Man on a Tightrope* (53).

KEATON Buster

American. 1895–1966. Son of vaudeville performers, he became part of their act at the age of seven. Appeared first in a number of Fatty Arbuckle shorts which, paradoxically, were too small for him. From 1920 Keaton was virtually his own director but, as he was hardly off the screen, he needed a co-director. It is fairly certain that most of the conception of the films was his. They are supreme examples of visual comedy allied to cinematic technique. The multitude of gags, impossible to describe in print, depend on cutting, camera set-ups and spacio-temporal tensions. His first independent feature, *The 3 Ages* (1923) parodied GRIFFITH's *Intolerance* (1916) and the pictorial splendour and feeling for landscape in his three historical films, *Our Hospitality* (1922), *Go West* (1925) and *The General* (1926) owe much to Griffith. In *Sherlock Jr.* (1924) he is a projectionist who finds himself in the films he is projecting, the perfect image for Keaton as director. One of the great geniuses of the cinema, he went broke, drank heavily and was forgotten for many years. Just before his death he was aware of the reassessment of his work and standing.

KEIGHLEY William

American. Born 1893. Former stage director and actor. Spent most of his career at Warners from 1934 where he was given some interesting assignments. Made a few first rate fast-paced crime melodramas with James Cagney (*G. Men*–1939, *Each Dawn I Die*–1939) and Edward G. Robinson (*Bullets or Ballots* – 1936) and some equally rapid comedies such as *Torrid Zone* (1940–Cagney and Ann Sheridan) and *The Bride Came C.O.D.* (1941–Cagney and Bette Davis). He also retained the sparkle of Kaufmann and Hart's stage comedy, *The Man Who Came To Dinner* (1942) with the aid of a superb cast including Monty Woolley, Bette Davis and Ann Sheridan. He was replaced by Michael CURTIZ on *The Adventures of Robin Hood* (1938) although he gets co-director's credit. It was Curtiz who made it a cut above anything Keighley ever directed. His last film, *The Master of Ballantrae* (1953) demonstrated it was time for him to retire. **Others:** *Babbitt* (34), *The Prince and the Pauper* (37), *Brother Rat* (38), *George Washington Slept Here* (42) *Honeymoon* (47), *Rocky Mountain* (50), *Close to My Heart* (51).

KELLY Gene

American. Born 1912. Former Broadway dancer-singer. His athletic and inventive dancing and choreography made him one of the most creative forces in the heyday of the film musical of the 50's. Contrasting the films he directed alone with those he made with Stanley DONEN, it would seem that he needed Donen for the overall conception, while he concentrated on the numbers. Whoever did what, *On the Town* (1949), *Singin' in the Rain* (1952) and *It's Always Fair Weather* (1955) are masterpieces of the genre. Of the seven movies he directed solo, only two are musicals. *Invitation to the Dance* (1956), a partially successful attempt to make an all-dancing film, contained three ballets, the last featuring a dance with Kelly and cartoon figures. There are glimpses of the old-time MGM musical magic in *Hello, Dolly* (1969), but it suffers from gigantism and the miscasting of Barbra Streisand. He directed the linking material in *That's Entertainment Part 2* (1976) like a TV special. That's Entertainment? His 'straight' movies have two left feet. **Others:** *The Happy Road* (56), *Tunnel of Love* (58), *Gigot* (63), *A Guide to the*

Gene Kelly in the title number from *Singin' in the Rain* (1952).

Married Man (67), *The Cheyenne Social Club* (70).

KENNEDY Burt

American. Born 1923. Served in the cavalry in World War II. Wrote TV Westerns and screenplays for four BOETTICHER-Randolph Scott movies. His own contributions to the Decline of the West are agreeable enough comedy Westerns, *Support Your Local Sheriff* (1969), *The Good Guys and the Bad Guys* (1969) and *Support Your Local Gunfighter* (1971) and unconvincing retreads of better Westerns. **Others:** *The Canadians* (61), *The Rounders* (65), *Return of the Seven* (66), *Welcome to Hard Times* (67), *The War Wagon* (67), *Young Billy Young* (69), *Dirty Dingus Magee* (70), *Hannie Caulder* (71), *The Train Robbers* (73), *The Killer Inside Me* (75).

KERSHNER Irvin

American. Born 1923. Former documentary film-maker and TV director, he has made fourteen pictures on various subjects and of variable quality since 1958. Erratic, eclectic and flashy, the films have little in common except a liking for the rebel. Sean Connery rants and raves as a radical poet in *A Fine Madness* (1966), George C. Scott turns on the charm as *The Flim Flam Man* (1967) and Barbra Streisand rebels against her domesticity in *Up the Sandbox* (1972) by having fantasies of being in a garish movie by Irvin Kershner. And yet *Loving* (1970) is a touching and sharp drama of a commercial artist (George Segal) rebelling against the routine of marriage and career, and *The Return of a Man Called Horse* (1976) gets closer to the Red Indian experience than most previous attempts. Then to the glossy gore of *The Eyes of Laura Mars* (1978) and the high tec games of *The Empire Strikes Back* (1980). Will the real Irvin Kershner stand up? **Others:** *Stakeout on Dope Street* (58), *The Young Captives* (59), *The Hoodlum Priest* (61), *A Face in the Rain* (63), *The Luck of Ginger Coffey* (64), *S.P.Y.S.* (74).

KIMMINS Anthony

British. 1901–1963. Actor/Writer/Producer/Director. Made mostly light comedies from the 30's, five with horse-faced ukelele-playing George Formby. *The Captain's Paradise* (1953) with Alec Guinness as a Ferry boat captain with a wife in two ports, is more amusing than the rest. *Bonnie Prince Charlie* (1948) is a pretty picture postcard version of history with a kilted David Niven in the title role. **Others:** *Mine Own Executioner* (47), *Flesh and Blood* (49), *Mr Denning Drives North* (51), *Who Goes There?* (52), *Smiley* (57), *The Amorous Prawn* (62).

KING Henry

American. 1888–1982. Born in a small town in Virginia. Actor and stage director before World War I. His best movies, in a career stretching from 1916 to 1962, are simple, idealistic, nostalgic evocations of rural and small-town America. *Tol'able David* (1921) established the tone. Richard Barthelmess' idyll in Greenstream Valley is disturbed by a family from outside who accuse him of cowardice. He defends the community, becomes a hero and wins the girl among the corn. *State Fair* (1933), *Carolina* (1934), *Way Down East* (1935 – a remake of the 1920 GRIFFITH film), *Maryland* (1940), *Chad Hanna* (1940), *Margie* (1946), *I'd Climb the Highest Mountain* (1951), *Wait 'Til the Sun Shines Nellie* (1952) are all some of the finest examples of Americana, as wholesome as a Norman Rockwell painting, extolling community life, honesty, humour and hard work. Fox (the studio where he worked for over thirty years) provided him with the subjects, the colour and the scope (later 'Scope) to paint his pictures. He also provided them with two tuneful period musicals, *In Old Chicago* (1938), ending with a spectacular fire, and *Alexander's Ragtime Band* (1938), two excellent Westerns, *Jesse James* (1939) and *The Gunfighter* (1950). Once outside America, King was no longer king. Three sluggish costume dramas with Tyrone Power (*The Black Swan* – 1942, *Captain from Castille* – 1947, *The Prince of Foxes* – 1949), Gregory Peck and Susan Hayward as *David and Bathsheba* (1951), a Biblical bore, and the sprawling, shallow versions of Hemingway and Fitzgerald, *The Snows of Kilimanjaro* (1952), *The Sun Also Rises* (1957) and *Tender is the Night* (1962). **Others:** *Romula* (24), *Stella Dallas* (25), *Lloyds of London* (35), *Seventh Heaven* (37), *Stanley and Livingstone* (39), *A Yank in the RAF* (41), *The Song of Bernadette* (43), *Wilson* (44), *A Bell for Adano* (45), *Twelve O'Clock High* (49), *King of the Khyber Rifles* (53), *Untamed* (54), *Love is a Many Splendored Thing* (55), *Carousel* (56), *The Bravados* (58), *This Earth is Mine* (59), *Beloved Infidel* (59).

KINUGASA Teinosuke
Japanese. Born 1896. Former child actor and leading oyama (female impersonator) who turned to direction when actresses were employed in films in 1922. Studied with Sergei EISENSTEIN. Virtually all his sound films are tales of the samurai. *Gate of Hell* (1953) is one of the few known in the West. The first Japanese film to use a Western colour process (Eastman colour), it makes a strong visual impact.

KLEISER Randal
American. Born 1948. Graduate of the University of Southern California Film school where he was a roommate of George LUCAS. Directed for some years on TV, including series such as *Marcus Welby MD*. *Grease* (1978) is bubble-gum for the eyes and ears with a fifties flavoring. *The Blue Lagoon* (1980) is a sea-blue movie, as soothing and undemanding as watching a tank of stupid fish.

KLUGE Alexander
Novelist. Assisted Fritz LANG on his two Indian films (1959). Made short documentaries, one on Nazi architecture (1960). Part of the new wave of German cinema, he wrote a manifesto criticizing 'Papas Kino' and demanding subsidies for young directors and the setting up of a film school. His films, influenced by early GODARD and often featuring his sister Alexandra Kluge, are witty, cerebral investigations into modern-day Germany and its relation to its recent past. **Others:** *Yesterday's Girl* (66), *Artists at the Top of the Big Top – Disorientated* (68), *Occasional Work of a Female Slave* (74), *Strongman Ferdinand* (76), *The Patriots* (79).

KOBAYASHI Masaki
Japanese. Born 1916. studied philosophy. Imprisoned by the Chinese during the war. His films, beautifully composed for the wide screen, often put into relief a human suffering that results from rigid codes of honour and obedience, while remaining true to the traditions of the period film. e.g. *Hara-Kiri* (1962) and *The Rebellion* (1967). *Kwaidan* (1964) tells four tales of the supernatural with haunting imagery derived from Japanese art. It was the most expensive Japanese film ever made.

KOPPLE Barbara
American. Born 1946. Editor, cinematographer and sound engineer on documentaries. She lived and worked with the Kentucky coal-miners and their families for over a year filming *Harlan County, USA* (1976), the Oscar-winning documentary on their struggles to establish a Union. Powerful, humane and committed cinema.

KORDA Alexander
British (naturalized). 1893–1956. Born in Hungary as Sandor Kellner. The first film-maker to be knighted. He certainly came closer than anyone in Britain to making quality films with an international appeal. Korda produced some of the finest British pictures, including films by Carol REED, David LEAN and Michael POWELL. The films he directed himself are less impressive. Directed his first film at the age of twenty-one and made over twenty features before leaving Hungary with his first wife, the actress Maria Corda. (He later married Merle Oberon.) After making films in Vienna, Berlin, Hollywood and Paris (where he directed *Marius* – 1931, the first of the PAGNOL trilogy), he settled in England in 1931. He formed his own production company – London Films – and built Denham Studios in an attempt to rival Hollywood. There, surrounded by other Hungarian exiles including his two brothers, Zoltan and Vincent, he made his personal historical biopics. *The Private Life of Henry VIII* (1933) with Charles LAUGHTON's superb burlesque King, Vincent Korda's sets and George Perinal's photography,

Charles Laughton and Elsa Lanchester (in real life Mrs. Laughton) as Anne of Cleves in Alexander Korda's *The Private Life of Henry VIII* (1933).

broke box-office records in America. Still better was the same team's *Rembrandt* (1936) with Laughton looking even more like the painter than he had the monarch. However, *The Private Life of Don Juan* (1934) with the ageing Douglas Fairbanks in his last film, was a disaster. **Others:** *The Private Life of Helen of Troy* (27), *Lady Hamilton* (41 – *That Hamilton Woman* US), *Perfect Strangers* (45 – *Vacation from Marriage* US), *An Ideal Husband* (48).

KORDA Zoltan
British (naturalized). 1895–1961. Born Hungary. Brother of Alexander. A soldier during World War I. Editor and cameraman in Germany in the 20's. Most of his films are exotic Kiplingesque adventures set in British colonial Africa and India while the sun shone high over the British Empire and when Paul Robeson in *Sanders of the River* (1935), Sabu and other assorted natives knew their place. *Elephant Boy* (1936), *The Drum* (1938), *The Four Feathers* (1939) and *The Jungle Book* (1942) are colourful and exciting story-book pictures. After four movies in Hollywood, including *The Macomber Affair* (1947), Hemingway softened and stretched, he made the stilted and well-meaning liberal view of apartheid in South Africa, *Cry the Beloved Country* (1952) and co-directed the risible remake of *The Four Feathers* called *Storm Over the Nile* (1955) as the sun set slowly on the Empire.

KOSTER Henry
American. Born 1905 as Hermann Kosterlitz, in Berlin. After making five films in Germany, he came to America at the invitation of Universal Studios. Spent his time, with producer Joe Pasternak, making six very successful musicals with well-scrubbed teenage soprano Deanna Durbin. i.e. *3 Smart Girls* (1936), *100 Men and a Girl* (1937), *3 Smart Girls Grow Up* (1939), *First Love* (1939), *Spring Parade* (1940), *It Started with Eve* (1941). When Pasternak, who had a taste for nubile sopranos and the popular classics, went to MGM, Koster followed. Laurence Melchior, Jose Iturbi and Kathryn Grayson provided the 'classics' in *Music for Millions* (1944 and *Two Sisters from Boston* (1946), stodgier and more sugary versions of the Durbin musicals. At Fox, he obligingly made most things that came along, whether Betty Grable fluff (*Wabash Avenue* –

1950 and *My Blue Heaven* – 1950), historical dramas (*Desiree* 1954 – BRANDO as Napoleon. *The Virgin Queen* 1955 – Bette Davis as Elizabeth I), feeble family comedies with James Stewart as a harassed father (*Mr Hobbs Takes a Vacation* 1962 etc) or Sunday School sermons (*A Man Called Peter* – 1955, *The Robe* – 1953, *The Story of Ruth* – 1960, *The Singing Nun* – 1965 etc) with the same schmaltzy cuteness. *The Robe* was the first yawning CinamaScope feature. **Others:** *The Unfinished Dance* (47), *The Bishop's Wife* (47), *The Inspector General* (49), *Come to the Stable* (49), *Harvey* (50), *No Highway* (51), *My Cousin Rachel* (52), *My Man Godfrey* (57), *The Naked Maja* (59), *Flower Drum Song* (61), *Take Her She's Mine* (63), *Dear Brigitte* (65).

KOTCHEFF Ted
Canadian. Born 1931. Resident in England in the 60's and the early 70's, he made nothing to write home to Canada about. *Billy Two Hats* (1973) is a Western filmed in Israel with Gregory Peck pretending to be Harry Lauder. On home ground, he made his best movie, *The Apprenticeship of Duddy Kravitz* (1974) helped enormously by Richard Dreyfuss's nervy *comic performance and Mordecai* Richler's script from his own novel. *Fun with Dick and Jane* (1977) and *Who is Killing the Great Chefs of Europe?* (1978) both with George Segal are tasteless and indigestible.

KOZINTSEV Grigori
Russian. 1905–1973. One of the founders of FEKS (Factory of the Eccentric Actor) with Leonid Trauberg and Sergei YUTKEVITCH, a theatre group that experimented in multi-media in 1921. With Trauberg, he made a number of eccentric short films and propaganda 'film posters'. *The New Babylon* (1929) follows the actions of a shop-girl and the various classes during the events leading to the collapse of the Paris Commune of 1871. The montage, lighting and episodic structure made it one of the most inventive silent films of the period. They went on to make the Maxim trilogy, *The Youth of Maxim* (1935), *The Return of Maxim* (1937) and *The Vyborg Side* (1939), a study in human terms of a worker caught up in the revolution. After the war, he parted from Trauberg and made three adaptations from classics. *Don Quixote* (1957) cleverly condensing the vast

book into a normal-length film, has fine use of colour evoking the Spanish landscape and a dominating performance from Nikolai Cherkassov (EISENSTEIN's Nevsky and Ivan). The two Shakespeare films, *Hamlet (1964)* and *King Lear* (1971), more problematic for English speakers (translations by Boris Pasternak) seem to lack depth and nuance, but have excellent performances and a real feeling for the Danish court and the 'blasted heath' respectively.

KRAMER Robert
American. Born 1940. An independent film-maker whose films are exclusively political in content with specific reference to the Vietnam War. Shot in 16mm as if they were documentaries with non-professional actors swapping political platitudes, they sometimes hit a raw nerve. **Titles:** *In the Country* (67), *The Edge* (68), *Ice* (70), *Milestones* (75).

KRAMER Stanley
American. Born 1913. Producer/Director. Worked as editor and script-writer at MGM before the war. As an independent producer in the 40's and early 50's, he made a number of economical, 'serious' films slightly outside the Hollywood mainstream, including three fine pictures by Fred ZINNEMANN (*The Men* – 1950, *High Noon* – 1952, *Member of the Wedding* – 1953). The films he directed are sluggish dinosaurs stuffed with wishy-washy liberal sentiments, tackling huge themes with impotent means. His heart is in the right place, but his camera isn't. *On the Beach* (1959), the threat of nuclear annihilation is reduced to an irksome interruption of a cocktail party attended by Gregory Peck, Ava Gardner and Fred Astaire; Nazism is the crime in the Perry-Mason-like courtroom drama of *Judgement at Nuremberg* (1961) with Judy Garland, Monty Clift and Marlene Dietrich as "star" witnesses (it has the obscenity to include actual film of concentration camp victims); a chain is the clanking symbol binding racist Tony Curtis to Sidney POITIER as two escaping prisoners in *The Defiant Ones* (1958); and in *Guess Who's Coming to Dinner?* (1967), Poitier is the Nobel Prize-winning black angel who wants to marry Katharine Hepburn and Spencer Tracy's WASP daughter. Religion (*Inherit the Wind* – 1960, *The Runner Stumbles* – 1979), Greed (*It's a Mad, Mad, Mad, Mad World* – 1963, *Oklahoma Crude* – 1973) and

pre-War European society (*Ship of Fools* – 1965) are all sunk by Kramer's big guns. **Others:** *Not as a Stranger* (55), *The Pride and the Passion* (57), *The Secret of Santa Vittoria* (69), *R.P.M.* (70), *Bless the Beasts and the Children* (71), *The Domino Principle* (77).

KUBRICK Stanley

American. Born 1928. Former journalist. Made two short films while working on Life Magazine. Kubrick has made ten features in twenty-seven years. The scrupulous care with which he chooses his subjects, his extremely slow method of working, the years of planning, the secrecy involved and the attendant speculation and publicity, his personality and the nature of his films build up an aura around every new work which ensures serious critical attention as well as interest from the general public. He has lived and worked in England for the last twenty years, making six deeply pessimistic movies about the present, past and

Stanley Kubrick directing a scene from *A Clockwork Orange* (1971).

future, striving to overcome technical and textual difficulties with each. The age of Nabokov's nymphet, *Lolita* (1962) was raised into the teens to make it more acceptable to cinema audiences thereby changing Humbert Humbert's 'perverse passion' into an acceptable one; this and the reduction in the importance of the American landscape in the novel (it was filmed in England) still did not detract from this acerbic comedy played to perfection by James Mason and Peter Sellers, with a witty screenplay by the novelist. If *Lolita* approaches a 20th century literary masterpiece, *Dr. Strangelove or How I Learned to Stop Worrying and Love the Bomb* (1963) gets as close to a 20th century nightmare as possible. Far more effective than more sombre efforts (*On the Beach, Fail Safe*), it elects to view the end of the world as the ultimate absurdity. George C. Scott and Sterling Hayden frighteningly embody Kubrick's anti-militarism, first revealed in the bitterly ironic and moving World War I drama, *Paths of Glory* (1957). Peter Sellers gives three brilliant caricature performances, especially the sinister doctor

with his artificial arm jerking into a Nazi salute. (Dr Strange Glove, Dr Strangle Love.) *Dr. Strangelove's* convincing message that there is no future, is contradicted by Kubrick's next two movies, *2001 — A Space Odyssey* (1968) and *A Clockwork Orange* (1971). For a film that wryly condemns a hyper-technological future, *2001* is a high-tec product in itself not far behind the futuristic world it depicts. Although technically light years ahead of many previous space odysseys, intellectually it lags behind. The simple message that man will become merely a machine of a machine (in this case the robot Hal 9000) is decked out with man's relationship with his primitive beginnings and an enigmatic ending which sees him regressing psychedelically through time. The use of Johann Strauss as an ironic counterpoint to the images seems like the many TV adverts it inspired. 'Singin' in the Rain' and Beethoven's 9th as a background to violence in *A Clockwork Orange* merely pinpoints the lack of invention and attitude to this self-conscious, over-emphatic interior decorator's view of the Britain

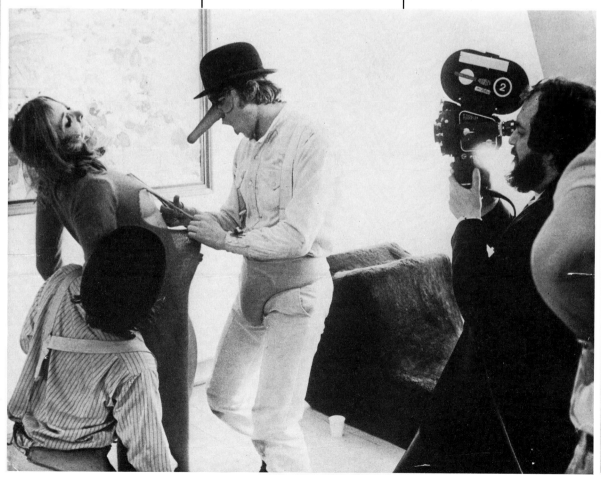

of the future. Much of its imagery has also been easily picked up by the advertisers. Far superior was the long, lavish and loving recreation of 18th century sensibility *Barry Lyndon* (1975), based on Thackeray's novel. Oscar winners, designer Ken Adam, cameraman John Alcott and art-director Roy Walker recreated the colours and lighting of the great English landscape and portrait painters. Kubrick starts each sequence in long shot as if looking at a painting and then gradually moves in to depict the often harsh life within the frame. From this elegant evocation of the Age of Reason, seen from a 20th century perspective, to the madness of *The Shining* (1980) where Kubrick again resorts to unsubtle shock treatment. There is a rare expectancy about every film he makes, and one can only hope he doesn't follow *The Shining* example with his next efforts. **Also:** *Killer's Kiss* (55), *The Killing* (56), *Spartacus* (60).

KULESHOV Lev

Russian. 1899–1970. Studied painting, architecture and sculpture. Entered films as designer. Worked on the agit-trains and formed a film collective. Wrote the first theoretical studies of montage. Using mobile cameras and quick cutting derived from American chase films, he made the gag-filled satire, *The Extraordinary Adventures of Mr West in the Land of the Bolsheviks* (1924). *Dura Lex* (1926 – *By the Law*), based on Jack London and set in the Yukon, is a strangely hypnotic work in five acts of three people locked together in a cabin for the winter with a riveting, stylised performance from Kuleshov's wife, Alexandra Khokhlova. Accused by the authorities of 'intellectualism', he was unable to make any further major films.

KUROSAWA Akira

Japanese. Born 1910. Best known of all Japanese directors in the West, but next to MIZOGUCHI or OZU he seems to have a coarsened sensibility. The popularity of his films abroad probably derive from their greater proximity to American movies than those of his compatriots. Logically, three of his films have been transferred easily into Westerns (the most famous being *The Magnificent Seven* – 1960 from *The Seven Samurai* – 1954), whereas some of his own

Kurosawa's *The Seven Samurai* (1954).

films are homages to the American Western. The twain also meet in *The Idiot* (51), *The Lower Depths* (1957), *Throne of Blood* (1957 from Macbeth), *The Bad Sleep Well* (1960 – from Ed McBain) and *Yojimbo* (1961 from Dashiell Hammett). *Rashomon* (1950) created a stir as it was the first Japanese film to be widely shown in the West. The films, often starring the powerful Toshiro Mifune, the engine room of the picture, generally work on one extrovert level, even in the tragic contemporary tales such as *Living* (1952), about the last days of a man dying of cancer, and *I Live in Fear* (1955). The style works best in the samurai adventures mixed with comedy and rich imagery like *The Seven Samurai, The Hidden Fortress* (1958) and *Sanjuro* (1962). *Dersu Uzala* (1975) contains a magnificent performance from Maxim Munzuk in the title role as a noble savage wise to the ways of nature, and one splendid set-piece (the building of a shelter during a storm) on the 70mm screen, but most of it is Disney adventure out of Robert FLAHERTY. The large screen is used again to frame the epic grandeur of *Kagamusha* (1980) with its red sunsets, vivid rainbows, the multi-coloured flags of soldiers, the dream-like battle scenes with horses and men dying in slow-motion, but there is something lifeless about the pictorial composition, the cutting and camera angles and the story never fulfils its Shakespearean promise. **Also:** *High and Low* (63), *Red Beard* (65), *Dodeskaden* (70).

L

LA CAVA Gregory

American. 1892–1949. Former cartoonist. Worked on early animation films. Although La Cava started directing features in 1921 and continued into the 40's, his name is synonymous with sophisticated screwball comedies of the 30's. Coming out of The Depression and into The New Deal, a favourite theme was the social contrasts of class, the idle rich learning how to be happy from the poor. Picture a huge Park Avenue mansion owned by a wealthy but bored family, butlers and maids scurrying around a central staircase. Enter a shop-girl or man of the people who puts their lives into perspective. Cast Irene Dunne, Carole Lombard, Ginger Rogers, Claudette Colbert, William Powell, Melvyn Douglas and Brian Aherne, giving them witty and worldly–wise lines and you have a La Cava comedy. *My Man Godfrey* (1936) is the best example. A variation of Barrie's 'The Admirable Crichton', it tells of a man (William Powell) from a shanty town who becomes butler to the Bullock family, straightens out their lives and marries their scatter-brained daughter (Carole Lombard). *She Married Her Boss* (1935) and *Fifth Avenue Girl* (1939) explored the same theme. *Stage Door* (1937), set in a boarding house for aspiring actresses (including Katharine Hepburn, Ginger Rogers), is best when it keeps on the flip side but, like La Cava's movies generally, founders when it becomes earnest. **Also:** *Gabriel over the White House* (33), *Private Worlds* (35), *What Every Woman Knows* (34), *Primrose Path* (40), *Lady in a Jam* (42), *Living in a Big Way* (47).

LACHMAN Harry

American. 1886–1975. Of all the movies he made in the 30's and 40's only *Dante's Inferno* (1935) stands out, mainly for its ten minute sequence of Spencer Tracy's dream of hell. Based on Gustav Doré's engravings for the poem and photographed by Rudolph MATÉ (his first American film) it recreated a horrific vision. **Also:** *Our Relations* (36) with Laurel and Hardy.

LAMONT Charles

American. Born 1898. Universal Studios second string director who was stuck with making Abbott and Costello meet . . . Ma and Pa Kettle in . . . Francis, The Talking Mule in . . . Not forgetting *Slave Girl* (1947), *Baghdad* (1949) and *Flame of Araby* (1951) with Yvonne de Carlo and Maureen O'Hara behind veils, where most of Lamont's movies should be.

LANDIS John

American. Born 1950. In his first feature, *Shlock* (1976), the director himself ran around in a monkey-suit trying to get laughs. *Kentucky Fried Movie* (1977) reached new hilarious depths of tastelessness, but *National Lampoon's Animal House* (1978) reached new depths without the hilarity or edge of the former. *The Blues Brothers* (1980) was a smashing musical i.e. cars, people and eardrums are smashed for 133 minutes. The metamorphosis of man into wolf in *An American Werewolf in London* (1981) is excellently achieved and for most of its hairy length, it is comic-horror at its best. College humour is alive and well.

LANFIELD Sidney

American. 1900–1972. Former jazz musician. Long at 20th Century Fox. Director of mostly lightweight vehicles, including two Alice Faye musicals (*King of Burlesque* – 1935, *Sing, Baby, Sing* – 1936); three thin ice-follies with Sonja Henie; two unctuous biopics (*Swanee River* – 1939 – Stephen Foster, *Follow the Sun* 1951 – Ben Hogan), a corny Astaire–Hayworth musicomedy (*You'll Never Get Rich* – 1941) and a couple of good Bob Hope comedies (*My Favorite Blonde* – 1942, *The Lemon Drop Kid* – 1950). **Others:** *Hound of the Baskervilles* (39), *Let's Face It* (43), *Skirts Ahoy* (52).

LANG Fritz

Austrian. 1890–1976. Studied architecture and painting in Vienna. Served in the Austrian army in World War I. Resembling a Prussian army officer, Lang looked on the world from behind his monocle with a grim detachment and strong moral sense through two careers — 1919 to 1932 in Germany and 1936 to 1956 in Hollywood. His reputation soon grew in Germany with his FEUILLADE–type serial *The Spiders* (1919–1920) and the two-part *Dr. Mabuse, The Gambler* (1922) about an evil genius of the underworld.

Peter Lorre in Fritz Lang's *M* (1931).

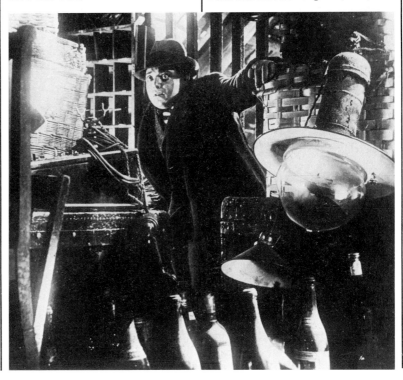

Fritz Lang

Made at a time of political turmoil, *Mabuse* is a masterly study of a decadent society. *Die Nibelungen* (1924), the German saga, also in two parts, makes impressive use of the stylised studio sets. The huge sets of *Metropolis* (1927) representing the futuristic city-factory where workers slave for rich masters, were inspired by the New York skyline. Despite its ridiculously naive ending, Capital and Labour reconciled by love, it is a potent allegory of totalitarianism. In his first sound film, *M* (1931), based on the actual case of the child killer of Dusseldorf, an ironic social comment is made on justice, capital punishment and mob-rule (a theme in *Metropolis* and *Fury*–1936) using elements from the theatre of Brecht. (Lang was later to work with Brecht on the stark anti-Nazi drama, *Hangmen Also Die*–1943, after his curious attempt at a Brecht–Weill singspiel, *You and Me* 1938.) In 1932, his wife Thea von Harbou, who co-wrote all of his films from 1920–1932, joined the Nazi Party. Goebbels then politely asked him to change the last reel of *The Last Will of Dr. Mabuse* (1932) in which Nazi slogans had been put into the mouth of the mad arch-criminal who uses his hypnotic powers in an effort to conquer the world. Lang realised that the monster he had created could now control him so he fled to France and then to the USA. In America he had dictatorial producers to deal with. MGM tacked on a happy ending to his first American film *Fury*. Warner Bros. did the same to *Cloak and Dagger* (1946) extracting from the film its anti-atomic energy message. For *Fury*, Lang wanted to make his anti-lynching statement stronger by using

a black man guilty of rape, but was forced to use an innocent white man (Spencer Tracy). The plea at the end of *M* ('Whatever you do to him is unimportant because it doesn't bring dead children back to life') is far more effective because Peter Lorre, the child-killer, is guilty. Yet, despite struggling against the Philistines of the big studios, he managed to make splendidly dark Langian films of murder, revenge and seduction such as *The Woman in the Window* (1944) and *Scarlet Street* (1945) both with Edward G. Robinson caught up with femme fatale Joan Bennett; *The Big Heat* (1953) and *Human Desire* (1954) with Glenn Ford and Gloria Grahame; and *Beyond a Reasonable Doubt* (1956) which uses a spare, uncompromising visual style. Working in America obliged Lang to be more economical and his German expressionism was contained and pared down. **Others:** *Liliom* (33), *You Only Live Once* (37), *The Return of Frank James* (40), *Man Hunt* (41), *Western Union* (41), *The Ministry of Fear* (44), *Secret Beyond the Door* (48), *Rancho Notorious* (52), *Blue Gardenia* (53), *Moonfleet* (55), *While the City Sleeps* (56), *The Tiger from Eschnapur* (59), *The 1000 Eyes of Dr. Mabuse* (61).

LANG Walter

American. 1898–1972. Graduate of Tennessee U. Served in World War I. Director at Fox from mid-30's until he retired in 1961. Responsible for cheering up people during the 40's with escapist Technicolor musical frolics, six of them starring the Forces favourite pin-up Betty Grable, including *Moon over Miami* (1941), *Coney Island* (1943) and *Mother Wore Tights* (1947). Leggy Betty couldn't act, sing or dance much, but she was as pretty as a picture by Walter Lang. However, *State Fair* (1945), his best musical of the period, has a freshness and gaiety missing from the Grable vehicles. *Sitting Pretty* (1948) and *Cheaper by the Dozen* (1950), both with prissy Clifton Webb, are perfect family comedies. A few years later, he was directing over-weight and gaudy musicals such as *Call Me Madam* (1953), *There's No Business Like Show Business* (1954), *The King and I* (1956) and *Can-Can* (1960). His last movie, *Snow White and the 3 Stooges* (1961), has little of the old Lang sign. **Others:** *The Blue Bird* (40), *Tin Pan Alley* (40), *The Great Profile* (40), *Weekend in Havana* (41), *On the*

Riviera (51), *With a Song in my Heart* (52), *Desk Set* (57), *Marriage Go Round* (60).

LATTUADA Alberto

Italian. Born 1914. Former writer and architect. Part of the neo-Realist movement. *The Bandit* (1946) looks at an ex-PoW who is forced to take to crime in post-war Italy and *Without Pity* (1948) tells of the relationship between a prostitute (Guilietta Masina, FELLINI's wife) and an American negro. He co-directed Fellini's first film, *Lights of Variety* (1950). He has not retained the status he once had. **Others:** *Anna* (51), *The Overcoat* (52), *Tempest* (57), *Mandrake* (65).

LAUGHLIN Tom

American. Born 1938. Directs himself under the name of T.C. Frank or Frank Laughlin, and writes with his actress wife (Delores Taylor) as Frank and Teresa Christina, but would smell as bad by any other name. *Billy Jack* (1971), *The Trial of Billy Jack* (1974) and *Billy Jack Goes to Washington* (1977) are about a half-breed (Laughlin) fighting for freedom and peace through violence. These films became popular with the young, but so did glue-sniffing. **Others:** *Born Losers* (67), *The Master Gunfighter* (75).

LAUGHTON Charles

British. 1899–1962. The great (and corpulent) actor directed only one film, a film which could easily fit into many people's ten-best list, *The Night of the Hunter* (1955) is an eerily beautiful parable of good and evil, written by James Agee, photographed atmospherically by Stanley Cortez with the creative use of Walter Schumann's music. The stylization, derived from German expressionism and American primitive paintings, also echoes GRIFFITH's rural dramas. The use of irises and other silent film techniques as well as the presence of Lillian Gish forces the comparison. Robert Mitchum as the psychopathic preacher-murderer hunting down the children as they take their boat down the river, Gish guarding the children like a mother hen and the murdered Shelley Winters' hair streaming out under water, are some of the most haunting and nightmarish images in all cinema.

LAUNDER Frank

British. Born 1907. Screenwriter for many years with Sidney GILLIAT. His films take place in an imaginary England and Scotland. The ghastly girls' school of St. Trinian's (inspired

Billy Chapin and Sally Jane Bruce in Laughton's *The Night of the Hunter* (1955).

by Ronald Searle's drawings) provided him with material for four films, the joke wearing thinner each time. *Geordie* (1955) and *The Bridal Path* (1959) are set in a touristy Technicolored Highlands. However, *The Happiest Days of Your Life* (1950) is a hilarious farce about a boys' school suddenly having to share quarters with a girls' school. **Others:** *Captain Boycott* (47), *The Blue Lagoon* (48), *The Belles of St. Trinians* (54), *The Great St. Trinian's Bank Robbery* (66).

LEACOCK Philip

British. Born 1917. Children are seen and heard in the majority of his films and, like children, they are sometimes good but more often bad. *The Kidnappers* (1953) is a touching tale set in Canada about two small boys, forbidden to have a dog, who take a lost baby as a pet. Three boys run away from home in *Escapade* (1955) to teach their parents a lesson and a diplomat's young son is closer to *The Spanish Gardener* (1956) than to his cold father. A Jewish girl and a Catholic boy teach adults a lesson in tolerance in *Hand in Hand* (1960), but kids imitate adults at war in *Reach for Glory* (1961) by playing dangerous war games of their own. **Others:** *The Brave Don't Cry* (52), *Appointment in London* (53), *Innocent Sinners* (58), *Let No Man Write My Epitaph* (59), *Take a Giant Step* (61), *The War Lover* (63), *Tamahine* (63), *Adam's Woman* (70).

LEACOCK Richard

British. Born 1922. Brother of Philip LEACOCK. Cameraman on Robert FLAHERTY's *Louisiana Story* (1948). Part of the 'direct cinema' documentary film movement which believed in filming events as they happen without interpretative editing or narration. Working mainly with Robert Drew and Donn Alan Pennebaker, he made *Primary* (1960) on the J.F. Kennedy campaign, *The Chair* (1963) showing a man sentenced to death, and *Happy Mother's Day* (1964) about the effect of the birth of quins on a small town. Also worked on one of the first rock-concert movies, *Monterey Pop* (1969) featuring Janis Joplin and Jimmy Hendrix.

LEAN David

British. Born 1908. Entered films in 1927 at the bottom. Gradually became an editor. Co-directed his first film, *In Which We Serve* (1942) with Noel Coward. Went on to make three further Coward subjects: *This Happy Breed* (1944), a smug and patronising saga of the lower middle-classes, *Blithe Spirit* (1945), a well-performed version of the supernatural farce and *Brief Encounter* (1945). The latter, based on a one-act play by Coward (who wrote the screenplay), must be one of the most telling juxtapositions of the romantic and the mundane in cinema. An illicit love story played out in realistic English suburbia over tea cups with Rachmaninov's 2nd Piano Concerto on the sound track, it echoes T.S. Eliot's 'Prufrock'–'Should I, after tea and cakes and ices, Have the strength to force the moment to its crisis?' The impeccable acting of Celia Johnson and Trevor Howard, the script beautifully balanced between the passionate narration and the clipped dialogue, and the fluid camerawork, make it Lean's brief encounter with greatness. He followed it with two of the finest adaptations of Dickens, *Great Expectations* (1946) and *Oliver Twist* (1948), both with almost Phizz-like photography (Guy GREEN), designs (John Bryan) and acting. Lean's skill was apparent in the three films he made with his wife, anaemic Ann Todd, *The Passionate Friends* (1949), *Madeleine* (1951) and *The Sound Barrier* (1952. *Breaking the Sound Barrier* – US); *Hobson's Choice* (1954) with three choice performances from Charles LAUGHTON, John Mills and Brenda De Banzie, and the not brief enough encounter in *Summer Madness* (1955 – *Summertime* – US) with Katharine Hepburn doing her scrawny, tearful spinster bit in a tourist brochure Venice. And thus did Lean become fat. There ensued four blockbusters, each less good than the last. Somewhere in the 2¾ hours of *The Bridge on the River Kwai* (1957) is a good film about the clash between two military men (Alex Guinness and Sessue Hayakawa) struggling to get out. The much longer *Lawrence of Arabia* (1962. 3¾ hours) has some stunning desert photography by F.A. Young, but in its straightforward narrative never approaches the ambiguities of the man despite Peter O'Toole's mystical gazes into the beyond. O'Toole's blue eyes were replaced by Omar Shariff's soulful brown eyes in *Dr Zhivago* (1966), an episodic and shallow version of Boris Pasternak's novel. *Ryan's Daughter* (1970) proved that big budgets are often

Celia Johnson and Trevor Howard in Lean's *Brief Encounter* (1945).

more detrimental to a film than small ones. Because of these gargantuan enterprises, Lean has made four films in the last twenty five years.

LEE Rowland V.
American. 1891–1975. A runaway orphan (Loretta Young) takes refuge in a *Zoo in Budapest* (1933) where, among the cages, she meets and falls in love with Gene Raymond who has spent his life there. A weird and gleamingly photographed love story in an unusual setting is Lee's only near masterpiece in a long career. *Son of Frankenstein* (1939) effectively uses the vast, grotesque castle where Basil Rathbone, in the title role, brings the monster (Boris Karloff) back to life with the help of Igor (Bela Lugosi). The basis for Mel BROOKS' parody *Young Franken-stein*, it still retains its menacing atmosphere despite absurdities like Lionel Atwill's police chief with an artificial arm similar to Peter Sellers' Dr Strangelove's. He also made a few entertaining costume adventures including *The Count of Monte Cristo* (1941) with Robert Donat and *Tower of London* (1939) with Rathbone and Karloff together again as a gruesome twosome. **Others:** *Cardinal Richelieu* (35), *The Three Musketeers* (36), *Son of Monte Cristo* (41), *The Bridge of San Luis Rey* (44), *Captain Kidd* (45).

LEE-THOMPSON J
British. Born 1914. Former actor. From 1950 to 1959, made a number of unassuming comedies and 'realistic' dramas. Aside from gripping suspenser, *Cape Fear* (1961), his films of the 60's are big budget, big screen fillers and time wasters with 'inter-national casts'. The very successful war adventure, *The Guns of Navarone* (1961) went to his head. From guns to 'bombs' such as *Taras Bulba* (1962), *Kings of the Sun* (1963), *John Goldfarb, Please Come Home* (1965), *MacKenna's Gold* (1968), and *The Chairman* (1969). Plus (or minus), *What a Way to Go* (1964), over two hours of 'kooky' Shirley MacLaine, and the fourth monkey tale, *Conquest of the Planet of the Apes* (1972). **Others:** *An Alligator Named Daisy* (55), *Yield to the Night* (56), *Woman in a Dressing Gown* (59), *Tiger Bay* (59), *North-West Frontier* (59), *Eye of the Devil* (66), *Before Winter Comes* (68), *The Reincarnation of Peter Proud* (74).

LEISEN Mitchell
American. 1897–1972. In the 30's, if MGM was the studio that reflected middle-class values and Warner Bros. the working classes, Paramount's mountain represented the upper crust. Ernst LUBITSCH established the studio style and Leisen continued the tradition with his chic, camp, witty, slightly dissolute sexual comedies written by Norman Krasna, Preston STURGES, Billy WILDER and Charles Brackett. The opulent sets, costumes and lighting embellished the stories of dynamic women in pursuit of men and power who found their dominance naturally diminished in the end. Given that the women were strong Claudette Colbert, Carole Lombard and Barbara Stanwyck and the men weak Fred McMurray and Ray Milland, role-reversal was in-evitable. A woman's place is at the centre of Leisen's pictures. He studied architecture and design, entering films as costume designer and art director. Three gems were *Hands Across the Table* (1935), Lombard as go-getting manicurist, *Easy Living* (1937), which starts with poor girl (Jean Arthur) receiving a mink coat thrown from a window . . ., and *Midnight* (1939). The latter is one of the most perfect comedies of the 30's, brilliantly plotted (Wilder and Brackett) and played (Colbert, John Barrymore) and set in a shimmering Paris. His perfumed soap operas (*Arise My Love* – 1940, *To Each His Own* – 1946) and couturier (rather than costume) dramas (*Frenchman's Creek* – 1944, *Kitty* – 1945), although skilful, do not match up to the earlier bitter comedies. He went into a sharp decline in the 50's, showing little of the panache he once had. **Others:** *Death Takes a Holiday* (34), *Murder at the Vanities* (34), *The Big Broad-casts of 1937 and 1938, Hold Back the Dawn* (41), *Take a Letter, Darling* (42), *The Lady is Willing* (42), *Lady in the Dark* (44), *Golden Earrings* (47), *Dream Girl* (48), *No Man of her Own* (50), *The Girl Most Likely* (57).

LELOUCH Claude
French. Born 1937. Made documen-taries from the age of nineteen. Operates his own camera. The film that made his international reputa-tion was *A Man and a Woman* (1966), the glossy women's magazine love story set at the *tres snob* seaside resort of Deauville. Racing driver (Jean-Louis Trintignant) and script-girl (Anouk Aimée), romp around in advertising images to Francis Lai's doo-bee-doo-bee-doo theme. Worse was *Live for Life* (1967) with Yves Montand as a documentary film-maker leaving his wife (Annie Girardot) for fashion model (Candice Bergen). The whole revolting enter-prise, including scenes of the Viet-nam war, was put together with the eye of a smooth huckster. **Others:** *La Bonne Annee* (73), *And Now My Love* (74), *Cat and Mouse* (75), *Second Chance* (76), *Another Man, Another Chance* (77), *Robert and Robert* (78).

LENI Paul
German. 1885–1929. Stage set de-signer for Max Reinhardt. His con-tribution to the horror genre was first established in Germany with the expressionistic *Waxworks* (1924), the lights, sets and stylized acting (Emil Jannings, Wilhelm DIETERLE) creating a sinister atmosphere. At

Universal Studios, he made the classic haunted-house movie, *The Cat and the Canary* (1927), *The Chinese Parrot* (1927), *The Man Who Laughs* (1929) and *The Last Warning* (1929) before dying of blood-poisoning at the age of 44. He believed that the art-director's role was paramount (or Universal) in provoking fear and, among other European imports, had a great influence on subsequent horror movies.

LEONARD Robert Z.

American. 1889–1968. Former actor. started directing in 1916. Joined MGM in 1925 where he remained for the rest of his career. Made many of their most beautifully wrapped packages with not very much inside. Three lavish Jeanette MacDonald-Nelson Eddy musicals (*Maytime* 1937, *The Girl of the Golden West* 1938, *New Moon* 1940), Gable and Garbo in *Susan Lenox* (1931), Gable and Crawford in the back-stage musical, *Dancing Lady* (1933); one of the studio's most expensive and prestigious movies, *The Great Ziegfeld* (1936) with elaborate production numbers and *Ziegfeld Girl* (1941) which borrowed sequences from the former movie. *In the Good Old Summertime* (1949), *Nancy Goes to Rio* (1950) and *The Duchess from Idaho* (1950) are smaller scale musicals handled in the same professional but colourless manner. **Others:** *The Firefly* (37), *Pride and Prejudice* (40), *Weekend at the Waldorf* (45), *The King's Thief* (55).

LEONE Sergio

Italian. Born 1921. Worked as assistant on dozens of features. Played a small role in DE SICA's *Bicycle Thieves* (1948). His first picture was *The Colossus of Rhodes* (1960), a successful spectacle with faded American actor, Rory Calhoun. Co-directed *Sodom and Gomorrah* (1961) with Robert ALDRICH, before embarking on his five parvenu Westerns. The great Westerns, such as John FORD's were carved out of America's frontier past, the myths growing organically from the material. Leone's Westerns self-consciously impose a mythology upon a foreign genre. He is playing at cowboys. His Westerns are about Westerns. His models are not even the best Westerns but films like *The Magnificent Seven* derived from KUROSAWA's *The Seven Samurai*

which in turn was inspired by the American Western. Leone's films are just as much sukiyaki Westerns as spaghetti ones. With their taciturn heroes (Clint EASTWOOD, Charles Bronson) patiently waiting for revenge, circular tracking shots, long silent close-ups, meaningful pauses and looks, final intricate shoot-outs and the Kabuki-like musical interruptions from Ennio Morricone, they are somewhere between caricature and a religious rite, the kind that provokes laughter in church. The 'Man with No Name' trilogy *A Fistful of Dollars* (1964), based on Kurosawa's *Yojimbo*, *For a Few Dollars More* (1965) and *The Good, The Bad and The Ugly* (1966) broke box-office records and made Clint Eastwood an international star. *Once Upon a Time in the West* (1968) is the apotheosis of the Leone style, glorious to some, vainglorious to others. **Also:** *Duck You Sucker* (71 — a.k.a. *A Fistful of Dynamite*).

LEROY Mervyn

American. Born 1900. In vaudeville in his youth. Began in films as wardrobe assistant. Directed thirty-eight movies at Warners from 1929 to 1938, and nineteen at MGM from 1940 to 1954. The sea change from Warners to Metro is a good example of studios imposing a style on directors, but also shows the difference between the harder-edged sensibility of the 30's and the softer 40's. At Warners, LeRoy's style was terse, tough and tense with a built-in social conscience. At MGM, he made slick, slow and sentimental entertainments. The final line of *Little Caesar* (1931) – 'Mother of Mercy, is this the end of Rico' – spoken by the dying Edward G. Robinson was just the beginning of Warners' series of crime-filled melodramas. Based on the character of Al Capone, the film made Robin-

Vivien Leigh and Robert Taylor in Mervyn LeRoy's *Waterloo Bridge* (1940).

Gloria Swanson with Mervyn LeRoy.

son a star and set the tone for the many gangster movies to follow. *I Am A Fugitive From A Chain Gang* (1932), one of the most uncompromising of social protest films, depicts the brutality of penal institutions in the South. The chilling ending is as famous as Rico's last words. Paul Muni, the fugitive of the title, asked how he survives, whispers, 'I steal.' Other powerful expressions of The Depression are *Two Seconds* (1932), the memories of a wife-murderer (Edward G. Robinson) during the two seconds on the electric chair 'between when the current hits him and his heart stops', and *They Won't Forget* (1937), a scathing attack on the lynch-law in the Deep South. Even the escapist musical, *Gold Diggers of 1933* carries a punch rare in the genre. At MGM, LeRoy swapped boxing gloves for kid gloves to handle ghastly Greer Garson tear-jerkers. *Quo Vadis?* (1951) took two years to make (in Rome) at immense cost. This over-long epic will be remembered for the spectacle of Peter USTINOV's cured-ham Nero. Back at Warners, he regained some of his form with the dynamic and brash, *Gypsy* (1962), arguably the best transposition of a Broadway musical to the screen. **Also:** *Five Star Final* (31), *Hard to Handle* (32), *Elmer the Great* (33), *Tugboat Annie* (33), *Oil for the Lamps of China* (35), *Anthony Adverse* (36), *Waterloo Bridge* (40), *Blossoms in the Dust* (41), *Random Harvest* (41), *Madame Curie* (43), *30 Seconds Over Tokyo* (44), *Little Women* (49), *Lovely to Look at* (52), *Million Dollar Mermaid* (52), *Rose Marie* (54), *Mr Roberts* (55), *The Bad Seed* (56), *The FBI Story* (59), *A Majority of One* (61).

LESTER Richard
American. Born 1932. In Britain since the 50's. Made TV commercials and comedy programmes. His first film was a silent short (with sound-effects), a visual equivalent of the surreal radio comedy series, 'The Goon Show', called *The Running, Jumping and Standing Still Film* (1959), a title (apart from the standing still) that aptly expresses Lester's style. Many of his films give the impression that if the director stood still for a moment he might wet his pants. The two Beatles' movies, *A Hard Day's Night* (1964) and *Help!* (1965) started the fashion for placing pop groups in various unlikely settings, using jump cuts and slow and speeded up motion. This worked to a certain extent with the "Fab Four", but was fatal to *A Funny Thing Happened on the Way to the Forum* (1966), Lester usurping the timing of a galaxy of old-time comedians, and *Royal Flash* (1975). Flash is the word to apply to *Petulia* (1968), a trendy 60's drama shot in San Francisco which time has now given the status of being an interesting and critical comment on the hippy era. *Robin and Marion* (1976), starring a grizzled Sean Connery and a simpering Audrey Hepburn, a sequel to the Robin Hood legend, monotonously repeats the theme of 'How old we've be-

come', whereas *Butch and Sundance, The Early Days* (1979) is a muted 'prequel' about 'How young we were!' Lester treats Dumas' heroes, *The Three Musketeers* (1973) and *The Four Musketeers* (1975) rather as he did the four Beatles, but there is much tongue-in-the-cheeky fun and the sets and costumes are suitably extravagant. *Superman II* (1981) is as spectacular and as entertaining as the first, despite some campy liberties with the spirit of the original comic book. However, his best movies are *The Knack* (1965), in which he plainly respects his players and material, and *The Bed Sitting Room* (1969), Goon Show humour extended into a post-nuclear war satire shot in sepia, with Ralph Richardson in the title role. **Also:** *The House on the Moon* (63), *How I Won the War* (67), *Juggernaut* (74), *The Ritz* (76), *Superman III* (83).

LEVIN Henry
American. Born 1909. Former theatre director. Made a few run-of-the-sword swashbucklers and low-budget thrillers for Columbia. Although not as good as *The Jolson Story*, *Jolson Sings Again* (1949) was another big box-office success for the studio. At Fox, he dealt lightly with sour Clifton Webb (*Mr Scoutmaster* – 1953, *The Remarkable Mr Pennypacker* –1959) and sweet Pat Boone (*Bernadine* – 1957, *April Love* – 1957, *Journey to the Centre of the Earth* – 1959). **Others:** *Cry of the Werewolf* (44), *The Return of Monte Cristo* (46), *Belles on Their Toes* (52), *The President's Lady* (53), *The Farmer Takes a Wife* (53), *The Gambler from Natchez* (54), *The Lonely Man* (57), *Where the Boys are* (60), *The Brothers Grimm* (62), *Genghis Khan* (65), *The Desperados* (69).

LEWIN Albert
American. 1894–1968. Entered MGM as screenwriter in 1924, becoming head of the story department and producer. Directed six films, four of which have their ardent admirers. The first three, *The Moon and Sixpence* (1942), *The Picture of Dorian Gray* (1945), and *The Private Affairs of Bel Ami* (1947), adaptations of Somerset Maugham, Oscar Wilde and Guy de Maupassant respectively and respectfully, star George Sanders at his suave best. Sanders' slightly perverse sophistication suited Lewin's own rococo tastes, and the films, like Wilde's Lord Henry Wootton, try to seduce one away

Brigitte Helm in Marcel L'Herbier's *L'Argent* (1928).

from bourgeois respectability. *Pandora and the Flying Dutchman* (1951) is another wicked fairy story told in arty colour images and silly dialogue. **Also:** *Saadia* (53), *The Living Idol* (57).

LEWIS Jerry

American. Born 1926. In 1946, joined Dean Martin in a cabaret act. Made their first screen appearance in *My Friend Irma* (1949). After sixteen movies together, they split up in 1956. Frank TASHLIN, who directed two of their final films and a couple of Lewis's early solo efforts inspired him to direct his own films. A talented comedian, he can make one wriggle with delight one moment and squirm with embarrassment the next. At his best when closest to his idol, Stan Laurel, but although Laurel cried a lot he was never as sentimental as Lewis. His first four movies as director are far superior to the rest. Abandoning a plot structure, they are a series of comic sketches linked by a tenuous theme (unusual in American comedy), often

using surrealistic visual gags. In *The Bellboy* (1960), homage is paid to Stan Laurel, *The Ladies' Man* (1961) makes brilliant use of a composite set, *The Errand Boy* (1961) has fun with a film-studio setting and in *The Nutty Professor* (1963), Lewis as Dr Jekyll turns into a Dean Martin – Mr Hyde. Inside every Jerry Lewis is a Dean Martin trying to get out. His last film, *The Day the Clown Cried* (1974) is still waiting for a release. Judgement remains pending, but the title and the setting — a Nazi concentration camp — do not bode well. **Others:** *The Patsy* (64), *The Family Jewels* (65), *Three on a Couch* (66), *The Big Mouth* (67), *One More Time* (69), *Which Way to the Front?* (70).

LEWIS Joseph H

American. Born 1900. An A–One B–movie director. Gangster films and Westerns are the most serendipitous. Three tough films noirs, *Undercover Man* (1949), *Gun Crazy* (1949 a.k.a. *Deadly is the Female*) and *The Big Combo* (1954); two Randolph Scott Westerns, *Lawless Street* (1955) and *7th Cavalry* (1956), and *The Halliday Brand* (1957) and *Terror in a Texas Town* (1958). *So Dark the Night* (1946) equals

Simenon in intensity and has a cast that even film buffs might not have heard of – Steven Geray, Ann Codee, Helen Freeman and Egon Brecher. **Others:** *My Name is Julia Ross* (45), *A Lady Without a Passport* (50), *Retreat-Hell* (52).

L'HERBIER Marcel

French. 1890-1979. Writer, musician, aesthete. Part of the post World War 1 avant-garde movement. Turned to the cinema as another means of exploring impressionistic imagery, hoping to create 'visual music'. His silent films are full of stylistic innovations. In *El Dorado* (1921), the blurred image (flou) is used and multiple superimpositions. Each set for *L'Inhumaine* (1924) was created by a different designer–CAVAL-CANTI, AUTANT–LARA, Fernand Leger, Mallet-Stevens and features dancers from the Ballet Suedois and music by Darius Milhaud. The acting is risible and the plot doesn't hold together, but it would be a good film to show at a modern art exhibition. *L'Argent* (1928) was the last of L'Herbier's silents and the most ambitious. The film, based on Zola, is a three hour condemnation of big business with an international cast moving through huge sets. Apart from the atmospheric adaptations of Gaston Leroux novels, *The Mystery of the Yellow Room* (1931) and *The Perfume of the Woman in Black* (1931), the rest of his sound films are rather conventional.

LITVAK Anatole
Russian. 1902–1974. Studied philosophy at St Petersburg. Worked as editor and director from 1929 to 1932 in Germany. The success of the romantic *Mayerling* (1936), made in France with Charles Boyer and Danielle Darrieux, led to a Hollywood career from 1937 to 1951 mostly at Warner Bros. where he continued to satisfy his taste for melodrama. He made two dullish Bette Davis tearjerkers, *The Sisters* (1938) and *All This and Heaven Too* (1940), two pale remakes, *Castle on the Hudson* (1940 – CURTIZ's *20,000 Years in Sing Sing* – 1933) and *The Long Night* (1947 – CARNÉ's *Le Jour se Lève* – 1939); an over-emphatic but disturbing view of a mental institution, *The Snake Pit* (1948) and the overwrought, *Sorry, Wrong Number* (1948) with Barbara Stanwyck miscast as a victim. Warners controlled some of his preachy prolixity, but five films he made from 1956 to 1967 brought out the worst in him. *Anastasia* (1956), *The Journey (1958)*, *Goodbye Again* (1961), *5 Miles to Midnight* (1962) and *The Night of the Generals* (1967) are long, ponderous, humourless, big screen dramas with international casts. Amazingly, over thirty years previously, he made a delightful comedy–thriller, *The Amazing Dr Clitterhouse* (1938) with Edward G. Robinson as an intellectual crook. **Also:** *Tovarich* (37), *City for Conquest* (40), *Out of the Fog* (41), *This Above All* (42), *The Deep Blue Sea* (55).

LLOYD Frank
American. 1889–1960. Born Scotland. Went to America at the age of twenty-one as an actor. As a director, he was known to be all at sea, his most famous film being *Mutiny on the Bounty* (1935), which won an Oscar for Best Picture. This lavish drama of the sea, took two years to make, 2¼ hours to watch the gripping clash between Charles LAUGHTON's sadistic Captain Bligh and Clark Gable's 'Mr Christian'. Most of it was shot expertly in a studio tank with only a few scenes in Tahiti. Other sea pictures he made were *The Sea Hawk* (1924), *The Eagle and the Sea* (1926) and *Rulers of the Sea* (1939). In fact, Lloyd had a long career on land with a penchant for literary adaptations, including *Oliver Twist* (1922 with Lon Chaney and Jackie Coogan), *East Lynne* (1931), *Cavalcade* (1934–Noel Coward's family saga pudding), *Berkeley Square* (1933) and *Under Two Flags* (1936). **Others:** *Wells Fargo* (37), *The Howards of Virginia* (40), *Blood on the Sun* (45), *The Last Command* (55).

LOACH Ken
British. Born 1936. Director of 'kitchen sink' TV dramas in the 60's. In 1968 left the BBC and set up Kestrel Films with Tony Garnett, to make films that 'clarify the lives of ordinary people'. *Poor Cow* (1968), in the Wednesday Play tradition was made in semi-documentary style about a girl trying to cope on a low income with a husband in jail. The principal theme of *Kes* (1969) is a young boy's escape from his deadly Northern Industrial environment through the training of a kestrel. Filmed entirely on location in Yorkshire and using mainly non-actors, it is a warm and beautifully observed piece of work. *Family Life* (1972–*Wednesday's Child* US.) is an effective but rather loaded exposition of the anti-psychiatry theories of R.D. Laing. **Also:** *Black Jack* (79), *The Gamekeeper* (80), *Looks and Smiles* (82).

LOGAN Joshua
American. Born 1908. Broadway director. Six out of his nine movies are adaptations from his own Broadway stage successes. The versions of two William Inge plays survived the journey better than the others. *Picnic* (1956) has an excellent cast (William Holden, Kim Novak, Rosalind Russell etc.) and a splendidly evoked Kansas town. *Bus Stop* (1956), although rather strident, is true to the Inge milieu and Marilyn Monroe is the least vulgar thing in it. *South Pacific* (1958), *Fanny* (1961), *Camelot* (1967) and *Paint Your Wagon* (1969) confirm the suspicion that Broadway musicals and Logan belong on Broadway. **Also:** *Sayonara* (57), *Tall Story* (60), *Ensign Pulver* (64).

LOSEY Joseph
American. Born 1909. Worked in the theatre for many years. Directed the New York premiere of Brecht's 'Galileo Galilei' in 1947. (He filmed it in 1972 with Topol, the unsatisfactory lead.) Losey claims to have been inspired by Brecht for most of his life. Very little of Brecht's dialogue, great clarity of mind and expression or irony is evident in Losey's obfuscating films. Brecht is all light, Losey is darkness, Brecht is unemotional, Losey merely cold, Brecht exposes the class system with a flood-light, Losey uses a candle. They both have a liking for allegory and were sent before the Un-American Activities House Committee. Losey was blacklisted for his leftist sympathies and moved to England in 1953. Before being caught in McCarthy's clammy hands, he made five features in

L to R: James Fox, Joseph Losey and Harold Pinter on the set of *The Servant* (1963).

82

Hollywood. *The Boy with Green Hair* (1948), a rather obvious fable on bigotry, *The Lawless* (1949), a murky drama about racism against Mexican–American fruit-pickers, and three tense low-budget thrillers, *The Prowler* (1951), *The Big Night* (1951) and *M* (1951), a remake of Fritz LANG's classic with David Wayne in the Peter Lorre role. Lorre is to Wayne what Lang is to Losey. Working under the names of Victor Hanbury and Joseph Walton, he made *The Sleeping Tiger* (1954) and *The Intimate Stranger* (1956) in England, two suspense tales as anonymous as their directors. In 1957, he came out of the closet and began to sign his name to his films. He also began to develop his baroque visual style using elaborate camera movements, shock angles and dramatic use of decor, particularly mirror reflections. *The Criminal* (1960–*The Concrete Jungle*–US), set in a prison, was Losey's first success in England. Part of the 'new realism' of British cinema, it now seems rather tame. Both *The Damned* (1962) and *Eve* (1962) were badly cut by the distributors and they survive as interesting failures. His collaborations with playwright Harold Pinter on three pictures, *The Servant* (1963), *Accident* (67), and *The Go-Between* (1971) are, on the whole, keen analyses of the English class structure, but Pinter's oblique dialogue seems to force Losey's style into an overloading of images in *The Servant* or a convoluted narrative style, surface detail and prettiness in the other two. *Boom* (1968) and *Secret Ceremony* (1968) confused mystification with significance, whereas the symbols that clutter up *Figures in a Landscape* (1970), *The Assassination of Trotsky* (1972) and *Mr Klein* (1976) are numbingly obvious. Free from the need for significance, the op and pop art *Modesty Blaise* (1966) is Losey's most enjoyable and relaxed movie. **Others:** *Time without Pity* (57), *The Gypsy and the Gentleman* (57), *Blind Date* (59), *King and Country* (64), *A Doll's House* (73), *The Romantic Englishwoman* (75), *Don Giovanni* (80), *The Trout* (82).

LUBIN Arthur

American. Born 1901. Made over one hundred movies from 1934, mostly for Universal, and what a camp mixture they are! Claude Rains and Nelson Eddy in *The Phantom of the Opera* (1943), Maria Montez and Jon Hall's exotic cavortings on the

Ernst Lubitsch

studio backlot in *White Savage* (1943) and *Ali Baba and the 40 Thieves* (1944), Turhan Bey as Aesop (!) in *A Night in Paradise* (1946), sinister Gale Sondergaard as *Spider Woman Strikes Back* (1946), Maureen O'Hara as *Lady Godiva* (1955) and 'Mr Universe' Steve Reeves in *The Thief of Baghdad* (1961) contain more laughs than his Abbott and Costello comedies and his 'Francis the Talking Mule' movies. **Also:** *Buck Privates* (41), *New Orleans* (47), *Rhubarb* (51), *South Sea Woman* (53), *The First Travelling Saleslady* (56).

LUBITSCH Ernst

German. 1892–1947. Acted in Max Reinhardt's stage company. In 1914, began acting, writing and directing a series of comedy shorts. His features in Germany included a number of ironic historical romances such as *Madame Dubarry* (1919) with Pola Negri, *Anne Boleyn* (1920) and *The Wife of Pharoah* (1922). Came to Hollywood in 1923 to direct Mary Pickford in *Rosita*. Among the five scintillating social comedies he made at Warners were *The Marriage Circle* (1924), a marital comedy of manners inspired by CHAPLIN's *A Woman of Paris, Lady Windermere's Fan* (1925), in which 'visual epigrams' were substituted for Wilde's verbal ones, and *So This Is Paris* (1926), all of which kissed the American public's hand with European sophistication. This bon-viveur brought continental manners and hedonism into puritan America. Left Warner Bros. because of a clash with Jack Warner. Two autocrats were too much for one studio. Lubitsch then established the Paramount Studio style of elegance, wit and cynicism in opulent surroundings. Jeanette MacDonald, making her film debut, was cast with Maurice Chevalier in *The Love Parade* (1929), Lubitsch's first sound film. He realized immediately that musical numbers should grow naturally out of the texture of the work and it paved the way for better musicals. MacDonald also appears in another film-operetta *Monte Carlo* (1930), in which she sings, 'Beyond the Blooo Horizon' from a train to happy, waving peasants in the fields. He was to direct two other musicals, *The Smiling Lieutenant* (1931), Chevalier in the title role singing 'Toujours L'Amour in the Army', and one of the most enchanting and polished of screen musicals, *The Merry Widow* (1934) with MacDonald and Chevalier. The many lighlights include a superb tracking shot outside their separate apartments as he sings, 'Maxim's', her change from widow's black to dazzling white (even the black dog is changed), and 'The Merry Widow Waltz' whirling through a mirrored ball-room shot from above. *Trouble in Paradise* (1932) and *Design for Living* (1933) are the jewels in the collection. Witty cutting, imaginative sets by Hans Dreier, perfect playing from the stars (Herbert Marshall, Miriam Hopkins, Kay Francis, Gary Cooper, Fredric March) and the priceless supporting actors (Edward Everett Horton, Charles Ruggles, Franklin Pangborn) treat the audience, for a rare moment in commercial cinema, as sophisticates. The 30's over and the world living through its darkest days, Lubitsch came up with one of Hollywood's great comedies. Not an escapist one, but *To Be or Not To Be* (1942), which took, of all subjects, the Nazi occupation of Poland. Jack Benny, Carole Lombard (in her final role) and Sig Ruman play it for bitter laughs. The famous 'Lubitsch Touch' has been variously defined, but the touch is that of a master chef who knows exactly the right amount of

(Left to right) Ronny Howard, Candy Clark and Charlie Martin Smith off the set of George Lucas' *American Graffiti* (1973).

spice or sugar to add to a dish. It is even more evident when one studies the films of his heirs, Otto PREMINGER, Joseph MANKIE-WICZ and Billy WILDER. **Others:** *Angel* (37), *Bluebeard's Eighth Wife* (38), *Ninotchka* (39), *The Shop Around the Corner* (40), *Heaven Can Wait* (43), *Cluny Brown* (46).

LUCAS George

American. Born 1944. Studied Film at the University of Southern California. Assistant to Francis Ford COPPOLA on *Finian's Rainbow* (1968) who produced his first movies. *THX–1138* (1971) was shot in San Francisco's unfinished subway system and in underground passages, but it's not an underground movie. It's a small-scale sci-fi film which creates an Orwellian society where sex is forbidden and all heads are shaven. Following the familiar pattern, an individual (Robert Duvall) escapes to the surface and stands out against the sun. The idea is not fully explored, but the use of sound and machines shows tech know-how. The box-office smash, *American Graffiti* (1973) is a dreamy vision of adolescent life in a small Californian town in 1962, before Vietnam and the drug scene. A time of comparative innocence. Using the rock 'n roll hits of the day on the sound track and with Haskell WEXLER's brilliant hyper-

realist photography, the film creates a finger lickin' golden past. It also draws on memories of teen-pix of the 50's, although how much cosier this nostalgia trip seems. *Star Wars* (1977) is a big toy for little boys. For all its barrage of technical show-offs, it has none of the menace, atmosphere, or intelligence of its sources. The metaphor of Good vs Evil is confused and echoes of every kiddie matinée are thrown in for bad measure. Lucas says it best. 'I like action, adventure, chases, things blowing up. I like comic books.' Comic books, yes. . . .

LUDWIG Edward

American. Born 1895. Hired himself out to a number of studios for mostly commonplace action movies. The best were set in exotic locations about men fighting over sultry women – Susan Hayward in China in *The Fighting Seabees* (1944), Gale Russell in the East Indies in *The Wake of the Red Witch* (1948), Yvonne de Carlo in the Bahamas in *Flame of the Islands* (1956). Also made the best version of *The Swiss Family Robinson* (1940) with Thomas Mitchell as the pater familias. **Others:** *That Certain Age* (38), *The Last Gangster* (39), *Big Jim McClain* (52), *Sangaree* (53).

LUMET Sidney

American. Born 1924. Former stage

and TV actor. Part of the first generation of TV directors who made it in the movies. Seven of his first nine movies, shot in black and white, are marked by heightened naturalism and theatricality. The first, *Twelve Angry Men* (1957) is an expertly contrived piece with Henry Fonda as the liberal conscience, trying to persuade the eleven other members of a jury to bring in a non-guilty verdict on a murder case. Much pleasure is derived from watching each showy actor do his turn. A trio of films adapted from plays by America's finest playwrights gain from some splendid acting, but suffer from slow and mannered direction. *The Fugitive Kind* (1959), Tennessee Williams' symbol-cluttered 'Orpheus Descending', has gutsy Anna Magnani and Joanne Woodward, but a soporific BRANDO; *View from the Bridge* (1961), Arthur Miller's over-emotional drama, has Maureen Stapleton and a steaming Brooklyn background, and in *Long Day's Journey into Night* (1962), Eugene O'Neill's masterpiece, Lumet was content to display the performances of Katharine Hepburn, Ralph Richardson, Jason Robards, and Dean Stockwell, without too much embellishment. *Fail Safe* (1963) is a straight-faced *Dr Strangelove* (1963), but less powerful. Powerful is what Lumet's films strenuously try to be.

Both *The Pawnbroker* (1965), Rod Steiger over-emoting in the title role of the nazi-victim now in Spanish Harlem, and *The Hill* (1965) doth protest too much. *The Group* (1966) totters between satire and soap opera, but did introduce eight bright new actresses to the screen. Lumet has always been basically a New York director, happiest when finding worms in the Big Apple, so with *Serpico* (1973), *Dog Day Afternoon* (1975) and *Prince of the City* (1981) he at last achieved the synthesis of style and content that had evaded him before. The vividly realized New York settings dictate the power and pace of the movies, all three based on true stories. Lumet is in his element among the cops, crooks and corruption of the city streets, and not with overblown woolly fables like *Network* (1976), *Equus* (1977) and *The Wiz* (1978). **Others:** *Stage Struck* (58), *The Deadly Affair* (67), *Bye Bye Braverman* (68), *The Seagull* (68), *The Anderson Tapes* (71), *The Offence* (72), *Murder on the Orient Express* (74).

LUMIÈRE Auguste and Louis

French. Auguste (1862–1954). Louis (1864–1948). There is a poetic congruity of their name and profession. Let there be Light, and there was Cinema. Developing Edison's Kinetoscope further, they patented a camera-projector called the Cinematograph. On 28th December 1895, they showed a twenty-minute programme of ten films of a train arriving at a station, a family meal, a boat sailing out of a bay, recorded with an immobile camera and occasional panning, is like viewing the Lascaux cave paintings. In the earliest film comedy, *L'Arroseur Arrosé,* a gardener gets water in his face from a hose, and in *The Demolition of a Wall,* the wall is rebuilt by reverse motion.

LUPINO Ida

American. Born 1918 in England. Daughter of Stanley Lupino, British comedian. An actress, who made her reputation in low-key, low-budget movies, directed five films of the same type. One of the few women directors in Hollywood, her films are hardly feminist in nature. Marriage offers a solution to dancer Sally Forrest whose career is destroyed when she gets polio in *Never Fear* (1950.a.k.a. *The Young Lovers*) and in *Hard, Fast and Beautiful* (1951) Sally Forrest as a tennis champion

Al Pacino in Lumet's *Dog Day Afternoon* (1975).

gives up her career when she realizes a home and husband are more important. Far better are *The Bigamist* (1953) and *The Hitchhiker* (1953) both with good, sweaty performances from Edmond O'Brien. **Also:** *The Trouble with Angels* (66).

LYNCH David

American. Born 1946. Studied Fine Arts and became a painter. His first feature, *Eraserhead* (1977) took five years to make. Shot in black and white, almost entirely at night with a sound track of fright, it is a disturbingly loathsome nightmare of a movie ripped untimely from the womb of Surrealist art and German Expressionist cinema. *The Elephant Man* (1981), a far more conventional film, begs the audience's pity and tolerance for the hideously deformed Victorian man, John Merrick (John Hurt under layers and layers of make-up).

McCAREY Leo

American. 1898–1969. There are three Leo McCareys. The first is the director of Laurel and Hardy shorts from 1927 to 1931. The second, from 1932 to 1937, is the man who made zany, wise-cracking comedies featuring Eddie Cantor, W.C Fields (*Six of a Kind*–1934), The Marx Brothers, Mae West (*Belle of the 90's*–1934), Harold Lloyd (*The Milky Way*–1936) and Cary Grant and Irene Dunne in *The Awful Truth* (1937). The third, beginning with *Make Way for Tomorrow* (1937), veers towards sentimentality in which those three sob-sisters, Religion, Family and Nation play important roles. He rose from gag-writer to production executive at the Hal Roach Studios and it was he who directed Laurel and Hardy in *Putting Pants on Philip* (1927), their first film together as a real duo. The Marx Brothers were so impressed by his work on *The Kid from Spain* (1932), a madcap musical with Eddie Cantor, that they got him for *Duck Soup* (1933), their most inspired movie. McCarey keeps the lunatic action going like an expert juggler keeping three screwballs in the air. Charles LAUGHTON gave his best comedy performance in *Ruggles of Red Gap* (1935) as the English butler won in a poker game by a Wild Westerner. Snappy, irreverent dialogue and comic timing from the leads makes *The Awful Truth* unequalled until HAWKS' *His Girl Friday*. As in the later movie, Ralph Bellamy is the perfect foil for the squabbling couple, Grant and Dunne. McCarey's sympathy, understanding and gentle handling of actors saves *Make Way for Tomor-*

row from bathos. The story of an elderly couple (touching performances from Victor Moore and Beulah Bondi) becoming a burden on their children, is poignant and comical in the right measures. The latter half of *Love Affair* (1939) drips with treacle, but the engaging performances (Charles Boyer, Irene Dunne) in this ship-board romance that ends sadly, redeem it. McCarey remade it in 1957 as *An Affair to Remember* with Cary Grant and Deborah Kerr, but the first half is broader and the second weepier. Comedy and tragedy sit uncomfortably together in *Once Upon a Honeymoon* (1942), one scene of which finds Cary Grant and Ginger Rogers in a Nazi concentration camp where Grant almost says, 'This is another fine mess you've got me into.' Bing Crosby appears as the lovable Father O'Malley in *Going My Way* (1944) and *The Bells of St Mary's* (1945) both done with enough manipulative skill to bring even an atheist to his knees. **Others:** *Good Sam* (48), *My Son John* (52), *Rally Round the Flag Boys* (58), *Satan Never Sleeps* (62).

MACHATY Gustav
Czechoslovakian. 1901–1963. One of the pioneers of soft porn. The nude scenes that caused a rumpus in the notorious *Ecstasy* (1933) are played by Hedy Kiesler (later Lamarr). The Pope protested when it was shown at the Venice Film Festival in 1934, the nude scenes were cut in the USA and Hedy's husband tried to buy up all the prints. It was much ado about nothing on. The film itself is full of pastoral beauty and Hedy's kiesler is not even seen. **Also:** *Erotikan* (29).

MacKENDRICK Alexander
American. Born 1912. Brought up in Scotland. Entered films as scriptwriter in 1937. After the war, joined Ealing Studios helping to form their particular comedy style with *Whisky Galore* (1949. *Tight Little Island*–USA), his first feature. Written by Compton Mackenzie and based on his novel, it tells of an island in the Outer Hebrides being deprived of its life-blood – whisky. The comedy is more effective by being rooted in a realistically observed background. *The Man in the White Suit* (1951) differs slightly from the Ealing tradition as it tends towards a satirical fable. Alec Guinness is an inventor who makes a fabric that will never wear out, thus bringing the wrath of both labour and management of the cloth-

ing industry upon him. *The Lady-killers* (1955) has a black edge to it. A gang of crooks attempt to bump off an old lady but find themselves (rather farcically) being eliminated one by one. It was the last Ealing comedy, bringing the golden age to an end. MacKendrick left Britain to make his first film in the country of his birth. *Sweet Smell of Success* (1957) is a biting duet played by Burt Lancaster's powerful newspaper columnist and Tony Curtis' obsequious press agent, against the jazzy dazzle of James Wong Howe's black and white images of New York by night. After three disappointing movies, he left the industry to become Dean of the film department at the California Institute of Arts. **Also:** *Mandy* (52), *The Maggie* (52 – High and Dry – USA), *Sammy Going South* (63), *High Wind in Jamaica* (65), *Don't Make Waves* (67).

McLAGLEN Andrew
American. Born 1925. Son of the actor, Victor McLaglen. The shadow of John FORD lies heavily over his work. Take away Ford's (remaining) eye for visual composition and poetry, play up his slapstick and sentimentality and you have a movie by McLaglen Junior. *Chisum* (1971) starts with John WAYNE silhouetted against the sky and ends the same way. Nothing in between justifies it except by reference to Wayne–Ford Westerns. However, with a good script and James Stewart's humane performance, *Shenandoah* (1965) captures the heartbreak of the Civil War. The rest of his Westerns and war movies, seem to have been directed by his father's Sergeant Quincannon, the bar-room brawler in Ford's cavalry trilogy. **Also:** *McLintock* (63), *The Rare Breed* (66), *The Way West* (67), *The Ballad of Josie* (68), *The Devil's Brigade* (68), *Bandolero* (68), *The Wild Geese* (78), *The Sea Wolves* (80).

McLAREN Norman
Canadian. Born 1914 in Britain. Settled in Canada in 1951. Known for the short, animated films he made for the National Film Board of Canada. Using many techniques such as drawing directly onto the film, mixing live action and drawings, pixillation, cutouts and diffused sound effects, the films have filled many a supporting programme at 'art-houses' throughout the world, delighting some and boring the pants off the many who'd much rather see Bugs Bunny. **Some**

titles: *Dots and Loops* (40), *Fiddle-de-dee* (47), *Neighbours* (52), *A Chairy Tale* (57) *Pas de Deux* (62).

McLEOD Norman Z.
American. 1898–1964. Former animator and gag writer. Made enjoyable comedies with The Marx Brothers (*Monkey Business* 1931, *Horse Feathers* 1932), Danny Kaye (*The Kid from Brooklyn* 1946, *The Secret Life of Walter Mitty* 1947), Bob Hope (*Road to Rio* 1947, *The Pale-face* 1948, *My Favorite Spy* 1951, *Casanova's Big Night Out* 1954, *Alias Jesse James* 1959), and the delightfully wry Constance Bennett (*Topper* 1937, *Topper Takes a Trip* 1939, *Merrily We Live* 1938). Plus *Alice in Wonderland* (1933) . . . according to Paramount with W.C. Fields (Humpty Dumpty), Cary Grant (Mock Turtle), Gary Cooper (White Knight) and Edward Everett Horton (Mad Hatter). **Also:** *Lady be Good* (41), *Panama Hattie* (42), *Let's Dance* (50), *Never Wave at a WAC* (52).

MAKAVEJEV Dušan
Yugoslavian. Born 1932. Former journalist and film critic. Virtually the only Yugoslavian film-maker to be known internationally, although his films have met official disapproval and some have never been shown commercially in his own country. He is an independent, anarchic, ironic spirit whose films are paradoxical essays using collage methods often juxtaposing a series of images in a humorous and dramatic manner. His first films, *A Man is not a Bird* (1965) and *The Switchboard Operator* (1967) use clips from documentaries, lectures, and animal film to contrast and comment on the lives of his 'fictional' characters. *W.R.-Mysteries of the Organism* (1971) –the title is meant to be misread– is a fusion of styles combining film of Wilhelm Reich and his sexually liberating practices and a fictional story, ambiguously comparing the West with Communist countries, Reich with Stalin. While seeming to admire Reich, he gives him and his disciples enough rope to beat each other with. The exploration into eroticism and society continued in the undisciplined *Sweet Movie* (1974) and *Montenegro* (81), in which a middle-class married woman in Sweden frees her libido with a gang of crazy Serbian immigrant workers. The flasher in Makavejev is subdued in *Innocence Unprotected* (1968). He cleverly took

the first Serbian feature ever made (1942) and recut it adding newsreel footage, animation and interviews with the original actors. Never snide, it is an amusing and affectionate homage to the brave and innocent film-makers.

MALICK Terrence

American. Born 1945. Studied philosophy at Harvard. A student at the American Film Institute. Of his two movies, *Badlands* (1974) is one of the best American films of the last decade and *Days of Heaven* (1978) one of the worst. Another film progeny of *Bonnie and Clyde* (1967), *Badlands* is an ironic, fatalistic and allusive picture of two semi-illiterate young outlaws (Martin Sheen, Sissy Spacek) in the 50's. The film has two narratives, a reading from the girl's diary of how she saw events and the contradictory objectivity of the director's narrative position. Unlike other contemporary cine-philiac movies, one feels it is the characters' actions that are influenced by movie heroes (such as James Dean) and fan mags and not the director's. For *Days of Heaven*, Malick and his cameraman Nestor Almendros sacrificed character, plot, development, and rhythm to the making of beautiful images. Based on the paintings of Andrew Wyeth, it could be called a series of tableaux vivantes, if it were not so dead. To be continued . . .

MALLE Louis

French. Born 1932. 'I'm always interested in exposing something, a theme, a character or situation which seems to be unacceptable. Then I try to make it work,' explained Malle. And he invariably does make it work. He has dealt with adultery, incest and child prostitution sympathetically, lifted the lid on French collaboration during the Occupation, made a fantasy which included a talking unicorn and filmed 110 minutes of two people having a dinner conversation. Like the title of one of his films, *Le Feu Follet* (1963), he is a will-o'-the-wisp director, a darting light shed over marshy ground. In his second film, *Les Amants* (*The Lovers*, 1957) he shot an adulterous couple making love to Brahms, causing a scandal, and making Jeanne Moreau into a star. This chic, erotic satire was called by Francois TRUFFAUT, 'The first night of love in the cinema.' Changing his skin, he bravely attempted in *Zazie dans le Metro* (1960) to find a visual equivalent to Raymond

Brooke Shields in Louis Malle's *Pretty Baby* (1978).

Queneau's eccentric syntax but, despite some ingenious cinematic tricks and a surreal view of Paris, it soon burns itself out. The solemnity of *Le Feu Follet*, a poignant study of the last few days in the life of an alcoholic, gives way to the gaiety of *Viva Maria* (1965) which wittily takes off the kind of big production it is i.e. large screen, colour, filmed on location in Mexico with stars Moreau and Brigitte Bardot. Courting scandal again, Malle delicately handled the subject of incest in *Le Souffle au Coeur* (1971. *Dearest Love*–GB. *Murmer of the Heart*–USA). However, it is basically a social comedy about the sexual education of an adolescent boy growing up in Paris in 1954 who, quite naturally, sleeps with his attractive mother (Lea Massari). Over twenty-five years after the Liberation, France was still touchy about the Occupation. *Lacombe Lucien* (1973) was one of the first features to reveal the unsavoury past, taking as its 'hero' a young French labourer who becomes a Fascist collaborator. *Black Moon* (1975), his first film in English, is a weird, beautifully shot (Sven Nykvist) Carollian fantasy. Not all of it comes off, but this Wonderland is full of surprising things including Joe Dalessandro singing Wagner. His first American film, *Pretty Baby*

Louis Malle (R) directing Benoit Fereux in *Le Souffle au Coeur* (1971).

(1978) caused the wrong sort of ruckus. In this recreation of a turn-of-the-century New Orleans brothel where the 12-year-old girl (Brooke Shields) is brought up, Malle avoids sensationalism. The prostitutes, the 'fleurs du Malle', are part of a bustling vibrant, comical-tragical community. The old and the new, the past and the present, the values of the old and the young are captured with a subtle eye for detail and lives lived in *Atlantic City* (1980). It doesn't always support the mythical structure imposed upon it, but the inter-relation of the characters against their tawdry environment and Burt Lancaster as a man from another age trying to survive on lies as walls collapse around him, carry the film. Malle's camera hovers around the table in *My Dinner with Andre* (1982), like a discreet maître d'hôtel listening to the absorbing conversation. Malle is married to the actress Candice Bergen and now lives in America. **Others:** *Lift to the Scaffold* (57), *Vie Privée* (62), *Le Voleur* (67).

MAMOULIAN Rouben

American. Born 1898 in Russia. Studied at the Moscow Arts Theatre. Went to America as a young man. Directed opera, operetta and plays. Continued to work on stage between films, directing the first productions of *Porgy and Bess*, *Oklahoma!* and *Carousel*. Invited to Hollywood at the beginning of sound, he immediately refused to be shackled by theatrical conventions, throwing himself into the new medium like a born cineaste. Whether musicals or dramas, his films have the rhythmic fluency of dance, full of visual and aural effects, sensuous lighting and

decor. On his first film, *Applause* (1929) he insisted on using two microphones on certain scenes, later mixing the sound. This story of an ageing Broadway burlesque queen (torch singer Helen Morgan's greatest role), who poisons herself, is full

of stunning camera movements rare in most early talking pictures. He uses skilful tracking shots, lighting, location photography and subjective sound in *City Streets* (1931) one of the first gangster movies. There were further innovations in *Dr Jekyll and Mr Hyde* (1932) such as the subjective camera at the beginning in which we first catch sight of Dr Jekyll (Fredric March) in the mirror, and the transformation scenes. In order to avoid dissolves and cuts, he devised a complex system of layers of coloured make–up and filters. When Jekyll becomes Hyde the camera revolves 360 degrees. *Becky Sharp* (1935) was the first film to use three–strip Technicolor, which allowed Mamoulian in this adaptation of 'Vanity Fair' to add another dimension to his cinematic gifts. Most striking was the ball scene when with the arival of the news of Waterloo the screen is drained of colour except for the red of the soldiers' uniforms. The chief pleasure of *Blood and Sand* (1941) is the voluptuous colour evok-

Maurice Chevalier performing the Poor Apache in Mamoulian's *Love Me Tonight* (1932).

ing the atmosphere of the bull–ring and the interiors styled after great Spanish painters. Sometimes his films are too ripe, too melodramatic, too mannered, but nothing mars the achievement of the black and white *Love Me Tonight* (1932), perhaps the most perfect and coherent of all screen musicals. The entire film is conceived in musical terms from the opening sequence of the noises of Paris awakening. By recording all the music before shooting, he was able to choreograph the actors and even animals to the music. The number, 'Isn't it Romantic?' starts with Maurice Chevalier humming the tune, it is picked up by a taxi driver, a composer in the cab writes it down, he adds words to it on a train, it is overheard by soldiers who are seen singing it on the march. A gypsy hears it, plays it on his violin and it is heard by Jeanette MacDonald so linking her by this musical chain to Chevalier before they have met. **Others:** *Song of Songs* (33), *Queen Christina* (34), *High, Wide and Handsome* (37), *Golden Boy* (39), *The Mark of Zorro* (40), *Summer Holiday* (47), *Silk Stockings* (57).

L to R: Bette Davis, Marilyn Monroe and George Sanders in Mankiewicz's *All About Eve* (1950).

MANKIEWICZ Joseph

American. Born 1909. Former journalist. Scriptwriter and Producer. (Produced Fritz LANG's first American film, *Fury*–1936). Directed his first eleven films from 1946 to 1952 for Fox. In the beginning was the Word according to Mankiewicz, and the screen is mostly a vehicle for his own literate, witty and satirical screen plays. The response required is similar to that of a theatre audience's, but although they are talky they are not photographed plays. Not a visual stylist certainly, but there are few movies that give as much pleasure as *A Letter to Three Wives* (1949) and *All About Eve* (1950). The first is a cleverly constructed story set in suburban America where the three wives (Jeanne Craine, Linda Darnell and Ann Southern) wonder which of their husbands is going off with the local vamp (the voice of Celeste Holm). The stringent solid comedy is derived as much from the dialogue and acting as the meticulously observed milieu. *All About Eve* is a poison pen letter to the New York theatrical world. High comedy played to the hilt by Bette Davis as the bitching, faded idol Margot Channing, George Sanders as the acid critic Addison de Witt, Anne Baxter as the cunning Eve and Celeste Holm, Thelma Ritter and Marilyn Monroe. *Five Fingers* (1952) is an absorbing espionage tale told in a semi-documentary style and *Julius Caesar* (1953) is an intelligent reading of the play, which avoids the temptation towards Hollywood spectacle and has performances of power from Marlon BRANDO as Mark Antony and John Gielgud as Cassius. His only musical (and Brando's) is the lively, lavish, *Guys and Dolls* (1955) with a fine use of an artificial Broadway setting. However, he over-reached himself in *The Barefoot Contessa* (1954), a soap opera despite the ironic narration, *Suddenly Last Summer* (1959), a ludicrous piece of Gothic (script by Gore Vidal from Tennessee Williams) with tentative flashbacks to break up the monologues, and the disastrous *Cleopatra* (1962). **Also:** *Dragonwyck* (46), *The Late George Apley* (47), *The Ghost and Mrs Muir* (47), *House of Strangers* (49), *No Way Out* (50), *People Will Talk* (51), *The Quiet American* (58), *The Honey Pot* (67), *There was a Crooked Man* (70), *Sleuth* (72).

MANN Anthony

American. 1906–1967. Real name Emil Bundsmann. Mann of the West. In the decade from 1950 to 1960, eleven of his eighteen movies were Westerns. Of the seven others, only *The Tall Target* (1951) is of much interest. The five Westerns with James Stewart are key films of the genre. Mann discovered a new Stewart, a tougher, more uncompromising and bitter Stewart than the drawling charmer of previous pictures. He relentlessly tracks down the man who stole his gun in *Winchester 73* (1950), shoots the man who betrayed him in *Bend of the River* (1952) and revenge is in his heart for the man who killed his brother in *The Man from Laramie* (1955). High in the Rockies, bounty hunter Stewart combats Robert Ryan and the brutality in himself in *The Naked Spur* (1953) and he is provoked into violence in *The Far Country* (1954). Each movie has the inevitability of a Jacobean tragedy. The plots are sharply delineated, full of tense love–hate relationships, violence with real pain, revenge and honour, set against brooding landscapes. The solemn rituals of the Western are not far from the medieval chivalric traditions of *El Cid* (1961) and with magnificent photography by Robert Krasker on location in Spain, Mann

James Stewart and Cathy O'Donnell in Anthony Mann's *The Man From Laramie* (1955).

creates an epic spectacle that towers above others of the same type including his own *The Fall of the Roman Empire* (1964). **Also:** *Thunder Bay* (53), *The Glenn Miller Story* (54), *The Last Frontier* (56), *Men in War* (57), *The Tin Star* (57), *God's Little Acre* (58), *Cimarron* (60), *Heroes of Telemark* (65).

MANN Daniel

American. Born 1912. Former jazz musician, actor, TV director. Shirley Booth (*Come Back, Little Sheba* 1953), Anna Magnani (*The Rose Tattoo* 1955) and Elizabeth Taylor (*Butterfield 8* 1960) all won Oscars for best actresses in a Daniel Mann movie. Susan Hayward gave one of her best all-stops-out performances in *I'll Cry Tomorrow* (1955) and Shirley Booth added weight to *About Mrs Leslie* (1954) and *Hot Spell* (1958). His theatrical TV–realist films of the 50's were the kind of showcases that produced large over-wrought acting from large, over-wrought actresses. His style naturally developed into soap. **Also:** *Teahouse of the August Moon* (56), *Ada* (61), *Five Finger Exercise* (62), *Our Man Flint* (65), *Judith* (65), *For Love of Ivy* (68), *A Dream of Kings* (69), *Willard* (70), *Matilda* (78).

MANN Delbert

American. Born 1920. Directed plays for the NBC TV Playhouse series from 1949 to 1955, some of them written by Paddy Chayefsky. When serious TV drama was drained from American TV, both Mann and Chayefsky entered the movies. His first feature *Marty* (1955) was adapted from the Chayefsky play he had directed on TV. This love story between two ordinary, unattractive people brought a new naturalism into Hollywood movies. Ernest Borgnine, sometime heavy, won the Oscar for his affecting performance of the Bronx butcher. Mann's other two collaborations with Chayefsky, *Bachelor party* (1957) and *Middle of the Night* (1959) continued to show that little people had real emotions. In the 60's, he left the drab black and white environment for fluffy, pink Doris Day comedies (*Lover Come Back* 1961, *That Touch of Mink* 1962) and the like. **Others:** *Desire Under the Elms* (58), *Separate Tables* (58), *The Dark at the Top of the Stairs* (60), *The Outsider* (61), *Dear Heart* (64), *Mr Buddwing* (65), *Fitzwilly* (67), *The Pink Jungle* (68), *David Copperfield*

(70), *Jane Eyre* (71), *Night Crossing* (82).

MARKER Chris

French. born 1921. Real name Christian Francois Bouche-Villeneuve — no name for a good socialist. Fought in the Resistance and with the American Air Force during the war. Wrote poems, short stories and film reviews, emerging from the post-war Left-Bank intellectual climate. The personal, poetic, lucid and committed Left wing documentaries he made from 1955 to 1966 established him as a major film-maker. *Letter from Siberia* (1958) uses cartoons, texts, and a sequence repeated three times with a different commentary questioning objectivity in films. *Cuba Si!* (1961) contains two long interviews with Fidel Castro and *Le Joli Mai* (1964) was compiled from fifty-five hours of interviews with the people of Paris with a linking commentary. His only fiction film was *Le Jetee* (*The Jetty* 1963), a thirty minute post-Third World War story, made up entirely of stills except for one brief moving shot. In 1966, he set up a company to produce new works called SLON (Societe de Lancement des Oeuvres Nouvelles) and only directs rarely. **Also:** *Sunday in Peking* (55), *Description of a Struggle* (60), *The Train Rolls On* (71), *Le Fond de L'air est Rouge* (77).

MARSHALL George

American. 1891–1975. Made over four hundred features from 1917 to 1969. A studio stalwart, most of his movies are on the light side, including six with Bob Hope, three Martin and LEWIS romps, three musicals with bawling blonde bombshell Betty Hutton and six drooping comedies with Glenn Ford. Best known for *Destry Rides Again* (1939), one of the most successful comedy Westerns with a witty script and engaging performances from James Stewart as the man who tames the town without guns and Marlene Dietrich as Frenchy singing 'See what the boys in the backroom will have.' Time and again Marshall tried unsuccessfully to repeat the winning formula, even remaking it as *Destry* (1954) with Audie Murphy and Mari Blanchard. **Others:** *The Goldwyn Follies* (38), *You Can't Cheat an Honest Man* (39), *The Ghost Breakers* (40), *Incendiary Blonde* (45), *The Blue Dahlia* (46), *The Perils of Pauline* (47), *My Friend Irma* (49), *Fancy Pants* (50), *Off-*

Limits (53), *Houdini* (53), *Red Garters* (54), *The Sheepman* (58), *The Mating Game* (59), *The Gazebo* (59).

MATÉ Rudolph

American. 1898–1964. Born in Cracow, Austria (now Poland). Brilliant cameraman on Carl DREYER's *The Passion of Joan of Arc* (1928) and *Vampyr* (1932). In Hollywood from 1935. His own uneven output offers many delights, but three gripping little thrillers stand out. *The Dark Past* (1948) has William Holden as a psychologist being held prisoner by a psychopathic killer. *D.O.A.* (1949 – *Dead on Arrival*) opens with Edmond O'Brien reporting a murder at a police station. 'Whose?' the cop asks. 'My own,' replies O'Brien. *Union Station* (1950) is set in and around the Chicago station (excellent use of location and a vast set) where William Holden ingeniously tries to trap a kidnapper. The incidental pleasures of the rest include Robert Mitchum, Linda Darnell and Jack Palance in conflict in a teetering cable car in *Second Chance* (1953), Tony Curtis as an English Knight from Brooklyn in *The Black Shield of Falworth* (1954) and the bliss of a deaf girl unable to hear Mario Lanza sing in his last film, *For the First Time* (1959). **Also:** *No Sad Songs for Me* (50), *The Prince who was a Thief* (51), *When Worlds Collide* (51), *The Mississippi Gambler* (53), *The Violent Men* (55), *The Rawhide Years* (56), *Miracle in the Rain* (56).

MAY Elaine

American. Born 1932. With Mike NICHOLS made up the brilliant satirical cabaret duo in the 50's and early 60's. After splitting up, she went into screen-writing (*Such Good Friends* 1971) and directing, successfully carrying over much of the scathing wit of their act. *A New Leaf* (1971) and *The Heartbreak Kid* (1973) are two of the most cruelly funny American comedies since the 30's. The horrendous females in both movies are played by Elaine May and her daughter respectively. In the former, she is the rich and blundering botanist whom Walter Matthau must marry in order to pay his debts, and in the latter Jeannie Berlin plays a young 'Yenta' who drives her husband on their honeymoon in Miami into the arms of WASP Cybill Shepherd. Her third movie, *Mickey and Nicky* (1976) is a film noir written for her friends, John CASSAVETES and Peter Falk which suppressed her greatest forté – humour.

MAYO Archie
American. 1891–1968. Directed for twenty years from 1926 to 1946, half the time at Warners. One of those invisible directors overshadowed by producers, stars, screenwriters and dance directors, his movies were as bad or as good as they were. He made musicals (*Go Into Your Dance* – 1935 – Al Jolson, Ruby Keeler. *Orchestra Wives* – 1942 – Glenn Miller's band), the unhypnotic *Svengali* (1931 with John Barrymore), Jack Benny as *Charlie's Aunt* (1941), a failed attempt at French poetic realism with Jean Gabin (*Moontide* 1942), the wooden *The Petrified Forest* (1936) and a likeable comedy of the theatre, *It's Love I'm After* (1937) both with Bette Davis and Leslie Howard and *A Night in Casablanca* (1946). **Others:** *Sonny Boy* (29), *The House Across the Bay* (40), *The Great American Broadcast* (41), *The Adventures of Marco Polo* (48).

MAYSLES Albert and David
American. Albert (born 1926) generally handles the camera. David (born 1932) is a sound expert. Part of the Direct Cinema movement believing the camera should unobtrusively record the 'truth'. Associated with Robert Drew, Donn Allan Pennebacker and Richard LEACOCK. it was Albert who named the movement. They started by making films on celebrities such as *Meet Marlon Brando* (1965) and *A Visit with Truman Capote* (1966). Their vivid document of the Rolling Stones Altamount Speedway free concert in December 1969 called *Gimme Shelter* (1971) caused a controversy because the stabbing of a black youth by a 'Hell's Angel' was caught on film. More questions are raised in *Gray Gardens* (1975), a fascinating 'nonfiction feature' on two eccentric women who may or may not be giving performances for the camera in their decaying Long Island mansion.

MAZURSKY Paul
American. Born 1930. Like FELLINI, a director he admires, there is a strong element of autobiography in his movies. His second film, *Alex in Wonderland* (1971), about a director trying to make his second film, includes a dream sequence in which he meets Fellini. (It's a bad dream.) Mazursky was born in New York, attended Brooklyn college, worked in a health-food restaurant, acted Off-Broadway, hung around the Village and had a small role in *Blackboard Jungle* (1955). The leading character in *Next Stop, Greenwich Village* (1975) is a young actor trying to make it in the theatre in New York. He works in a similar restaurant and gets a part as a juvenile delinquent in a movie. It is affectionate and funny (even getting away with a monstrous Jewish momma joke in the form of Shelley Winters), sometimes teetering on the edge of sentimentality. But he admits he likes to work on 'the verge of corn'. Both *Bob and Carol and Ted and Alice* (1969), his first feature, and *Blume in Love* (1973) have audaciously corny endings which somehow work against one's better judgement. After an abortive attempt at wife–swapping in the former, the two couples realize that love and fidelity are more important than sex and join the other characters and crew in a Felliniesque parade to the strains of Dionne Warwick's 'What the world needs now is love . . . .' In *Blume in Love*, George Segal, who has refused to accept that his wife has left him, catches up with her in Venice and as the Liebestod plays on the Florian orchestra and various couples get together (including Aschenbach and Tadzio), they rush into each others' arms. *An Unmarried Woman* (1977) continues in the line of gently satirical character studies, although this witty and observant portrait of a woman (Jill Clayburgh) making her life anew after being left by her husband, rings false when she meets the man of her dreams. Despite miscalculations, Mazursky is to be cherished like Woody ALLEN, for bringing New York Jewish humour and sensibility into a crass Californian industry. **Also:** *Harry and Tonto* (74), *The Tempest* (82).

MEDVEDKIN Alexander
Russian. Born 1900. Member of the Red Army during the Civil War. In 1932, took charge of the film train that travelled all over the Soviet Union making films on the spot and showing them to the local people. Virtually unknown outside Russia until Chris MARKER's *Le Train en Marche* (1971 – *The Train rolls on*) about the train, including an interview with Medvedkin as a prelude to *Happiness* (1934) which dealt with collective farming using burlesque, surrealism, music-hall jokes and satire, surprising during the period of strict Socialist Realism. The silent film, with a musical score, succeeds in producing what the title promises.

MÉLIÈS Georges
French. 1861-1938. Conjuror, cartoonist, inventor and mechanic. In 1896, he built France's first film studio. Trick photography, including superimposition, and stop-motion, is used as if part of a magician's act, with himself as the illusionist. For example in *The Melomaniac* (1903) he plays a music master who removes his head only to be replaced by another and another. Throwing his heads on a telegraph wire, they form

Melies' *20,000 Leagues under the Sea* (1907).

musical notes. *A Trip to the Moon* (1902), *20,000 Leagues Under the Sea* (1907) and *New York to Paris by Car* (1908) are among the hundred or so films extant that still astonish and amuse.

MELVILLE Jean-Pierre
French. 1917-1973. Real name Jean-Pierre Grumbach. Changed his name because of his enthusiasm for the works of the great American writer, Herman Melville. But it was the American gangster novel and the film noir that were the greatest influences on his films. His favourite film was *The Asphalt Jungle* (1950) directed by John HUSTON, the maker of *Moby Dick* (1956). He always wore a stetson and dark glasses in public. In order to retain his independence, he set up his own production company in 1946, making his first films on low budgets. Shooting on location in Paris and New York respectively for *Bob le Flambeur* (1956) and *Two Men in Manhattan* (1959), he achieved a certain gritty free-wheeling style that brought something new to the crime thriller. His later films move ceremoniously through sleazy bars, hotels and nightclubs as backgrounds to double-crossing and killing. *The Samurai* (1967) follows the last day of a cold-blooded hired killer (Alain Delon) who nevertheless has a code of honour as does the gangster (Lino Ventura) in *Second Breath* (1966) who dies after ratting on his friends. One's reaction to these romantic and formal films depends on how one reacts to Ventura's epitaph. 'He is a danger to society, but he has preserved a sort of purity.' Eight of his thirteen films were crime thrillers which re-established the popularity of the film noir in France. However, they have been submerged by a welter of poor French gangster movies trying to imitate him as much as he imitated himself. Of his other films, *Le Silence de la Mer* (1947) succeed in transposing Vercors' almost unfilmable parable of the Resistance to the screen. Melville was himself in the *maquis* and *Leon Morin, Priest* (1961) and *L'Armee des Ombres* (1969 *Shadow Army*) are austere and tragic views of the Resistance. *Les Enfants Terribles* (1950), narrated and written by Jean COCTEAU, shot almost entirely on the stage of the Theatre Pigalle, recreated the strange and enclosed world of the novel. **Others:** *Le Doulos* (62), *L'Aine des Ferchaux* (63 – *The Magnet of Doom*), *Le Cercle Rouge*

(70), *Un Flic* (72–*Dirty Money*).

MENZEL Jiri
Czechoslovakian. Born 1938. Attended the Prague Film School. His first feature–length film was the Oscar-winning *Closely Observed Trains* (1966). Set during the Nazi occupation of Czechoslovakia, it follows the days of a young trainee at a country railway station whose main desire is to lose his virginity. Balanced perfectly between comedy and tragedy, it is a closely observed and touching anti-heroic film. **Also:** *Capricious Summer* (68).

MENZIES William Cameron
American. 1896-1957. Art director on many lavish productions including *Gone with the Wind* (1939). Out of the twelve films he directed, only *Things to Come* (1936) has much merit. Realising that H. G. Wells' futuristic novel 'The shape of things to come' needed imaginative art-direction, Alexander KORDA got Menzies to design and direct it. The sets, photography (Georges Perinal) and music (Arthur Bliss) help to counter-act the lack-lustre direction and stilted performances. **Also:** *The Green Cockatoo* (40), *Invaders from Mars* (53).

MEYER Russ
American. Born 1923. Started by making nudie quickies before breaking into the more commercial soft-core skin-flick market with garish, grotesque and gruesome comic-strip erotica such as *Vixen* (1968), *Cherry, Harry and Rachel* (1969), *The Seven Minutes* (1971) (i.e. the time it takes a woman to have an orgasm), *Super Vixens* (1973), *Up* (1976). *Beyond the Valley of the Dolls* (1970) is thought, by some respected critics, to be one of the greatest American movies of the last fifteen years. **Also:** *Faster Pussycat* (67), *Kill! Kill!* (67).

Battle scene from Milestone's *All Quiet on the Western Front* (1930).

MESZAROS Marta
Hungarian. Born 1931. Formerly married to Miklos JANCSO. She has received international recognition for her penetrating, uncomfortable, intimist films on the female condition. **Some titles:** *Riddance* (73), *Adoption* (75), *Nine Months* (76), *The Two of Them* (77).

MILES Christopher
British. Born 1939. Brother of actress Sarah Miles. D. H. Lawrence, Jean Genet and Jean Anouilh have been subject to his misinterpretations. Too busy creating atmosphere and pretty shots to make stories or acting convincing, he has made *The Virgin and the Gypsy* (1970 – from a Lawrence novella), *Time for Loving* (1971 – Anouilh trilogy), and *The Maids* (1974). *Priest of Love* (1981), about the last years of D.H.'s life, is a living waxworks show.

MILESTONE Lewis
American. Born 1895 in Russia. Former film editor. Served in World War I. Came to America in 1917. Started directing in 1925. His second sound film, *All Quiet on the Western Front* (1930), based on Erich Maria Remarque's novel, was a milestone in anti-war movies. Told from the German side, it follows seven boys who leave school full of patriotic fervour who are thrown into the horror of trench warfare. Particularly effective were the tracking shots of soldiers attacking the enemy lines and the counter-attacks with deaths on both sides. So realistic were these sequences that they have often been used in actuality films of the war. Skilful use is made of the single track sound system, crane shots, music and photography (Arthur Edeson). The famous last scene where the boy (Lew Ayres) is killed while reaching for a

butterfly, was shot by Karl FREUND using Milestone's own hand. He was to make seven more war movies of variable quality during his career. *Edge of Darkness* (1943), set in Norway in World War II, has some extraordinary camerawork in the action sequences. *A Walk in the Sun* (1945), *The Halls of Montezuma* (1951) and *Pork Chop Hill* (1959) failed to avoid the guts 'n' glory clichés of the genre, despite powerful moments. Some of his 'peace' movies are interesting. *The Front Page* (1931), one of the first rapid-fire wisecracking comedies, is now overshadowed by HAWKS' version of the Hecht–MacArthur play, *His Girl Friday*. A restless camera and the agitated performances of Joan Crawford and Walter Huston livened up Somerset Maugham's slushy *Rain* (1932). *Hallejulah I'm a Bum* (1933), the only musical directly about the Depression with rhyming–couplet dialogue and starring Al Jolson and Harry Langdon, was a noble failure. Also part of his best period (the 30's) was *The General Died at Dawn* (1936), a STERNBERGian drama atmospherically created among a superb studio China and *Of Mice and Men* (1939), an excellent adaptation of the John Steinbeck story, gave Burgess Meredith and Lon Chaney Jr their best film roles. **Also:** *Anything Goes* (33), *The North Star* (43), *The Purple Heart* (44), *The Strange Loves of Martha Ives* (46), *Arch of Triumph* (48), *Kangaroo* (52), *Les Miserables* (52), *Melba* (53), *Oceans II* (60), *Mutiny on the Bounty* (62).

MILIUS John
American. Born 1944. Studied Film at the University of Southern California. His macho interests include surfing, the martial arts, hunting, guns, Hemingway, 'Bully' Teddy Rooseveldt, Generals Patton and MacArthur, Admires Japanese samurai films and pre-Bonnie and Clyde gangster movies. After writing scripts for a number of films including two *Dirty Harry*'s, he made *Dillinger* (1973), a sardonic, romanticized and extremely violent crime thriller which played up the love-hate rivalry between cop (Ben Johnson) and crook (Warren Oates). Told with a certain wide-screen sweep, *The Wind and the Lion* (1975) is a Kiplingesque adventure story for admirers of strong leaders and those with a nostalgia for Empire or kiddie matinees at the Empire. *Big Wednesday* (1978) is a meandering, mawkish up-dated

'beach party', buddy-buddy movie with some splendid surfing sequences. **Also:** *Conan the Barbarian* (82).

MILLER David
American. Born 1909. Thankfully, he has made only twenty movies in over forty years. However, *Sudden Fear* (1952) is a suspenseful drama with Jack Palance trying to kill Joan Crawford, and *Lonely are the Brave* (1962) is an interesting Western with Kirk Douglas as the 'last cowboy' being hunted portentously over the highways by helicopters and trucks. **Also:** *Billy the Kid* (41), *Love Happy* (50), *Diane* (55), *The Opposite Sex* (56), *The Story of Esther Costello* (57), *Midnight Lace* (60), *Back Street* (61), *Captain Newman MD* (62), *Executive Action* (73).

MILLER George
Australian. Medical doctor who practised in Melbourne for some years. Directed TV series, including *The Sullivans*. *Mad Max* (1980), a big money spinner, proved that an Aussie film could out-bike, out-stunt, out-CORMAN, out-cult any Yankee exploitation movie. *Mad Max 2* (1982), also set in a future where gasoline is the only currency, was made with American money and the effects come even more like a punch down under. Derived, no doubt, from his medical days, Miller has a dramatic cutting technique and doesn't flinch from blood.

MINNELLI Vincente
American. Born 1910. A name that conjures up a world of fantasy, brilliant colours, stylish decor and costumes, where Fred Astaire, Judy Garland, Gene KELLY, Cyd Charisse and Leslie Caron dance and sing. He had worked in New York as designer and director of ballets and musical-comedies before Arthur Freed, the MGM producer, asked him to come to Hollywood. From 1943 to 1953, he made seven of the screen's finest musicals. His film debut was the all-black musical, *Cabin in the Sky* (1943) which, by creating real characters out of the whimsy, transcends the negro stereotypes and gets Lena Horne, Ethel Waters, Duke Ellington and Eddie 'Rochester' Anderson to give of their best. Using Technicolor for the first time in *Meet Me in St. Louis* (1944) he was able to paint the four seasons in the year of a St. Louis family between 1902-1903 with a loving eye for period detail. Magical moments include a radiant Judy Garland (then Minnelli's wife) singing 'The Boy Next Door' and the rhythmically staged 'Trolly Song', both of which advanced the plot. Both *Yolanda and the Thief* (1945) and *Ziegfeld Follies* (1946) have remarkable dream ballets featuring Fred Astaire. In the former, amid the soggy screenplay, there is an audacious sixteen minute surreal ballet and in the latter the Lime-House Blues number is a highlight. *The Pirate* (1948) purposely

L to R: Fred Astaire, Nanette Fabray and Jack Buchanan in the Triplet Number from Minnelli's *The Band Wagon* (1953).

goes for theatrical, stylised settings and performances but the editing, colour photography and the Cole Porter numbers performed by Garland and Gene Kelly refuse to make it stagey. *The Band Wagon* (1953) gave Fred Astaire his finest screen role. A scintillating, warm and witty tribute to the back-stage musical, it not only plays on Fred's persona but contains a dig at Minnelli's own 'artiness' in the shape of Jack Buchanan's hammy actor-director. It is full of visual and aural delights including the spoof Mickey Spillane ballet, 'Girl Hunt' and the number that sums up what Minnelli's musicals are all about, 'That's Entertainment'. Of the later CinemaScope musicals only *Gigi* (1958) is the same league, despite over-indulging his taste for decoration. *Brigadoon* (1954) and *Kismet* (1955) are top-heavy studio-bound Broadway transfers, but *The Bells are Ringing* (1960) and *On a Clear Day You Can See Forever* (1970) have moments that recall better days. His 'straight' films are over-heated airless melodramas in which the actors chewed the delicious decor. However, the recreation of Van Gogh's paintings in *Lust for Life* (1956) and Kirk Douglas's physical likeness to the artist is hallucinatory. All but three of his films were made for MGM. He seemed to need the studio machinery and security and when the studio system evaporated, so did he. Liza Minnelli is his daughter by Judy Garland. **Others:** *The Clock* (45), *Madame Bovary* (49), *Father of the Bride* (50), *The Bad and the Beautiful* (52), *Cobweb* (55), *Tea and Sympathy* (56), *Design-*

ing Woman (57), *Some Came Running* (58), *Home from the Hill* (60), *Four Horsemen of the Apocalypse* (61), *Two Weeks in Another Town* (62), *The Courtship of Eddie's Father* (63), *The Sandpiper* (65), *A Matter of Time* (76).

MIZOGUCHI Kenji

Japanese. 1898-1956. Former painter and journalist. Out of over eighty films, only about a dozen have been seen in the West. These are enough to establish him as one of the greatest directors of all time. From 1922 to 1936 he was, on the whole, forced to make many films in which he had little interest, but he gradually developed his own style and subject matter. Like many Japanese directors, he had to turn to period dramas because of the regime's restrictions on contemporary subjects. His

Mizoguchi's *Ugetsu Monogatari* (1953).

humanist view of the brutality of feudal Japan is mainly concerned with the sufferings of women. It is through women that he approaches the world. Like the women of the period, his camera watches calmly from a discreet distance. It is a style of long takes, long shots and gentle camera-movements, delicately avoiding the need for cutting by using slow dissolves, and minimum use of close-ups. At moments of crisis or violence, the effect of moving away to a medium or long shot deepens the sympathy for the characters. His best known work is *Ugetsu Monogatari* (1953. *Tales of the Pale Moon after Rain*) based on two 16th century ghost stories told in beautiful and intense images with the underlying theme of women's endurance and love. Other masterpieces are *Sisters of the Gion* (1936), *The Story of the Last Chrysanthemum* (1939), *The Life of O'Haru* (1952), *Sansho, the Bailiff* (1954), and his first colour film, *The Empress Yang Kwei Fei* (1955). His last work, *Street of Shame* (1956) returns to the contemporary subject of prostitution in Tokyo.

MONTGOMERY Robert

American. 1904-1981. Smooth, romantic leading actor in films from 1929. Directed five movies of which the first, *The Lady in the Lake* (1946) is the most notorious. Based on one of Raymond Chandler's finest novels, he uses a gimmicky subjective camera for Philip Marlowe so that the whole story is literally seen through his eyes. Mercifully, it is the only commercial feature to use this technique. **Others:** *Ride the Pink Horse* (47), *Once More, My Darling* (49), *Eye Witness* (50), *The Gallant Hours* (60).

MORRISSEY Paul

American. Born 1939. After the attempt on Andy WARHOL's life in 1968, he is credited with the direction of films that came out of the Warhol 'factory'. Narratively more conventional than Warhol's experimental movies, they have been shown commercially. The titles of the first three, featuring beefy Joe Dalessandro as a male hustler, sum them up. *Flesh* (1968), *Trash* (1970) and *Heat* (1971) are amusing camp exercises in the best of bad taste, filmed in a simple, unfussy manner. These sympathetic and direct movies peopled by junkies, hookers and drag queens were overtaken in the mid-70's by the sexploitation movie. **Others:** *Women*

in Revolt (72), *Forty Deuce* (82).

MULLIGAN Robert

American. Born 1925. If an old-fashioned liberal-minded Irish-American New York cop (as played by Pat O'Brien) directed films, Mulligan's are the type he'd make. He is, in fact, the son of a New York policeman. Graduated from directing TV dramas to his first feature, *Fear Strikes Out* (1957), Alan J. PAKULA's first production and Anthony Perkins' first starring role. A highly strung movie about the crack-up of a baseball player, it's an interesting triple debut despite being rather simple about complexes. However, what followed were a number of cosy, well-meaning, competently made sentimental dramas. A touching belief in the basic benevolence of people as in *To Kill a Mockingbird* (1963)–lawyer Gregory Peck defends a black accused of rape in a small Southern town, and *Up the Down Staircase* (1967) was schoolteacher Sandy Dennis overcoming hostility from delinquent pupils, tends towards easy solutions and even complacency. *Summer of '42* (1971), about a young boy's sexual education, has soft-focus photography, a soft-hearted screenplay and soft-centred direction. **Also:** *The Rat Race* (60), *Come September* (61), *The Spiral Road* (62), *Love with the Proper Stranger* (63), *Baby, the Rain Must Fall* (65), *Inside Daisy Clover* (66), *The Other* (72), *Same Time Next Year* (78).

MUNK Andrzej

Polish. 1921–1961. After only three features and in the midst of a fourth, one of Poland's most promising directors was killed in a car crash. The amputated film, *The Passenger* (1961) showed every sign of being his best. Three episodes were put together plus a montage of stills with music and commentary over. The powerful and haunting sequences take place in Auschwitz, told in flashback on board a liner where a former female guard meets one of her prisoners many years later. The play of past and present, guilt and memory suggested many layers of meaning. A student at Lodz Film School (at the same time as POLANSKI and SKOLIMOWSKI), he made a series of documentaries on Polish industry. *Eroica* (1957), his second feature, was an ironic two-part study of heroism during the war. **Also:** *Man on the Track* (57), *Bad Luck* (60).

MURNAU F.W. (Frederich Wilhelm)

German. 1889–1931. Real name Frederich Wilhelm Plumpe. Studied philosophy, music and art at Heidelberg. Acted with Max Reinhardt. Made his debut as film director in the year of Robert WIENE's *The Cabinet of Dr. Caligari* (1919), the first complete example of Expressionism in the cinema and a great influence on German films of the next decade. Murnau's early features were similar supernatural tales, including *Nosferatu* (1922). The first appearance on the screen of Bram Stoker's Dracula, it was pirated from the novel and different names were used. Negative film and speeded-up motion suggest a ghostly ride and the photography of Fritz Arno Wagner and the spectral, gaunt figure of Max Schreck's Count Orlock (Dracula) make it the eeriest and most magical of the genre. *The Last Laugh* (1924), although expressionistic in manner, moved nearer the Kammerspielfilm (chamber film) which dealt with ordinary people and events with an element of social criticism. The whole story of an old hotel doorman (Emil Jannings) reduced to lavatory attendant, is told without any inter–titles. The camera tracking through the hotel corridors, the distortions, the subjective shots, the drunken dream sequences make words superfluous. Jannings was the imposing star of *Tartuffe* (1925) and *Faust* (1926), lavish studio productions with imagery derived from Old Masters. The sets were constructed in pieces related to the camera set-ups to avoid any staginess. In 1926, he left for Hollywood to make *Sunrise* (1927). It tells the simple story of a farmer (George O'Brien) who tries to kill his devoted wife (Janet Gaynor) because of another woman. Memorable is the long ride on a trolly towards the city without back-projection, the farmhouse scenes lit like Dutch interiors, and the virtuoso long take as the man goes to meet the vamp at night by the lake. The blend of German and Hollywood techniques, the lighting, the fluidity of the camera and Gaynor's moving per-

Janet Gaynor and George O'Brien in Murnau's *Sunrise* (1927).

NEAME Ronald

British. Born 1921. Cinematographer from 1935 to 1945. Producer of four of David LEAN's earlier films. Despite having the dead hand of the British Film Industry in the 50's on his shoulder, his three films with Alec Guinness, *The Card* (1952), *The Horse's Mouth* (1959) and *Tunes of Glory* (1960) are lively examples of indigenous film-making. *The Prime of Miss Jean Brodie* (1968) was a good showcase for Maggie Smith's 'creme de la creme' performance, but Judy Garland deserved better for her final movie than the hackneyed, *I Could Go On Singing* (1962). Neame followed the money to America where he had a success with *The Poseidon Adventure* (1972) in which any direction was submerged by the impressive sets and special effects. **Others:** *The Million Pound Note* (53), *The Man that Never Was* (56), *The Seventh Sin* (57), *Escape from Zahrain* (61), *The Chalk Garden* (63), *Mister Moses* (64), *Gambit* (66), *Scrooge* (70), *The Odessa File* (74), *Meteor* (79), *First Monday in October* (81).

NEGULESCO Jean

American. Born 1900 in Rumania. Painter and theatrical designer in Paris. Emigrated to the USA in 1927. Joined Warners as scriptwriter in 1937. Most of the eight movies he made for them are good examples of the studio's style. *The Mask of Dimitrios* (1941), *The Conspirators* (1944) and *Three Strangers* (1946) are in the best traditions of *The Maltese Falcon* and *Casablanca*, all three featuring the irrepressable duo of Peter Lorre and Sydney Greenstreet, while *Humoresque* (1947) is a superior melodrama made with panache and starring Joan Crawford at her most predatory and John Garfield as the violinist (the hands were Isaac Stern's) she desires. Heart strings were plucked a little too hard in *Johnny Belinda* (1948) with Jane

formance make it a poetic masterpiece. However, a happy ending and some comedy scenes were imposed upon it, and his two other Hollywood films suffered greatly from studio interference. It was as a reaction to this that he and Robert FLAHERTY formed their own company and took off for the South Seas to make *Tabu* (1931). Murnau laid his own conception on the film in which he used the people and settings of a shimmering paradise of Tahiti to tell a fictional story – a young fisherman falls in love with a virgin dedicated to the gods. Murnau was killed in a car crash on his way to Paramount to take up a contract. **Also:** *Phantom* (22), *City Girl* (29).

Wyman winning the Oscar for her role as the deaf-mute. Moving over to 20th Century Fox, he was soon swallowed up by empty CinemaScope extravagances. These candy floss movies – pretty to look at and sticky inside – were generally concerned with three girls, looking for rich men (*How to Marry a Millionaire* 1953), seeking romance in Rome (*Three Coins in the Fountain* 1954), advancing their husbands' business careers (*Woman's World* 1954) or battling their way up in a firm (*The Best of Everything* 1959). **Also:** *Deep Valley* (47), *Road House* (48), *The Mudlark* (50), *Titanic* (53), *Daddy Long Legs* (55), *The Rains of Ranchipur* (55), *Boy on a Dolphin* (57), *A Certain Smile* (58), *Count Your Blessings* (59).

NEILAN Marshall
American. 1891-1958. Former film actor. Directed many of Mary Pickford's best pictures including *Rebecca of Sunnybrook Farm* (1917), *The Little Princess* (1918) and *Daddy Long Legs* (1919). The demon drink caused his downfall and he was often fired from projects because he was drunk. He was out of work by the 40's. He had a small part in KAZAN's *A Face in the Crowd* (1957), a year before his death. **Others:** *Penrod* (22), *Dorothy Vernon of Haddon Hall* (24), *Tess of the D'Urbervilles* (24), *The Lemon Drop Kid* (34).

NEILL Roy William
American. 1890-1946. Born in Ireland. Produced and directed almost all the Basil Rathbone-Nigel Bruce Sherlock Holmes movies with a nice sense of atmosphere, pace, economy and wit. **Also:** *Frankenstein Meets the Wolf Man* (43), *Black Angel* (46).

NELSON Ralph
American. Born 1916. Former stage actor, playwright, theatrical producer and TV director. His first feature, *Requiem for a Heavyweight* (1962) – an adaptation of Rod Serling's TV play which won Nelson an Emmy – is too ham-fisted and the degradation of the boxer (Anthony Quinn at his whimpering worst) is piled on too relentlessly to be moving. The same style was applied to specious Westerns (*Soldier Blue* 1969, *The Wrath of God* 1972), tearjerkers (*Soldier in the Rain* 1969, *Lillies of the Fields* 1963) and tedious comedies (*Father Goose* 1964). The tendentious *Charly* (1968) won an

Oscar for Cliff Robertson as a retarded man who gets a new brain. The director should be so lucky.

NEUMANN Kurt
German. 1908-1958. In Hollywood from 1925. Director of mostly second features. Made the first three movies of eight-year-old boy soprano Bobby Breen, RKO's answer to Shirley Temple. One of his last films was the enjoyably improbable, *The Fly* (1958) in which a scientist accidently swaps heads with a fly. **Some Titles:** *Rainbow on the River* (36), *Island of Lost Men* (39), *Tarzan and the Leopard Woman* (46), *Rocket Ship XM* (50), *Son of Ali Baba* (53), *Carnival Story* (54), *Mohawk* (56).

NEWMAN Joseph M
American. Born 1909. Mostly made competent B movie actioners. Spectacular fire-fighting sequences in *Red Skies of Montana* (1952), the bang-bang of cops and robbers in *The Human Jungle* (1954), good special effects of meteors attacking a planet in *This Island Earth* (1955) and the clash of swords in *Kiss of Fire* (1955) are enough to keep most spectators awake. **Also:** *Lucky Nick Cain* (51), *The Outcasts of Poker Flat* (52), *The Big Circus* (59), *The George Raft Story* (61).

NEWMAN Paul
American. Born 1925. A star for over sixteen years, he has directed three movies, two of which, *Rachel-Rachel* (1968) and *The Effect of the Gamma Rays on Man-in-the-Moon Marigolds* (1972) are sensitive, intelligent, over-elaborate vehicles for his wife Joanne Woodward's neurotic and comic talents. *Sometimes a Great Notion* (1971) sometimes doesn't make a great film.

NIBLO Fred
American. 1874-1948. Former stage and film actor. Started making films for Thomas INCE. Directed Douglas Fairbanks in his first swashbucklers, *The Mark of Zorro* (1920) and *The Three Musketeers* (1921), Valentino as the great toreador in *Blood and Sand* (1923), Garbo in *The Temptress* (1927) and *The Mysterious Lady* (1928) and Norma Talmadge in *Camille* (1927). The interest of these movies does not lie in the basic direction but in the personalities of the stars. The interest of *Ben Hur* (1927) is the second unit direction of B. Reeves Eason in the sea-battle (a few extras were said to have lost their lives) and in the breathtaking chariot race (copied in the 1959 version). The rest of this silent spectacle drags terribly.

NICHOLS Mike
American. Born 1931 in Berlin as Michael Igor Peschowsky. Part of a satirical cabaret act with Elaine MAY in the 50's and early 60's. One of their sketches was of a Jewish mother's shock at her son's choice of profession. 'Can you imagine me saying, "There goes my son the nurse." She might have said, 'There goes my son the movie director. First he made a picture with a lot of dirty talk with Elizabeth Taylor as Virginia Woolf or somebody. Then there was this nice Jewish boy sleeping with a shikseh called Mrs. Robinson. "Carmel knowledge", I thought was about Israel but it was about sex again. Then there's this movie about a talking fish. I tell you it's enough to break a mother's heart.' *Who's Afraid of*

Dustin Hoffman and Anne Bancroft in Nichols' *The Graduate* (1967).

Virginia Woolf? (1966) is a workable adaptation of the Edward Albee play, but it remains essentially a piece of theatre, *The Graduate* (1967) had a great appeal among middleclass college kids, but Dustin Hoffman's skin-deep rebel is now a member of the New Right, *Catch-22* (70) could possibly have worked if made by Stanley KUBRICK. **Also:** *Carnal Knowledge* (71), *The Day of the Dolphin* (73), *The Fortune* (75).

NICHOLSON Jack
American. Born 1937. An actor who embodied early 70's rebellion and has grown in stature over the years. His two movies as director have a lot in common with his own energetic, nervous, quirky and chaotic acting persona. *Drive, He Said* (1970) is a counter-culture campus comedy-drama that tries too hard to be *the* statement about America during the Vietnam war, but there are some good satirical anti-Jock moments. *Goin' South* (1978) is a comedy-Western which with more restraint on his own acting and the mannered camerawork (Nestor Almendros) would have been more effective.

NORMAN Leslie
British. Born 1911. Producer-director. Father of Barry Norman, fast-talking film pundit on British TV. *The Night My Number Came Up* (1956) and *X-The Unknown* (1957) are modest but effective thrillers, but the big-production *Dunkirk* (58) was flatly directed. **Also:** *The Shiralee* (58), *The Long and the Short and the Tall* (60), *Summer of the 17th Doll* (61).

NUGENT Elliot
American. Born 1900. Broadway actor and playwright in the 20's. Went to Hollywood as an actor and writer in 1929. From 1934, directed mostly at Paramount concentrating on comedy. Harold Lloyd's penultimate movie, *Professor Beware* (1938) is a hectic farce; five films with Bob Hope included *The Cat and the Canary* (1939), a reasonably good remake of Paul LENI's 1927 old, dark house movie; and Danny Kaye made his St Vitus Dance debut in *Up in Arms* (1944), the highlight being Kaye's patter song, 'Manic-Depressive Pictures Presents', the very opposite of Nugent's carefree pictures. Away from the Hopes, the Crosbys and Kayes, he made some genuinely poetic little romantic comedies such as *Two Alone* (1934).

Some titles: *Three-cornered Moon* (33), *The Great Gatsby* (1949), an unpretentious, anecdotal approach to the novel with Alan Ladd in the title role, was more watchable than the hollow glitter of the 1974 version; *Love in Bloom* (35), *Enter Madame* (35), *Splendor* (35), *My Favorite Brunette* (47), *Welcome Stranger* (47), *My Girl Tisa* (48), *Mr Belvedere Goes to College* (49), *Just for You* (52).

OLIVIERA Manoel de
Portuguese. Born 1908. Spent most of his life managing the family factory of industrial machinery. The six features he has made since 1942 have been unknown until recently. Each of his films is stylistically different although they are tenuously linked by the theme of doomed love. *Past and Present* (1972) is a bourgeois family drama told with black humour, the camera roaming around the talkative characters in their opulent settings. The camera hardly moves in *Francisca* (1981), but the rich, beautifully composed colour images are never static throughout its 2¾ hours. These many-layered films are some of the most original of the last decade. **Also:** *Ill-Fated Love* (1978).

OLIVIER Laurence
British. Born 1907. This great actor's main contribution to cinema are his three Shakespearean films in which he played the title roles. The best, *Henry V* (1945), made on the eve of Britain's invasion of occupied France, made much of the patriotic

Laurence Olivier as *Hamlet* (1948).

fervour of the play. Splendidly photographed by Robert Krasker with effective music by William Walton, it opens in the Globe Theatre in Elizabethan London and when the Chorus invites us to take 'imagined wing', the film shifts to France with stylised sets derived from medieval paintings. The Battle of Agincourt, however, inspired by Uccello and EISENSTEIN's *Alexander Nevsky*, was filmed on location. The film comes full circle at the end, returning to the 'Wooden O'. *Hamlet* (1948) is somewhat reduced to a tragedy of 'a man who couldn't make up his mind', but Olivier's masculine Prince, the use of the soliloquies as interior monologues and the atmospheric set, carry the drama. As *Richard III* (1955) he gives his greatest screen performance in one of the best productions (stage or screen) one could wish to see. The *Prince and the Showgirl* (1957) needed a LUBITSCH to give it life. It is an insipid romance between Olivier (at his mannered worst) and a bewildered Marilyn Monroe.

A scene from Ernanno Olmi's *The Tree of Wooden Clogs* (1978).

OLMI Ernanno
Italian. Born 1931. Worked for many years in the film section of the film section of Edison-volta. There he made over forty documentaries on the workers at the plant. His first feature, *Time Stood Still* (1959) was financed by the company. A virtual two-hander, it was shot during winter at a hydro-electric dam in the mountains and meticulously describes the existence of two men guarding the dam. The use of non-actors and real settings puts him squarely in the Italian Neo-Realist tradition, while avoiding the tendency to preach or sentimentalize the characters. *Il Posto* (1961 – The Job) used the Edison building and its employees in a humourous and astute study of white-collar workers, contrasting the dehumanization of the work with their humanity. *I Fidanzati* (1963 – The Engagement) concerns the separation of a young engaged couple when the man has to go to Sicily for work, subtly highlighting the problems of industrialism. When he moved higher up the social scale or used professional actors as in the reverent *A Man Called John* (1965 – Rod Steiger as Pope John XXIII) he was less original or convincing. *The Tree of Wooden Clogs* (1978), a three-hour study on peasant life in Bergamo in North Italy at the end of the 19th century, was based on stories told to him by his grandmother. He does not impose an interpretation on the hard life they led, letting the real peasants, speaking in their own dialect, re-enact the life of their forebears. **Others**: *One Fine Day* (68), *In the Summertime* (71), *The Circumstance* (74).

OPHULS Marcel
French. Born 1927 in Germany. Son of Max OPHULS. Assistant to his father on *Lola Montes* (1955). After two minor features, he joined French TV (ORTF) where he made a 3½ hour documentary on the Munich crisis juxtaposing newsreels and interviews, a technique he continued throughout his other work. *The Sorrow and the Pity* (1969) was commissioned by ORTF who declined to show it. Its 4½ hours of newsreel footage and extended interviews build up a complex picture of Clermont-Ferrand during the German Occupation. Collaborators, resistance fighters, observers and leaders all come before the camera to reveal things unspoken of in public before. *A Sense of Loss* (1972) on the people in Ulster and *The Memory of Justice* (1975) which compares German war crimes with Algeria and Vietnam attempts more to persuade than to reveal.

OPHULS Max
German. 1902-1957. Real name Max Oppenheimer. At the beginning of *La Ronde* (1950), the Master of Ceremonies (Anton Walbrook) walks through a film studio onto a fin-de-siècle set, changes into an opera cloak, begins to sing an Oscar Strauss waltz and spins a merry-go-round. He is Ophuls's alter ego and the films are merry-go-rounds, moving to the sound of a waltz or a rondo capricio as the camera tracks and circles. A masked dancer sweeps into a dance hall in *Le Plaisir* (1952) the camera moving with him, he whirls and whirls as the music gets livelier until he falls. In the centre of a huge circus ring, the ringmaster (Peter USTINOV) cracks his whip, as *Lola Montès* (1955) reminisces and the camera revolves 360 degrees to reveal her past. The past and present are joined like the couples in *La Ronde* changing partners and the earrings of *Madam De . . .* (1953) are passed from hand to hand until they come full circle. The past returns in *Liebelei* (1932) as the camera tracks around the room where the dead couple were happy, she having jumped to her death after he is killed in a duel. Similarly, the past is relived as the concert pianist reads the *Letter from an Unknown Woman* (1948) who is dead, and for whom he will be killed in a duel. Love is Ophuls' theme and, as it is transitory, it exists in the past, the tracking, circling camera suggests time passing. He does not wallow in nostalgia but summons up 19th Century Vienna or the Second Empire as part of the whirl of destiny in a danse macabre. After five films in Germany including *The Bartered Bride* (1932), the Smetana opera, and *Liebelei*, less ironic than the Arthur Schnitzler play, but with more emphasis on music and sound than dialogue, he made eight films in France. Sometimes, like Viennese coffee, there's much whipped cream on top of the bitterness. In 1941, he went to America where the only film he made that suggests the European period

Fernand Gravey and Danielle Darrieux in Max Ophuls' *La Ronde* (1950).

was *Letter from an Unknown Woman*, in which turn-of-the-century Vienna is lovingly created. *Caught* (1949) and *The Reckless Moment* (1949) are two suspenseful melodramas both with James Mason as romantic doctor and slimy blackmailer respectively, rare instances of Ophuls dealing with a contemporary setting. Returning to Paris in 1949, he made *La Ronde* with a terrific French cast making a meal out of Vienna Schnitzler, *Le Plaisir* based on three Maupassant stories, *Madame De . . .*, a witty confection and his final and best film, *Lola Montès*, the only one in colour. With an extraordinary treatment of space on the Cinema-Scope screen (using masking and other devices), it tells the story of Lola (Martine Carol), now a circus attraction, in a series of flashbacks of her love affairs with Liszt, a student and King Ludwig of Bavaria. The crane shots and elaborate camera movements have the virtuosity of a Liszt sonata. **Also:** *La Signora di Tutti* (34), *Divine* (35), *La Tendre Ennemie* (36), *Werther* (38), *De Mayerling`a Sarajevo* (40), *The Exile* (47).

OSHIMA Nagisa

Japanese. Born 1932. Graduated in law. Former editor and scriptwriter. Started directing at the time of the French New Wave and came under their influence, especially GODARD's. His first film to gain a reputation abroad was *Death by*

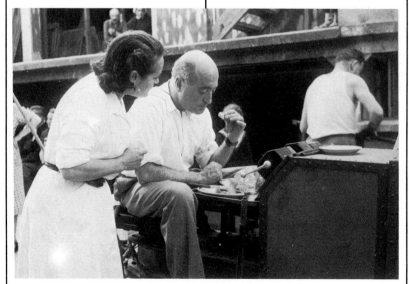

Max Ophuls taking a break on the set of *Le Plaisir* (1952).

Hanging (1968). Beginning like a documentary on the death penalty, it becomes more and more unreal when the condemned man's body refuses to die. Using Brechtian intertitles, the characters act out the man's story. Colour, black and white-inter-titles and Brechtian–type songs make up *The Diary of a Shinjuka Thief* (1969). *Boy* (1969), structurally more conventional, tells of how a boy's parents train him to be knocked down by cars so they can sue the drivers and *The Ceremony* (1971) uses the oppressive family as a microcosm of Japanese society. They are all stimulating, irritating, provocative and chilling metaphors of present-day Japanese values. More commercially successful was *In the Realm of the Senses* (1976) which, for many, is in the realm of pornography, dealing with the obsessive love-making between a gangster and a prostitute. Sex and death are linked, ending with her castrating him. His control of the medium is evident in *The Empire of the Passions* (1978), a ghost story set at the turn of the century, but the social conviction and complexity of his earlier films seems to have evaporated and he now keeps one eye on the audience's emotions and the other on the box-office.

OSWALD Gerd
American. Born 1916 in Germany. Son of German director Richard Oswald. Among the fourteen movies he made between 1956 and 1970, only two need detain us. *A Kiss Before*

Dying (1956) is a compelling, ironic thriller with Robert Wagner as a psychopathic momma's boy who kills his pregnant girl-friend and *Crime of Passion* (1957), a superbly paced film noir. Barbara Stanwyck kills the boss of her husband, nice cop Sterling Hayden, and Sterling, investigating the murder, closes in on his wife. It makes one wonder how an industry can allow a man who directed these two movies to make *Screaming Mimi* (1958) with Anita Ekberg and Gypsy Rose Lee, *Paris Holiday* (1958) a feeble farce with Bob Hope and Fernandel, and the painful *Bunny O'Hare* (1970) with bank robbers Bette Davis and Ernest Borgnine dressed as hippies. Leaving the debris behind him, Oswald went into TV. **Also:** *Valerie* (57), *Brainwashed* (61).

OZU Yasujiro
Japanese. 1903-1963. Joined the Shochiku Film Company in 1923 as assistant and writer, remaining with them for the rest of his career. He never married and lived with his mother all his life. He tried to use the same actors and technicians from film to film. Kogo Noda wrote almost all the screenplays and the actor Chishu Ryu appeared in all but two of his fifty-four films. Almost the same age as Ozu, Ryu often played the director's alter ego. Stylistically and thematically the films are very much alike and even their titles are confusingly similar: *Late Spring* (1949), *Early Summer* (1951), *Early Spring* (1956), *Late Autumn* (1960), *Early Autumn* (1961), *An Autumn Afternoon* (1962). The seasons in the titles refer to the age of the main characters. Apart from his early films which were light, ironic comedies, all his films are about middle-class family relationships told through the traditional Japanese concept of 'sympathetic sadness'. He has no interest in plots, it is the interplay of the characters that absorbs him. After 1930, he never used a dissolve. The camera moves seldom, remaining fixed about three feet from the floor at the level of the eyes of the people sitting. Each sequence is of great formal beauty, often punctuated by short exterior shots and intensified by music. Ozu never used the wide screen and came to sound and colour late. It is difficult to describe an Ozu film without making it sound dull, inert and trivial. But, within his chosen parameters, they are rich in humour, emotion, psychological and social insights. His is one of the most consistent and rewarding oeuvres in cinema. **Other titles:** *The Flavour of Green Tea over Rice* (52), *Tokyo Story* (53), *Twilight in Tokyo* (57), *Equinox Flower* (58), *Good Morning* (59).

Ozu's *Good Morning* (1959).

PABST G.W. (Georg Wilhelm)
Austrian. 1887-1967. Acted and directed in the theatre. Interned in France during World War I. It is per-

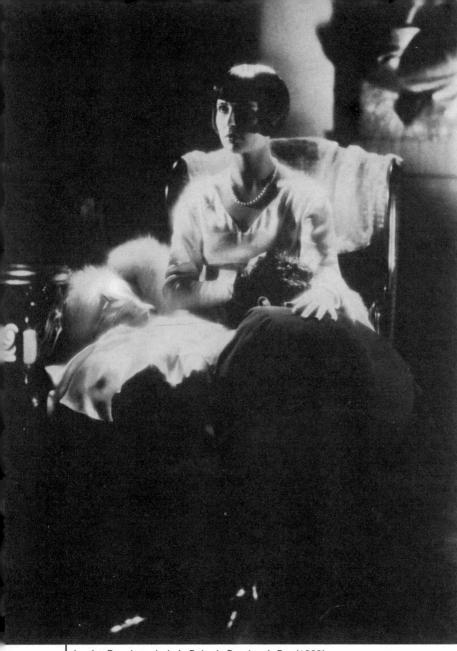

Louise Brooks as Lulu in Pabst's *Pandora's Box* (1928).

haps unfair to Pabst that when one recalls his best films, the actresses in them spring to mind. The 20-year-old Greta Garbo on the brink of prostitution contrasted with the middleaged, fallen woman Asta Nielsen in *Joyless Street* (1925), Brigitte Helm uncharacteristically cast as the lonely blind girl in *The Love of Jeanne Ney* (1927), Lotte Lenya in *The Threepenny Opera* (1931) and, above all, Louise Brooks in *Pandora's Box* (1928) and *Diary of a Lost Girl* (1929). Coming out of a Germany of rapid inflation and the rise of Nazism, these depictions of human degradation in a corrupt society reveal Pabst's left-wing sympathies. *Joyless Street*, despite its melodramatic story, seemed to bring a change from Expressionism to Realism in the German cinema. The coolly observed

descent of a middle-class girl (Garbo) forced into prostitution caused the film to be banned in Britain and cut in other countries. It was after seeing Louise Brooks in Howard HAWKS' *A Girl in Every Port* (1928) that Pabst asked her to play Lulu, the woman who destroys men and meets her death at the hands of Jack the Ripper, in *Pandora's Box*, adapted from two of Franz Wedekind's plays. The black, bobbed hair framing a pale kittenish face, the intense eroticism of each expression and gesture, has made her one of the icons of the cinema and inspired Pabst to his greatest film. *Diary of a Lost Girl* again explores the social and economic breakdown of post-war Germany with its depiction of a girls' reform school and the inevitable brothel. Brecht and Kurt Weill were to do the screenplay for

The Threepenny Opera, but their desire to give it even more anti-bourgeois bite than the stage version, proved too strong for Pabst and the film company. The realism doesn't work as well against the stylised settings, but the performances and songs retain much of the pungency of the original. Both *Westfront 1918* (1930) and *Kameradschaft* (1931) plead the cause of international brotherhood, using the French and German languages. The former ends with a French soldier clutching the hand of a dead German and the latter tells of German miners rescuing their French comrades trapped in a mine on the French-German border. From a cynical 1980's standpoint, they now seem naive and do not have enough visual impact to sustain them. In France from 1934 he made interesting commercial films including *Don Quichotte* (1934), episodes from the novel punctuated with songs, starring the great Russian bass Chaliapin. Returning for family reasons to Vienna in 1939, he made three historical films under the Nazis. As an atonement his last films were about anti-semitism (*The Trial* – 1948) and Hitler's final hours in *The Last Ten Days* (1955).

PAGNOL Marcel

French. 1894-1974. Born near Marseilles. A popular playwright and screenwriter before directing his first films. In the beginning, he considered the sound cinema as a means of getting his plays seen by millions, but once in the business he devoted himself almost entirely to films. In 1934, he set up his own film company and studios near Marseilles. From there came a series of films redolent of the sights and sounds of Provence; the rich Southern accents, the sun-bleached hills, the vineyards, anisette, the chirping of crickets, petanque. The scripts were by himself, original or adapted from his plays, or from Jean Giono stories, with music by Vincent Scotto and featuring Raimu, Fernandel, Pierre Fresnay, Charpin and Orane Demazis. The first two parts of the 'Pagnol trilogy', *Marius* (1931) and *Fanny* (1932) were directed by Alexander KORDA and Marc ALLEGRET respectively but every savorous word and incident were his. He directed the third and weakest *Cesar* (1936), the only one to have been written directly for the screen. Taking his camera out into the small towns of Provence for *Angele* (1934)

Pagnol's *The Baker's Wife* (1938).

and using direct sound, he made what Vittorio DE SICA and Roberto ROSSELLINI felt to be the first neorealist film. The backgrounds and the acting (especially by Fernandel) transcend the melodramatic plot of a fallen woman giving up her child. *The Baker's Wife* (1938) combines the best of Pagnol's humour with sympathetic characterisations of Provençal life. When the wife runs off with a young shepherd, the baker (Raimu) is too distraught to make bread. The villagers attempt to get the wife back if he promises not to reproach her. When she returns he welcomes her warmly but reviles her cat for having been away, the kind of masterstroke seen throughout his films. **Also:** *Harvest* (37), *Topaz* (51), *Manon of the Springs* (52).

PAKULA Alan J.
American. Born 1928. Majored in Drama at Yale. Worked as producer in the Warner Bros. cartoon department. Began producing feature films in 1957 with *Fear Strikes Out*, the first of seven films he produced directed by Robert MULLIGAN. His own first three pictures are psychological studies in the form of college movie (*The Sterile Cuckoo* 1969 – *Pookie* GB) with an unendurable Liza Minnelli as a crumbling Kookie, thriller (*Klute* – 1971) and romantic comedy (*Love and Pain and the Whole Damn Thing* – 1972), the whole . . . has Maggie Smith and Timothy Bottoms suffering love and pain in Spain. Gordon Willis's photography, an attempt at film noir in colour, and an 'adult' script make *Klute* more interesting than its TV series plot and situations merited. Donald Sutherland in the title role is at his most soporific as a detective investigating a murder, and Jane

Fonda pulls out all her mannerisms trying to make the middle-class call-girl believable. His two best movies are political thrillers. *The Parallax View* (1974) is an extremely disturbing no-holds-barred look at an assassination cover-up with a down–beat ending and *All the President's Men* (1976) is a more straightforward view of the complex Watergate issue, meticulously reconstructing the building up of evidence against the conspirators by the Washington Post's ace reporters, Woodward and Bernstein (Robert REDFORD and Dustin Hoffman self-consciously playing down their film star personae). However, this superior Lou Grant episode doesn't come to any significant conclusions. Jane Fonda plays Henry Fonda in a slow, incoherent Western, *Comes a Horseman* (1978) and *Starting Over* (1979) is a passable triangle comedy with the plus factor of Burt REYNOLDS, Jill Clayburgh and Candice Bergen, but Pakula still needs to prove he can deliver something more than smart commercial packages. **Also:** *Rollover* (82), *Sophie's Choice* (83).

PARADJANOV Sergei
Russian. Born 1924 in Georgia, of Armenian parents. Imprisoned in the Soviet Union in 1974 for various 'crimes'. He was released in 1977 and has not made a film since. His first, *Shadows of Our Forgotten Ancestors* (1964) shows a talent for lyrical extravagance. A copy of *The Colour of Pomegranates* (1969 – *Sayat Nova*) was smuggled into the West for a limited showing. It is an extraordinarily original visual experience, its eloquent imagery illustrating in a series of tableaux, the poems of the Georgian poet Aruthin Sayadin, who was known as Sayat Nova (1712-95).

As a friend of his remarked, 'Paradjanov made films not about how things are, but how they would have been had he been God.'

PARKER Alan
British. Born 1942. Worked in advertising for some years. made commercials, some of them spoofing old movies. His first feature, *Bugsy Malone* (1976) is rather like an extended commercial for candy with kids playing at Chicago gangsters of the 20's. Despite its inherent cuteness, the numbers are well staged (dubbed by good adult singers) and Our Gangsters are talented and likeable enough to appeal to all but paedophobes. Xenophobes are well catered for in *Midnight Express* (1978) which arrives at the sagacious conclusion that the Turks are 'a nation of pigs'. This sadomasochistic, manipulative movie is based on the true story of Billy Hayes, a young American jailed for drug smuggllng in Istanbul, but Parker's technique is as subtle as the Turkish jailors' methods of brutalising the prisoners. *Fame* (1980) begins with the good idea of following eight young people through four years at the American Academy of Performing Arts, but develops into a series of trite confessionals with awkwardly interposed musical numbers. 'Something wonderful's happening to me, mama,' says one of the budding actresses, 'I'm growing up.' Parker's attempts at growing up in his first film about adults, *Shoot the Moon* (1981) is a Kramer vs Ordinary People divorce drama, hysterically directed and acted by Albert Finney and Diane Keaton. **Also:** *The Wall* (82).

PARRISH Robert
American. Born 1916. Hollywood juvenile who appeared in a number of films including *All Quiet on the Western Front* (1930) and *City Lights* (1931). Editor and assistant director to John FORD. His first two films were fast, tough gangster movies, *The Mob* (1951) and *Cry Danger* (1951). A couple of good brooding Westerns, *Saddle the Wind* (1958) and *The Wonderful Country* (1959) survived the limited Julie London as their heroines; and Gregory Peck survives in the wilds of Burma in *The Purple Plain* (1954) after his aircraft crashes in this very British endurance movie. Parrish, however, did not survive the 60's when even his rather journeyman talents failed him. **Also:** *My Pal Gus* (52), *Lucy Gallant* (55),

Fire Down Below (57), *In the French Style* (63), *Up from the Beach* (65), *The Bobo* (67), *Duffy* (68).

PASCAL Gabriel

Hungarian. 1894-1954. Produced films in Europe before coming to England in 1935. Somehow persuaded George Bernard Shaw to sell him the film rights of his plays. He produced four films of Shaw plays, directing two of them. *Major Barbara* (1941) has an excellent cast (Wendy Hiller, Rex Harrison, Robert Morley etc), good photography (Ronald NEAME) and sets (Vincent Korda), but the opening out of the play is contrived. *Caesar and Cleopatra* (1945), despite lavish sets and costumes remains stubbornly theatrical. Nevertheless, most of the words remain intact and Claude Rains and Vivien Leigh are perfect casting. The othe two adaptations were *Pygmalion* (1938 – Anthony ASQUITH) and *Androcles and the Lion* (1952 – Chester Erskine).

PASOLINI Pier Paolo

Italian. 1922-1975. Studied art history and literature. A well-known novelist, poet, short-story writer and screenwriter before directing his first film, *Accatone* (1961) which drew on his knowledge of sub-proletarian Rome and revealed his attraction for the social outcast. Accatone is a reformed pimp who, after trying to make an honest living, takes to thieving and is killed while escaping arrest. Using non-actors, the realistic depiction of a derelict urban landscape is counterpointed ironically by the use of Bach's St. Matthew Passion on the soundtrack. *The Gospel According to St. Matthew* (1964) seemed a strange choice for a Marxist, but this is an attempt to take Christ away from the opulent church and make him into an ordinary Italian peasant, an outcast like Accatone. It was shot in Calabria using non-professional actors, including Pasolini's mother as the Virgin Mary, with every word taken directly from the scriptures. In its sombre, realistic way, it highlights other interpretations of Christ, but upholds the basic tenets of the Church. The two vagabonds in *The Hawks and the Sparrows* (1966) are caught, like many Italians, between The Church and Marxism. The couple of delightful innocents (played by Toto and Pasolini's curly-haired, clown-faced mischievous angel, Ninetto Davoli) reappear in two similar surrealist comic short films. Pasolini deals with the hated middle-classes for the first time in *Theorem* (1968) and *Pigsty* (1969). They are filmed with such calm beauty and underlying disgust that the rather silly parables gain in significance. A young man (Terence Stamp) sleeps with each member of an industrialist's family and the maid in *Theorem*. Their liberation from a bourgeois existence drives them all mad, because sex is the one thing the middle classes don't control. Similarly in *Pigsty*, an industrialist is ruined when he discovers his son's sexual attraction for pigs. This was the last of his contemporary subjects although *Oedipus Rex* (1967), while faithful to Sophocles, has a prologue and epilogue set in modern times. Ravishingly filmed in Morocco using the desert landscapes and Moorish architecture, it ends with the blind Oedipus on the arm of his daughter Antigone, walking through the streets of modern Rome like a common beggar. The trilogy, *The Decameron* (1971), *The Canterbury Tales* (1972) and *The Arabian Nights* (1974) concentrate on the more scatological episodes. Untramelled by any Freudian or religious guilt, they capture the free spirit of the originals. This uncomplicated sexuality disappears in *Salo or the 120 Days of Sodom* (1975), Pasolini's last film before he was murdered. An updating of Sade's novel to the days of the Salo Fascist Republic of 1944, it is set in a vast mansion where a party of Fascists have rounded up a group of young people to satisfy their depraved desires. An almost unbearable film to watch (if it weren't there would be something wrong with the spectator or the film) it never sets out to titillate nor does it ever relish the horrors, but clinically exposes the exploitation of human beings by others. The last ten minutes are among the most horrifying, memorable and beautiful in cinema.

PASSER Ivan

Czechoslovakian. Born 1933.

Pier Paolo Pasolini as Giotto in *The Decameron* (1972).

A typical scene from Sam Peckinpah's *The Wild Bunch* (1969).

Studied at the Prague Film School. Boyhood friend of Milos FORMAN for whom he co-wrote four films. Made two features in Czechoslovakia before leaving for the USA like Forman. *Intimate Lighting* (1966) is a tender, well-observed comedy about the everyday pleasures of life, set in a provincial town where friends meet to drink, eat, play music and reminisce. This gentle humour concealing regret continued into the harsher world of his American movies. *Born to Win* (1977) and *Law and Disorder* (1975), two comedy-dramas set in New York, didn't quite find the right blend of European and American sensibilities. By using the trappings of the film noir in *Cutter's Way* (1981), Passer has made his most cohesive American picture. Because colour is a commercial pre-requisite, it is again pressed into service to remind one of black and white in this tale of a horribly crippled Vietnam Vet (John Heard) seeking his revenge on the local bigwig whom he suspects of murder. The plot is left open-ended, but it is basically a mood piece and character study with three fervid performances from Heard, Jeff Bridges as his buddy and Lisa Eichhorn as his alcoholic wife.

PASTRONE Giovanni

Italian. 1883-1959. His biggest venture and one of the most expensive films to date was *Cabiria* (1914), a huge spectacle about the adventures of a slave girl during the Second Punic War. The titles were written by Gabriele d'Annunzio, the most famous Italian writer of the day. It contained innovations such as dolly and crane shots. Its great success in America inspired D.W. GRIFFITH to embark on his large-scale productions.

PECKINPAH Sam

American. Born 1926. Born and brought up on a ranch in California. Attended military school and had a spell in the Marines. His films reflect his background, a masculine world where one's manhood and independence can only survive through violence. Hence the nostalgia for the 'Old West' where men were men and women were nowhere. No matter how unpalatable one may find this philosophy, he expresses it with passionate intensity. The recurring theme of 'unchanged men in a changing land' appears in *Ride the High Country* (1962. *Guns in the Afternoon* GB) with Randolph Scott and Joel

McCrea as ageing gunfighters against an autumnal landscape, escorting a cargo of gold to the banks has more to do with nostalgia for the Old Western than the Old West. William Holden and his gang in *The Wild Bunch* (1969) in 1914, try to live as outlaws from another age, although the scenes of carnage reflect the year the film was made. *The Ballad of Cable Hogue* (1970) is another elegy for the West and Steve McQueen in *Junior Bonner* (1972), rather touchingly, feels an anachronism (like the director?) in the new-style West. He tries to scrape a living as a rodeo rider while his brother makes money by selling properties and exploiting the Old West for its tourist possibilities. In the end, his father (Robert Preston) leaves for Australia where he hopes to find some of the forgotten frontier values. Peckinpah's Westerns, photographed superbly by Lucian Ballard, splattered with symbols and blood, do have a lyrical disenchantment. Away from the controlling mythology of the Western, his blood-dimmed vision lacks all conviction. It is at its most unpleasant in *Straw Dogs* (1971) where the man of reason (Dustin Hoffman) is forced into violence against those who raped his wife (Susan George), exulting in the eye-for-an-eye slaughter with the complicity of the director-audience. However, as much violence has been done to his films as to his characters. He has continued a running battle with producers and film companies whom he sees as the bad guys. **Also:** *Major Dundee* (65), *The Getaway* (72), *Pat Garrett and Billy the Kid* (73), *Bring Me the Head of Alfredo Garcia* (74), *The Killer Elite* (75), *Cross of Iron* (77), *Convoy* (78).

PEERCE Larry

American. Son of opera singer Jan Peerce. His father used to sing a sentimental ballad called 'The Blue Bird of Happiness' with a sob in his voice. A number of Peerce Junior's movies are filmic equivalents of that kind of song. *One Potato, Two Potato* (1966) is quite a moving story of the problems of an inter-racial marriage, but *The Other Side of the Mountain* Parts I and II (1975 & 1978) are too self-consciously tear-jerky to feel for the woman skier paralyzed in a ski accident and her boy-friend killed in a plane crash. *Goodbye Columbus* (1969) is a good adaptation of Philip Roth's novel starring Richard Benjamin making his debut. **Also:** *The Sporting Club* (71), *A Separate Peace* (73), *Ash Wednesday* (74), *Two-Minute Warning* (76), *The Bell Jar* (78).

PENN Arthur

American. Born 1922. Studied at the Actor's Studio New York. Directed plays on TV and Broadway. Continued to alternate between stage and screen. His strong sympathy with the outsider and an anti-Establishment stance had an impact on the anti-draft, anti-Vietnam, middle-class college students at the end of the 60's. *Bonnie and Clyde* (1967) was one of the most influential American movies of the last decades in its amoral attitude to 'the outlaw' seen from a modern psychological and social viewpoint, and its recreation of the Depression era (sepia photographs, carefully selected music, decor etc). The script, the photography, the players (Warren BEATTY, Faye Dunnaway etc) and Penn's controlled direction move the black comedy ineluctably towards the much imitated ending (hundreds of bullets pump into the miscreant pair who die in slow motion). The Depression is referred to in Woody Guthrie's songs heard in *Alice's Restaurant* (1969) which mixes fact and fiction with Arlo

Faye Dunnaway and Warren Beatty in Arthur Penn's *Bonnie and Clyde* (1967).

Guthrie (Woody's son) playing himself in this extension of his talking blues, 'The Alice's Restaurant Massacree.' Its ballad form and studied improvisational technique had an obvious appeal for those who could identify with this communal haven of hippies. *Little Big Man* (1970) too-consciously views the past from a modern standpoint seeing the Cheyenne as 'ethnic' hippies contrasted favourably with white civilisation. This demystification of legends such as Custer is done in too simplistic a manner, a process begun in Penn's first feature, *The Left Handed Gun* (1958) where Paul NEWMAN plays a crazy mixed-up Billy the Kid with Method mannerisms. *The Chase* (1966) is linked in its plodding way with the law/outlaw theme of *Bonnie and Clyde* and the Billy the Kid movie, with Marlon BRANDO's fair-minded sheriff trying to stop the inhabitants of a small Texas town

from lynching Robert REDFORD. The ending echoes the killing of Lee Harvey Oswald. The Kennedy assassination and the Vietnam war underlie Penn's platitudinous portrait of those Significant Sixties in *Four Friends* (1982) about another outsider (a Yugoslav immigrant like its screenwriter Steve Tesich) growing up in an Indiana steel town, wanting a share of the American Dream. Perhaps the most significant outsider of all is the blind, deaf and dumb Helen Keller in *The Miracle Worker* (1962) desperately trying to communicate in some way. But, whatever his shortcomings, Penn is not afraid to take risks. **Also:** *Micky One* (65), *Night Moves* (75), *The Missouri Breaks* (76).

PERRY Frank

American. Born 1930. Former theatre director. His wife, Eleanor Perry wrote the screenplays for all his films up to 1970 before their divorce. *David and Lisa* (1962) and *Last Summer* (1969), both about teenagers under stress, are potentially sensitive character studies squeezed into Freudian or allegorical formulae. The parable in *The Swimmer* (1968-completed by Sydney POLLACK) of a man who swims each of his wealthy neighbour's pools, does not hold water as a comment on suburbia. (It works better in the cold print of John Cheever's story), but Burt Lancaster almost makes it convincing. The movies Perry made without his wife are self-consciously clever and fail on all counts. **Also:** *The Diary of a Mad Housewife* (70), *Doc* (71), *Play it as it Lays* (72), *Man on a Swing* (73), *Rancho Deluxe* (75), *Mommie Dearest* (81).

PETRI Elio
Italian. 1929-1979. His nine films mainly reflect the political and social climate of industrial, middle-class Italy in the 60's and early 70's. *The Assassin* (1961) and *Investigation of a Citizen above Suspicion* (1970) are the most successful, being criticisms of society by representing a corrupt police force, although they suffer from a flashy style, insistent symbolism and a superficial reading of Kafka.

PETRIE Daniel
American. Born 1920. Even camp followers of soap opera would be sorely tested by trashy efforts such as *The Bramble Bush* (1959) – a sub 'Peyton Place', *Stolen Hours* (1963) a cloying remake of *Dark Victory*, *The Idol* (1966), *Buster and Billie* (1974) and *The Betsy* (1977). **Also:** *A Raisin in the Sun* (61), *The Main Attraction* (62), *The Spy with the Cold Nose* (67), *The Neptune Factor* (73), *Lifeguard* (75), *Fort Apache, the Bronx* (81), *Six Pack* (82).

PEVNEY Joseph
American. Born 1920. Former stage and film actor. Worked mostly for Universal Pictures. If the names Jeff Chandler, George Nader and Julie Adams cause any frisson, then Pevney's commonplace action movies are just the thing. Chandler's grey, curly hair and earnest tanned features were seen in over half a dozen of his movies; boxing to kill in *The Iron Man* (1951), winning Rhonda Fleming with a sword in *Yankee Pasha* (1954), wooing Jane Russell in *Foxfire* (1955) and winning

the war in *Away All Boats* (1956). For the rest, there were bland, family comedies, including *Tammy and the Bachelor* (1957) with Debbie Reynolds. *Man of a Thousand Faces* (1957) contains an excellent performance from James Cagney as Lon Chaney, but the lustreless direction fails to recapture the style of the period or Chaney's movies. In the 60's, he went into TV which probably suits his conveyor-belt type direction. **Also:** *Meet Danny Wilson* (51), *Twilight for the Gods* (58), *Cash McCall* (60), *The Crowded Sky* (60).

PIALAT Maurice
French. Born 1925. Working within the naturalistic tradition and using an unobtrusive camera and discreet editing, he studies the everyday existence of ordinary people, generally at a moment of crisis. In *L'Enfance Nue* (1968) a foster child takes to petty crime, *Nous ne Veillirons pas Ensemble* (1972) shows the break-up of a marriage and *La Gueule Ouverte* (*The Mouth Agape* 74) harrowingly describes how a family copes when faced with a mother dying of cancer. The technique sometimes becomes lax as when he allows the rather empty young people to have their head in *Passe Ton Bac d'Abord* (1976), but is effective in the Zolaesque *Loulou* (1981) where a girl (Isabelle Hupert) leaves her middle-class husband and takes up with an unemployed lay-about (Gerard Depardieu) because he's good in bed. He seems to work equally well with stars and unknowns.

PICHEL Irving
American. 1891-1954. Acted in many films at Paramount from 1930 to 1939. The only film of much interest he directed (with Ernest B. SCHOEDSACK) was his first, an excellent atmospheric thriller, *The Most Dangerous Game* (1932. *The Hounds of Zaroff* – GB). The game of the title refers to the hunting of people like animals by a crazy sportsman, but also to man being the most dangerous beast to hunt. Most of his other movies are sentimental comedies and minor melodramas made during the 40's, generally related to the effects of the war such as *The Pied Piper* (1942) with Monty Woolley leading children away from the Nazis and *The Moon is Down* (1943), based on Steinbeck's novel about the German occupation of Norway. **Also:** *A Medal for Benny*

(45), *Tomorrow is Forever* (46), *The Bride Wore Boots* (46), *Temptation* (46), *Mr Peabody and the Mermaid* (48), *Destination Moon* (50).

PIERSON Frank R.
American. Born 1925. Wrote a number of good screenplays, notably *Dog Day Afternoon* (1975). His first movie was a murky spy thriller, *The Looking Glass War* (1969) based on John Le Carré, and his third, *King of the Gypsies* (1979), a hopelessly muddled load of crystal balls. He took over from Jerry SCHATZBERG during the shooting of *A Star is Born* (1976) and was just an obedient chauffeur on this over-weening Barbra Streisand ego-trip.

POITIER Sidney
American. Born 1924. The first black actor to break away from the demeaning pop-eyed negro stereotypes. The films he directed and starred in were aimed at a black middle-class family audience. The best were *Uptown Saturday Night* (1974) and *Let's Do It Again* (1975), two amusing black buddy-buddy movies with Bill Cosby and Poitier. Both were box–office smashes, but they have only prepared the way for more ambitious black directors. **Also:** *Buck and the Preacher* (1971), *A Warm December* (1972), *A Piece of the Action* (77), *Stir Crazy* (81).

POLANSKI Roman
French (Naturalized). Born 1933 in Paris of Polish parents. They returned to Poland inopportunely and were sent to a concentration camp where his mother died. No wonder his films, told with the absurdist

Roman Polanski

107

humour that comes out of adversity, make little distinction between nightmare and reality. 'This is not a dream. It is reality,' Mia Farrow screams in *Rosemary's Baby* (1968) when she believes she has been impregnated by Satan. We witness the 'reality' of Catherine Deneuve's breakdown as the walls of her room come alive and a man rapes her in *Repulsion* (1965). The totally realistic settings of New York (*Rosemary's Baby*), London (*Repulsion*), Paris (*The Tenant* – 1976) and Los Angeles (*Chinatown* – 1974) gradually become horrifying deathtraps. Like the figure of K in Kafka's novels, the victim in each case uncomprehendingly believes himself to be partly responsible. Polanski himself plays the tormented K character in *The Tenant*, and in *The Fearless Vampire Killers* (1967. *Dance of the Vampires* – GB) he is trapped in a Transylvanian castle with vampires, one of them played by his wife Sharon Tate. In 1969, Sharon Tate was brutally murdered in macabre circumstances by the demonic disciples of Charles Manson in their Hollywood home. Two years later, Polanski was showing the gruesome murders in *Macbeth* (1971), the most blood-soaked of all Shakespeare's plays and one with an undercurrent of supernaturally evil forces. 'Fair is foul and foul is fair,' expresses Polanski's world and life is art and art is life. His second role as K was played at his arrest and trial in Hollywood for apparently having had sex with a girl of thirteen. In *Knife in the Water* (1962), his only Polish feature, a simple sailing trip turns into an absurdist drama of sexual rivalry. *Repulsion* is on sexual disgust, *Cul-de-Sac* (1966) on sexual humiliation, *What?* (1972) has an Alice in a Wonderland of sexual perversions and incest is played up at the end of *Chinatown*. Married couples are disturbed (in two senses) by an intruder or intruders in *Knife in the Water*, *Cul-de-Sac*, *Rosemary's Baby* and *Macbeth*. Polanski started as an actor on stage and in films (he appeared in four of Andrzej WADJA's). He spent five years at the Lodz film school. His first short films were influenced by surrealism and the theatre of the absurd, a strain that continued into his feature films. **Also:** *Tess* (79).

POLLACK Sydney
American. Born 1934. Former TV actor and director. His glossy commercial movies about important

Michael Sarrazin and Jane Fonda in Sydney Pollack's *They Shoot Horses, Don't They?* (1969).

social issues are made by someone who wishes to be considered a serious Hollywood artist. For those who believe that is a contradiction in terms, Pollack proves them right. The basic material of the films is often daring and powerful, but in his hands it turns to pulp. *They Shoot Horses, Don't They?* (1969) has a lot of self-pitying characters suffering through a marathon dance contest in what is supposed to be a microcosm of the Depression; *The Way We Were* (1973) is the worst kind of radical chic, being neither radical nor chic and *Bobby Deerfield* (1977) is more mawkish than morbid. As in *Three Days of the Condor* (1975) and *Absence of Malice* (1981), issues are raised in order to be skirted. Robert REDFORD appears in four of Pollack's movies and his good-looking, superficial earnestness perfectly reflects the films themselves. **Also:** *This Property is Condemned* (66), *The Scalphunters* (68), *Castle Keep* (68), *Jeremiah Johnson* (72), *The Yakuza*

(75), *Tootsie* (82).

POLONSKY Abraham
American. Born 1910. Wrote the script for Robert ROSSEN's *Body and Soul* (1947) after working as a journalist and on radio. His first film *Force of Evil* (1949) seemed to promise an interesting career, but it had hardly been released when he was blacklisted by the studios following the McCarthy anti-communist hearings. It was twenty years before he directed another picture. *Force of Evil* is a complex, rather impenetrable, film noir built poetically into an allegory of capitalism. It was too long an absence to pick up where he let off, but *Tell Them Willie Boy is Here* (1969) is a forceful Western despite its rather weighted Message. **Also:** *Romance of a Horse Thief* (1971).

PONTECORVO Gillo
Italian. Born 1919. His documentary film experience came in useful for his best known film, *The Battle of Algiers*

(1965). Banned in France for some years, it is a reasonably balanced and telling account of Algeria's fight for independence, made in a pseudo-documentary style, mixing actors with the actual participants. *Kapo* (1960) strains towards documentary realism, but the concentration camp setting is disagreeably used as a background to a bad melodrama. **Also:** *Queimada* (1968).

PORTER Edwin S.
American. 1869-1941. Born in Scotland. Made many films for the Edison Company. *The Great Train Robbery* (1903) was the first American film to tell a definite story. Its ten minutes contain fourteen scenes, each continuous and unedited, and filmed in a long shot except the final scene when the gang-leader is revealed in close-up firing at the audience. It was the most successful and influential of early films. D.W. GRIFFITH made his screen debut as an actor in *Rescued from the Eagles's Nest* (1907) which includes close-ups and cross-cutting. By the time Porter made his last film in 1915, he was completely overshadowed by the films of Griffith.

POST Ted
American. Born 1925. Former TV director. His films are slick, sick and second-hand. *Hang 'Em High* (1968) is a stringy American spaghetti Western with hang-dog Clint EASTWOOD out to get those who tried to hang him; *Beneath the Planet of the Apes* (1970) is beneath *The Planet of the Apes*; *Magnum Force* (1973), script by John MILIUS and Michael CIMINO, the second Dirty Harry movie with Clint Eastwood, is a repulsive two hours of relentless bloodletting; *Whiffs* (1975) with Elliott Gould is T*R*A*S*H; and *Go Tell the Spartans* (1978) or tell it to the marines, is an ordinary war movie but the Vietnam setting gave it a topical kick. **Also:** *The Baby* (73), *The Harrad Experiment* (73) *Good Guys Wear Black* (79).

POTTER H.C.
American. Born 1904. Former Broadway director. Came to Hollywood in 1935 and in over twenty years made a number of pleasant comedies, a few weepies and tepid musicals. *Hellzapoppin* (1941), one of the looniest of American movies, never really goes far enough but much of

Olsen and Johnson's anarchic gags from their Broadway show remain as well as quite a few cinematic ones. Less frantic but equally funny is *Mr Blandings Builds His Dream House* (1948) with Cary Grant and Myrna Loy struggling against architects, lawyers and builders in an attempt to get their suburban retreat built. His best weepie was *Shopworn Angel* (1938) with the ever-suffering Margaret Sullavan in the title role and James Stewart as the naive soldier who doesn't know she's shopworn. It begins with a splendid World War I montage by Slavko Vorkapich. **Also:** *The Story of Vernon and Irene Castle* (39), *Blackmail* (39), *Second Chorus* (40), *Mr Lucky* (43), *The Farmer's Daughter* (47), *The Time of Your Life* (48), *The Miniver Story* (50), *Three for the Show* (55).

POWELL Michael
British. Born 1905. Assistant to Rex INGRAM at his Nice studios.

(Left to right) Leonide Massine, Anton Walbrook and Eric Berry in Powell (and Pressburger's) *The Red Shoes* (1948).

Michael Powell

Worked with Alfred HITCHCOCK in the late 20's. In 1939, he collaborated with the Hungarian scriptwriter Emeric Pressburger for the first time on *The Spy in Black*, thus beginning one of the closest creative partnerships in cinema. So close was their working relationship that, although Pressburger's contribution was mostly writing and Powell was in charge on the studio floor, they received joint directorial credit on their films from 1939 to 1956. This may account for their curious blend of the very British with the very Middle-European. There is a mystical love for the nation in *A Canterbury Tale* (1944) and *I Know Where I'm Going* (1945), patriotism and courage in *One of Our Aircraft is Missing* (1942) and *The Small Back Room* (1948) and yet the most sympathetic characters in *The Spy in Black* (1939), *Contraband* (1940 and *The Life and Death of Colonel Blimp* (1943) are Germans. *A Matter of Life and Death* (1946), *The Red Shoes* (1948) and *The Tales of Hoffmann* (1951) are closer to the world of Vincente MINNELLI's Hollywood musicals, influenced themselves by European design, than to any British film. In fact, all their films go against the British realist tradition. Out of the twelve they made between 1943 and 1956, nine were in colour. The sensuous use of Technicolor (photography by Jack CARDIFF or Christopher Challis), the flamboyant sets and designs (Hein Heckroth and Alfred Junge) help to make for eccentric, extravagent, intelligent, witty fantasies. Junge's sets for *Black Narcissus* (1947) breathtakingly create the atmosphere of a convent high up in

the Himalayas where the nuns struggle against desire. A heady mixture of religion and eroticism also runs through the wondrously strange *A Canterbury Tale*. Powell's most fascinating solo effort *Peeping Tom* (1959) about a psychopathic murderer who photographs his women victims at the moment of their death, is rich in levels of interpretation. (Powell himself appears in it as a cruel father.) In 1941, Powell and Pressburger formed Archer Films which began with an arrow hitting the bull's-eye of a target. There are few British directors who have aimed so high and hit the bull's eye so often. Francis Ford COPPOLA installed Powell in his Zeotrope studios as adviser. **Also:** *The 49th Parallel* (41), *Gone to Earth* (50, *The Wild Heart* – USA), *The Elusive Pimpernel* (50), *The Battle of the River Plate* (56), *Honeymoon* (58), *The Queen's Guards* (61).

PREMINGER Otto

American. Born 1906 in Vienna, Austria. His father was a Public Prosecutor so he watched many trials as a young man. Worked as an actor and assistant to Max Reinhardt. Went to the USA in 1935. Signed a contract with Fox in 1943 as producer-director where he stayed for ten years. His best films were the moody, ambiguous, enclosed crime melodramas of the 40's and early 50's. Using a cool interrogatory method, they are puzzles put together like pieces of evidence in a trial where the interest lies not in the verdict but in the characters who reveal themselves through their obsessions. The director never sits in judgement, hardly ever getting beyond a reasonable doubt. A dreamlike atmosphere is contrasted with the prosaic investigations of murder in the haunting *Laura* (1944), detective Dana Andrews falls in love with the 'dead' Laura (Gene Tierney) from her portrait, her perfume and the title song; *Fallen Angel* (1945), Dana Andrews is the murder suspect; *Whirlpool* (1949), Gene Tierney under hypnotic influence is suspected of murder. Andrews and Tierney come together again in *Where the Sidewalk Ends* (1950) in which he is a cop guilty of murder. A whole town is put on trial in *The Thirteenth Letter* (1951) and the sequence of these masterfully narrated thrillers ends with *Angel Face* (1952), Jean Simmons giving her finest performance as the murderess in the ambivalent title

L to R: Clifton Webb, Vincent Price, Judith Anderson, Dana Andrews and Gene Tierney (in painting) in Preminger's *Laura* (1944).

role. Less interestingly, trials in a court are more central to later films such as *The Court Martial of Billy Mitchell* (1955. *One Man Mutiny* – GB), *Saint Joan* (1957) and *Anatomy of a Murder* (1959). In the latter, we are not told whether the accused (Ben Gazzara) is really guilty or not. His movies after becoming an independent producer in 1953 are an odd lot, generally given a boost by Saul Bass's credit titles and posters. *The Moon is Blue* (1953), once thought daring because it used the words 'virgin' and 'seduce' (it was banned in several States) is a tame, stagey comedy. *The Man with the Golden Arm* (1956) also had trouble with censorship because of its treatment of drug addiction. Its seedy atmosphere, jazz score and Frank Sinatra and Kim Novak's performances still pack a certain punch, even though the attitudes are outdated. Preminger discovered Jean Seberg and put her in the inadequate *Saint Joan* and in the

elegant, CinemaScope, black and white/colour soap opera, *Bonjour Tristesse* (1958). His over-long comic-strip epics on huge subjects (*Advise and Consent* – 1962 on American politics, *The Cardinal* 1963 on religion, *In Harm's Way* 1964 on War and *Exodus* 1960 on the birth of Israel) try to please all of the people all of the time. One sympathises with Mort Sahl's cry half-way through *Exodus* of 'Let my people go!' The films of the last few years have been unqualified disasters, except the brilliantly harsh comedy, *Such Good Friends* (1971). **Also:** *Centennial Summer* (46), *Forever Amber* (47), *Daisy Kenyon* (47), *Lady Windermere's Fan* (49), *River of No Return* (54), *Carmen Jones* (54), *Porgy and Bess* (59), *Bunny Lake is Missing* (65), *Hurry Sundown* (67), *Skidoo* (68), *Tell me you love me, Julie Moon* (68), *Rosebud* (75), *The Human Factor* (79).

PRÉVERT Pierre

French. Born 1906. Director, actor and scriptwriter. Appeared in Luis BUNUEL's *L'Age d'Or* (1930). *L'Affaire est dans le Sae* (1932) and *Voyage Surprise* (1946) are two delightful medium-length satirical burlesques written by his brother Jacques Prévert

PUDOVKIN V. (Vsevolod)

Russian. 1893-1953. Studied at the Moscow State Film School under KULESHOV. Published two very influential books on the cinema, 'Film Technique' and 'Film Acting'. His dynamic montage is used to great comic effect in a short film, *Chess Fever* (1925) which combines shots from the actual Chess championships with a fictional narrative. His first feature, *Mother* (1926) takes Gorky's rambling novel and turns it into a tightly constructed narrative. It tells of a mother's conversion to communism during the abortive 1905 Revolution. Water is a constant visual metaphor as in the scene of blocks of ice flowing rapidly in the river as the May Day demonstrators run through the streets. Taking the same subject as EISENSTEIN's *October* (1927), *The End of St. Petersburg* (1927) is more human and less stylised. Showing the effect of the events of 1917 on an uneducated peasant boy, it has an emotional impact. His last great silent film was *Storm Over Asia* (1928) which tells the story of a Mongolian nomad who, discovering he is heir to Genghis Khan, leads his people against the British occupying forces. (It was banned in Britain for some years.) It ends with a tremendous storm symbolizing revolutionary forces. A film of visual beauty (photographed by Anatoli Golovnya, as were the others), humour and compassion. Pudovkin was never very happy with sound. In 1935, he was injured in a car crash and did not work for a long period. When he returned to directing, the world had changed and his films were historical reconstructions that toed the Party line.

A scene from Pudovkin's *Storm Over Asia* (1928).

QUINE Richard

American. Born 1920. Hollywood juvenile and dancer in films such as *Babes on Broadway* (1941) and *My Sister Eileen* (1942). Spent ten years directing at Columbia. Six of his first eleven movies were so-so musicals co-written with Blake EDWARDS, including two starring barrel-chested belter Frankie Laine (*The Sunny Side of the Street* 1951, *Rainbow Round my Shoulder* 1952) and two bargain-basement *On the Towns*, *All Ashore* (1953) and *So This is Paris* (1954). *My Sister Eileen* (1955) was the pick of the bunch due mainly to Betty Garrett and the dance direction of Bob FOSSE. His comedies up to the mid-60's were bright and breezy puffballs such as the two with Judy Holliday (*Full of Life* 1957, *The Solid Gold Cadillac* 1956) and *Sex and the Single Girl* (1964). The best of Quine were the four pictures he made with ice-cold ash-blonde Kim Novak with whom (it is plain to see) he was in love, especially two uncharacteristic dramas, *Pushover* (1954), a gripping little thriller about a cop (Fred MacMurray) falling into Novak's clutches, and *Strangers When We Meet* (1960) of adultery in suburbia. **Also:** *Drive a Crooked Road* (54), *Operation Madball* (57), *Bell, Book and Candle* (58), *It Happened to Jane* (59), *The World of Suzie Wong* (60), *The Notorious Landlady* (62), *Paris When it Sizzles* (63), *How to Murder Your Wife* (65), *Hotel* (67), *The Moonshine War* (70), *The Prisoner of Zenda* (79).

RAFELSON Bob

American. Born 1934. Nephew of Samson Raphaelson, playwright and screenwriter. In the late 60's, youth movies identified with the draft-dodging campus rebels disillusioned by their elders and the war in Vietnam. Yet, it was no James Dean that embodied this counter-culture but Jack NICHOLSON, a thirty-three-year-old actor with thinning hair and vulpine smile and Bob Rafelson, a director pushing forty. They were not father figures or Big Brothers, but hip uncles. Rafelson became a TV story editor after drifting around, spending a period in the services and working as a disc-jockey. His first movie *Head* (1968) featured The Monkees, those plastic Beatle replicas. It is a plotless, surrealistic romp that has its moments, such as the group playing dandruff in Victor Mature's hair. His second and best picture, *Five Easy Pieces* (1970), a picaresque tale of a middle-class drop-out (Nicholson), reacting against his stifling Seattle family, Mozart and Mathematics, moves impressively from place to place, giving each scene equal weight. The innovative use of Country and Western music stresses the characters' need for liberty, so do the nicely observed set-pieces: Nicholson playing the piano on a removal truck, trying to get a waitress to bend the rules, and meeting with his ailing father. *The King of Marvin Gardens* (1972), opening with a cleverly sustained monologue by Nicholson as an FM disc-jockey (the oracles of pop culture). Set in Atlantic City in winter (well captured by Laszlo Kovacs' photography), it soon gets weighed down by self-conscious symbolism and a striving for mythic resonances. With the days of the

Jack Nicholson in Bob Rafelson's *Five Easy Pieces* (1970).

youth movie over and the rebels of 1968 now insurance salesmen, he turned to the classical structure of the much-filmed, *The Postman Always Rings Twice* (1981). Despite the photography of Sven Nykvist, the playing of Jack Nicholson and Jessica Lange, and its attempt to be true to James Caine's novel, it has too many loose ends and a loose ending and doesn't seem to engage the director as much as his contemporary films did. **Also:** *Stay Hungry* (76).

RAPPER Irving

American. Born 1898. Former theatre director. Spent over six years as assistant to, among others, Michael CURTIZ and William DIETERLE at Warner Bros. Directed at Warners from 1941 to 1950, returning for two films in the late 50's. They reflect the influence of the studio and the directors he was apprenticed to. His biopics: *One Foot in Heaven* (1941) on Methodist Minister William Spence and *The Adventures of Mark Twain* (1944), both with Fredric March, and *Rhapsody in Blue* (1945) with the colourless Robert Alda (Alan's father) supposedly playing George Gershwin, are duller than Dieterle's. His adaptations from plays: *The Corn is Green* (1945) with a padded Bette Davis in a studio mock-up Welsh village, *The Voice of the Turtle* (1947), Ronald Reagan as a lonely soldier wooing Eleanor Parker, *Anna Lucasta* (1949), the all-white version with Paulette Goddard, and *The Glass Menagerie* (1950) with a miscast of Gertrude Lawrence, lack imagination. In *Now Voyager* (1942), immaculate performances from Bette Davis as the plain, introverted spinster who, in the best wish-fulfilment manner, blossoms into an attractive woman, Paul Henreid creating an erotic tremor by lighting two cigarettes at the same time and handing her one of them, Claude Rains and Gladys Cooper, Max Steiner's score and Casey Robinson's screenplay all came together to produce the classic Hollywood weepie. The last line could be Rapper's epitaph; 'Let's not ask the moon, when we have the stars.' **Also:** *Deception* (46), *Forever Female* (53), *Bad for Each Other* (53), *The Brave One* (56), *Marjorie Morningstar* (58), *The Miracle* (59).

RATOFF Gregory

American. 1897-1960. Born in St Petersburg, Russia. In Hollywood from the mid-thirties as actor and director. With his thick, Russian accent he usually played domineering impresarios in a hammy manner. Ham, schmaltz and corn are the ingredients that make up his films as director, which include seven leftover musicals for Fox. Ingrid Bergman made her Hollywood debut in *Intermezzo* (1939), a remake of the Swedish film she made three years earlier, as the music student in love with married violinist, Leslie Howard, the usual mixture of sentimentality and classical music. Ratoffs last film, *Oscar Wilde* (1960) with Robert Morley, was released at the same time as Ken HUGHES' movie on the same subject. Ratoff's effort was a faded lily. **Also:** *Rose of Washington Square* (49), *Adam Had Four Sons* (41), *The Corsican Brothers* (41), *Footlight Serenade* (42), *The Heat's On* (43), *Irish Eyes are Smiling* (44), *Paris Underground* (45), *Where Do We Go from Here?* (45), *Do You Love Me?* (46), *Carnival in Costa Rica* (47), *Black Magic* (49).

RAY Nicholas

American. 1911-1979. Born Raymond Nicholas Kienzle. Studied architecture with Frank Lloyd Wright. Worked in the theatre as actor and director with Elia KAZAN among others. Directed early TV drama for John Houseman who produced his first feature, *They Live By Night* (1947) for RKO. A pre-credit title sequence introduces us to the young couple (Farley Granger and Cathy O'Donnell) with the subtitle, 'This boy, this girl were never properly introduced to the world we live

Nicholas Ray

in'. This seems applicable to most of Ray's characters and to the director himself. The doomed outlaw lovers of *They Live By Night*, the boy (John Derek) from the slums on trial for

Natalie Wood, Sal Mineo and James Dean in Ray's *Rebel Without a Cause* (1955).

murder in *Knock on Any Door* (1949), Humphrey Bogart, the isolated screenwriter with sadistic tendencies in *In a Lonely Place* (1950), the misanthropic cop (Robert Ryan) and the blind girl (Ida Lupino) in *On Dangerous Ground* (1951), Sterling Hayden, 'I'm a stranger here myself' as *Johnny Guitar* (1954), James Dean, Natalie Wood and Sal Mineo in *Rebel Without a Cause* (1955) and James Mason, hooked on cortisone, in *Bigger Than Life* (1956) are all strangers, alienated from society, trying to make contact with the world. They are caught in bigger-than-life situations and the constantly moving camera and editing express this. Ray managed to get an intensity from his actors, helped by dynamic framing and later a dramatic use of colour and the CinamaScope screen. The colour and almost choreographic action sequences suggest a musical form. There are songs and dances in the excessive gypsiana of *Hot Blood* (1956), Johnny Guitar sings to fiery Joan Crawford, and Cyd Charisse dances in *Party Girl* (1958). There is something off-beat about most of his films, even within the Hollywood context. The neurotic male leads in *In a Lonely Place* and *On Dangerous Ground*, the insecure, lonely rodeo rider (Robert Mitchum) in *The Lusty Men* (1952), ballad-like structures of the Westerns, *Johnny Guitar* and *The True Story of Jesse James* (1957), the anthropology of *The Savage Innocents* (1960), the ecology of *Wind Across the Everglades* (1958) and the disenchanted cry of youth in *Rebel Without a Cause*. His brooding, violent, romantic side was stifled in the two interminable Samuel Bronston produced epics, *King of Kings* (1961) and *Fifty-Five Days to Peking* (1963). Ill and disillusioned, he forsook Hollywood and commercial film-making for ever in 1963. In the last weeks of his life, Wim WENDERS filmed the one-eyed, cancer-eroded shell of a man in *Lightning Over Water* (1980), a younger director's dubious hommage to an older one. **Also:** *A Woman's Secret* (49), *Born to be Bad* (50), *Run for Cover* (55), *Bitter Victory* (58).

RAY Satyarjit
Indian. Born 1921. Born in Calcutta, Bengal. Out of an industry almost entirely dominated by formula, escapist Hindi musical films, Ray suddenly appeared on the international scene with a masterpiece, *Pather Panchali* (1955), in the minority language of Bengali. He had a Western education, studied Fine Arts and became an established commercial artist. In 1950, he met Jean RENOIR in India shooting *The River*, who encouraged him to make *Pather Panchali*, the first of a trilogy based on a popular book by Bhibuti Bashan Bannerjee. He had great difficulty in raising the money, until he was aided with funds from the West Bengal Government. He shot the film in natural surroundings with non-professionals. The title means 'Little song of the road' and the motif throughout is one of travel, of something beyond the tiny, rural community where the boy Apu grows up with his tightly-knit family. There are the travelling players viewed with wonder and delight by the child, and the sound of the train taking people to the big cities. In a lyrical moment, Apu and his sister run through the long grass towards the railway line and he sees the reality of the locomotive close up for the first time. In the second part, *The Unvanquished* (1956), Apu goes with his mother to Benares and then returns to the village. He begins to get an education and will break away from the traditional values of his family. It ends with the death of his mother. In the last part, *The World of Apu* (1959), he is a young man in the big city. After his arranged marriage and the death of his wife, he scatters the pages of the novel he had written over a mountain at dawn. Observed with great insight and attention to social detail, they are told at a leisurely pace in which actions count for more than dialogue. Most of the themes of Ray's films are in the trilogy, most noticeably the effect of change on individuals. The music of Ravi Shankar plays an important role in the trilogy and Ray himself has written the music for many of his films. This is central to *The Music Room* (1958) which focuses on a declining, reclining aristocrat in the decaying mansion, who spends all his money on performances of Indian classical music. The 19th century Maharajah of Lucknow in *The Chess Players* (1977), who is being dethroned by the British East India Company, is a musician and poet and the director obviously sympathises with these effete creatures trying to stem the tide of change. The collision between traditional and modern beliefs comes out forcefully in *The Big City* (1963), a study of a young wife's efforts to reconcile the role of domestic servant with career woman and *Charaluta* (1964 – *The Lonely Wife*), a poignant view of a middle-class marriage at the turn of the century. Perhaps he has avoided some of the complexities of Indian life, but his films are firstly stories that follow a classical structure in the Indian tradition, offering no easy answers, showing the human face of that vast country. **Also:** *Devi* (60), *The Adventures of Goopy and Baghda* (68), *Days and Nights in the Forest* (69), *Distant Thunder* (73).

REDFORD Robert
American. Born 1937. Matinee idol of the 70's. *Ordinary People* (1980), his first movie as director, is an elegantly filmed, not terribly original or ambitious, WASP family drama with a sentimental solution. The mixed-up kid, deprived of his mother's love and blamed for the death of his brother, embracing his father with 'I love you', loses its effect as he had already hugged his psychoanalyst in a similar manner a little earlier. Mary Tyler Moore is well cast against type as the monster mother and Timothy Hutton gives an excellent perky performance as the son, despite his false sleepless-night makeup.

REED Carol
British. 1906-1976. Former stage actor and producer. Became dialogue director at Ealing Studios in the thirties. In the forties, he directed a number of skilful dramas with excellent actors, rich in atmosphere and milieu, often using expressionistic lighting and shock camera angles to heighten tension. *Odd Man Out* (1947) tells of the last hours of a wounded Irish gunman (James Mason in one of his best roles) on the run during The Troubles in Dublin. The suspense is brilliantly sustained, although the style is sometimes excessive. The peak of Reed's career was reached in the two films scripted by Graham Greene. *The Fallen Idol* (1948) is set almost entirely in a large foreign embassy and the enclosed arena and small cast lend power to the story of a small boy left in the care of the butler (Ralph Richardson in top form) while his parents are away. When the butler's wife is killed, the boy involuntarily puts the blame on the butler, whom he idolizes. Although Harry Lime (Orson WELLES) only appears two-thirds into *The Third Man* (1949), the spirit and presence of Welles lurks somewhere in the shadows throughout.

Through the streets of war-torn Vienna, Joseph Cotton goes hither and zither looking for his friend believed dead. A cat meows in a doorway. Cotton turns and, as the theme of Anton Karas's effective zither music swells we see the cat licking a pair of shoes. The camera rises and Welles's face emerges into the light. Robert Krasker's location photography is admirable, despite Reed's apparent request never to keep the camera straight. He made a faltering attempt to recapture the atmosphere of *Odd Man Out* and *The Third Man* with *The Man Between* (1953) starring James Mason and returned to Graham Greene with the slight, *Our Man in Havana* (1960), (six of his films have 'Man' in the title), which contains a series of subtle performances from Alec Guinness, Ralph Richardson and Noel Coward. There was an evident decline as he moved into larger projects. Of *The Agony and the Ecstasy* (1965), featuring Charlton Heston as Michelangelo getting a pain in the neck while painting the Sistine Chapel, Time magazine commented, 'Heston hits the ceiling!'. Reed hit the jackpot with *Oliver!* (1968). This long-winded, tuneless, well-scrubbed musical inexplicably won six Oscars. **Also:** *Bank Holiday* (38), *The Stars Look Down* (39), *Night Train to Munich* (40), *Kipps* (41), *The Young Mr Pitt* (42), *The Way Ahead* (44), *A Kid for Two Farthings* (55), *Trapeze* (56), *The Key* (58), *The Running Man* (63), *Flap* (70), *Follow Me* (71).

REINER Carl
American. Born 1922. Comedy actor, writer and director. Appeared in Sid Caesar's TV show in the 50's. Wrote *The Dick Van Dyke Show* from 1961-1966. His films are enjoyable show-busy comedies that make perfect in-flight movies. *Enter Laughing* (1967), adapted from his semi-autobiographical Broadway play, tells of a Jewish boy from the Bronx who wants to make it big in show-business, *The Comic* (1969) is about a silent-screen comedian (Dick Van Dyke), *The One and Only* (1978) tells of a chutzpanik (Henry Winkler) who dreams of becoming a Broadway star but ends up as the next best thing: an all-in wrestler. In *Oh God!* (1970), the Supreme Being is played by the supreme stand-up comic, George Burns and *Dead Men Don't Wear Plaid* (1982) is an ingenious pastiche in which gumshoe Steve Martin (the star of Reiner's *The Jerk* – 1979) plays scenes with Alan Ladd, Bogart, Veronica Lake etc in interwoven extracts from 40's and 50's thrillers. *Also: Where's Poppa?* (1970), *The Man With Two Brains* (83).

REINIGER Lotte
German. 1889-1981. Animator of silhouette cartoons adapted from Chinese shadow theatre. Her first feature was *The Adventures of Prince Ahmed* (1926). Many others were of well-known fairy tales and operas. She created the shadow play in RENOIR's *La Marseillaise* (1938).

REIS Irving
American. 1906-1953. Former radio writer and director. Gave Orson WELLES his first chance on radio. While Welles was making *Citizen Kane* and *The Magnificent Ambersons* at RKO, he was directing three of the B-picture Falcon series with George Sanders at the same studio. Other films include a likeable comedy with Cary Grant and nineteen-year-old Shirley Temple as *The Bachelor and the Bobbysoxer* (1947), a well-acted version of Arthur Miller's *All My Sons* (1948) with Edward G. Robinson and Burt Lancaster and a pale musical, *Dancing in the Dark* (1949). Ended his twelve-year career with the smug two-hander, *The Four Poster* (1952) starring Rex Harrison and Lilli Palmer (then husband and wife) enacting scenes from married life *around* the bed of the title, enlivened only by UPA cartoon interludes. **Also:** *The*

Joseph Cotton (L) and Orson Welles as Harry Lime in Reed's *The Third Man* (1949).

Big Street (42), *Enchantment* (48), *Three Husbands* (50), *Of Mice and Music* (51).

REISZ Karel

British. Born 1926 in Czechoslovakia. Came to Britain as a child. Read chemistry at Cambridge. Became part of the Free Cinema group with Lindsay ANDERSON and Tony RICHARDSON. Published an influential book entitled 'The Technique of Film Editing' (1955). His first feature, *Saturday Night and Sunday Morning* (1960) is the best of the British New Wave movies which dealt with working-class life. Albert Finney's 'angry young man' gives the film a punch as he reacts against his drab Northern industrial surroundings. Reisz's interests obviously lay elsewhere as he quickly abandoned social concerns for films with a psychological bent. *Night Must Fall* (1964) makes the mistake of updating Emlyn Williams' play, decking it out with heavy Freudian symbols and *Morgan: A Suitable Case for Treatment* (1966) is as schizophrenic as its protagonist and now looks as trendy-artificial as *Saturday Night and Sunday Morning* looks trendy-natural. *Isadora* (1968) is a muddled, lethargic biopic of Isadora Duncan, who must have danced better than Vanessa Redgrave to win such acclaim. In America, both *The Gambler* (1974) and *Who'll Stop the Rain?* (1978. *Dog Soldiers* GB) are too bound by literary scripts and a need to give every action significance, although both have a certain manic quality. *The French Lieutenant's Woman* (1981) fails more in intention than in execution. The film within a film device is not a satisfactory equivalent to John Fowles' reconstructed/deconstructed 19th century novel and emerges as a polite, cold and handsomely mounted exercise.

RENOIR Jean

French. 1894-1979. Son of Auguste, Renoir, the great Impressionist painter. Spent much of his childhood in Provençe surrounded by a loving family and a warm circle of friends. Renoir's career is almost the history of cinema, from the expressionism of the early silents to neo-realism, committed cinema, film noir, Hollywood studio productions, Technicolor period spectacles to fast TV techniques. If one had to save only one director's oeuvre for posterity, it would have to be Renoir's. His films manage like no-one else's to blend a

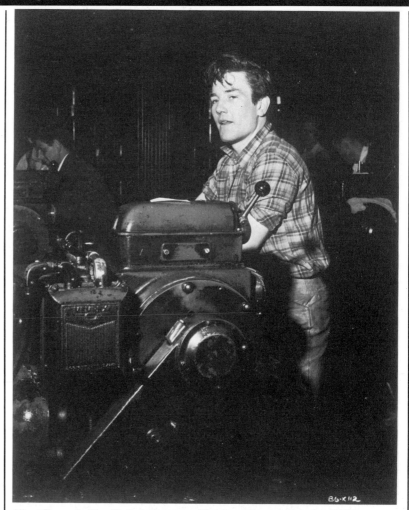

Albert Finney in Karel Reisz's *Saturday Night and Sunday Morning* (1960).

variety of emotions and moods, realism, fantasy, tragedy and farce. The illusion of the theatre is a constant metaphor. His characters are seen in the round. There are no heroes or villains. Each is stupid and wise, noble and petty. Renoir's cinema is egalitarian. Scenes are balanced between the characters, as the camera moves with them. 'The terrible thing about this world is that everybody has his reasons,' says a character in *La Règle du Jeu* (1939. *The Rules of the Game*), the most archetypal and perfect of Renoir's films. The word 'terrible' takes away any complacency from his humanism. Events and people are never taken at face value. Individuals are trapped by the rules of the social game; masters and servants, bosses and workers, officers and men, bourgeois and clochard. It is his understanding and love of actors that gives force to the democratic view. His films are collective works, made by a group of friends with the same goal. He often adapted

the roles to suit the actors' personalities instead of the other way round. His use of deep focus, natural sound and settings, of colour and lighting are always at the service of the actors, whether the unknown players in *Toni* (1935) or Michel Simon, Jean Gabin, Pierre Renoir (his brother), Anna Magnani, Ingrid Bergman or Jean-Louis Barrault. The characters are never seen in isolation from their environment. There is a reverence for nature as strong as in his father's paintings. Renoir entered films after his marriage to one of his father's models, Catherine Hessling, in order to make her a star. She displayed her strange automaton-like movements and white face in his first five films, notably *Nana* (1926) influenced by STROHEIM. He then made four films with the extraordinary simion-faced Michel Simon: *Tir au Flanc* 1928, *On Purge Bebe* 1931, his first sound film based on Feydeau, *La Chienne* 1931 with a brilliant use of direct sound, and *Boudu Sauvé des*

Eaux 1932 – *Boudu Saved From Drowning*. In the latter, Simon as a tramp is the spirit of anarchy almost trapped into a bourgeois marriage before regaining his liberty on the banks of the Seine. *The Crime of Monsieur Lange* (1936), written by Jacques Prévert, expresses workers' solidarity and the Popular Front in the form of an ironic black comedy. The three prisoners of war in *La Grande Illusion* (1937) are working class (Jean Gabin), middle-class (Dalio) and aristocratic (Pierre Fresnay). Erich von Stroheim as the German commandant of the camp tries to persuade Fresnay that class loyalty is stronger than national ties. Fresnay, in fact, dies so that his fellow prisoners can escape. *La Regle du Jeu*, made on the eve of the outbreak of war, shows a society being disrupted from within. Renoir took the comedies of Beaumarchais and Musset as his models. In America during the war, he managed to preserve much of his style, even persuading the studios to shoot a great deal of *Swamp Water* (1941) and *The Southerner* (1945) on location. Despite an upbeat ending and painted sets, *The Diary of a Chambermaid* (1946) is French in feeling, full of

Jean Renoir (L) and Julien Carette in *La Règle du Jeu* (1939).

humour and social comment. His first film in colour, *The River* (1950) was made in India and beautifully shot by his nephew Claude Renoir. On his return to Europe, he made three stylish Technicolor operetta-like romances, *The Golden Coach* (1953) with Anna Magnani, *French Can Can* (1955) with Gabin and Francoise Arnoul and *Elena et les Hommes* (1956) with Ingrid Bergman, each about a woman who has to choose

between three men and the theatre. His last film and testament *The Little Theatre of Jean Renoir* (1971) brought together many of the themes and subjects with which he had been associated. **Also:** *The Little Match Girl* (28), *La Nuit de Carrefour* (32), *Madame Bovary* (34), *Une Partie de Campagne* (36), *The Lower Depths* (36), *La Bête Humaine* (38), *La Marseillaise* (38), *This Land is Mine* (43), *The Woman on the Beach* (47),

Jean Gabin and Simone Simon in Renoir's *La Bête Humaine* (1938).

Le Dejeuner sur L'Herbe (59), *The Vanishing Corporal* (62), *The Testament of Doctor Cordelier* (61).

RESNAIS Alain

French. Born 1922. Began in films as an editor before directing a series of short art films on *Van Gogh* (1948), *Gaugin* (1950) and Picasso's *Guernica* (1950). The poet Paul Eluard wrote the commentary for the latter which, by interpolating photos, newspaper headlines and shots of contemporary Spain, was able to place the painting in a wider context. Already noticeable is the creative editing, the importance of the word and the intermingling of past and present. The opening lines of T.S. Eliot's 'Burnt Norton' express the main theme of Resnais's films. 'Time present and time past are both perhaps present in time future, and time future contained in time past.' The long exploratory tracking shots, which were to become characteristic of his films, wander over the present-day ruins of Auschwitz in *Night and Fog* (1955), a thirty-minute documentary. The scenes in colour, the controlled narration (written by Jean Cayrol, himself a deportee) and the gentle music is contrasted with newsreels of the concentration camp victims. He continued to work with leading contemporary writers, treating sound, words, music and images on an equal basis. In *Hiroshima Mon Amour* (1959), a French actress is having an affair with a Japanese architect. Around them is the rebuilt Hiroshima, still living with the horror of the past, while images of her past in Nevers during the war, where she was in love with a German soldier, flash into her mind. The images and the text (by Marguerite DURAS) make up a masterful expression of subjective time. Rejecting a chronological structure, *Last Year in Marienbad* (1961) mingles memory, imagination, past and present, desire and fulfilment as a man tries to convince a woman guest (Delphine Seyrig), in a vast baroque mansion with geometrically designed gardens, that they had met the year before. The screenplay by Alain ROBBE-GRILLET, the stylised playing, the organ music, the tracking shots down endless corridors, the decor, the 'flash-ins', are elements of this haunting and erotic poem. *Muriel* (1963) seems more realistic on the surface, but it is as stylised and metaphysical as the previous films. Using over-lapping sounds and dialogue (by Jean Cayrol) and ethereal music by Hans Werner Henze, a group of characters are placed in mundane situations but tortured by their memories, in a Boulogne shot in visionary colour. These three masterpieces are almost equalled, three films and fourteen years later by *Providence* (1977). In the interim, he gave us *La Guerre est Finie* (1966), a simplistic one-note

Delphine Seyrig and Giorgio Albertazzi in Resnais' *Last Year in Marienbad* (1961).

portrait of an ageing exile from Franco's Spain; *Je t'aime, Je t'aime* (1968), which puts a man in a time machine, is rather like revealing the mechanics behind a magician's act and *Stavisky* (1974), about the death of an epoch, is as beautiful to look at but as dead as a stuffed peacock. *Providence* is basically a nightmare lived by a dying novelist (John Gielgud in his finest screen role) inhabited by four members of his family. The next morning everything is bathed in light as they all come together joyously to celebrate his birthday. The thin dividing line between fact and fiction, dream and reality has hardly ever been better conceived. From this peak, Resnais plunged into the numbing banality of *My American Uncle* (1979) which illustrates the determinist theories of one Dr Henri Laborit who tells us we are only what society makes us.

REYNOLDS Burt
American. Born 1936. His cool, devil-may-care brawn established him as the Clark Gable of the 70's. His films as director reflect his mock-macho image to a certain degree *Gator* (1976) is a compendium of cliches – corrupt Southern politicians, bent cops, bootleggers and car chases. *Sharkey's Machine* (1982), a sleak, cops 'n pushers crime movie contrasts with *The End* (1978), a tasteless, black comedy with quite a few death-rattle laughs on the way.

RICHARDSON Tony
British. Born 1928. In the late 50's and 60's, there emerged in England a movement of playwrights, novelists and film-makers who were labelled 'angry young men'. In 1956, Richardson directed the stage production of the key work of the movement, John Osborne's 'Look Back in Anger'. In 1958, Karel REISZ, Osborne and Richardson set up Woodfall Films with which to vent their anger. Richardson's first two features were versions of Osborne plays. *Look Back in Anger* (1959) suffers from unsubtle direction and Richard Burton's blasting performance while *The Entertainer* (1960) gains from Laurence OLIVIER's ogling, run-down music-hall comedian and the evocation of a seedy English seaside resort. His busy direction, scavenging from the French *nouvelle vague*, took the bite out of Shelagh Delaney's *A Taste of Honey* (1962) and Alan Sillitoe's *The Loneliness of the Long Distance Runner* (1962). John Osborne script-

ed *Tom Jones* (1963) which transformed Henry Fielding's great mock-heroic 'novel of manners' into a simple-minded, bawdy romp. Thirteen years later, he returned to Fielding with *Joseph Andrews* (1976), a pathetic attempt to recapture the box-office success of the previous film. The rest of his films give the impression of someone desperately running to jump on a band-wagon and falling flat on his face. Jeanne Moreau, Mick Jagger, Anna Karina, Jack NICHOLSON, Marguerite DURAS, Jean Genet, Nabokov, Evelyn Waugh, William Faulkner have all been victims of Richardson's ineptitude. **Also:** *Sanctuary* (61), *The Loved One* (65), *Mademoiselle* (66), *The Sailor from Gibraltar* (67), *The Charge of the Light Brigade* (68), *Laughter in the Dark* (69), *Ned Kelly* (70), *The Border* (82).

RICHTER Hans
German. 1888-1976. Painter involved in cubism, futurism, but his heart belonged to Dada. His experimental abstract and surrealist films were a great influence on avant-garde film-makers. He taught in America for fifteen years from 1942. **Some titles:** *Rhythmus 21,22,23* (21-23), *Ghosts Before Noon* (27), *Dreams that Money Can Buy* (44), *8 × 8* (56), *Alexander Calder* (63).

RIEFENSTAHL Leni
German. Born 1922. Trained as a ballet dancer and studied painting. She appeared in four of Arnold FANCK's mountain films. Her first feature, *The Blue Light* (1932) was of a similar kind, emphasising a Germanic mystical union with nature. Hitler was impressed and asked her to make a short film for the National Socialist Party called *Victory of Faith* (1933). She was then given over forty cameramen and many technicians to film the 1934 Nuremberg Rally under the title, suggested by the Führer, *Triumph of the Will* (1934). Despite her later protestations that it was merely a record of history and not a propaganda film, the event was shaped into a great, mythic spectacle with Hitler as a Wagnerian hero descending upon the medieval town to save *das volk*. Ecstatic faces stare up at him as the sun catches his head like a halo. Using dramatic editing, the people become a dehumanized mass moving through Busby BERKELEY routines in a 'Springtime for Hitler' show. It established her as Germany's foremost 'ideological propagandist'. As a result she was commissioned to film the 1936 Olympic Games in Berlin. This became, *Olympia* (1938) a four-hour documentary in two parts that took two years to edit. The beauty of many of the images do not compensate for much of the grandiose bad taste of Nazi art. If these two films do stir audiences today, it is not, as many claim, despite their fascism but *because* of it. She was blacklisted by the Allies in 1945 and could not work again for seven years. In 1954, she

Leni Riefenstahl's *Triumph of the Will* (1934).

completed *Tiefland*, begun in 1935, a melodrama shot in thirties black-and-white textures, based on the opera by D'Albert and starring herself as a gypsy dancer. She lives in East Africa where she has been trying to finish two anthropological films for many years. There is no sign they will ever be completed.

RITCHIE Michael

American. Born 1939. Studied literature and history at Harvard. Worked on TV for some years, directing episodes from Dr Kildare and The Man from U.N.C.L.E., among others. Robert REDFORD was impressed by one of his TV films and got him to direct *Downhill Racer* (1969). By using a semi-documentary style, mixing 16mm with 35mm, it gives a rare insight into the sport of Olympic skiing. The laconic script and Redford's character border on the sententious, but it is in the downhill races that interest mounts.

Ritt's *Hud* (1963).

Ritchie continued his theme of competition in *The Candidate* (1972) and *Smile* (1975), semi-satires on Middle America that take one idea and hammer it into the ground. The first never gets beyond the surface irony and realistic reconstruction of a Presidential campaign, although Redford is well cast in the vapid title role. *Smile* is fixed in its superior view of the thirty-three contestants of the Young American Miss Pageant beauty competition. There is a much lighter touch in *The Bad News Bears* (1976), a delightfully wry comedy containing the un-American message that winning isn't everything. The Little League baseball team is the most individualized bunch of kids since 'Our Gang', cute in the sense of smart, while Walter Matthau as their misanthropic coach, never noticeably plays for laughs nor tries to be lovable. *Semi-Tough* (1977) has a witty, free-wheeling quality for most of the way and pro football is only one target of Ritchie's sharpened satire. **Also:** *An Almost Perfect Affair* (79), *The Island* (80).

RITT Martin

American. Born 1920. Former stage actor who studied with Elia KAZAN. Acted and directed on TV. Taught at the Actors' Studio where his students included Paul NEWMAN, Joanne Woodward and Rod Steiger. Ritt is a sensitive, idealistic director whose sensitivity can become sentimental, his idealism idealization. He has persisted disarmingly with unfashionable liberal themes throughout his career. *Edge of the City* (1956 — *A Man is Ten Feet Tall* GB), *The Great White Hope* (1970), *Sounder* (1972) and *Conrack* (1974) all deal with the effect of racial hatred on individuals. *Norma Rae* (1979) has Sally Field gutsily helping to form a union of textile workers. Touching as these films are, they lead to easy solutions and the idea that social and political problems are merely a matter of good guys vs bad guys. Woody ALLEN is *The Front* (1976) paid to put his name to the work of blackballed writers during the McCarthy era. Quite a few of the people involved in the film had been blacklisted, Ritt, Walter Bern-

PAUL NEWMAN IS "HUD"!

THE MAN WITH THE BARBED WIRE SOUL!

"Brutally frank... superbly acted... magnificently filmed..." —BOB CONSIDINE

A SALEM-DOVER PRODUCTION · CO STARRING MELVYN DOUGLAS · PATRICIA NEAL · BRANDON DeWILDE · PANAVISION® · PRODUCED BY MARTIN RITT AND IRVING RAVETCH · DIRECTED BY MARTIN RITT · SCREENPLAY BY IRVING RAVETCH AND HARRIET FRANK Jr. · FROM A NOVEL BY LARRY McMURTRY · MUSIC SCORED BY ELMER BERNSTEIN · A PARAMOUNT RELEASE

Copyright© 1962 by Paramount Pictures Corporation, Salem Productions, Inc. and Dover Productions, Inc.

stein (scriptwriter), Zero Mostel and Joshua Shelley (actors). Too brightly wrapped to really probe that sordid period of American history, it ably lifts a few stones. All one's misgivings about Ritt's well-meaning, slightly old-fashioned work are dispelled in *Hud* (1963) in which the theme of realism vs idealism is eloquently expressed. For once, having a cynical, irresponsible character at the centre, he is able to balance his precepts better. Set on a declining cattle ranch in modern Texas, it has superb black-and-white photography by James Wong Howe, a truthfully modulated script from Irving Ravetch and a moving quartet of performances from Paul Newman, Melvyn Douglas, Patricia Neal and Brandon de Wilde. **Also:** *No Down Payment* (57), *The Long Hot Summer* (58), *The Sound and the Fury* (59), *Paris Blues* (61), *The Outrage* (64), *The Spy Who Came in from the Cold* (65), *Hombre* (67), *The Brotherhood* (68), *The Molly Maguires* (69), *Pete 'n Tillie* (73), *Casey's Shadow* (78).

RIVETTE Jacques
French. Born 1928. A member of the original group of critics on the influential Cahiers du Cinema magazine who later became directors. After four shorts, he struggled to make his first feature, *Paris Nous Appartient* (1960, *Paris Belongs to Us*). Because of lack of funds, it was made over a period of years and strangely reflects the struggles of creation against all odds. A group of amateurs come together in a deserted Paris in summer to stage a performance of Shakespeare's Pericles. Its austere style builds up an atmosphere of doom as deaths occur and there is fear of a conspiracy. Paris is the constant background to his films, seen as realistically as possible but where fantastic things take place. In *L'Amour Fou* (1968) a theatre group prepares to stage Racine's Andromaque while being filmed by a TV team. This four-and-half hour film was developed from improvizations with the actors and technicians. *Out One* (1971) originally ran twelve hours and forty minutes, but was cut down to *Out One: Spectre* (1973) of four hours and twenty minutes. In it, two plays by Aeschylus are being rehearsed separately by a man and a woman who used to live together. These films break with traditional methods of filming (virtually no shooting script), almost capturing the film during its genesis. As they do not

seek to reach any conclusion, they could continue for ever. Less cabalistic and approachable than his other films is *Celine and Julie Go Boating* (1974. *Celine et Julie vont en bateau*), a brilliantly comic meditation on the nature of fiction. Two girls, a magician and a librarian, meet in Montmartre and get involved in an endless theatrical melodrama being played out in a suburban house. Their efforts to alter the course of the drama are as fruitless as the audience's wish to influence the characters in a film they are watching. **Also:** *La Religieuse* (65), *Duelle* (75), *Noroit* (76), *Le Pont du Nord* (82).

ROBBE-GRILLET Alain
French. Born 1922. Novelist of the *nouveau roman* movement in the 50's which repudiated objective reality and chronological narratives. Wrote the script for Alain RESNAIS's *Last Year in Marienbad* (1961). His own films, complex erotic fantasies, are like scripts in search of a Resnais to articulate them. **Some titles:** *L'Immortelle* (63), *Trans-Europ Express* (66), *L'Homme qui ment* (68), *L'Eden et aprés* (70).

ROBSON Mark
American. Born 1913 in Canada. Started in Hollywood as editor. Worked with Robert WISE on the cutting of *Citizen Kane* (1941). Both began their careers directing shadowy spine-tinglers for RKO producer Val Lewton, both made two big boxing dramas, both gained a certain reputation for realism, both leapt into sentimental blockbusters and disaster movies and both are reasonably proficient craftsmen. Are Robert Wise and Mark Robson one and the same? No. Robson's *Champion* (1949) was released in the same month as Wise's *The Set-Up* and suffered in comparison because of the over-dramatized prize-fights and the sentimental approach to the subject. It happened again in 1956 when Wise's *Somebody up There Likes Me* opened at the same time as Robson's *The Harder They Fall*. The first was a successful celebration of the benefits boxing can bring, the latter was a hard-hitting exposé of professional boxing that left too many questions unanswered. In boxing, at least, it's better to be Wise. *The Harder They Fall* was Humphrey Bogart's last picture. Robert Donat also died soon after the release of *The Inn of the Sixth Happiness* (1958) in which Ingrid Bergman and a group of

children try to escape Malcolm Arnold's pursuing music. (Wise topped it later with *The Sound of Music*.) **Also:** *The 7th Victim* (43), *Isle of the Dead* (45), *Home of the Brave* (49), *Bright Victory* (51), *Phffft* (54), *The Bridges of Toko – Ri* (55), *The Little Hut* (57), *Peyton Place* (57), *From the Terrace* (60), *Nine Hours to Rama* (62), *The Prize* (63), *Von Ryan's Express* (65), *Valley of the Dolls* (67), *Earthquake* (74), *Avalanche Express* (78).

ROCHA Glauber
Brazilian. 1938-1981. Former journalist and film critic. Leader of the group Cinema Novo, a co-operative set up in the late 50's. It's aim was to make radical films freed from North American influence. The Brazilian film industry suffered a blow with the military coup in 1964 and in 1970, Rocha was forced to work abroad. His films draw on the mystic cultural traditions of his country, often contrasting the primitive and the modern, using ritualized theatrical techniques and political texts. *Black God, White Devil* (1964) and *Antonio Das Mortes* (1969) are both set in the arid north-west of Brazil where the starving peasants are exploited by bandits, multinationals and the church. The films he made in Europe and Africa such as *Lions Have Seven Heads* (1970) move further into anarchy and madness, only seeming to add to the burdens of the Third World. **Also:** *Age of the Earth* (80).

ROEG Nicholas
British. Born 1928. Cameraman on CORMAN's *The Masque of the Red Death* (65) and TRUFFAUT's *Fahrenheit 451* (1966). Should cameramen be allowed to direct their own films? No great cinematographer who took to direction has made much impact. The cameraman is the eye, the director the brain. Roeg's films are all eye and no brain. *Performance* (1970) and *The Man who Fell to Earth* (1976), both featuring outrageous pop-stars (Mick Jagger and David Bowie), are content to observe their stars' striking features in an assortment of arty visuals. *Don't Look Now* (73) and *Bad Timing* (80) are aimless, morose allegories of identity weighed down by endless mirror images. **Also:** *Walkabout* (71), *Eureka* (82).

ROGOSIN Lionel
American. Born 1924. Made docu-

Francoise Fabian and Jean-Louis Trintingnant in Rohmer's *My Night With Maud* (1968).

---

mentaries on location before the introduction of light 16mm cine and sound equipment. Despite the un-wieldiness of the camera and lack of fluidity, *On the Bowery* (1957) gives a desolate picture of the tramps and drunks who live in the heart of afflu-ent Manhattan. *Come Back, Africa* (1959) was shot clandestinely in South Africa and reveals the degra-dation of apartheid. Both films suffer from stilted staged incidents, but were forerunners of Direct Cinema. **Also:** *Good Times, Wonderful Times* (66), *Woodcutters of the Deep South* (73).

ROHMER Eric

French. Born 1920. Real name Maurice Scherer. Wrote for Cahiers du Cinema from 1951, becoming editor from 1958 to 1963. With Claude CHABROL, he published 'Hitchcock' in 1957, which saw the director's work from a Catholic view-point. In his 'Six Moral Tales', the characters are defined ethically by their relationships with the opposite sex, rather in the manner of the dis-course in 18th century novels or tales. In Rohmer's words, he is 'less con-cerned with what people do than what is going on in their minds while they are doing it.' Most of the action

in the films is in the dialogue, but they are far from being static conversation pieces. The sumptuous, hedonistic settings and the seductive women are essentially what the conversations, narrations, diary and letter extracts are all about. For films that deal with the resistance to temptation, they are tantalizingly erotic. The male pro-tagonists might reject the physical pleasures, but the films embrace them. In each, a man renounces hav-ing sex with a woman, in order to prove his fidelity to his wife or fiancée who represent stability or a home. The renunciation brings as much re-lief to them as an orgasm, figuratively 'pulling out' just in time. In *La Collectioneuse* (1966), an intellectual rejects the advances of a promiscuous bikini-clad nymphette in the sensu-ous summer surroundings of St Tropez for the sake of his English girl-friend waiting for him in a cold climate: the Catholic engineer (Jean-Louis Trintignant) in *Ma Nuit Chez Maud* (1968) spends a chaste night with the beautiful, dark, free-thinking Maud (Francoise Fabian) because he is already committed to marrying devout, blonde Marie-Claude Barrault; the diplomat (Jean-Claude Brialy), spending a summer in the shimmering lake–side resort of Annecy, permits himself the ex-

quisite pleasure of embracing *Claire's Knee* (1970), as erotic a moment as any heavy-breathing bed play, before giving himself to his fiancee; and the husband in *L'Amour L'Apres Midi* (1972) sees himself in the mirror while about to submit to the charms of the independent Chloe (Zouzou) and runs back to the safe arms of his middle-class wife. *The Aviator's Wife* (1981) is the first of a series called 'Comedies and Proverbs'. The characters are less articulate than in the Moral Tales, but still weigh up their actions; as the Musset-like sub-title of the film suggests, 'on ne saurait penser a rien' (one can't think of nothing). It is a delightful comedy of errors concerned with the illusions of love, shot in Paris with a ravishing centre piece in a verdant park. **Also:** *The Marquise of O* (76), *Perceval le Gallois* (78), *Le Beau Marriage* (82).

ROMERO George A

American. Born 1939. Director of exploitation pictures that are part of the late night 'cult circuit' in the States. Lurid, loathsome and repug-nant horror movies, full of slavering zombies, ghouls and vampires. **Some titles:** *Night of the Living Dead* (68), *The Crazies* (73), *Hungry Wives* (73), *Martin* (78), *Dawn of the Dead* (79), *Knightriders* (81).

ROMM Mikhail

Russian. 1901-1971. After script-writing, he made his first feature *Boule de Suif* (1934), the last Russian silent film, an elegant, well-acted version of Maupassant's novel. *Lenin in October* (1937) and *Lenin in 1918* (1939) are lively, hagiopics starring Lenin look-alike Boris Shchukin. The years of Stalinism weighed heavily on his films, but after the thaw, he came back with *Nine Days of the Year* (1961), an interesting work about young scientists, and *Ordinary Fascism* (1965), a compilation film on the rise of the Nazis.

ROSENBERG Stuart

American. Born 1925. Worked for some years in TV. A tough, factual crime thriller, *Murder Inc* (1960) was his first movie of an ill-assorted group. Of his four films with Paul NEWMAN, *Cool Hand Luke* (1967) is the best, a brutal but less dark chain-gang movie than most. The others with Newman were the tedious, *WUSA* (1970), the tepid *Pocket Money* (1972) and the turgid, *The Drowning Pool* (1975). **Also:** *The April Fools* (69), *Move* (70), *The Laughing Policeman* (73), *Voyage of the Damned* (76).

ROSI Francesco

Italian. Born 1922. Worked in theatre for two years. Assistant director and scriptwriter for ten years. Assisted Luchino VISCONTI on *La Terra Trema* (1948). Most of his films are taken from actuality and attempt to divide fact from fiction. They show a concern with social issues, especially the effect of Italian politics and justice on the individual. His investigations into the lives and deaths of the Sicilian bandit, *Salvatore Giuliano* (1962), the Italian industrialist Mattei in *The Mattei Affair* (1972) and gangster, *Lucky Luciano* (1973), are made up of flashbacks, interviews, newsreels in a semi-documentary form. *The Moment of Truth* (1965) featured one of Spain's most famous matadors, Miguel Mateo Miguelin. By using a tele-photo lens, he was able to show the bull-fighter slaughtering bulls in close-up without using a double. Lately, he has turned back to neo-realist subjects, reminiscent of Visconti's exercises in that style. *Christ Stopped at Eboli* (1979) is based on the book by Carlo Levi, doctor, painter and writer, who was exiled from Turin to a primitive peasant village by Mussolini and *Three Brothers* (1981), one a judge, one a teacher (called Rocco) and the third a factory worker, symbolise the cultural split between North and South Italy. Rosi's style, often fragmented and flashy, studiously 'aesthetic', is never quite equal to the content. **Also:** *Hands across the City* (63), *Cinderella-Italian Style* (67), *Illustrious Corpses* (73).

ROSS Herbert

American. Born 1927. Former dancer, choreographer and New York stage director. This background of ballet and Broadway reflect in his films. Entered the movies as dance director on *Funny Girl* (1968) which included Barbra Streisand's ugly duckling Swan Lake parody. He directed Streisand again in *The Owl and the Pussycat* (1970), a loud and conventional comedy, and in the not-so-hot sequel to *Funny Girl*, *Funny Lady* (1975), with a draggy plot interrupting the snappy numbers. Funny writer Neil Simon linked with Ross on *The Sunshine Boys* (1975), *The Goodbye Girl* (1977), and *California Suite* (1978) with unimaginative results, but containing savorous turns from George Burns, Richard Dreyfuss, Maggie Smith and Michael Caine. Ballet is the subject of *Turning Point* (1977) and *Nijinsky* (1980). Mikhail Baryshnikov impresses in the former, a clichéd story turning on a cattish pas-de-deux by Anne Bancroft and Shirley MacLaine that sets out to prove ballet is butch. Not even the dance sequences are good in *Nijinsky*, a soap-ballet that sets out to prove ballet is gay. *The Last of Sheila* (1973) and *The Seven-per-cent Solution* (1976) are enjoyable puzzles to solve, and *Play it Again, Sam* (1972) makes clever use of nebbish Woody ALLEN's Bogart-Casablanca fantasies. The contrast between songs like 'We're in the Money' and the harsh reality of the Depression is dazzlingly realized in *Pennies from Heaven* (1982) which, with, the best production numbers for many a year, expresses how escapist musicals were perceived in the 30's.

ROSSELLINI Roberto

Italian. 1906-1977. Editor and scriptwriter in the thirties. Although the term 'neo-realist' was first applied to VISCONTI's *Ossessione* (1942), it was Rossellini's three films on the Resistance, the Liberation, and the post-war turmoil that established the style. Shot with minimum resources in natural surroundings with actors and local people, they depict historic events in human terms. A rough and ready immediacy add to their intensity, bringing real situations and fiction together. *Rome, Open City* (1945) tells of a Resistance leader hunted by the Germans in occupied Rome. He is betrayed by his mistress and he and a priest are shot. *Paisa* (1947) contains six episodes which take place from the first Allied landings in Sicily to the day of victory. The best episode is of the meeting between a black American soldier and an urchin boy who steals his boots. With an avoidance of sentimentality, the children emerge as the nucleus of suffering. In *Germany, Year Zero* (1947), a boy in occupied post-war Germany tries to feed his family. He takes the advice of his Nazi teacher (now a black marketeer) to poison his ailing father in order to save on food. Isolated from other children and society, the boy throws himself off a ruined building. The films do not avoid melodrama or naivety, but passion and humanity vibrate through them. The pessimism of these three films gives way to spiritual regeneration in the rest of his work. In 1950, he married Ingrid Bergman. Like a postulant, she took off her make-up, stripped herself of the trappings of Hollywood stardom and placed herself in his hands. She is at the centre of *Stromboli* (1949), *Europa '51* (1952), *Journey to Italy* (1953) and *Fear* (1954) seeking salvation on top of a volcano, by tending the poor and the sick, and by witnessing a miracle. The sequence of these much-admired spiritual melodramas was interrupted by *The Flowers of St Francis* (1950) which illustrated the life of the saint. After his divorce from Bergman, he seemed to take on the cloak of a holy teacher, making films of saints in a direct and realistic manner in order to humanize them. *The Rise to Power of Louis XIV* (1966) shows the man beneath the wig. **Also:** *General della Rovere* (59), *Viva L'Italia* (60), *Vanina Vanini* (61), *The Age of the Apostles* (68), *Socrates* (70), *Augustine of Hippo* (72).

ROSSEN Robert

American. 1908-1966. Wrote and directed for the theatre. His play 'The Body Beautiful' (1934) got him a contract with Warners where he stayed for six years as screenwriter, contributing to their socially committed movies. His second feature as director, *Body and Soul* (1947) used boxing as the perfect metaphor for a

Robert Rossen (left) on the set of *The Brave Bulls* (1951) with Mel Ferrer (far right).

dog-eat-dog society and a symptom of capitalism. A great deal of the film is powerful despite the over-insistent direction and script (Abraham POLONSKY) and the obligatory happy ending that dodged the issues raised. Its main quality lies in the film noir camerawork by James Wong Howe and the expressive bullish performance by John Garfield as the boxer owned body and soul by the system. Soon after its release, Rossen, Polonsky and Garfield were brought before the Un-American Activities hearings, marking them for life. He was able to make *All the King's Men* (1949) before being blacklisted. This rather heavy-handed tale of political corruption, effectively blended location photography and studio work and benefited from hard-hitting performances

from Broderick Crawford as the Huey Long-type politician and Mercedes McCambridge. He formed his own company abroad making, among others, *The Brave Bulls* (1951), a gloomy bull-fighting picture with well-defined black and white photography from Howe again, and the over-long, over-serious epic, *Alexander the Great* (1956) with Richard Burton in a blond wig. His third film, after returning to Hollywood in 1957, was *The Hustler* (1961) which he wrote, produced and directed. The black and white Cinama-Scope photography (Eugene Shuftan) beautifully captures the poolrooms, bars, furnished rooms and diners of the milieu and the editing makes the game of pool as exciting as any sport on film. Paul NEWMAN in the title role suggests arrogance, vulnerability, the seedy and the romantic, and all the other parts are taken expertly. His last film was the strange and intelligent study of schizophrenia, *Lilith* (1963) in

which Jean Seberg and Warren BEATTY are directed to perfection. **Also:** *Johnny O'Clock* (47), *Island in the Sun* (57), *They Came to Cordura* (59).

ROSSIF Frederic
French. Born 1922 in Yugoslavia. Known for his forceful, often facile subjective compilation films such as *Le Temps du Ghetto* (1961) made up of footage of the Warsaw ghetto, *To Die in Madrid* (1962) on the Spanish Civil War and *October Revolution* (1967).

ROUCH Jean
French. Born 1917. Ethnologist and anthropologist who set up the International Ethnographic Film Committee in 1952. Began using film as part of his research into the tribes of West Africa. For his first feature, *Moi, Un Noir* (1958), he allowed a group of people on the Ivory Coast to dictate the content of a film on their lives. The camera not only follows their

daily existence but the acting out of their fantasies. The development of lightweight sound and cinę equipment led to what was described as 'cinema verite' (derived from Dziga VERTOV's Kino Pravda). Rouch believed that the camera's intervention stimulated people to greater spontaneity, expression and truth without asking them, as in the American Direct Cinema, to act as though the camera was not there. *Chronique d'un Ete* (*Chronicle of a Summer* 1961), made with the sociologist Edgar Morin, edited down twenty-five hours of interviews with a cross-section of Parisians, many of them replying to the question, 'Are you happy?'. This ethnological approach to the French and Africans alike makes for fascinating and revealing documentaries. **Also:** *La Pyramide Humaine* (59), *La Chasse au Lion a L'Arc* (65), *Jaguar* (67), *Petit`a Petit* (69).

ROUSE Russell
American. Born 1916. 'Bomb' manufacturer who writes most of his own films with Clarence Greene. They 'wrote' *The Thief* (1952) which has no dialogue. This suicidally crazy idea was meant in earnest, unlike Mel BROOKS's *Silent Movie*. The houses in the titles of *House of Numbers* (1957) and *A House is not a Home* (1964) are a prison and a brothel. In the first, Jack Palance hopes to get out by changing places with his twin brother (Jack Palance) and the second has Shelley Winters as the 'Madam'. Poor Stephen Boyd had to wade through *The Oscar* (1965) Rouse can dream, can't he? and *The Caper of the Golden Bulls* (1966).

ROWLAND Roy
American. Born 1910. Directed mostly for MGM, Mediocre Gooey Movies. Little Margaret O'Brien cried through three of his pictures, Jane Powell warbled pleasantly through *Two Weeks with Love* (1950) and *Hit the Deck* (1955) and Mario Lanza almost flattened *The Seven Hills of Rome* (1958) with his bellowing. His work outside the cosy confines of MGM was more interesting and quirky and included *The 5000 Fingers of Dr T.* (1952), a bizarre and vulgar extended dream sequence of a young boy's nightmare of a piano school where 500 boys are kept prisoner by the evil Dr T. and *The Girl Hunters* (1963) in which Mickey Spillane plays his own Mike Hammer. **Also:** *Our Vines have Tender Grapes* (45), *Killer McCoy* (47), *Excuse My Dust* (51), *Bugles in the Afternoon* (51), *Affair with a Stranger* (53), *Rogue Cop* (54), *Meet Me in Las Vegas* (56).

RUGGLES Wesley
American. 1889-1972. One of the original Keystone Kops. Brother of comic character actor, Charles Ruggles. Worked at Paramount for many years directing romantic comedies with polished performers such as Claudette Colbert, Jean Arthur, Carole Lombard, Fred McMurray and Melvyn Douglas. *No Man of Her Own* (1932) was Gable and Lombard's only co-starring movie and *I'm No Angel* (1933) has Mae West's immortal line, 'Beulah, peel me a grape'. This high camp movie led to the introduction of the Hays Code the following year. **Others:** *Bolero* (34), *I Met Him in Paris* (37), *True Confession* (37), *Sing you Sinners* (38), *My Two Husbands* (39), *London Town* (46).

RUDOLPH Alan
American. Born 1944. Protégé of Robert ALTMAN who produced his first films. *Welcome to L.A.* (1977) or 'The City of One-Night Stands' is about the fouled up love lives of the denizens of tinsel town with the Altman stock company including Keith Carradine, Sally Kellerman, Geraldine Chaplin and Sissy Spacek. Miss Chaplin turns up in the effective but far-fetched revenge movie called *Remember My Name* (1978) in which she persecutes her angular ex--husband Anthony Perkins. **Also:** *Roadie* (81)

RUSH Richard
American. Born 1931. Graduate of UCLA Film Department. Started by making commercial and industrial films before working his way down to exploitation movies (including three with Jack NICHOLSON). They were directed under the pseudonym of Eli Cross, the name given to the director in *The Stunt Man* (1979) played by Peter O'Toole. A film full of visual surprises, tries to trick the audience once too often, and ponderously plays with notions of Illusion and Reality. Unfortunately, Rush had to tout the project around for so long that it lost its topical impact (the Vietnam war) on release. Ingmar BERGMAN, no less, liked the dated counter-culture college movie, *Getting Straight* (1970) and cast Elliott Gould in *The Touch* because of it.

Freebie and the Bean (1974) is the perfect movie for lovers of comedies with cretinous cops wrecking cars.

RUSSELL Ken
British. Born 1927. Former ballet dancer, actor, photographer. The short films he made for BBC TV, while displaying Philistinism as to the nature of creation and art, brought a fresh approach and visual flair to bear on the lives of Prokoviev, Elgar, Debussy, Richard Strauss, Delius and Isadora Duncan. His dilettantism became magnified ten-fold on the big screen, and images that had livened up 'the box', grew flaunting, crude and gaudy. Every stale cinematic trick was vomited up into the public's faces. The lives of Tchaikovsky (*The Music Lovers*, 1971), Gaudier-Brzeska (*Savage Messiah*, 1972), *Mahler* (1974), Liszt (*Lisztomania*, 1975) and *Valentino* (1977) were all grist to his run-of-the-mill talent. Even The Who's morbid rock-opera, *Tommy* (1975) was taken beyond bad taste and Sandy Wilson's modest 20's pastiche *The Boy Friend* (1971) was turned into an all-ogling, all-winking, all-nudging musical. It is the cinema of loathing. Loathing for his material, his actors, music, literature, art, the audience and perhaps himself. **Also:** *French Dressing* (63), *Billion Dollar Brain* (67), *Women in Love* (69), *The Devils* (71), *Altered States* (81).

RYDELL Mark
American. Born 1934. Former TV director and actor. His first two features were good-looking faithful adaptations from minor works by D.H. Lawrence (*The Fox* 1968) and William Faulkner (*The Reivers* 1969). The first, filmed in Canada, tells without sensationalism of a lesbian relationship disturbed by a man, the second is a folksy, family movie despite the presence of golden-hearted whores. *The Cowboys* (1972) is also meant for the family, although its story of how youngsters between the ages of nine and fifteen learn to become killers after their protector John WAYNE is murdered, is less than edifying. Fans of raunchy, gutsy singer Bette Midler are well catered for in *The Rose* (1979), based on the life of Janis Joplin, but the story comes over as the usual 'A Star is Bored' stuff. Gerontophiles, anglers and those who cherish the memory of old movies with Henry Fonda and Katharine Hepburn will love *On Golden Pond* (1981).

S

SAGAN Leontine

German. 1899-1974. Taught at Max Reinhardt's theatre school. Acted in and produced many plays. *Madchen in Uniform* (*Girls in Uniform* 1931), based on a play she had produced, is set in an oppressive boarding school for the daughters of Prussian officers. Made on the eve of the Nazi's accession to power, it is not only anti-authoritarian, but it treats the lesbian relationship between a girl and a teacher with a radical sense of sexual and personal liberty. She made only one other film, *Men of Tomorrow* (1932), for Alexander KORDA in England before returning to the stage.

ST. CLAIR Malcolm

American. 1897-1952. Writer and director for Mack SENNETT until 1921. Made two Buster KEATON shorts, *The Goat* (1921) and *The Blacksmith* (1922). Started directing features with the 1000-dollar-a-week canine star Rin-Tin-Tin in the 20's and ended his career making four appalling Laurel and Hardy movies at the end of theirs. i.e. *Jitterbugs* (1943), *The Dancing Masters* (1943), *The Big Noise* (1944), *The Bullfighters* (1945). In between were a few sophisticated silents such as *Gentleman Prefer Blondes* (1928), jazz-age musicals with Joan Crawford and Helen Kane and second-feature comedies. **Others:** *Montana Moon* (30), *Dangerous Nan McGrew* (30).

SAKS Gene

American. Born 1921. Comic actor and Broadway director whose films are adaptations of stage hits. The three Neil Simons are as good or as bad as the plays. *The Odd Couple* (1967) has Walter Matthau and Jack Lemmon comically at odds, *Barefoot in the Park* (1967) has Robert REDFORD and Jane Fonda as an odd couple and *The Last of the Red Hot Lovers*, with Alan Arkin as a Don Jewan who owns a fish restaurant, stinks. **Also:** *Cactus Flower* (69), *Mame* (74).

SANDERS Denis

American. Born 1929. With his brother Terry, wrote the screenplay for Raoul WALSH's *The Naked and the Dead* (1958). As independent producers, they gave George Hamilton and Robert REDFORD their first screen roles in *Crime and Punishment USA* (1958) and *War Hunt* (1962) respectively, both slightly off-beat projects that seemed to bode well for the future. Prognostications were wrong. **Also:** *Elvis: That's The Way It Is* (70).

SANDERS-BRAHMS Helga

German. Born 1940. Former announcer on German TV. Made documentaries for TV. Her films generally centre on women's place in an alienating society. Best known for *Germany, Pale Mother* (1980), a symbolic, committed and melodramatic account of her own mother's experiences during World War II and after. *No Mercy, No Future* (1981) is a harrowing portrait of a schizophrenic German girl based on the autobiographical writings of an actual girl. **Also:** *Shirin's Wedding* (76), *Heinrich* (77).

SANDRICH Mark

American. 1900-1945. At RKO between 1934 and 1938 where he made *The Gay Divorcee* (1934), *Top Hat* (1935), *Follow the Fleet* (1936), *Shall We Dance?* (1937) and *Carefree* (1938). Fred Astaire and Ginger Rogers gliding over a black, glass floor against art-deco sets by Van Nest Polglase, facing the music by Irving Berlin, Jerome Kern or George Gershwin and dancing cheek to cheek night and day, momentarily changing partners, suggesting they call the whole thing off but, with a 'shall we dance?', they come together again doing the Continental, the Piccolino or the Yam while on the sidelines are Eric Blore, Edward Everett Horton and Helen Broderick. Whatever else Sandrich did, they can't take that away from him. After a dispute with RKO, he left for Paramount and Fred and Ginger went their own ways. At Paramount, he made *Holiday Inn* (1942) with Crosby and Astaire, packed with songs including 'White Christmas' and *Here Come the Waves* (1944), a likeable wartime musical with Crosby and Betty

Fred Astaire and Ginger Rogers dancing 'Cheek to Cheek' in Sandrich's *Top Hat* (1935).

Hutton. **Also:** *Love Thy Neighbour* (40), *Skylark* (41), *So Proudly We Hail* (43), *I Love a Soldier* (44).

SANTELL Alfred

American. 1895-1981. Former architect. Director and writer for Mack SENNETT in the 20's. Usually second-string director who got to make a few 'big' pictures, such as *Daddy Long Legs* (1931) with Janet Gaynor, Maxwell Anderson's ponderous *Winterset* (1936) in which Burgess Meredith made his film debut, and Eugene O'Neill's *The Hairy Ape* (1944) with William Bendix as the stoker lusting for rich bitch Susan Hayward on deck. **Also:**

Having Wonderful Time (38), *Aloma of the South Seas* (41), *Beyond the Blue Horizon* (42).

SARAFIEN Richard C.
American. Born 1925. Much TV work. Made a couple of films in England, *Run Wild, Run Free* (1969) about a mute boy and a dumb animal, and *Fragment of Fear* (1970), psychological whodunnit hokum with David 'Blow Up' Hemmings. Back in the USA, he offered *Vanishing Point* (1971) a 100-minute car chase to a rock score, *The Man Who Loved Cat Dancing* (1973), a spoof Western, and *The Next Man* (1976), a spy saga showing off the shape of sharpshooter, Cornelia Sharpe. **Also:** *Man in the Wilderness* (71), *Lolly Madonna XXX* (73).

SARGENT Joseph
American. Born 1925. Handled a couple of tense, commercial suspense thrillers adeptly. *The Forbin Project* (1969), a mechanophobe movie about computers taking over the world and *The Taking of Pelham 123* (1974), a fast-paced yarn of gangsters taking hostages on a New York subway train. **Also:** *White Lightning* (73), *MacArthur* (77).

SAURA Carlos
Spanish. Born 1932. Studied at the Madrid Film Institute. Professional photographer until 1957. The films he made in Franco's Spain often contain oblique criticisms of the regime. He analysed the Spanish bourgeoisie, the church, the army and sexual taboos in *The Hunt* (1965), *Peppermint Frappe* (1967) – the first film of many to feature his future wife, Geraldine Chaplin – *The Garden of Delights* (1970) and *Anna and the Wolves* (1972). Films such as *Cria!* (1975. *Cria Cuervos*), *Elisa, My Life* (1976) and *Cousin Angelica* (1974) have a shifting chronology and an obsession with childhood. 'For years I've been studying . . . how memory, imagination and close reality form a complex and fascinating whole,' he says. Although he often achieves his goal, his films are more complex than fascinating. Franco's death seems to have, for the time being, deprived his films of an element of danger. **Also:** *Los Golfos* (59), *Blindfolded* (78), *Mother's 100th Birthday* (79), *Blood Wedding* (81).

SAVILLE Victor
British. 1897-1979. Produced and directed in England from 1927 and in Hollywood from 1945 to 1955. The English period included three musicals with Britain's top musical-comedy star, Jessie Matthews, notably *Evergreen* (1934) in which she sings 'Dancing on the Ceiling'. She became a star in *The Good Companions* (1933), a pleasant version of J.B. Priestly's novel, and appeared with a delightful array of stars in the compendium film, *Friday the 13th* (1933). In Hollywood, he was given British assignments. The 'London-can-take-it' wartime musical with Rita Hayworth, *Tonight and Every Night* (1945) which includes a number danced to a Hitler speech, A.J. Cronin's *The Green Years* (1946) in a studio Scotland, the frightfully MGM British of *If Winter Comes* (1947) with Walter Pigeon and Deborah Kerr, Kipling's *Kim* (1950) and seventeen-year-old Elizabeth Taylor's first adult role in *The Conspirator* (1949). Paul NEWMAN made his screen debut in Saville's last film, *The Silver Chalice* (1955), a wooden 144-minute CinemaScope spectacle about which Newman still blushes. **Also:** *Storm in a Teacup* (37), *Green Dolphin Street* (47), *Calling Bulldog Drummond* (51), *24 Hours of a Woman's Life* (52), *The Long Wait* (54).

SCHAFFNER Franklin
American. Born 1920. Five years war service. Worked on documentaries including 'The March of Time' and TV series such as 'The Defenders', and 'Jackie Kennedy's Tour of the White House'. The perfume of the White House pervades *The Best Man* (1964), a witty political piece by Gore Vidal, shot in a semi-documentary style. Politics also figures in *The War Lord* (1965), not an unsuccessful stab at 11th century England with Charlton Heston in the title role, *Planet of the Apes* (1967), Heston bares his chest again in this cumbersome allegory, *Patton* (1969), an ambiguous biopic on a modern war lord with a growling George C. Scott and *Nicholas and Alexandra* (1971), a tedious, simplistic Tsar-trek. *Islands in the Stream* (1976) develops into sentimental tosh and false heroics but George C. Scott comes as near to the Hemingway persona as one could wish. Gregory Peck and Laurence OLIVIER compete for the worst accent of the year award in *The Boys from Brazil* (1978), enjoyable send-in-the-clones nonsense.

SCHATZBERG Jerry
American. Born 1927. Former fashion photographer on 'Vogue'. For the prejudiced, that says it all. There is an element of the photographer and glossy mag reporter in *Puzzle of a Downfall Child* (1970), a modish story of a muddled model (Faye Dunaway) and *The Panic in Needle Park* (1971), a modish story of muddled junkies with Al Pacino in his first starring role. After *Scarecrow* (1973), a well-acted (Gene Hackman and Pacino) and photographed (Vilmos Zsigmond), 'Of Mice and Men'-type hobohemian buddy-buddy movie. He hit the road again with the country-and-western song-in-the-heart, tear-in-the-eye *Honeysuckle Rose* (1980) featuring Dyan Cannon and Willie Nelson. **Also:** *The Seduction of Joe Tynan* (79), *Misunderstood* (83).

SCHERTZINGER Victor

American. 1880-1941. Concert violinist, composer, song-writer, film director. A musician who made films or a director who composed. Naturally, he was associated with musicals. Wrote the music for Ernst LUBITSCH's first sound film, *The Love Parade* (1929). Also wrote the title songs of the two musicals he directed starring ex-Met soprano Grace Moore, *One Night of Love* (1934) and *Love Me Forever* (1935). Made the first two Crosby-Hope-Lamour Road pictures, *Road to Singapore* (1940) and *Road to Zanzibar* (1941). His last two movies were both with Crosby and Mary Martin, *Rhythm on the River* (1941) and *The Birth of the Blues* (1941). He died soon after completion of the latter.

SCHLESINGER John

British. Born 1926. Former actor and TV director. Directs theatre and opera productions. *A Kind of Loving* (1962) and *Billy Liar* (1963) introduced fresh, young players such as Alan Bates, Tom Courtenay and Julie Christie in modest films set in accurate working-class surroundings.

Jon Voight (L) and Dustin Hoffman (far R) in Schlesinger's *Midnight Cowboy* (1969).

As the 'kitchen sink' sank to be replaced by 'Swinging London', Schlesinger moved into the upper echelons with *Darling* (1965), an attempt at a cynical morality tale about a society the writer (Frederic Raphael) and the director seem to relish. *Far From the Madding Crowd* (1967) seldom gets beyond a picturesque illustration of Hardy's novel. New York is seen in *Midnight Cowboy* (1969) and *Marathon Man* (1976) as a caricatural wicked city, as one-dimensional as the characters. In the former, the stud and the con-man are superficially and sentimentally conceived with Dustin Hoffman in the Margaret Sullavan role dying just as he reaches Miami, the place of his dreams. *Marathon Man* is a tawdry affair with each image heavily emotive and significant and a plot with as many holes as in Dustin Hoffman's teeth after Laurence OLIVIER's Nazi dentist is through with him. Peter Finch and Glenda Jackson suffer exquisitely to 'Cosi Fan Tutti' in *Sunday, Bloody Sunday* (1971) because they're both in love wuth the same vapid boy. *Yanks* (1979), an old-fashioned boy-meets-girl in wartime England story, would have been better in five half-hour episodes on TV. His hamfistedness is most evident in his steam-rolling of Nathaniel West's classic, *Day of the Locust* (1975) and *Honky Tonk Freeway* (1981).

SCHLÖNDORFF Volker

German. Born 1939. Studied in Paris. Assistant to MALLE, RESNAIS and MELVILLE. Worked for French TV. Documentaries on Algeria and Vietnam. His analytical style and a liking for parables is especially suited to social and political subjects. His first feature, *Young Torless* (1966) is an accomplished transposition of the Robert Musil novel of embryonic Nazis at a boys' boarding school. Günter Grass's World War II parable, *The Tin Drum* (1979), however, loses its complexity and yet becomes muddied, but David Bennent as the boy who refuses to grow beyond the age of three effectively brings the book's character to life. Other forceful investigations into Germany past and present are *The Sudden Fortune of the Poor People of Kombach* (1971) set in 1891 when a group of peasants rob a local tax cart, made starkly without too many period embellishments, and *The Lost Honour of Katerina Blum* (1975), based on Heinrich Böll's novel of an innocent woman accused of terrorism, needed more distance to make it less self-righteous. Like a few of his other films, it was co-directed by his wife, Margaretta von Trotta, a director in her own right (*The German Sisters* 1981). The documentary side of *Circle of Deceit* (1982), actually filmed on location in war-torn Beirut, is more compelling than the story of a German reporter concerned about objective journalism and the break-up of his marriage. **Also:** *Baal* (70), *Summer Lightning* (72), *Coup de Grace* (76).

SCHOEDSACK Ernest B.

American. 1893-1979. At 17 worked for Mack SENNETT as cameraman. Filmed battles during World War I. Met Merian C. COOPER in Kiev in 1926. They combined to make documentaries in Iran and Thailand and two features, *The Four Feathers* (1929) and *King Kong* (1933), their greatest success. With Irving PICHEL, he made *The Most Dangerous Game* (1931), but took solo credit for *Son of Kong* (1933), a poor chimp off the old block, *The Last Days of Pompeii* (1935), the destruction worth waiting over an hour for and *Mighty Joe Young* (1949) another Kong rip-off. The latter depends almost exclusively on Willis O'Brien's special effects (aided by Ray Harryhausen) for its impact. The nightclub scene when the giant gorilla breaks out of his cage is especially spectacular. He last worked on *This is Cinerama* (1953). (See COOPER and PICHEL.)

SCHRADER Paul

American. Born 1946. Son of strict Calvinist parents. Going to the movies was forbidden, but young Paul broke away and guiltily saw his first film at the age of seventeen. A strong puritan streak remains, revealing itself in his screenplay for *Taxi Driver* (1976), and his second film as director, *Hard Core* (1979) follows a Calvinist midwesterner (George C. Scott) in search of his daughter through the porn world of L.A. seen with a cold eye. *American Gigolo* (1979), a well-designed morality play about a stud (Richard Gere) who satisfies rich women but not himself, lacks rhythm and reason. 'As reality becomes more depressing, we regress into fantasy,' Schrader says to justify the making of *Cat People* (1982) about people who turn into black leopards at sundown. Full of lurid images, it hints at hidden sexual fears, but is less effective than Jacques TOURNEUR's 1942 movie of the same title. His first feature,

David Bennent in Schlöndorff's *The Tin Drum* (1979).

Blue Collar (1978) has all the makings of a real proletarian picture, but rapidly loses its way in melodrama. One-time divinity student and graduate of UCLA, Schrader wrote a book called 'Transcendental Style: BRESSON, OZU, DREYER'.

SCHULTZ Michael

American. Born 1938. Part of the new wave of black directors working within the Hollywood system. Directed on the New York stage and TV. His first movie was the bouncy black *American Graffitti* called *Cooley High* (1975) which led on to *Car Wash* (1976). A funny, funky film with a disco beat, it depicts a day at an L.A. car wash in a series of sketches almost like a string of numbers in a musical. Richard Pryor, one of the most original comedians around, had an amusing cameo in *Car Wash*, but was wasted in the conventional bio-pic, *Greased Lightning* (1977), the story of Wendell Scott, the first black stock–car champion, and in *Which Way is Up?* (1977), an orange pickin' mess of a movie. He failed to return to the form of his first two movies with the all-white musical, *Sgt. Pepper's Lonely Heart's Club Band* (1978), an embarrassingly feeble fantasy built around some thirty Beatles' hits.

SCORSESE Martin

American. Born 1942. Spent a bed-ridden asthmatic childhood in the Sicilian-Catholic family in Little Italy, New York. This restless, nervy, black-bearded little man still gives the impression of being obsessed by his background, although he claims to have exorcised the demons of his childhood by making *Mean Streets* (1973). It was shot on a small budget in and around Los Angeles with only one week in New York. Filmed in dark tones, it inhabits the twilight world of pool-rooms, bars and night-clubs where two small-time hoods, Harvey Keitel and his sidekick, Robert De Niro, try to survive. Religious and family rituals cover the violence and gun lore seething beneath. The smooth bonhomie between members of the Mafia, the spaghetti meals, Italian arias and machismo is familiar stuff, but the relationship between Keitel and De Niro (who has a tour-de-force monologue) is one of the strengths of the movie. It foreshadows the hellish vision of New York in *Taxi Driver* (1976). Travers (De Niro) has no friends. He is the typical, paranoid

Robert de Niro in Scorsese's *Mean Streets* (1973).

loner, alienated from urban society. A Vietnam Vet, he sees New York as 'an open sewer'. Dangerous identification with the character is created by the apocalyptic view of the city, steam hissing out of the streets, the sordidness of 42nd Street, the incessant noise of the traffic and the wailing sirens, and the narration from his diary. 'Listen you fuckers, you screwheads, here is someone who would not take it anymore.' After killing a pimp (Keitel) as a step to cleaning up the city and to rescue the young prostitute (Jodie Foster), the camera tracks over the bloody walls, guns and corpses and out into the street in a typical end-shot. But De

Niro emerges alive and well, driving his cab and considered a hero. *Raging Bull* (1980), the story of Jake La Motta, world middleweight boxing champion from 1949 to 1951, alternates monotonously between professional and domestic fights in another of Scorsese's explorations into the close-knit Italian-American community with the underlying rigid and sentimental codes of masculinity. The boxing is treated as an excuse for some splendid black and white images, but not even De Niro (Scorsese's *primo uomo*) can make such a completely unattractive protagonist into Samson Agonistes. However, in these three almost expressionistic movies, he has shown an exciting, excitable, dark and obsessive talent that makes him the Celine of the cinema. If the New York of

these films is the city of 40's films noirs, *New York, New York* (1977) is the wonderful town of 40's musicals, and although overlong and lacking narrative drive, it is an entertaining pastiche with the redoubtable duo of Liza Minnelli and De Niro. Scorsese's inventiveness was first noticed as editor and virtual director of *Woodstock* (1970), *the* rockumentary. Roger CORMAN helped him make his first feature, *Boxcar Bertha* (1972), a reasonable apprentice work with a fine sense of locale. **Also:** *Alice Doesn't Live Here Anymore* (74), *The Last Waltz* (78), *King of Comedy* (82).

SCOLA Ettore
Italian. Born 1931. Former screenwriter. Made a number of lively, mainstream comedy-dramas, mainly concerned with Italian sexual stereotypes often featuring Vittorio Gassman and Marcello Mastroianni Some of the minor appeal of *A Special Day* (1976) was in the casting against type of Sophia Loren as a frumpy housewife and Mastroianni as a homosexual drawn together on the day of Hitler's visit to Rome. **Also:** *Let's Talk About Women* (64), *A Drama of Jealousy* (69), *We All Loved Each Other So Much* (75), *The Night of Varennes* (81).

SCOTT Ridley
British. Born 1939. Studied at the Royal College of Art in London. Stage designer and set designer for TV. Set up his own production company to make commercials. A brilliant designer, he prepares a shot-for-shot storyboard before filming. He was his own cameraman on his first feature, *The Duellists* (1978), based on a Conrad story, which almost outdoes *Barry Lyndon* in period, pictorial beauty, but does not have the unifying social relevance of KUBRICK's method, and its mixed American-British cast is awkward. Following along Kubrick's lines, he made it big with two Sci-fi blockbusters dependent on hardware. *Alien* (1979) is a Space Exorcist 2001 with a B movie plot of the 50's and actors like robots speaking 70's language and spewing up horrific creatures. *Blade Runner* (1982), based on Philip K. Dick's 1968 novel 'Do Androids Dream of Electric Sheep?' about robots going berserk, has splendid special effects and a LANGian nightmarish metropolis.

SEARS Fred F.
American. 1913-1957. Second features director of standard oaters, conventional crime stories and *Earth vs the Flying Saucers* (1956), a close encounter of the banal kind, except for some Ray Harryhausen special effects. Sears, however, takes his dubious place in social history as the director of the first rock 'n roll movie, *Rock Around the Clock* (1956) and its sequel, *Don't Knock the Rock* (1957) both featuring kiss-curled Bill Haley and his Comets. **Also:** *Ambush at Tomahawk Gap* (53), *Chicago Syndicate* (55), *Calypso Heat Wave* (57).

SEATON George
American. Born 1911. Former stage actor and director. Spent twelve years as screenwriter. William Perlberg produced Seaton's films at Fox which included a couple of assembly-line Betty Grable musicals, *Billy Rose's Diamond Horseshoe* (1945) and *The Shocking Miss Pilgrim* (1946); two exercises in whimsy, *Miracle on 34th Street* (1947) and *For Heaven's Sake* (1950), and the apple-pie family entertainment, *Chicken Every Sunday* (1949). Formed an independent partnership with Perlberg going in for rather plodding, sentimental dramas such as *Little Boy Lost* (1953) with Bing Crosby, and *The Country Girl* (1954) starring Crosby as an alcoholic and Grace Kelly as his dowdy wife. (She won an Oscar for not wearing makeup.) *Airport* (1970) was the first and best of the fear-of-flying-inducing movies with all-star passenger lists. **Also:** *The Proud and the Profane* (56); *Teacher's Pet* (58), *The Pleasure of his Company* (61), *The Counterfeit Traitor* (61) *Showdown* (72).

SEDGEWICK Edward

American. 1893-1953. Routine director of second features, he made eight of Buster KEATON's first films at MGM, watching as 'The Great Stone Face' disintegrated. *The Cameraman* (1928) and *Spite Marriage* (1929) were the last of Keaton's great period with gags to equal the earlier successes, but the others are painful to see. *Free and Easy* (1930), Buster's first sound film, was the beginning of the end, followed by *Doughboys* (1930), *Speak Easily* (1931), *Parlor, Bedroom and Bath* (1932), *The Passionate Plumber* (1932) and *What, No Beer?* (1933).

SEILER Lewis

American. 1891-1964. All-purpose Warner Bros. director from 1938 to 1953. Previously made many lively Tom Mix silent Westerns. At Warners directed five crime thrillers with Humphrey Bogart in the same role, the same suit and hat, often co-starring The Dead End Kids. e.g. *Crime School* (1938), *King of the Underworld* (1939), *The Big Shot* (1942). Ronald Reagan suffers from double vision and epilepsy as baseball star Grover Alexander in *The Winning Team* (1952), a laboured biopic. At Fox for a short period, he made three gossamer Vivian Blaine-Carmen Miranda musicals. i.e. *Something for the Boys* (1944), *Doll Face* (1946), *If I'm Lucky* (1946). **Also:** *Hell's Kitchen* (39), *Dust Be My Destiny* (39).

SEITER William A.

American. 1891-1964. After many silent movies he made mostly light comedies and musicals in the 30's and 40's that pleasantly helped audiences escape The Depression and The War. Shirley Temple displayed her considerable talents in *Dimples* (1936) and *Stowaway* (1936), in which she impersonates Eddie Cantor, Al Jolson and Ginger Rogers dancing with a Fred Astaire doll. The real Fred and Ginger are seen in five Jerome Kern numbers in *Roberta* (1935) and Fred and Rita Hayworth go through some splendid dance routines (also to Kern's music) in *You Were Never Lovelier* (1942). Plus three Deanna Durbin movies and the Marx Brothers in *Room Service* (1938) to dispel the gloom. **Also:** *Sunny* (30), *Sally, Irene and Mary* (38), *Four Jills in a Jeep* (44), *It's a Date* (40), *Nice Girl?* (41), *Up in Central Park* (48), *One Touch of Venus* (49), *Dear Brat* (51).

SEITZ George

American. 1888-1944. The serial king. From 1913 made Pearl White serials and directed and acted in *The Sky Ranger* and others. Made many features for MGM from 1933, including most of the popular Andy Hardy series starring Mickey Rooney, and a couple of good thrillers, *Woman Wanted* (1935) and *Kind Lady* (1935). **Also:** *Kit Carson* (40), *Sky Murder* (40).

SEMBENE Ousmane

Senegalese. Novelist and film-maker. Studied film with DONSKOI in Moscow. His novel, 'Le Docker Noir' (1957) was based on his experiences as a trade union organizer in Marseilles. One of the founders of African cinema, most of his films are in Wolof, a language of the Senegalese people and are comedy-dramas that dig deeply into African society and its colonial past, drawn from popular forms of entertainment and local culture. **Some titles:** *Black Girl* (66), *The Money Order* (68), *Emitai* (72), *Xala* (74), *Ceddo* (77).

SEN Mrinal

Indian. Born 1923 in Calcutta. A Bengali like Satyajit RAY, but in opposition to Ray's European humanism. A Marxist, his films attack the poverty and exploitation in Indian society. He has been called the 'Bengali GODARD'. Influenced by the French New Wave, he abandoned orthodox narrative cinema in the 70's, but has returned in his later work to more local story-telling techniques. *Bhuvan Shome* (1969), the first low-budget film to be financed by the Indian government, is a shrewd comedy about a bureaucrat who falls for a village girl. He entered a more political phase with his 'Calcutta Trilogy' consisting of *Interview* (1971), a man loses a job because he cannot get a suit to wear, *Calcutta '71* (1972), forty years in the history of social deprivation told with Brechtian rigour, and *The Guerilla Fighter* (1973) an analysis of the extreme left. 'I wanted to make disturbing and annoying films, not artistic ones,' he said. *The Royal Hunt* (1976) and *And Quiet Flows the Dawn* (1979) are less agit-prop films, but are still powerful, unsentimentalised political parables which try to come to terms with the complexities of his country. **Also:** *Chorus* (74), *The Outsiders* (77), *Man with the Axe* (78).

SENNETT Mack

American. 1880–1960. Born in Canada of Irish extraction. Real name Michael Sinnott. Took parts in burlesque plays before joining the Biograph Company in 1909. He learned methods of directing and editing from D.W. GRIFFITH. Began directing and acting in comedies for Biograph and then for the Keystone Company. In five years, he established the type of rapid, irreverent, crazy slapstick comedy forever associated with his name. Using speeded-up action, reverse motion and other camera and editing tricks, the films usually ended with a chase full of death-defying thrills executed by the comics themselves and stuntmen. Sennett filmed the throwing of the first custard pie by Mabel Normand at Fatty Arbuckle in *A Noise from the Deep* (1913), and created the Keystone Kops. *Tillie's Punctured Romance* (1914) was the first feature-length comedy (1¼ hours) and starred Marie Dressler, Mack Swain and Charlie CHAPLIN. He gradually delegated most of the directing to others, remaining a producer.

SHAVELSON Melville

American. Born 1917. Wrote comedy screenplays from the early 40's mainly with Jack Rose. Many of his films propound the principle of family planning. i.e. plan to have a large family. Wrote *Room for One More* (1952), about a soft-hearted couple who can't stop adopting children. Continued the doctrine of the more the schmaltzier in *The Seven Little Foys* (1956), vauldevillian widower Bob Hope puts his kids into his act, *Houseboat* (1958), widower Cary Grant gets Sophia Loren to look after his three kids, *Yours, Mine and Ours* (1968), widower Henry Fonda with ten kids marries widow Lucille Ball who has eight, *Mixed Company* (1974), a couple adopt three children of different races as they only have three of their own and *The War Between the Men and the Women* (1972), bachelor Jack Lemmon marries a woman with three kids, a dog and an ex-husband. He wrote of his experiences while making *Cast a Giant Shadow* (1966), Israeli propaganda hokum, in a book called 'How to make a Jewish movie'. **Also:** *Beau James* (57), *The Five Pennies* (59), *A New Kind of Love* (63).

SHERMAN George

American. Born 1908. Made mostly

standard action movies, colour Westerns and swashbucklers. Flame-headed Maureen O'Hara appeared with Errol Flynn in *Against All Flags* (1952), with Jeff Chandler in *War Arrow* (1954) and with John WAYNE in *Big Jake* (1971). **Also**: *The Bandit of Sherwood Forest* (46), *The Golden Horde* (51), *Son of Robin Hood* (58).

SHERMAN Lowell

American. 1885-1934. A sophisticated film actor who appeared in GRIFFITH's *Way Down East* (1920) and in CUKOR's *What Price Hollywood?* (1932) as the alcoholic film director. Directed thirteen movies from 1930 until his death at the age of 49, most of them sex comedies full of innuendo. It was *She Done Him Wrong* (1933), the first film to give Mae West the star treatment, that saved Paramount from bankruptcy. She invites Cary Grant to 'come up and see me some time' in one of her wittiest and sauciest films. Katharine Hepburn won her first Oscar as the stage-struck actress in *Morning Glory* (1933), a sharp comedy-drama with its share of clichés. 'You don't belong to any man now . . . You belong to Broadway.' **Also:** *Bachelor Apartment* (31), *The Greeks Had a Word for Them* (32), *Born to be Bad* (34), *Broadway Thru a Keyhole* (34).

SHERMAN Vincent

American. Born 1906. Former stage actor. Wrote screenplays before becoming one of Warners top directors in the 40's. His best films were *All Through the Night* (1942), a comedy spy thriller with Humphrey Bogart, Conrad Veidt and Peter Lorre, and two Bette Davis vehicles, *Old Aquaintance* (1943) and *Mr Skeffington* (1945). The former has a running cat fight between Davis and Miriam Hopkins and the latter is a lavish soap opera with Davis as a selfish society woman who loses her looks after a bout of diphtheria, but it's okay because her long-suffering husband, Claude Rains, returns home blind from a concentration camp. Errol Flynn's high living lost him his looks, but Sherman managed to make him look good in *The Adventures of Don Juan* (1949), a tongue-in-the-cheek swashbuckler. Films with Ann Sheridan, Ida LUPINO, Ava Gardner and Rita Hayworth proved he could show off beautiful women if nothing else. He continued with

melodramas into the 60's with *The Young Philadelphians* (1959) and *Ice Palace* (1960). **Also:** *Nora Prentiss* (47), *The Unfaithful* (47), *The Hasty Heart* (49), *Lone Star* (51), *Affair in Trinidad* (52), *The Garment Jungle* (57).

SHINDO Kaneto

Japanese. Born 1912. Screenwriter from 1934. Assistant to MISO-GUCHI. *Children of Hiroshima* (1952) and *Dobu* (1955) both dealt starkly with the effects of the Atom Bomb. He became justifiably renowned in the West for *The Island* (1960), a tale, told without dialogue, of the hard life of a peasant family trying to scrape a living on a barren island. His reputation declined, but *Onibaba* (1964) is a strange and violent folk story.

SIDNEY George

American. Born 1911. Former musician. Made shorts at MGM in the 30's. Most of his feature films are musicals, less inventive and stylish than those of his contemporaries at MGM, Vincente MINNELLI, Stanley DONEN and Charles WALTERS. Nevertheless, for producer Arthur Freed, he made the pleasant Wild West musicals, *The Harvey Girls* (1946) with Judy Garland, and *Annie Get Your Gun* (1950) with Betty Hutton replacing Garland and Sidney replacing both Busby BERKELEY and Walters, and the splendid *Show Boat* (1951), the first version in Technicolor with a touching touched-up Ava Gardner in a role that ideally should have gone to Lena Horne. He directed 'more stars than there are in the heavens' in *Thousands Cheer* (1943) and Gene KELLY and Frank Sinatra in *Anchors Aweigh* (1945), both weighed down rather by Joseph Pasternak's kitschy production approach. However, two of his best movies were lively, colourful, choreographed non-musical swashbucklers, *The Three Musketeers* (1948) with Gene Kelly as D'Artagnan and *Scaramouche* (1952) which, *tout proportion gardé*, is not far from RENOIR's *The Golden Coach* made in the same year. At Columbia, his three movies with Kim Novak, *The Eddie Duchin Story* (1956), *Jeanne Eagles* (1957) and *Pal Joey* (1957) were inferior to his earlier work. The one latterday musical to recapture the verve of the MGM days was *Bye*

Bye Birdie (1963). **Also:** *Bathing Beauty* (44), *Holiday in Mexico* (46), *Cass Timberlaine* (47), *Kiss Me Kate* (53), *Jupiter's Darling* (55), *Pepe* (60), *Viva Las Vegas* (64), *The Swinger* (56), *Half-a-Sixpence* (67).

SIEGEL Don

American. Born 1912. Studied at Cambridge University, England and The Royal Academy of Dramatic Art. Directed montage sequences for Warners and wartime documentaries. In the 50's, made a name for himself as director of forthright, cynical, tough, low-budget thrillers. Moved into larger scale productions in the late 60's, but retained the same

Clint Eastwood in Don Siegel's *Dirty Harry* (1971).

themes, drive and economy. *Riot in Cell Block II* (1954) and *Escape from Alcatraz* (1979) and *Crime in the Streets* (1956) and *Coogan's Bluff* (1968) are not that far apart, except for the gradual swing from a liberal standpoint to a more right-wing law-and-order stance. Richard Widmark as *Madigan* (1968) is typical of his uncompromisingly independent heroes, suspicious of all organizations. A dedicated cop, he has no time for the niceties of the law. Clint EASTWOOD, the cop hero of *Coogan's Bluff* and *Dirty Harry* (1971) is a loner, an outsider working within the system, but he is as cold-blooded and expressionless as the 'pod' people in Siegel's atmospheric allegory, *Invasion of the Body Snatchers* (1956), in which people are taken over and lose their feelings and identities. Eastwood as Harry Callahan moves inscrutably from one dirty job to the next 'always getting the shit end of the stick', hating 'spics, niggers, wops and kikes', treating women despicably and only handling his Magnum 44 with affection. By making his prey a whining, ugly, long-haired hippy type with a CND badge who calls cops 'pigs' and shoots at a 'Jesus Saves' neon sign, it panders to every member of the Moral Majority, gun-fetishist and budding vigilante. Despite the disclaimers, the film is loaded in favour of the Eastwood character. Terse, tense and slickly made, it is dangerously persuasive. John WAYNE goes out shooting in his final film, *The Shootist* (1976), a morbid, self-indulgent Western in which he plays an old gunfighter dying of cancer (like the actor). Away from the macho world of which Siegel is a past master, he made one of his most interesting and atypical pictures, *The Beguiled* (1970), a Gothic romance with Eastwood as a wounded soldier who takes refuge in a girls' school during the Civil War. For once, the women are characters and not merely murder victims or 'pieces of ass'.
Also: *The Big Steal* (49), *Baby Face Nelson* (57), *The Gun Runners* (58), *The Line-Up* (58), *Hound Dog Man* (59), *Flaming Star* (60), *Hell is for Heroes* (62), *The Killers* (64), *Two Mules for Sister Sara* (69), *Charley Varrick* (72), *Telefon* (77).

SILVER Joan Micklin

American. Born 1935. Studied at Sarah Lawrence College, New York State. Wrote scripts for educational films and for Mark ROBSON's wait-

ing wives Vietnam movie, *Limbo* (1972). Her husband financed her first two films. Her first, *Hester Street* (1974), shot in black and white and set in New York at the turn of the century, is an intelligent and gentle story of a young Jewish girl (Carol Kane) from the old country adapting to the American Way of Life. Her narrative skill, off-beat humour and way with actors is also evident in *Between the Lines* (1977), about the rise and fall of a radical weekly newspaper, and *Head Over Heels* (80), her first studio-backed film, a romantic comedy. She manages, on the whole, to circumvent the clichés and soft-centredness inherent in the subjects.

SILVERSTEIN Eliot

American. Born 1927. TV director. His first feature, *Cat Ballou* (1965) is a reasonably amusing spoof Western with Lee Marvin winning an Oscar for his double role. Some unintentional laughs in *A Man Called Horse* (1969), which is mostly an effective Swiftian tale of an English aristocrat (Richard Harris) captured by Sioux Indians in 1825 who rises from being a beast of burden to espousing their cause. **Also:** *The Happening* (67), The Car (77).

Robert Siodmak (R) directing (L to R) Melvyn Douglas, Gregory Peck and Ava Gardner in *The Great Sinner* (1949).

SIODMAK Robert

American. 1900-1973. Born in Memphis, Tennessee. His parents went to live in Germany when he was a year old. Studied at the University of Marburg. Became an actor and stage director. Co-directed (with Edgar ULMER) his first film, *Menschen am Sontag* (1929, *People on Sunday*), a co-operative venture (screenplay by Billy WILDER, photography by Eugene Schufftan) depicting twenty-four hours in the lives of working-class Berliners. He then made a few psychological dramas influenced by Expressionism, but when Goebbels criticized *The Burning Secret* (1933) for its 'dubious moral implications', he left for France, virtually at the same time as Fritz LANG and Wilder. In France, he made unexceptional vehicles for stars such as Edwige Feuillere, Danielle Darrieux, Jouvet and Harry Bauer, but *Pieges* (1939. *Snares*) with its police investigation and seedy characters prefigures his American period. It is for the few Hollywood

134

movies made from 1944 to 1949, in a career that stretched from 1929 to 1969, that Siodmak will be remembered. He brought a Germanic atmosphere of ominous shadows, expressionistic lighting and claustrophobic settings into the American film noir. *Phantom Lady* (1944) is the first of his 'night city' films, full of deceptive appearances. A man walks the mean streets, goes into dimly lit bars and dives, searching for the one woman who can prove him innocent of the murder of his wife. A mute servant girl is trapped in a mysterious house with a maniac in *The Spiral Staircase* (1945), an archetypal Siodmak thriller with a startling use of mirrors, corridors and the staircase of the title. *The Dark Mirror* (1946) also uses the mirror image where Olivia de Havilland plays identical twins, one good, the other a killer. (The same *doppelganger* theme is used in *Cobra Woman* – 1944 – with Maria Montez as twins.) The neon-lit crime thrillers *The Killers* (1946), *Cry of the City* (1948) and *Criss-Cross* (1949) also deal in repressed passions in a paranoiac city. The last of the 40's films noirs was *The File on Thelma Jordan* (1949) with a strong, smouldering performance from Barbara Stanwyck. After casting off the shadows for the bright, swashbuckling spoof, *The Crimson Pirate* (1952), he returned to the mists of Europe where his best film was *The Devil Strikes at Night* (1957) about a strangler of fifty women during the Nazi period. **Also:** *Son of Dracula* (43), *Christmas Holiday* (44), *The Suspect* (44), *The Strange Affair of Uncle Harry* (45), *Time Out of Mind* (47), *The Great Sinner* (49).

SIRK Douglas

American. Born 1900 in Germany of Danish parents. Real name Hans Detlef Sierck. Former journalist. Worked in the theatre in Germany as actor, producer and director. Made a few films, costume melodramas, before going to America. No matter how minor the movie, they were always done with impeccable style, paying attention to lighting, sets and costumes. Directed suave George Sanders in three atmospheric period pieces, *Summer Storm* (1944), *A Scandal in Paris* (1946) and *Lured* (1947); a few unpretentious family pictures including a colourful and witty musical, *Meet Me at the Fair* (1952); and Barbara Stanwyck submitting in *All I Desire* (1953) and *There's Always Tomorrow* (1956) to

the ideology of 'a woman's place is in the home'. However, it is with the four, rich and ripe, Universal Technicolor melodramas of the 50's that he really came into his own. In *The Magnificent Obsession* (1954), Rock Hudson (who appeared in eight of Sirk's films) becomes an eye-surgeon in order to restore the sight of Jane Wyman whose blindness he had caused in an auto accident; Middleaged, middle-class widow Jane Wyman in *All That Heaven Allows* (1955) flies in the face of convention by marrying her gardener, Rock Hudson, a much younger man; alcoholism, impotence, disease and destruction are rife in the oil-rich pre-Dallas family in the baroque *Written on the Wind* (1956), and the close friendship between Lana Turner and a black woman, Juanita Moore, in *Imitation of Life* (1959) provides a weepy end to the golden age of Hollywood melodrama. They have all the ludicrous extravagances of plot used time and again in TV soap opera, but when Sirk was making his bold and lush movies, TV had yet to discover sexual and social themes. The fluid camerawork, the inventive use of colour, the intensity of the performances, a genuine compassion for the characters and an implicit condemnation of a hypocritical and decaying social structure, transcend the material. This is what attracted the radical Rainer Werner FASSBINDER to Sirk's work. **Also:** *Hitler's Madmen* (43), *The Lady Pays Off* (51), *Weekend with Father* (51), *Has Anybody Seen My Gal?* (52),

Take Me to Town (53), *Sign of the Pagan* (54), *Captain Lightfoot* (55), *Battle Hymn* (57), *Interlude* (57), *Tarnished Angels* (57), *A Time to Live and a Time to Die* (58).

SJOBERG Alf

Swedish. Born 1903. One of Sweden's great theatre directors. Former head of the Royal Dramatic Theatre of Stockholm. After making his first feature, *The Strongest* (1929), a poetic drama of seal hunters filmed in natural settings, he returned to the stage for eleven years before making another. *Frenzy* (1944) instigated a renaissance of Swedish cinema, leading to the films of Ingmar BERGMAN (who wrote the script), and introduced Mai ZETTERLING to international audiences. She plays an adolescent girl victimized by a sadistic schoolmaster and misunderstood at home, who turns to prostitution. This highly-charged work, expressionist in style, prefigures some of BERGMAN's early films. *Miss Julie* (1951) loses some of the claustrophobia of the Strindberg play, but it has a remarkable performance from Anita Bjork and a complex flashback–flashforward technique in which characters from the past appear in scenes with those of the present. Another powerful female performance is given by Eva Dahlbeck in *Only a Mother* (1949), a saga of a woman's life. **Also:** *Karin Mansdotter* (54), *The Father* (69).

SJOMAN Vilgot

Swedish. Born 1924. Well-known

Lana Turner and John Gavin in Douglas Sirk's *Imitation of Life* (1959).

novelist. Wrote scripts for a number of films. Assistant to Ingmar BERGMAN. He is interested in exposing social and sexual taboos. A girl is raped by a dog in *491* (1964) and *My Sister, My Love* (1966) takes the incestuous love affair from 'Tis Pity She's a Whore' as its basis. He caused a *succes de scandale* with *I am Curious Yellow* (1967) and *I am Curious Blue* (1968) which contain a measure of shock tactics, explicit sex and lesbianism. Their loose narrative structure and the use of newsreel material, reflect part of the changing political climate in Europe in the late 60's, but they are rather more heavy going than heavy breathing. *I Am Blushing* (1982) is Sjoman's answer to COPPOLA's *Apocalypse Now* (1979), made in the Philippines, based on Conrad's 'Victory' with the director as a shaven-headed BRANDO and Larry 'J.R.' Hagman representing American corruption. The title may be the result of foresight.

SJOSTROM Victor

Swedish. 1879-1960. Director and actor. The most influential director, with Mauritz STILLER, of early Swedish cinema. Showing a preference for social problems and filming in natural settings, he illustrated the Swedish literary tradition of the relationship of the landscape and climate with the psychology of the characters. *The Phantom Carriage* (1921) is an eerie story of the supernatural, with excellent special effects, shot mainly outdoors and starring himself. He was brought to Hollywood in 1923 where he directed nine films under the name of Victor Seastrom, during an unhappy six-year stay. He got Lon Chaney to give his most naturalistic performance in the first MGM movie *He Who Gets Slapped* (1924), the story of a scientist who becomes a circus clown, and directed fellow Swedes Greta Garbo and Lars Hanson in *The Divine Woman* (1928), but the two films he made with Lillian Gish and Hanson, *The Scarlet Letter* (1926) and *The Wind* (1928) are his finest achievements in America. The former is a fine adaptation of Hawthorne's novel and the latter is a powerful melodrama, shot on location in the heat of the Mojave Desert. Gish, giving the performance of her life, alone in a desert shack, kills an intruder and buries him in the sand, but the incessant wind almost drives her mad and exposes the hand of the dead man.

The force of nature and its effect on the psyche have seldom been better portrayed. MGM interfered with the editing and added a sound track. Sjostrom returned to Europe where, after directing a couple of films, returned to acting. He is remembered as the old professor in BERGMAN's *Wild Strawberries* (1957).

SKOLIMOWSKI Jerzy

Polish. Born 1938. Studied literature, art and ethnography at Warsaw University. At Lodz film school, he co-wrote scripts for POLANSKI's *Knife in the Water* (1962) and WAJDA's *Innocent Sorcerers* (1959), in which he played one of the leads. In his three Polish films, he confronts the problems of the post-war generation, existing in a dehumanized society with he himself playing an outsider bitterly caught in an age of anxiety. In *Walkover* (1965), Skolimowski, a former amateur boxer, plays a rootless thirty-year-old who decides to return to boxing. An equivocal film, it creates a feeling for the industrial locale and poses questions about competition and ageing. *Barrier* (1966) is an assured surrealistic satire of a young medical student's journey across a strangely conceived Warsaw, while *Hands Up!* (1967) sees Poland as a country full of trains taking Poles to unknown destinations against their will. The authorities banned the film and he left the country to become, like Polanski, an itinerant filmmaker. He carried his vision and acid humour with him. In Belgium, he made *Le Depart* (1967), a very French New Wave comedy, in Yugoslavia *The Adventures of Gerard* (1970), a rather heavy big-budget farce based on Conan Doyle, in Munich, *King, Queen, Knave* (1972), an uneven version of Nabokov's novel and *Deep End* (1970) was shot in London and Munich. A young boy who works at a run-down swimming pool in a London suburb is obsessed by a girl, finally going off the deep end by killing her. The simple story is conceived in short, vibrant scenes that manage to capture the world as seen through the adolescent's eyes, revealing something about London that few British directors have succeeded in doing. In *The Shout* (1979), based on a story by Robert Graves, he expoits the underlying menace of the seeming innocence of the English countryside. London is an alien city for four Polish workmen, only one of whom speaks English, in *Moonlighting* (1982), a brilliantly economical

Alan Bates in Skolimowski's *The Shout* (1979).

film (it was shot in five weeks) which obliquely refers to the Polish crisis. Skolimowski has turned the state of exile to his advantage.

SMIGHT Jack

American. Born 1926. TV and film director. His style, or lack of it, is interchangeable in both media. *Harper* (1966), an attempt to recapture the feel of private-eye pictures of the 40's, is pure 60's slick and *Kaleidoscope* (1966), set in swinging sixties London, is a jokey, pop art, heist movie. Rod Steiger shows a rare comic flair in *No Way to Treat a Lady* (1968), playing seven parts, more than in his whole career, but is back to his mannered, morose self in *The Illustrated Man* (1969), a pretentious science-fiction morality play with Steiger as a tatooed tramp with each tatoo telling a story. **Also:** *I'd Rather Be Rich* (64), *The Third Day* (65), *The Secret War of Harry Frigg* (67), *Airport 75* (74), *Rabbit Run* (75), *Midway* (76).

136

in colour, 70mm and stereophonic sound, are full of eye-boggling rhetorical images which convey the impression of a rapturous dream dreamed by the sleeping giant of Russian cinema.

SPIELBERG Steven

American. Born 1947. The Peter Pan of movies. Some are born childish, some achieve childishness and some have childishness thrust upon them. Spielberg's films are scrumptious, mindless, enjoyable, hard-back comic-book fare for kiddies and grown-ups who want to regress and escape the real world. He has plundered worthless Saturday matinee material, spent a fortune refurbishing it and presenting it as precious metal. He is a raider of the lost RKO. Since *Jaws* (1975), apart from the gargantuan flop of *1941* (1979), his pictures have broken all box-office records, making him the Messiah of the industry. Rubber Spielberg dolls are sold everywhere as a tie-in with the movies. His success is out of this world or E.T. Son of an electrical engineer and computer expert, he took an English degree at California State College, Long Beach. Directed TV series, including the first Columbo episode. His TV movie,

SNOW Michael

Canadian. Born 1929. Painter, sculptor, jazz musician. A prominent figure in the American Underground and one of the most advanced 'structural' film makers, he attempts to redefine our way of seeing by exploring new spatio-temporal concepts. *Wavelength* (1966–1967) is effectively a single 45-minute zoom starting from a high viewing position in an empty loft (people enter and a murder is committed), finally focussing on a photograph of the sea. A camera mounted on a machine able to move in multiple directions was set up in an area of N. Canada for the three-hour *La Region Centrale* (1970–1971) and the result is a continually changing landscape seen through the eye of the revolving, panning, tilting and swirling camera.

SOLNTSEVA Yulia

Russian. Born 1901. Widow of DOVZHENKO who filmed the posthumous screenplays left by her husband. Difficult to judge how much was detailed in the scripts and how much was her own work. However, the trilogy, *Poem of the Sea* (1958), *The Flaming Years* (1961) and *The Enchanted Desna* (1965), made

Harrison Ford (right) in Spielberg's *Raiders of the Lost Ark* (1981).

Duel (1971) is an immensely effective man vs machine thriller of a driver being chased across country by a menacing truck. *The Sugarland Express* (1974) is also about a chase, this time about a young couple pursued by the police and is probably the last time Spielberg treated people with any depth. *Jaws* is best when the shark is not visible as in the expert sequence on the beach when panic ensues after a swimmer disappears and only frantic legs are seen in the water. When the famous, mechanical monster is trundled in, cleverly edited with footage of real sharks, it becomes less menacing. (Compare it to HITCHCOCK's *The Birds*.) Even 'Bruce' the shark machine is more interesting than the pompous characters. Special effects are again the stars of *Close Encounters of the Third Kind* (1977), a quasi-religious ecstatic fantasy of a flying saucer coming down in America and choosing ordinary guy, Richard Dreyfuss to take off with them. We are not alone in the Universe, but are accompanied by soppy, little green men. *Raiders of the Lost Ark* (1981) lacks the tatty charm of its sources, but the masterful sets, cutting and effects make up for it. *E.T. – Extra-Terrestial* (1982) is an expert and entertaining amalgam of all the elements of children's literature and movies of the past. Seen entirely from the child's viewpoint it is the apotheosis of cuteness. Loveable foetus-faced 'E.T.' has been marooned on wicked Earth but finds a friend in a human boy before having to return to his home in the sky. This star-child has replaced Lassie, Toto, Dumbo, Bambi and C–3PO in the hearts of the fickle movie-going public.

Who's directing whom? Francois Truffaut and Steven Spielberg on the set of Spielberg's *Close Encounters of the Third Kind* (1977).

STAHL John M.

American. 1886–1950. Former stage and screen actor. Spent ten years at Universal Studios making mainly 'women's pictures', dealing with novelettish material tastefully and tactfully, getting marvellous performances from Irene Dunne (*Back Street* 1932, *Magnificent Obsession* 1935, *When Tomorrow Comes* 1939), Margaret Sullavan (*Only Yesterday* 1933) and Claudette Colbert (*Imitation of Life* 1934), using apt close-ups and two-shots. Douglas SIRK remade three of Stahl's films for the same studio in the '50's, but his approach was less restrained and more baroque excepting *Leave Her to Heaven* (1945) which Stahl made for Fox. Revelling in colour for the first time, he presents a lurid, operatic tale of a woman (Gene Tierney) whose jealousy ruins those around her. Here he was able to pull out all the stops, before retreating into the polite and cosy world of *The Foxes of Harrow* (1947), *The Walls of Jericho* (1948) and *Oh, You Beautiful Doll* (1949), a Tin Pan Alley June Haver musical. **Also:** *The Immortal Sergeant* (43), *The Eve of St. Mark* (44), *Keys of the Kingdom* (44).

STALLONE Sylvester

American. Born 1946. Son of a Sicilian father and French mother. Studied drama at Miami University and worked as an actor off-Broadway. Had small parts in a number of films before starring in *Rocky* (1976. Directed by John G. ALVILDSEN). It was one of the most profitable movies for twenty years and a personal success for Stallone, who claims to have written the script in three-and-a-half days. He wrote, directed and starred in *Paradise Alley* (1978), set in the year of his birth, but influenced by 'every goddam Warner Brothers epic' of the 30's and twice as loud and corny. *Rocky II* (1980) continues where *Rocky* left off and structurally the films are very much alike. Stallone believes in the principle that 'if at first you succeed then try, try again,' so along comes *Rocky III* (1982) with the same irresistible, simple emotions and situations, proving they do make movies like they used to. *Rocky* IV, V, VI, VII to come?

STERNBERG Josef von.

American. 1894-1969. Born in

138

Vienna as Jonas Sternberg. Served in the American army in World War I. Worked in Hollywood as editor, writer and assistant director in his 20's. Both Sternberg and Marlene Dietrich existed before and after their work together, but then so did Laurel and Hardy, Gilbert and Sullivan and Marks and Spencer. Sans Dietrich, he made *Underworld* (1927), one of the few silent American films to deal with organized crime and *The Docks of New York* (1928) treats urban squalor with poetic realism obtained by the soft lighting (Sternberg's trademark) and stylized performances. *The Last Command* (1928) with Emil Jannings in another masochistic role as an exiled Russian general forced to become an extra in a Hollywood film about the Revolution, sets up a strange double image between the exotic Russian past and the present studio set. The two versions of classics, *An American Tragedy* (1931) and *Crime and Punishment* (1935) have imaginative moments, but are basically straightforward and flat,

Josef von Sternberg

containing some pretty hammy performances. Most of his other work was bread and butter stuff, excepting *The Saga of Anatahan* (1953) showing what can be done with a simple studio set and lighting and *The Shanghai Gesture* (1941), a throwback to his golden days at Paramount with its

magical realization of an Oriental gambling den, only lacking the erotic presence of Dietrich. They 'came' together in *The Blue Angel* (1930), *Morocco* (1930), *Dishonored* (1931), *Shanghai Express* (1932), *Blonde Venus* (1932), *The Scarlet Empress* (1934) and *The Devil is a Woman* (1935), seven of the most sensuous, bizarre, exotic and unnaturalistic films in cinema. The iconographic figure of Dietrich, the illusory vision of Woman, the eternal femme fatale appearing in different guises as Lola-Lola, Amy Jolly, Spy X27, Shanghai Lily, Catherine the Great, or Concho Perez, inhabiting a phantasmagoric Berlin, Morocco, Spain, Russia, China or America, conjured up by sets, make-up, wigs, costumes, light and shadow. The absurd dime-novel plots, whether colonial adventure, spy story or historical romance, the dreadful dialogue delivered at a languorous pace and the stereotyped characters are transformed by Sternberg's pictorial splendour. He claimed to have written and photographed all his films, but Jules

Marlene Dietrich as Catherine the Great in Sternberg's *The Scarlet Empress* (1934).

Furthman is credited with the screenplay of six and Lee Garmes as cameraman was probably responsible for many of the chiaroscuro effects. **Also:** *The King Steps Out* (36), *I Claudius* (37–unfinished), *Jet Pilot* (51), *Macao* (52).

STEVENS George

American. 1904-1975. Began directing Laurel and Hardy two-reelers for Hal Roach. In the 30's and early 40's, he made a wide range of polished comedies, dramas and a couple of musicals. During the war, he filmed with the 6th Army in Europe, including the liberation of Dachau. After the war, his films were more personal, his working methods slower (he would shoot from every possible angle before assembling the film in the cutting-room) and his style more deliberate. Katharine Hepburn's main preoccupation in *Alice Adams* (1935), *Quality Street* (1937) and *Woman of the Year* (1942) is to catch a man and keep him. The latter was the first pairing of Hepburn with Spencer Tracy. Barbara Stanwyck realises she can't get a man with a gun in the episodic, *Annie Oakley* (1935) and Jean Arthur appears in the excessively talkie, *The Talk of the Town* (1942) and in the lively comedy, *The More the Merrier* (1943). From the colonial derring-do of *Gunga Din* (1939) to the ikky, *Penny Serenade* (1941), he proved himself an excellent craftsman with a liking for the arty cut and a slow build-up. Of the pre-War movies, *Swing Time* (1936) stands out as one of the finest Fred Astaire and Ginger Rogers musicals, and *A Damsel in Distress* (1937) is a delightful musical-comedy based on P.G. Wodehouse starring Fred without Ginger but no lack of zip. *I Remember Mama* (1948), the first post-War movie, is a warm-hearted comedy-drama with a gallery of beautifully observed characters, full of movement and atmosphere. The second screen version of Dreiser's 'An American Tragedy' called *A Place in the Sun* (1951), is virtually the only Stevens' film in which sex plays a part, but the tastefulness smooths out the story, although it is for the closeups of Monty Clift, Shelley Winters and Elizabeth Taylor that the film should be seen. The measured pace adds to the building up of tension in the classic Western, *Shane* (1953). Alan Ladd is the lone gunfighter who rides in from nowhere, defends the homesteaders by shooting the vicious hired-gun in

George Stevens

black (Jack Palance) and rides off again. It is seen mainly through the eyes of the hero-worshipping boy, Brandon de Wilde and, as Ladd leaves, the camera follows the boy as he runs after him with the landscape echoing his shouts of 'Shane, Shane'. *Giant* (1956) manages to contain Edna Ferber's sprawling novel of Modern Texas into a coherent three-hour's epic story-telling, although the second half deteriorated due principally to the failure of Rock Hudson, Elizabeth Taylor and James Dean (in his last role) to age convincingly. *The Diary of Anne Frank* (1959) is well-meaning, dull and badly cast and *The Greatest Story Ever Told* (1965) is a three-hour-forty-minute Jesus Christ Superbore blockbuster filled with dreary cameo appearances from a horde of Hollywood stars. **Also:** *Vivacious Lady* (38), *Something to Live For* (52), *The Only Game in Town* (69).

STEVENSON Robert

American. Born 1905 in Britain. Made a film a year for twenty years from 1937 without dishonour, before becoming the Disney Studios director par excellence. The pre-Disney period included *King Solomon's Mines* (1937) with Paul Robeson singing against the painted backdrops, *Tom Brown's Schooldays* (1940) with

Freddie Bartholomew as the proper little Victorian gentleman, *Back Street* (1941), a good remake of the John STAHL 1932 weepie, starring Margaret Sullavan, and *Jane Eyre* (1943) with Orson WELLES as a perfect, brooding Rochester. As head elf in the Disney family-picture factory he directed the two flying rubber movies, *The Absent-Minded Professor* (1961) and *Son of Flubber* (1963), the flying nanny (Julie Andrews' screen debut) in *Mary Poppins* (1964), an enjoyable mixture of live-action and animation, and the flying bedstead in *Bedknobs and Broomsticks* (1971), all giving almost as much pleasure to children as his literary namesake. **Also:** *My Forbidden Past* (51), *Old Yeller* (57), *Kidnapped* (60), *In Search of the Castaways* (62), *That Darn Cat* (65), *The Gnome-Mobile* (67), *The Love Bug* (69), *Herbie Rides Again* (73).

STILLER Mauritz

Swedish. 1883–1928. Former violinist. Actor in the Swedish and Finnish theatre. His first films were sophisticated sex comedies such as *Erotikon* (1920), anticipating BERGMAN's *Smiles of a Summer Night*. Under the influence of his friend Victor SJOSTROM, he moved nearer the more sombre Swedish literary tradition with films based on the novels of Selma Lagerlof drawn from folk tales in which the close relation between the landscape and the characters is explored. *The Saga of Gosta Berling* (1923), almost a series of historical tableaux, is famous for Greta Garbo's first appearance in a feature film. It was Stiller who discovered Greta Gustafson, renamed her, got her to lose ten kilos and created her mystique. In 1925, Louis B. Mayer invited Stiller and Garbo to Hollywood, but he obviously only wanted Garbo and took on Stiller as part of the package. He was not chosen to direct her first American film, was replaced after only ten days on her second, but remained to coach her off the set. He made two films at Paramount, *Hotel Imperial* (1926) and *The Woman on Trial* (1927) as vehicles for Pola Negri. He returned to Sweden where he died a couple of months later, leaving his protegée to go on to greater glory. **Also:** *Love and Journalism* (16), *Thomas Graal's Best Film* (17), *Sir Arne's Treasure* (19), *Song of the Scarlet Flower* (19).

STONE Andrew
American. Born 1902. Started directing serials, which accounts for his taste for cliff-hangers. It is musicals, however, that lie at both ends of his career. Thankfully, the songs override the silly plots of *The Great Victor Herbert* (1939) and *Stormy Weather* (1943), the latter a worthwhile showcase for some of the best black talent around including Lena Horne, Bill Robinson, Fats Waller and Cab Calloway. Unfortunately, nothing could save the poisonous treacle of *Song of Norway* (1970) and *The Great Waltz* (1972), ludicrously fanciful biopics on the lives of Edvard Grieg and Johann Strauss. In 1943, he formed his own production company with his wife Virginia Stone and generally specialized in preposterous suspensers, many of them forerunners of the 'disaster' movies of the 70's. Shooting mainly on location, they preferred to blow up real trains, crash planes and sink ships than use models. Doris Day brings down an airplane singlehandedly in *Julie* (1956), though she's never flown before; passengers are trapped in a sinking ship in *The Last Voyage* (1960) and a terrifying forest fire is the climax of *Ring of Fire* (1961). **Also:** *The Steel Trap* (52), *A Blue-Print for Murder* (53), *Cry Terror* (58), *The Decks Ran Red* (58), *The Password is Courage* (63).

STRAUB Jean-Marie
French. Born 1933 in Metz, France, before it was annexed by Germany. Studied film in Paris. Assistant to BRESSON and RIVETTE. Left for Germany during the Algerian War to escape military service. All his films have been made in collaboration with his wife, Daniele Huillet, mainly in Germany and Italy. His first works were short films based on Heinrich Böll, *Bonn Diary-Machorta-Muff* (1963) and *Nicht Versohnt* (1965 *Not Reconciled*) the latter a fifty-three minute decomposition of the long novel about three generations of a German family in which past and present coexist, making the point that Nazism runs through the generations. All the roles in *The Chronicle of Anna Magdalena Bach* (1967) are taken by professional musicians (except for Huillet in the title role) led by Gustav Leonardt who plays Bach, the musician and the music. Using direct sound and extremely long takes, it is really a documentary on musicians at work today and in the 18th century as well as a concert in which the frozen images do not detract from the music. Both *Othon* (1972) and *History Lessons* (1973) are Brechtian exercises, placing history in relation to modern political life. Brecht spoke of 'the theatre whose stage is the street' and in *Othon*, Straub places his non-French speaking, non-professional actors on the terrace of the Palatine Hill in Rome, getting them to read the Corneille play against the sound of traffic. In *Fortini/Cani* (1977) the left-wing Italian Jewish writer Franco Fortini examines his thoughts on the Israeli-Palestinian conflict and *From the Clouds to the Resistance* (1979), based on two works by Cesare Pavese, takes the form of six dialogues between mythological figures on the partisan movement in Piedmont during the war. Schoenberg's religious and philosophical opera, *Moses und Aron* (1975) was filmed in Italy using direct sound. Despite an unconvincing Act II orgy, it is a faithful rendering of the opera with its obvious attractions to Straub of pure thought vs image, reason vs emotion, silence vs communication, idea vs verbal expression. Like Moses, Straub's austere minimalist cinema is concerned with these issues.

STRICK Joseph
American. Born 1923. Former journalist on the Los Angeles Times. Filmed mainly in his spare time for about eight years. *The Savage Eye* (1960), co-directed with Ben Maddow and Sidney Meyers, is a semi-documentary that looks at the more bizarre aspects of life in L.A., although the eye is more jaundiced than savage. His attempts to scale the heights of twentieth century literary masterpieces is like a pole-vaulter with a walking-stick. *The Balcony* (1963), Genet's symbolic play set in a brothel is tame; *Tropic of Cancer* (1969) erroneously updates Henry Miller's 1934 diary of sexual adventures in Paris and miscasts Rip Torn as the writer. Some of the quality of *A Portrait of the Artist as a Young Man* (1977), Joyce's youthful masterwork comes through, although the dialectic is minimised, but Strick's attempt to film the unfilmable *Ulysses* (1967) . . . 'No, I said No I won't No.'

STROHEIM Erich von
American. 1885-1957. Born in Vienna of middle-class parents. Emigrated to USA in his early twenties and from 1914 played small

parts in films, including GRIFFITH's *Birth of a Nation* (1915) and *Intolerance* (1916). Became one of Griffith's assistants. He added the 'von' to his name, claiming to be an ex–army officer of noble descent. His screen persona became inseparable from his real self and, by playing a succession of brutal Prussian officers, gained the title of 'the man you love to hate'. Stroheim directed nine films in his whole career, but only his first two, *Blind Husbands* (1918) and *The*

Devil's Passkey (1919 – a lost film), were released without considerable studio interference. It is true that he was profligate with studio money (he rebuilt almost the whole of Monte Carlo on the Universal backlot for *Foolish Wives* 1921) and Irving Thalberg, head of production at Universal and later MGM, called him a 'footage fetishist', but the luxuriousness of settings was essential to his vision of European decadence. Yet, despite the vandalism committed on his art, he remains one of the great figures of cinema influencing, among others, Jean RENOIR. In *Blind Husbands, Foolish Wives* and *The Wedding March* (1926), he plainly enjoys his role of the seductive, seducing aristocrat in these cynical, witty, erotic Ruritanian melodramas, rich in social and psychological detail, in which love crosses class barriers and lust remains unconsummated. The camera moves seldom, but a long shot generally dissolves into a medium shot and then a close-up of a character. He depended a great deal on extended shots to build up dramatic intensity, character and atmosphere, preferring irises and fades to conventional editing. *Queen Kelly* (1928), produced by Joseph Kennedy and its star, Gloria Swanson, is a truncated but, nevertheless, delirious sado-masochistic masterpiece played against lavish decor being gnawed by the worm of evil. Even *The Merry Widow* (1925), based on the Lehar operetta, has a whiff of decay among the romanticism. Unlike his other silent films, *Greed* (1923) was filmed almost entirely on location, often the exact settings of Frank Norris's novel 'McTeague'. Stroheim wanted to make it with complete fidelity, 'picturalising' each sentence. The climax was actually shot in Death Valley with the actors really suffering from the heat. In its original ten-hour version, it remains the greatest film never seen, in its two-and-a-half hour version, it is the longest and greatest trailer ever made. ZaSu Pitts, wide-eyed and pale-faced, personifying the film's title, gives one of the finest of silent screen performances against a brilliantly observed social milieu. Not long after being prevented from completing his one sound film, *Walking Down Broadway* (1933) – released in mutilated form as *Hello Sister* – he left for France where he spent the rest of his life as an actor. Returning to Hollywood after many years, he is seen poignantly directing Gloria Swanson once more in Billy WILDER's *Sunset Boulevard* (1950).

STURGES John

American. Born 1911. Made documentaries during the war while in the air corps. Generally associated with action movies, particularly Westerns for which his cool style, use of long shot and interest in the individual pitting his strength against outside forces, is best suited. *Escape from Fort Bravo* (1953), *Gunfight at the O.K. Corral* (1957), *The Law and Jake Wade* (1958), *Last Train from Gun Hill* (1958) and *The Magnificent Seven* (1960) are all robust Westerns with gritty performances, made with skill and not much depth. There's plenty of action too in the far-fetched *The Great Escape* (1963) and *The Eagle Has Landed* (1976). One of his best and one of his worst films feature Spencer Tracy. In *Bad Day at Black Rock* (1954), Tracy plays a one-armed stranger who descends on a small town to uncover its secrets in a well-paced, intriguing yarn and one of the few films to touch on the problems of the Japanese-Americans during the war. Although filmed with Hemingway's guidance, in the actual locations of the book, *The Old Man and the Sea* (1958) completely defeated Sturges and his screenwriter, who grappled with the short parable-novel and came up with a skeleton. **Also:** *The Magnificent Yankee* (50), *Kind Lady* (51), *The People Against O'Hara* (51), *Jeopardy* (53), *Underwater* (54), *Backlash* (56), *Never So Few* (59), *Sergeants Three* (62), *The Satan Bug* (65), *The Hallelujah Trail* (65), *Hour of the Gun* (67), *Ice Station Zebra* (68), *Marooned* (69), *Joe Kidd* (72), *McQ* (74).

STURGES Preston

American. 1898-1959. Real name Edmund P. Biden, a name that could have been given to one of his characters. After some success as a playwright, he worked as screenwriter in Hollywood throughout the 30's. He wrote the scripts of all twelve films he directed. His America is a giddy, corrupt, bustling country, full of characters who throw off the bonds of convention, and eccentrics (played by William Demarest, Raymond Walburn, Franklin Pangborn and Eugene Pallette). The witty lines, visual gags and comic timing form part of his acerbic view of American life, although the misanthropy is tempered with a certain affection for his characters. In *The Great McGinty* (1940), a hobo (Brian Donlevy) becomes State governor by craft and graft in one of the best political satires. American values are entertainingly drubbed in *Christmas in July* (1940) in which Dick Powell goes on a frenzied spending spree thinking he has won a coffee slogan contest with the dreadful, 'If you can't sleep, it isn't the coffee, it's the bunk.' Barbara Stanwyck is *The Lady Eve* (1941), a card sharp on a Trans-Atlantic liner who catches shy, sappy, rich boy, Henry Fonda, in this stunning sex comedy. The serious uprightness of Joel McCrea is cleverly counterpointed by the absurd goings on around him in three of Sturges's films. In *Sullivan's Travels* (1941), he plays a successful director of film comedies who becomes a tramp in order to have first hand experience of social deprivation for a drama he wishes to make. Things turn nasty and he ends up in a chain gang. One night, the sullen prisoners shuffle in to see a movie, but they are soon laughing uncontrollably at a Mickey Mouse cartoon. This convinces Sullivan that to make people laugh is the finest achievement. The satire on Hollywood is effective, but the message is too pat and the autobiographical element uncomfortable.'. He continued his mission to make people laugh with the quintessential Sturges screwball comedy, *Palm Beach Story* (1942) in which Claudette Colbert takes off by train for Florida to get a divorce from her husband (Joel McCrea) and marry a rich man. On the train she meets millionaire J.D. Hackensacker III (Rudy Vallee) who proposes to her. The plot is resolved in typically nutty fashion. His two satires on small-town America *The Miracle of Morgan's Creek* (1944) and *Hail the Conquering Hero* (1944) starring klutzy Eddie Bracken, milk the sacred cows of motherhood and war-hero worship for laughs. His last four films were a curious mixture. Straight biopic, *The Great Moment* (1944), the throwback comedy, *Mad Wednesday* (1946) with Harold Lloyd in his final role, the inventive but unfunny, *Unfaithfully Yours* (1948), a hectic Betty Grable musical, *The Beautiful Blonde from Bashful Bend* (1949) and the made-in-France, *The French They are a Funny Race* (1956. *The Diary of Major Thompson*-GB) both Sturges's and Jack Buchanan's last film. The film she is not funny.

SUTHERLAND Edward A.

American. 1895-1974. Former stunt-man and actor. Married to Louise Brooks from 1926 to 1928 whom he directed with W.C. Fields in *It's the Old Army Game* (1926). Fields also starred in *International House* (1933) with a hilarious all-star cast gathered to watch a demonstration of a new invention, television; *Mississipi* (1935) with Fields stealing the film from Bing Crosby and *Poppy* (1936). Directed Eddie Cantor in *Palmy Days* (1931), Mae West in *Every Day's a Holiday* (1937), Laurel and Hardy in *Flying Deuces* (1939) and Abbott and Costello's first feature, *One Night in the Tropics* (1940), none of these films being near the comedians' best pictures. His last movie, before going into TV was the indigestible spuds and matzo balls *Abie's Irish Rose* (1946). **Also:** *Diamond Jim* (35), *The Boys from Syracuse* (40), *Dixie* (43), *Follow the Boys* (44).

SWIFT David

American. Born 1919. Worked mostly on radio and TV as writer-producer-director. Hayley Mills melts the hardest hearts in *Pollyanna* (1960) and appears as twins in *The Parent Trap* (1961), both bright Disney family entertainments. Jack Lemmon is worth watching in the somewhat tired comedies, *Under the Yum Yum Tree* (1963) and *Good Neighbour Sam* (1964), but *How to Succeed in Business Without Really Trying* (1967) is a felicitous Broadway transfer with imaginative staging of the Frank Loesser numbers, although Robert Morse fails to tone down his performance for the screen.

SYBERBERG Hans-Jurgen

German. Born 1935. As a young man, he filmed Brecht's Berliner Ensemble in rehearsal and the influence of the great German dramatist is evident in his films. They derive from Brecht's epic theatre and *lehrstücke*, fusing the formal with the ideological in an attempt to demystify Germany's cultural and historical past. A blend of theatre techniques such as back projections and back drops in *Ludwig-Requiem for a Virgin King* (1972), *Ludwig's Cook* (1973), history from below stairs in which we are taken on a cook's tour of his master's palaces, *Karl May* (1974), a biopic collage of the adventure writer and *Hitler* (1977), a

four-part seven-hour view of its subject from every possible angle. Any further fascination with the Nazi *Weltanschauung* is satisfied by the five-hour interview of *Winifried Wagner* (1975), the composer's daughter-in-law. **Also:** *Parsifal* (82).

SZABO Istvan

Hungarian. Born 1938. Studied at the Academy for Film Art in Budapest. Part of the Hungarian New Wave in the 60's. Gained world-wide attention with his second feature, *Father* (1967), a technically masterful exploraton of the younger generation's relationship to the past, symbolized by a growing boy's dreams of his dead father. The problems of the artist in a totalitarian state are presented forcefully in *Mephisto* (1981), based on the novel by Klaus Mann, about an actor who sells his soul by continuing to practise his art under the Nazis. Visually splendid in evoking the mood of the period, it is a subtle portrait of an opportunist, brilliantly relating the play in which the actor becomes famous with the rise of Nazism. Klaus Maria Brandauer as the flamboyant actor gives a remarkable many-faceted performance.

TANNER Alain

Swiss. Born 1929. Worked in TV and documentary films. An exact contemporary and friend of Claude GORETTA. His committed cinema has attempted to wipe the smug smile off the Swiss face by looking at alternative life styles. His first feature, *Charles, Dead or Alive* (1969) was the first Swiss film in more than two decades to be shown widely abroad. Charles (Francois Simon, Michel's son), a middle-aged watch company executive turns his back on his work and goes off to live in the country, but his family commit him to a mental home. In *Return to Africa* (1973), a young couple who wished to

settle in Algeria remain in Geneva and make of it their own foreign world. In collaboration with left-wing writer John Berger, he made *The Middle of the World* (1974), a parable of the conflict between rich and poor, male and female and North and South, told in a series of long takes, and *Jonas who will be 25 in the year 2000* (1976), a political comedy about the possibilities of change. In the controversial (and irritating) *Messidor* (1977), two young girls hitch-hike around Switzerland and kill a man who tries to molest them. Tanner emerged from a heart operation claiming to have finished with didacticism and presented his first film in English, *Light Years Away* (1981), a wordy folk tale set in Ireland starring Trevor Howard. Tanner and others have given the lie to those that say Switzerland only produces cuckoo-clocks and chocolate, although chocolate is easier to digest. **Also:** *La Salamandre* (71).

TARKOVSKY Andrei

Russian. Born 1932. Studied at the Soviet State Film School under Mikhail ROMM. His five films in twenty years are some of the most intensely personal and visually powerful statements to have come out of Eastern Europe for many years. His rich pictorial sense was already evident in his first film, *Ivan's Childhood* (1962), the story of an orphan boy working for the partisans during the war. The medieval painter *Andrei Rublev* (1966) is seen creating his masterpieces while around him barbaric acts are being enacted. It ends with a sequence of icons to which the colour and CinemaScope screen does justice. *Solaris* (1971), a striking science-fiction film, without

Tarkovsky's *The Stalker* (1980).

reliance on special effects, is weighed down somewhat by turgid philosophic discussions as the cosmonauts are forced into self-examination, while *The Mirror* (1975), full of dream-like images, is an impenetrable evocation of the director's life. There is a long section in *The Stalker* (1980) in which a philosopher and scientist discuss their differing viewpoints in terms of bad 30's didactic drama, but the rest tells of a nightmarish journey through a forbidden wasteland undertaken by the shaven-headed stalker of the title and his two companions. Shot in eerie sepia colour, it remains to haunt the mind.

TASHLIN Frank

American. 1913–1972. Former animator, cartoon story writer and gag man. Became head of Columbia's Screen Gems cartoon department in 1941. Wrote feature film scripts, including *Paleface* (1948) with Bob Hope and *Love Happy* (1950) with the Marx Brothers. He continued to see life in terms of cartoon films in which he treated Jerry LEWIS and others as animated drawings, which accounts for much of the cruel and mechanical humour, but also for the crazy flights of fantasy. He seems impatient and unhappy when having to play a scene straight. When a patient in *The Disorderly Orderly* (1965) complains to Jerry Lewis about snow on her TV screen, he opens the machine only to be knocked down by a blizzard. When Jayne Mansfield walks down the street in *The Girl Can't Help It* (1956), a man's spectacles crack and two bottles of milk held suggestively in a milkman's hands, boil over, and Anita Ekberg is referred to in the title of the Martin and Lewis comedy, *Hollywood or Bust* (1956). Often offensive, crudely unfunny, and hardly ever straying from the caricatural, Tashlin's films are still full of enough surprising visual gags to keep one awake during the flat bits. **Also:** *Son of Paleface* (52), *Susan Slept Here* (54), *Artists and Models* (55), *The Lieutenant Wore Skirts* (56), *Will Success Spoil Rock Hunter?* (57), *Rock-a-bye Baby* (58), *The Geisha Boy* (58), *Cinderfella* (60), *Bachelor Flat* (62), *The Glass-Bottom Boat* (66), *The Alphabet Murders* (66), *Caprice* (67).

TATI Jacques

French. Born 1908. Real name Jacques Tatischeff. Started entertaining at rugby club dinners by doing mimes of sportsmen, which he extended for the music-hall stage. Appeared in a number of shorts in the 30's. Unlike the films of CHAPLIN and KEATON, his are not built around himself. Although he often triggers off certain incidents, he is mainly peripheral to the action, the observer of the absurdities of modern life and the idiosyncrasies of people. He doesn't seem to invent gags, but is on the spot when they happen. His 'M. Hulot' picks his way through a mine-field of gadgets, which everyone else takes for granted. Six foot four inches tall, almost always wearing a hat, overcoat and rather too short trousers and smoking a pipe, he walks as if against a strong wind, his legs desirous of going in the opposite direction. The films have virtually no dialogue, the humour residing in the body language of ordinary people as well as in the eloquent and meticulously organized sound effects; a woman's heels across a tiled floor, the belching of machines, the growl of motor-cars, the squeak of glass doors. His first two films are set outside the big city, but make reference to it. In *Jour de Fête* (1947), Tati plays a village postman who tries to imitate the high-speed delivery of American mailmen as seen in a documentary, and *M. Hulot's Holiday* (1953) shows, with comic realism, the urban population at play by the sea. *Mon Oncle* (1958) and *Traffic* (1970) deal with the ridiculous aspects of the human's relationship with machines and architecture. The first involves a gadget-oriented house in which the family almost become robots themselves and the second views the motor-car and high-ways with suspicion. There is a simplistic, sentimental, humanist philosophy that runs through the films, a nostalgia for the old, petit bourgeois Paris with its picturesque *quartiers*, the corner bistro, accordian music. The kind of district where M. Hulot lives in *Mon Oncle* in contrast to the modern house of his businessman brother-in-law where his nephew lives miserably. But Tati sees that the reality is the Paris of commerce, skyscrapers, neon-lit drugstores and traffic jams. The Paris of *Playtime* (1967) where the tourists only glimpse old Paris in postcards or as a reflection in the glass doors of a concrete building. *Playtime*, with its vast sets through which the tourists scurry, uses the space and possibilities of the 70mm screen as never before. Its nature can be perceived by comparing it to the shifting themes of a symphony. A gag is stated, then developed while others begin to take shape in the background. Sometimes there are variations on the gag or it disappears only to be hinted at again. Like music, it cannot be fully absorbed the first time. Tati, who spends some years preparing each film has had difficulty in finding money. The world will be poorer if he is unable to make another, but we still have five comic masterpieces to enjoy.

TAVERNIER Bernard

French. Born 1941 in Lyons. Former journalist and press officer. Co-wrote 'Thirty Years of American Cinema'.

Jayne Mansfield and Joan Blondell in Tashlin's *Will Success Spoil Rock Hunter?* (1957).

Jacques Tati in *M. Hulot's Holiday* (1953).

His well–crafted, intelligent and commercial films attempt to combine American narrative technique with pre–War French film styles, dealing with crises of confidence in his smug characters. Unwittingly, they come out as complacent films about complacency. He made his name with his first feature, *The Watch Maker of Saint Paul* (1974), based on a Simenon novel and set in Lyons with his favourite actor Philippe Noiret, as the watchmaker whose son kills a factory owner, and who realizes he never really knew his son. **Also:** *Let Joy Reign Supreme* (75), *The Judge and the Assassin* (76), *Spoiled Children* (77), *A Week's Holiday* (80), *Death Watch* (80), *Clean Slate* (82).

TAVIANI Paulo and Vittorio.

Italian. Paulo born 1931. Vittorio born 1929. Started making documentaries in 1954. Their films have intrinsically interesting subjects such as the education of a Sardinian shepherd who lived without language until he was twenty in *Padre Padrone* (1977), or the last days before the liberation in Italy in 1944 in *The Night of Lawrence* (1982), but are often undermined by overstating their case, letting music supply much of the emotion and resorting to gimmickry. **Also:** *Allonsanfar* (74).

TAUROG Norman

American. 1889-1981. Former child actor. A studio-hopping director with a special affinity for children and young people's subjects. Worked with Mickey Rooney on the preachy, syrupy, *Boys' Town* (1938); the likable small-fry biopic, *Young Tom Edison* (1940); a strained comedy, *A Yank at Eton* (1942) that could only have harmed Anglo-American relations, *Girl Crazy* (1942) in which Mickey and Judy Garland perform some snappy Gershwin numbers and *Words and Music* (1948) with Rooney as Lorenz Hart dying of a broken heart and cigars in the corny, mendacious story between the many starry numbers. The melodramatic tale of an abandoned wife with a large family about to be evicted from her house in *Mrs Wiggs and the Cabbage Patch* (1934), is made moving and comic by the detailed set-pieces and the richly enjoyable performances by W.C. Fields, ZaSu Pitts and Donald Meek. The Selznick-produced, *The Adventures of Tom Sawyer* (1938) in story-book, early Technicolor, is the best Twain on film. Taurog continued to make films for the youth market at the end of his career, including six identical Elvis Presley musicals, *G.I. Blues* (1960), *Tickle Me* (1965), *Speedway* (1967), *Double Trouble* (1967), *Blue Hawaii* (1962), *It Happened at the World's Fair* (1963).

Also: *We're Not Dressing* (34), *Strike Me Pink* (36), *Mad About Music* (38), *Broadway Melody* (40), *The Hoodlum Saint* (46), *The Bride Goes Wild* (48), *Room for One More* (52), *Living It Up* (54), *Bundle of Joy* (57).

TESHIGAHARA Hiroshi

Japanese. Born 1927. Studied painting. Made documentaries, including one on the painter *Hokusai* (1953) and another in New York on the boxer, *Jose Torres* (1959). He is best known for *Woman of the Dunes* (1964), a heavily symbolic erotic drama of a man and a woman trapped at the bottom of a sandpit, until they almost become part of the landscape. **Also:** *The Face of Another* (66), *Man without a Map* (68).

TETZLAFF Ted.

American. Born 1903. Former cinematographer. Made around a dozen moderately good low-budget films between 1941 and 1955. Pat O'Brien foils crooks trying to take over an oil field in *Riffraff* (1947), opens an orphanage for newsboys in *Fighting Father Dunne* (1948), faces George Raft in *A Dangerous Profession* (1949), while Raft cleans up a smuggling ring in *Johnny Allegro* (1949). *The Window* (1949) is a tense little thriller about a child who witnesses a murder but his parents don't believe him. **Also:** *World Premiere* (41), *The White Tower* (50), *Under the Gun* (50), *Gambling House* (50), *Terror on a Train* (53. *Time Bomb –* GB), *Son of Sinbad* (55).

THOMAS Gerald

British. Born 1920. Made a living, directing(!) dozens of crude comedies(?) in the *Carry On . . .* series which consist of ancient, dirty jokes, lavatorial schoolboy humour, a double-entendre a line, and a string of hammy, campy actors (Sidney James, Charles Hawtrey, Kenneth Williams, Kenneth Connor, Joan Sims, Barbara Windsor, Hattie Jacques) telegraphing each jest with pursed lips, rolling eyes and a snigger. There is *Carry on . . . Sergeant* (59), *Nurse* (60), *Cleo* (65), *Spying* (65), *Camping* (72), *Doctor* (72) etc etc. **Also:** *The Duke Wore Jeans* (58), *Watch Your Stern* (60), *Follow That Camel* (67).

THOMAS Ralph

British. Born 1915. Directed mainly hollow lightweight exercises, principally for producer Betty Box and the Rank Organisation. What Gerald

THOMAS was to the *Carry Ons*, Ralph Thomas was to the *Doctor* series, most of them starring Dirk Bogarde in his matinee idol days. *Doctor . . . In the House* (54), *. . .At Sea* (56), *. . . At Large* (57), *. . . In Love* (62), *. . . In Distress* (63), *. . . In Trouble* (70) all about shy, young doctor up against his bombastic chief (James Robertson Justice) and getting into trouble with girls (not vice versa). Rank contract star Bogarde also appeared in two feeble adventures, *Campbell's Kingdom* (1957) and *The Wind Cannot Read* (1958), a tired spy spoof, *Hot Enough for June* (1964 – *Agent 8¾* – USA) and as Sidney Carton in *A Tale of Two Cities* (1958). It was a far, far better thing that Bogarde did when he left Thomas and Rank, than he had ever done. He might have ended up playing in *Percy* (1971) and *Percy's Progress* (1974), limp comedies about a penis transplant. A real shmuck plays the title role stiffly. **Also:** *The Clouded Yellow* (51), *Above Us the Waves* (55), *The Iron Petticoat* (56), *The Thirty-Nine Steps* (59), *No Love for Johnnie* (61), *Some Girls Do* (68), *The Love Ban* (73).

THORPE Richard

American. Born 1896. A studio drudge, long time with MGM. Directed some of their biggest productions in the 50's, including three cumbersome costumers starring boring, expressionless Robert Taylor: *Ivanhoe* (1952), *Knights of the Round Table* (1954) and *Quentin Durward* (1956), but the jousts are well-staged. There is more sword-play in *The Prisoner of Zenda* (1952), an almost frame-for-frame Technicolor remake of the 1937 version, with Stewart Granger holding his own in a double role. There are as many cliches as arias in *The Great Caruso* (1951) sung and acted (in that order) by Mario Lanza. Lanza's voice comes bellowing incongruously out of the slim frame of Edmund Purdom in *The Student Prince* (1954). The step from the lungs of Lanza to the pelvis of Elvis in *Jailhouse Rock* (1957) was taken in Thorpe's stride, making one of the better Presley musicals. **Also:** *Night Must Fall* (38), *The Adventures of Huckleberry Finn* (39), *Tarzan Finds a Son* (39), *Tarzan's New York Adventure* (42), *Fiesta* (47), *The Sun Comes Up* (48), *Malaya* (49), *The Prodigal* (55), *Fun in Acapulco* (63), *The Truth About Spring* (65).

TOBACK James

American. Born 1944. Harvard graduate. Teacher of literature at New York U. Wrote the screenplay for Karel REISZ's *The Gambler* (1974). Admits to being an obsessive about gambling and sex. His first feature, *Fingers* (1977) is about a Mafia debt-collector (Harvey Keitel) who'd rather be a concert pianist, despite his cassette player blaring out hard rock. He has a strained prostate gland, he rips out the genitals of the gangster who killed his father, and he has his brains blown out at the end. In *Love and Money* (1979), Ornella Muti sings the Star-Spangled Banner to Ray Starky to help him get a hard-on. The film, produced by cosmetics company Brut and dropped by them because it stank, features veteran director, King VIDOR. *Exposed* (1982) has similarities with *Fingers*. Harvey Keitel plays a terrorist who blows up a Paris restaurant killing the mother of concert violinist, Rudolph Nureyev, who swears revenge. It is said that Toback is a 'comer' in more ways than one.

TORRE-NILSSON Leopoldo

Argentinian. 1924-1978. Son of film director, Leopoldo Torres Rio. Began working with his father at the age of fifteen. Scriptwriter and assistant on many of his father's films. His own films, most of them adaptations of the novels of his wife, Beatriz Guido, broke away from the staple Argentinian product of superficial comedies and melodramas. *House of the Angel* (1957), *The Fall* (1959) and *Hand in the Trap* (1961) are studies of a bourgoisie repressed by a suffocating Catholic morality and its effect on adolescents faced with original sin. The Gothic, claustrophobic and crumbling world echoes Luis BUNUEL's without the biting irony. *Summer Skin* (1961) and *The Terrace* (1963) show teenagers creating a world of their own away from the stifling mansions of their parents. By the mid-60's, he found it more and more difficult to make the films he wanted because of the political and economic climate of his country. **Also:** *The Eavesdropper* (1964).

TOURNEUR Jacques

French. 1904-1977. Son of Maurice TOURNEUR. Assisted on many of his father's films. Went to Hollywood in 1934 where, as second-unit director he worked on *A Tale of Two Cities* (1935) with Val Lewton. When Lewton became producer at RKO in

Tourneur's *I Walked with a Zombie* (1943).

1942, he immediately got Tourneur to direct for him and together they established a unique style of low-budget horror films. Tourneur's reputation rests almost entirely on the three pictures he made with Lewton in 1943, *Cat People*, *I Walked with a Zombie* and *The Leopard Man* which, with inventive use of light and shadow, space and movement, rely on the suggestion of horror rather than its depiction. Without resorting to shock effects, an underlying fear of the supernatural invests each scene. The fact that Tourneur claimed to have believed in the supernatural gives the films a particular conviction. The mystery is tangible, as in the sequences when the cat-woman (Simone Simon) visits the zoo or, is in pursuit down the city streets in *Cat People*, or in the extraordinary nocturnal walk through the fields towards a voodoo meeting in *I Walked with a Zombie* interrupted by the elongated, black features and staring eyes of the zombie guardian of the crossroads. He returned to the supernatural fourteen years later with *Night of the Demon* (1957. *Curse of the Demon* USA) made in Britain with Dana Andrews as a psychologist refusing, at first, to believe in an ancient curse. The subtle evocation of the macabre is ruined by the appearance of a ridiculous monster in the end, added by the studio against

Tourneur's wishes. The rest of his work consists of competent Westerns and adventure tales and a classic film noir, *Out of the Past* (1947. *Build My Gallows High*–GB) with the archetypal Robert Mitchum as a private eye ambling laconically through a murky atmosphere of double-cross and murder. **Also:** *Canyon Passage* (46), *Berlin Express* (48), *The Flame and the Arrow* (50), *Anne of the Indies* (51), *Way of the Gaucho* (52), *Appointment in Honduras* (53), *Wichita* (55), *The Comedy of Terrors* (63).

TOURNEUR Maurice

French. 1876-1961. Former stage actor. Worked as a book illustrator and poster designer. In America from 1914 to 1926. His films are remarkable for their decors and pictorial composition, well suited to fantasies such as *The Wishing Ring* (1914), *Trilby* (1915) and *The Blue Bird* (1918). He also made adaptations of literary classics, notably *Victory* (1919), *Treasure Island* (1920), *The Last of the Mohicans* (1921) and *Lorna Doone* (1922). Refusing to compromise in his work, he returned to France. His sound films do not equal his silent movies and only *Volpone* (1940), with Harry Bauer, is of much interest. He directed until 1949 when he was seriously injured in a car crash.

TRNKA Jiri

Czechoslovakian. 1912-1969. Animator and puppeteer. He made several cartoons, but is best known for his short, imaginative puppet films. His features include *A Midsummer Night's Dream* (1958), shot in Eastman Color and CinemaScope, a good antidote to the Muppets. **Also:** *The Emperor's Nightingale* (49), *Song of the Prairie* (49), *The Good Soldier Schweik* (54).

TROELL Jan

Swedish. Born 1931. Former schoolteacher. Well-known for his successful, slushy saga of Swedes who emigrated to America in the 19th century, *The Emigrants* (1972) and *The New Land* (1973) starring Max von Sydow and Liv Ullmann as a loving couple bravely surviving disasters against beautiful landscapes. **Also:** *Here is Your Life* (66), *For Better, For Worse* (74), *The Flight of the Eagle* (82).

TRUFFAUT Francois

French. Born 1932. 'Are films more important than life?' asks Jean-Pierre Léaud in *Day for Night* (1973. *La Nuit Amercaine*). For Truffaut the answer must be in the affirmative. The enthusiasm he feels for filmmaking communicates itself in *Day for Night*, dedicated to the Gish sisters, with Truffaut himself playing a film director trying to get a film complete on time despite all the physical and psychological problems he encounters. He is at the centre, soothing everyone and convincing them of the importance of the film *Meet Pamela*, even though it doesn't seem worth the trouble. At night, he dreams of stealing stills of *Citizen Kane* from a cinema. *Shoot the Pianist* (1960) is a tribute to American film noir, *Jules and Jim* (1961) is full of cinematic allusions (one to CHAPLIN's *The Kid*), but is a homage to Jean RENOIR. The courtyard in *Bed and Board* (1970. *Domicile Conjugale*) refers to Renoir's *Le Crime de Monsieur Lange*; *Stolen Kisses* (1968) opens with a shot of the Paris Cinemateque, *The Bride Wore Black* (1967) and *The Mississipi Mermaid* (1969) are HITCHCOCK inspired, and he named his daughters, Eva and Laura after films by LOSEY and PREMINGER. But, for all that, Truffaut is no pasticheur, and many of his films have an immediacy and freshness uncluttered by ciné culture. They have the lucidity and freedom of expression of someone who wishes to retain a certain innocence. It is best seen in his semi-autobiographical series of five films with Jean-Pierre Léaud as his alterego Antoine Doinel. Truffaut had been in a reform school, deserted from the army and spent some time in various prisons. *The 400 Blows* (1959) shows the twelve-year-old Antoine, neglected by his parents and taking to petty crime. He is placed in a reform school but escapes to the coast. The film ends with a freeze as he runs towards the sea, which he had never seen. There was an extraordinary rapport between the fourteen-year-old Léaud and his director, which continued as Antoine gets older, falls in love, marries, has a child, divorces, and finally becomes a writer in the last Doinel film, *Love on*

Truffaut and Jean Pierre Cargol in Truffaut's *L'Enfant Sauvage* (1968).

the Run (1978). These lightweight films, hiding a pain at the loss of youthful spontaneity and the difficulties of love, are set in an endearing Paris as essential to their spirit as in those of René CLAIR or Jacques BECKER. His art is a fragile one, sometimes falling into archness, academicism and cuteness but, from the invigorating tale of friendship and love, *Jules and Jim*, the futuristic nightmare of *Fahrenheit 451* (1966), the didacticism of *L'Enfant Sauvage* (1968. *Wise Child*), the romanticism of *Anne and Muriel* (1971. *Les Deux Anglaises et le Continent*), the austerity of *The Green Room* (1978) and the Occupation therapy of *The Last Metro* (1980), he demonstrates a wide range of styles and subjects. **Also:** *Silken Skin* (64), *A Gorgeous Bird Like Me* (72), *The Story of Adele H* (75), *Small Change* (76), *The Man Who Loved Women* (77), *The Woman Next Door* (81).

TUTTLE Frank
American. 1892-1963. Graduate of Yale. Former journalist. Active in Hollywood from early 20's at Paramount, where he stayed for most of his career. His silent films included four with Bebe Daniels and six with the 'It' girl, Clara Bow. His sound films ranged from five inconsequential Bing Crosby musicals, and Eddie Cantor dreaming himself into Ancient Rome in *Roman Scandals* (1933) to Dashiell Hammett's *The Glass Key* (1935) with George Raft, and *This Gun for Hire* (1942), a tense tale based on Graham Greene that paired Alan Ladd and Veronica Lake for the first time. **Also:** *The Big Broadcast* (32), *College Holiday* (36), *Doctor Rhythm* (38), *Paris Honeymoon* (39), *The Hour Before Dawn* (44), *The Great John L.* (45), *The Magic Face* (51), *Hell on Frisco Bay* (55).

ULMER Edgar G
American. 1900-1972. Born in Vienna. Studied architecture and became a stage designer. Co-directed with Robert SIODMAK, *Menschen am Sondag* (1929. *People on Sunday*). Assistant to MURNAU on his four American films. His Germanic background, mixed with that of American hard-boiled literature is evident in his B minus features. After *The Back Cat* (1934), a bizarre, necrophiliac horror movie with Boris Karloff and Bela Lugosi for Universal, he made few films until he joined PRC, not Poverty Row Company but Producers Releasing Corporation. He made eleven quickies for them between 1942 and 1946 with titles like *Girls in Chains* (1943), *Jive Junction* (1943) and *My Son, the Hero* (1943). It was astonishing that he was able to do so much with so little in *Bluebeard* (1944), a period piece shot in six days with John Carradine as a puppeteer who strangles girls, and *Detour* (1945) which, despite its cheap look, wretched back-projection and zombie-like acting, is a tightly-packed fatalistic drama of sex and money. *Ruthless* (1948) surprisingly expresses anti-capitalist sentiments in a story of the rise and fall of a business-tycoon (Zachary Scott) who ruins the lives of different people (conveniently all gathered at a party for flashbacks) including ex–partner Sidney Greenstreet in his most demanding role. 'He wasn't a man, he was a system', is Scott's epitaph. *The Naked Dawn* (1954), a precise caper movie and *The Man from Planet X* (1951) contribute to the making of Ulmer into a cult figure. For some film buffs, he's ready for canonization. **Also:** *The Wife of Monte Cristo* (46), *Carnegie Hall* (47), *Babes in Baghdad* (52), *Daughter of Dr. Jekyll* (57), *The Amazing Transparent Man* (60), *Beyond the Time Barrier* (60).

USTINOV Peter
British. Born 1921. Corpulent, cosmopolitan, hammy actor, rarely successful playwright, opera producer and ideal talk-show personality. Directed three films while still in his 20's, including the mild anti-war comedy, *Private Angelo* (1949) starring and written by himself. His lukewarm cold-war satire, *Romanoff and Juliet* (1961) was adapted from his stage play with himself as the ruler of a mythical country. *Lady L* (1965), expensively set in turn-of-the-century Paris, is a tiresome romp with Sophia Loren, Paul NEWMAN, and David Niven and *Hammersmith is Out* (1972) is a picture worthy of its stars, the most boring couple of the 60's and 70's, Richard Burton and Elizabeth Taylor. *Billy Budd* (1962), based on Melville's allegory, is far too literal but it does have a chilling performance from Robert Ryan as evil personified.

VADIM Roger
French. Born 1928. Real name Roger Vadim Plemmiankov. Former journalist on Paris Match. Met Brigitte Bardot while working as assistant on Marc ALLEGRET's *Future Vedettes* (1954). He married her and began to cock-tease less fortunate males by putting her into his first feature *And God Created Woman* (1956). And Vadim created Bardot, the 'sex kitten'. His Bardotlatry continued with *Heaven Fell That Night* (1957) and *Warrior's Rest* (1962). He displayed his second wife, Annette Stroyberg in *Les Liaisons Dangereuses* (1959), an updated version of Laclos's 1782 novel of libertinism. The cool, ironic tone and Gerard Philipe and Jeanne Moreau as the orgiasts, make it one of his better efforts. Catherine Deneuve, mother of one of his children, appears in *Vice and Virtue* (1962), a maladroit adaptation of two de Sade novels set during the Occupation. His attempts to make his third wife, Jane Fonda, into a sex object a la BB in *La Ronde* (1964), *La Curee* (1966) and *Barbarella* (1968) was laughable but unfunny. His arty, soft-porn salivations went from bed to worse in *Pretty Girls All in a Row* (1971), his first American film starring Rock Hudson as a college counsellor who murders campus nymphettes, and *Don Juan 1973* (1973) with thirty-nine-year-old Bardot in the title role, bedding beauties. Vadim sees himself as akin to the 18th century licentious *conteurs*, but his work is far more sad than Sade.

VAN DYKE W.S. 'Woody'

American. 1887-1943. Former child actor, gold-miner and lumberjack who became one of MGM's most prolific and proficient directors. A studio technician, bound to bring in a film on schedule, he was called 'One Shot Woody'. Made dozens of silent Westerns and then a series of movies with exotic locations such as *White Shadows in the South Seas* (1928. Begun with Robert FLAHERTY), *The Pagan* (1929), *Trader Horn* (1931) and the first talkie Tarzan film, *Tarzan, the Ape Man* (1932) which introduced Johnny Weissmuller and his jungle cry to the screen. He brought Jeanette MacDonald and Nelson Eddy together for the first time in *Naughty Marietta* (1935) and was instrumental in getting the studio to cast William Powell and Myrna Loy, both of whom he had directed in *Manhattan Melodrama* (1934), as Nick and Nora Charles in *The Thin Man* (1934), a perfect pairing in a series of six Thin Man movies, four of them directed by Van Dyke. He directed Jeanette MacDonald in seven pictures, the most famous being the disaster musical, *San Francisco* (1936) where she stood among the excellent special effects and sang. **Also:** *Cuban Love Song* (31), *Rose Marie* (36), *The Devil is a Sissy* (36), *Rosalie* (37), *Marie Antoinette* (38), *Sweethearts* (38), *Bitter Sweet* (40), *I Married an Angel* (42), *Cairo* (42).

VAN PEEBLES Melvin

American. Born 1932. The first of the generation of black movie directors. Spent ten years in France, painting and writing. He produced, wrote, directed and composed the music of *The Watermelon Man* (1970), a broad but vigorous fantasy about a white, racist, insurance salesman who turns black overnight. *Sweet Sweetback's Baadasssss Song* (1971), dedicated to 'All the Brothers and Sisters who have had enough of The Man', stars Van Peebles as a stud who kills a white cop and is pursued relentlessly across the country. One of the best of Blaxploitation movies, it proved it was possible to make a film outside the system and still make money.

VARDA Agnes

French. Born 1928. Worked as a still photographer. Made her first film, *La Pointe Courte* (1955), claiming never to have been to the cinema. Edited by Alain RESNAIS, it was shot in a small fishing village in the South of France and tells two stories concurrently. Its interest today, if any, lies in its being a forerunner of the Nouvelle Vague. Her short films for the French Tourist Board, showed a keen eye and a sense of humour. *Cleo from 5 to 7* (1962) observes two hours in the life of a night-club singer who is told she might die soon. Every trivial incident takes on a significance for her and Paris is seen as if for the last time. Jean Rabier's camera captures the sheen of the city, but there is far less than meets the eye. The advertising prettiness of *Happiness* (1965. *Le Bonheur*) is used as an ironic reflection on the title. It tells of a carpenter who wants his wife to accept that he can be happily married and love his mistress. The wife drowns herself and he lives happily ever after with his mistress and children. Like the carpenter, Varda wants her gateau and eats it, by swamping the statement in Mozart and idyllic colour landscapes. In *One Sings, The Other Doesn't* (1977), a feminist film for romantic housewives, and a birth-control tract that elevates the pleasures of motherhood, two girls are supposed to represent aspects of the woman's movement from 1962 to 1976. The one sings songs about pregnancy called 'It's beautiful to be a balloon'. Also full of hot air is *Lion's Love* (1969) with Shirley CLARKE playing an avant-garde film director in this modish, Pirandellian exercise. Varda is married to Jacques DEMY. **Also:** *The Creatures* (66).

VARNEL Marcel

French. 1894-1947. Came to England via Hollywood in the 30's where he made some of the most British of British comedies featuring Will Hay, George Formby and The Crazy Gang. Outstanding are the Gainsborough comedies with the self-important, blissfully ignorant Will Hay, and his side-kicks, fat boy Graham Moffatt and toothless codger Moore Marriott in *Oh, Mr Porter* (1937), *Ask a Policeman* (1939) and *Where's the Fire?* (1939). **Also:** *Gasbags* (40), *Let George Do It* (40), *Hi Gang* (41), *The Ghost of St. Michaels* (41).

VERTOV Dziga

Russian. 1896-1954. Real name Denis Kaufman. His parents fled to Russia from Poland when the Germans invaded in 1915 with their three sons, Denis, Mikhail and Boris. (Boris beame a celebrated cameraman in the USA and France, Mikhail worked with Vertov.) Denis became a futuristic poet and, at twenty, while working for the Revolutionary Cinema Committee, changed his name to Dziga Vertov (Ukranian words that evoke spinning and turning). Became editor of newsreels in 1918, using footage sent in to Moscow from the agit-trains all over the Soviet Union. *Kino-Pravda* (*Cinema Truth*) and *Kino Glaz* (*Camera Eye*) were a series of documentary films made between 1922 and 1925, constructed from newsreel sequences to which he added slow or reverse motion, animation, texts and still photographs. His first full-length film, *The Man with a Movie Camera* (1929) is a spectacular constructivist film poem to the city of Moscow, displaying all the techniques of the cinema at his disposal. Documentary and underground film-makers still acknowledge its influence. Vertov was part of the explosion of experimental art in the early, heady days of the Russian Revolution. Although he believed in Lenin's phrase that the function of the cinema is to maintain revolutionary fervour, he was later attacked for formalism and made few other feature-length films. **Also:** *Three Songs for Lenin* (34).

VIDOR Charles

American. 1900-1959. Born in Budapest. Former opera singer. A leading director at Columbia from 1939 to 1948. Throughout his long career, he made glamorous, colourful, sentimental, over-produced, trashy romances, but can be forgiven for bringing out the best in the gorgeous, redheaded 40's sex goddess, Rita Hayworth. Married to nasty, scar-faced casino owner, George McCready in *Gilda* (1946), she sings 'Put the Blame on Mame' after a few drinks, peeling off her long gloves as Glenn Ford and millions of hot-blooded men all over the world lusted for her. She was later to say, 'Every man I knew had fallen in love with Gilda and wakened with me.' She shines through the dull plot of *Cover Girl* (1944) with Gene KELLY, and is a sexy Carmen to Glenn Ford's Don Jose in the listless, Bizetless, *The Loves of Carmen* (1948). 'Discontinue that so-called Polonaise jumble you've been playing for days,' says Merle Oberon's George Sand to Cornel WILDE's Chopin in *A Song to Remember* (1945). Chopin turns up again in the banal biopic of Liszt called *Song Without End* (1960). Vidor died of a heart attack before shooting ended and George CUKOR completed it. **Also:** *The Lady in Question* (40), *New York Town* (41), *The Tuttles of Tahiti* (42), *Hans Christian Anderson* (52), *Rhapsody* (54), *Love Me or Leave Me* (55), *The Swan* (56), *The Joker is Wild* (57), *A*

Ronald Colman and Kay Francis on the set of King Vidor's *Cynara* (1931).

Farewell to Arms (57).

VIDOR King

American. 1896-1982. Began as a projectionist and then worked for a newsreel company. Joined MGM as director in 1922 and, after a few successful but impersonal films, he was able to make *The Big Parade* (1925), one of the first films to deal with the horrors of World War I. His technical virtuosity is apparent in the editing of the battle scenes and the film began what he hoped would be 'a series of films depicting episodes in the lives of the average American man and woman'. The average man in *The Crowd* (1928) comes to New York hoping to be somebody. John marries Mary and they dream of settling down in 'an ideal home for an ideal couple'. But they are faced with unemployment and poverty and the 'ideal home' becomes a miserable tenement. The expressionistic sets and the fluid camerawork stress the alienation of the big city. The film picks them out from the ant-hill life of New York but, in the last shot, the camera pulls back from them until they are just specks lost in the crowd. John and Mary appear again in *Our Daily Bread* (1934) where they join a farm co-operative with other unemployed people hit by the Depression.

Although politically ambiguous, it was a brave, if raw, attempt to inject contemporary issues into the escapist American cinema of the 30's. *Hallelujah* (1929) is another pastoral idyll and Vidor's first sound film. Much of this innovative all-black musical was shot on location, the sound being dubbed in later in order to retain the visual poetry of silent cinema. The three different themes of 'Hell hath no fury . . .', 'the opening up of America' and 'a man can rise in America by his own efforts' found respectively in *Stella Dallas* (1937), a classic Barbara Stanwyck weepie that comes down on the side of social respectability, *North-West Passage* (1940), an injun' killing epic with Spencer Tracy, and *An American Romance* (1944), an inspirational tribute to the self-made man played by uninspiring Brian Donlevy, come together in the frenzied tetralogy of lurid melodramas made between 1946 and 1952. The Selznick-produced *Duel in the Sun* (1946) – a demented, delirious Western of sibling rivalry (upright Joseph Cotton and amoral, miscast Gregory Peck) for the love of tempestuous half-breed Jennifer Jones, played mostly against blood-red skies, is Hollywood high romanticism at its peak. 'What a dump!' says Bette Davis when she arrives newly-married at country-doctor husband Joseph Cotton's house in *Beyond the Forest* (1949) and continues on her ruthless way committing adultery and finally murder and in *Ruby Gentry* (1952), Jennifer Jones wildly seeks revenge on the man she loves, seeing him die face-downwards in the mud of the marshes. *The Fountainhead* (1949) is a long way from the days of *The Crowd*. Based on Ayn Rand's Nietzschian novel of an uncompromising architect (Gary Cooper), Vidor's stylized direction follows the lines of the modern architecture the film upholds, the camera rising to join Cooper as he sits on the top of a building above the masses he despises. **Also:** *The Patsy* (28), *Show People* (28), *Billy the Kid* (30), *Street Scene* (31), *The Champ* (31), *The Citadel* (38), *Man with a Star* (55), *War and Peace* (56), *Solomon and Sheba* (59).

VIGO Jean

French. 1905-1934. Son of an anarchist who died in prison in 1917. Inherited his father's anti-clericism, anti-militarism and anti-authoritarian ideas. Spent an unhappy time at

boarding school. Caught TB as a child. Died before completing his only full-length feature at the age of twenty-nine. Started in films as assistant cameraman at the Nice studios where he met Boris Kaufman (VERTOV's brother) who was to shoot all his films. *Apropos de Nice* (1929), influenced by Vertov's experiments in montage, is a forty-minute documentary that brilliantly elaborates the simple contrast between the rich tourists and the poorer inhabitants of Nice. A woman suns herself until she becomes a skeleton, people walking along the promenade are compared to animals, a girl at a cafe is stripped nude in a series of dissolves and a croupier rakes up passengers just arrived by train. Little money and not much experience account for the rough edges of *Zéro de Conduite* (1933), but this only adds to the strange, anarchic poetry of the film. Set in a dreadful boarding school, four boys organize an uprising because of the petty restrictions imposed on them. It has a fresh, child's-eye view of authority and adults seen as perverse, hypocritical, corrupt and oppressive members of the Establishment. The head-master is played by a long bearded dwarf, looked down upon by the boys. The most celebrated sequence is the dormitory pillow-fight that beomes a snowy wonderland of feathers. Any telling of the simple story of *L'Atalante* (1934) cannot do justice to the richness of Vigo's last work. A young barge captain takes his bride to live on his barge that plies the canals around Paris. Much of it was shot on location in difficult conditions, but it captures the life on board with realism and fantasy. The everyday life is filled with magical moments; Michel Simon as the mate telling fantastic stories of his travels, a waltz from a phonograph acompanying the movement over the water, the man searching for his sweetheart under water and the joy of reconciliation.

VISCONTI Luchino

Italian. 1906-1976. A man of contradictions, all of which reflect in his work. 'Art is ambiguous. It is ambiguity made a science, 'says Aschenbach's friend in *Death in Venice* (1971). Aristocrat, Marxist, homosexual, theatre and opera director, neo-realist, decadence-monger. As a Marxist, in principle, he should be dedicated to the destruction of the class and culture he represents, and yet it is bourgeois European art that

attracts him; Wagner, Mahler, Bruckner, Thomas Mann, D'Annunzio, Lampedusa. He is both repelled and drawn to a decaying society which he depicts in such impressively loving detail. The Prince Salina (Burt Lancaster) in *The Leopard* (1963) reflects sadly throughout on the death of the aristocratic world and the rise of the crass bourgeoisie during the Rissorgimento; Ludwig II of Bavaria (Helmut Berger) in *Ludwig* (1972) fights against the philistines who cannot appreciate Wagner's genius, and the cholera in *Death in Venice* regretfully threatens to sweep away the luxury of the 'Hotel des Bains' on the Lido. *The Damned* (1969) sets out to examine the rise of German fascism, but gets hypnotised by the Nazi regalia and becomes positively jack-boot kissing as Helmut Berger in Dietrich drag romps with the Boys in the Bund. Just as the come-hither boy, Tadzio, wakens Dirk Bogarde's fussy Aschenbach out of his academic trance in *Death in Venice*, so ham Berger, Visconti's fallen angel, disturbs the tranquillity of Professor Burt Lancaster in *Conversation Piece* (1975). Lancaster is quite happy with his art collection and classical music until a nouveau-riche Marchese, her 'kept boy' (guess who?) and children move into the flat above, and like those eggheads in a 40's screwball comedy, he learns to come to terms with modern life and let his hair down. Visconti hardly ever did the same. Although his reputation was gained as a neo-realist (the term was coined to describe his first feature, *Ossessione* – 1942) only *Le Terra Trema* (1948) comes close to the neo-realist ideal in its picture of the wretched economic conditions of Sicilian fishermen, shot in the real locations with the local people enacting their story. It is difficult not to be moved, despite Visconti's approaching it as a realistic production of *Cavallerina Rusticana*. It is really through the conventions of opera that Visconti works as in the lush Verdian spectacle of *Senso* (1954). Instead of giving us a three-hour soap opera about King Ludwig, he might have filmed a Wagner opera with James King and Christa Ludwig or instead of sentimentalizing and distorting Mann's novella with its lashings of Mahler used like Max Steiner, he might have filmed Britten's opera. *Rocco and his Brothers* (1960) was an attempt to return to neo-realism in a saga of a family who go to Milan to

escape the poverty of the South, but it falls into melodramatic gestures, becoming Rococo and his brothers. **Also:** *Bellisima* (51), *White Nights* (57), *Sandra* (64), *The Stranger* (67), *The Innocent* (76).

WAJDA Andrzej

Polish. Born 1926. Son of a cavalry officer killed in World War II. Joined the resistence at the age of sixteen. Graduate of the Lodz film school. Polish cinema burst upon the world with his war-trilogy, *A Generation* (1954), *Kanal* (1957) and *Ashes and Diamonds* (1958). Wajda was the voice of those who were teenagers during the war. A generation later, he has become the voice of Poland today, struggling to survive political and economic turmoil. Even in his historical films, by the use of symbolism and ironic allusions, he was able to comment on contemporary Poland. *A Generation* forcefully expresses a youthful bitterness and an anti-romantic attitude to the war. *Kanal* starkly creates the claustrophobic nightmare of Polish patriots escaping the Nazis in the sewers of Warsaw during the uprising of 1944. The crown of the trilogy and perhaps Wajda's finest work, *Ashes and Diamonds*, takes place on the last day of the war. The brilliant young actor, Zbigniew Cybulski, embodied the sceptical, new generation in his anti-heroic role of a nationalist ordered to kill a Communist leader. Its enigmatic, twilight world communicated the 'Polish experience' beyond the frontiers as few films have done. Cybulski also appeared in *The Innocent Sorcerers* (1960), an ironic sex comedy which uncompromisingly dealt with modern Polish youth, further establishing his reputation as the Polish James Dean. Cybulski was killed running for a train in 1967 at the age of forty and *Everything for Sale* (1968) is an earnest attempt to make a film-within-a-film tribute to the actor, played by his less charismatic successor, Daniel Olbrychski. Driven by 'censorship behind closed doors', Wajda's films from the mid-60's to the mid-70's are mainly esoteric, overworked, literary adaptations of Polish allegorical novels. With the relaxation of censorship, he returned to contemporary subjects, first with *Man of Marble* (1976), a bold, no-frills, no-holds-barred story on the life of a worker-hero of the Stalinist 50's who falls from official favour. *Man of Iron* (1981) leaps off the screen like today's headlines. Taking the personal story of the son of the *Man of Marble* (played by the same actor, Jerzy Radziwiowicz), he sets it against the wider struggle for the recognition of Solidarity. The interest of these films depends to a large extent on their political topicality and as Wajda uses a straightforward, unfussy narrative technique, they might soon seem as dated as yesterday's headlines. **Also:** *Lotna* (59), *Siberian Lady Macbeth* (62), *Ashes* (65), *Landscape After Battle* (70), *The Birch Wood* (71), *The Wedding* (72), *Land of Promise* (74), *The Young Ladies of Wilko* (79), *The Conductor* (80).

WALKER Hal
American. 1896-1972. Former stage director who made nine pictures for Paramount in a short career, including two Road pictures (*Road to Utopia* 1945, *Road to Bali* 1952) and four Dean Martin-Jerry LEWIS comedies. (*My Friend Irma Goes West* 1950, *At War with the Army*

Zbigniew Cybulski in Wajda's *Ashes and Diamonds* (1958).

1950, *That's My Boy* 1951, *Sailor Beware* 1951.)

WALSH Raoul
American. 1887-1981. Started in films as an actor. Played Lincoln's assassin in GRIFFITH's *Birth of a Nation* (1915). Director of over two hundred pictures dating back to 1912. He lost his right eye in an accident while making *In Old Arizona* (1929). Made few films outside Warner Bros. from 1939. His forte was for loud, extrovert, unpretentious, fast-paced adventure movies that rarely omit a fist fight. He never lets a scene go on longer than necessary and is much given to the long shot where action can be seen in its entirety against the landscape. His outstanding silent films were *The Thief of Baghdad* (1924) with Douglas Fairbanks and some magical trick photography, and *What Price Glory?* (1926), a rumbustious comedy that turns into an anti-war drama with Victor McLaglen and Edmund Lowe fighting each other and the Germans. His tough-guy assignments at Warners included *The Roaring Twenties* (1939), a documentary style evocation of the gangster era with James Cagney as a bootlegger. *High Sierra* (1941) revealed a deeper side to Walsh and gave Humphrey Bogart his first three-dimensional role. He remade it as *Colorado Territory* (1949), a genuinely tragic Western with Joel McCrea and Virginia Mayo dying hand in hand. Errol Flynn starred in seven of Walsh's robust adventures, notably as Custer in *They Died With Their Boots On* (1941) and *Gentleman Jim* (1942). His best period ended with Cagney as the murderer with a mother-fixation in

White Heat (1949) standing on the top of a blazing oil-tank and screaming, 'Made it, Ma! Top of the World!' He continued to make action movies, but larger production values weigh them down and cliches are thicker on the ground. **Also:** *Me and My Gal* (32), *The Bowery* (33), *Klondike Annie* (36), *They Drive By Night* (40), *Manpower* (41), *Strawberry Blonde* (41), *Objective Burma* (45), *The Man I Love* (46), *Pursued* (47), *Captain Horatio Hornblower* (51), *Distant Drums* (51), *World in his Arms* (52), *A Lion is in the Streets* (53), *Battle Cry* (55), *The Tall Men* (55), *The Revolt of Mamie Stover* (56), *Band of Angels* (57), *The Naked and the Dead* (58), *Esther and the King* (60), *A Distant Trumpet* (63).

WALTERS Charles
American. 1911-1982. Former dancer and director of stage musicals. Joined MGM as choreographer in 1942, staging some imaginative numbers in musicals such as *The Harvey Girls* (1945) and *Summer Holiday* (1947) before being given the chance to direct. His first film was the zestful campus musical, *Good News* (1947) where he displayed a light touch and the ability to build a number on screen. Elegant Fred Astaire danced through three graceful musicals, with Judy Garland in *Easter Parade* (1948), with Ginger Rogers for the first time in ten years in *The Barkleys of Broadway* (1949) and with Vera-Ellen in *The Belle of New York* (1952). The plot of *Summer Stock* (1950) might have been slim, but Judy Garland was definitely overweight. Walters did his utmost to make her look good, but the best number 'Get Happy' was shot three months after completion when Garland had slimmed down. Other pleasing musicals were two Esther Williams aquatic vehicles, *Dangerous When Wet* (1953) and *Easy to Love* (1953), Leslie Caron as *Lili* (1953), and *High Society* (1956). His few non–musical movies seem to cry out for production numbers. Both Cary Grant and Walters called it a day after *Walk, Don't Run* (1966). **Also:** *Torch Song* (53), *The Glass Slipper* (55), *The Tender Trap* (55), *Don't Go Near the Water* (57), *Ask Any Girl* (59), *Please Don't Eat the Daisies* (60), *Jumbo* (62), *The Unsinkable Molly Brown* (64).

WARHOL Andy
American. Born 1928. A leading figure in the American Pop Art

movement. Over eighty films have come out of his New York 'factory'. Like his celebrated 'Campbell's Soup Cans', they are reclaimed dispensable objects. Film a man sleeping for six hours in *Sleep* (1963) or the Empire State Building from a fixed position for eight hours in *Empire* (1964) and call them works of art. Why not? Warhol's movies reach the parts other films don't wish to. Why should Hollywood have all the stars? Warhol creates his own 'superstars', Viva, Candy Darling, Holly Woodlawn and Joe Dellasandro. Drag-queens, male and female hustlers who get together and improvise their own uncensored Hollywood fantasies in the films called *Blow Job* (1964), *Harlot* (1964), *My Hustler* (1965), and *Blue Movie* (1968). *Chelsea Girls* (1966) has two screens on which to watch them perform and *Lonesome Cowboys* (1968) shows what HAWKS's male heroes might have got up to with each other had they been allowed to. (See Paul MORRISSEY.)

WATKINS Peter
British. Born 1937. TV and film director. The controversial *The War Game* (1966) was made for the BBC who refused to show it when they realized it might give the public the mistaken impression that nuclear war is horrendous. Using a vigorous newsreel style and non-professional actors, it shows in detail what would happen if a nuclear bomb fell on London, although it doesn't go far enough. Hysterical reportage techniques are used in the feature films, *Privilege* (1967), a very 60's fantasy of the manipulation of pop stars and *Punishment Park* (1971) about a neofascist government taking over the USA. Cassandra had nothing on Watkins. **Also:** *The Gladiators* (69), *Edvard Munch* (75).

WATT Harry
British. Born 1906. His outdoorsy features were strongly influenced by his background in documentaries. Assistant to Robert FLAHERTY on *Man of Aran* (1934), co-directed *Night Mail* (1936 with Basil Wright) and *London Can Take It* (1940 with Humphrey JENNINGS). Made British Westerns in Australia, *The Overlanders* (1946), *Eureka Stockade* (1948) and *The Siege of Pinchgut* (1959); and shot *Where No Vultures Fly* (1951) and *West of Zanzibar* (1954) in Africa with uneven scripts, acting and colour, but there are plenty of animals running around.

WAYNE John
American. 1907-1979. Appeared in over a hundred and fifty movies, becoming *the* cowboy supreme. Often the butt of the sophisticated, he was a fine screen actor whose roles were far more subtle than his own simplistic, rightist beliefs. Best to remember him in the films of Howard HAWKS and John FORD than as star-director of his two flag-waving efforts, *The Alamo* (1960) and the inept guts 'n glorification of the Vietnam War, *The Green Berets* (1968. Helped by Ray Kellogg and Mervyn LEROY).

WEGENER Paul
German. 1874-1948. A leading actor with Max Reinhardt's company. Took the lead in the first version of *The Student of Prague* (1913). He co-directed (with Henrik GALEEN) and played the monster in *The Golem* (1914). His lumbering gait was imitated by Boris Karloff in James WHALE's *Frankenstein* (1931). He directed and played the Golem again in *The Golem and the Dancer* (1917) and in the remake, *The Golem* (1920) using expressionistic sets and chiaroscuro to create a Gothic effect. Directed until 1937, but continued to act in films of the Nazi period. **Also:** *The Pied Piper* (1916).

WEILL Claudia
American. Born 1948. Graduate of Yale. Distantly related to the composer Kurt Weill about whom she is planning a film. Worked on TV's 'Sesame Street' and made many documentaries including *The Other Half of the Sky: A China Memoir* (1975) on a woman's delegation to China led by Shirley MacLaine. Her first feature, *Girl Friends* (1978) is a warmly observed comedy of human relationships with a smart, comic performance from Melanie Mayron, a female Woody ALLEN. Together with her second film, *It's My Turn* (1980) about a feminist maths professor who falls for a macho type, she has proved that sophisticated feminist comedies can be made, just as Hollywood churned out hundreds of anti-feminist ones in the 30's and 40's.

WEIS Don
American. Born 1922. Worked as scriptwriter, dialogue director and assistant on many Stanley KRAMER-produced movies. A greater contrast between Kramer's strained seriousness and Weis's own bouncy, lightweight pictures would be hard to find. At MGM, the accent was on youth and he directed cheerful Debbie Reynolds in both *I Love Melvin* (1953) with Donald O'Connor, and *The Affairs of Dobie Gillis* (1953) with young dancers Bobby Van and Bob FOSSE. After leaving MGM, his films went on the slide, but he continued to work with young people. After the ghastly, *Did you ever hear the one about the traveling saleslady?* (1968) he disappeared into the anonymity of TV. **Also:** *The Gene Krupa Story* (59), *Critic's Choice* (63), *Pajama Party* (64), *Billie* (65), *The Ghost in the Invisible Bikini* (66).

WELLES Orson
American. Born 1915. The picture of an ursine Welles, a pathetic, bloated actor and has-been director, prostituting himself on beer commercials, whose first film was one of the greatest ever made but never directed another good one, still persists in people's minds. The image is false. Few Hollywood directors could boast finer films. Had he been any different and conformed to the system, he might have become another Mark ROBSON or Robert WISE. He has not made a film that is not a personal statement. 'My name is Orson Welles' is like COCTEAU's signature or HITCHCOCK's fleeting appearances. In *F for Fake* (1973), he plays himself, a dazzling magician who tells anecdotes about art forgers with relish. 'Art is the lie that makes us see the truth,' he demonstrates. What is a story-teller but a great liar. As the old wealthy merchant in *The Immortal Story* (1968), he wishes to make a sailor's myth come true. He holds us with his glittering eye as he tells of how he pays a young sailor to sleep with a women he thinks is the merchant's wife so that at least one sailor will be telling the truth. That Lord of Misrule, Falstaff, is one of the magnificent liars of literature and Welles's portrayal gives him dignity in the splendid comic poem and historical epic, *Chimes at Midnight* (1966), welding material from five Shakespeare plays. There is a poignant aptness in the actor born to play the king, as fool at the feet of the newly crowned Henry V, his younger self. 'I know thee not, old man.' Mysterious millionaire Mr Arkadin laughs when he sees the Beckettian figure of Akim Tamiroff in *Confidential Report* (1955). 'What's funny?' Tamiroff asks. 'Old age,' Welles-Arkadin replies in this

Orson Welles as *Citizen Kane* (1941).

minutes to 88, but it remains a haunting, ironic, exuberant portrait of Booth Tarkington's declining aristocratic family in the late 19th century. *Citizen Kane* (1941) broke all the rules. The Hearst-like newspaper tycoon is seen from many viewpoints, going against chronological narrative conventions. The use of wide-angle and deep focus lenses, the innovative use of sound, narration and overlapping dialogue, Bernard Herrmann's music, the great set-pieces, the performance of Welles and his Mercury players, Gregg Toland's camerawork, all in pursuit of the meaning of the word 'Rosebud'. Perhaps there is a self-destructive streak in Welles, perhaps with more money and fewer restrictions he might have made more and better films including the unfinished, *Don Quixote*, but as Marlene Dietrich says at the end of *Touch of Evil*, 'He was some kind of a man. What does it matter what you say about people?' **Also:** *The Stranger* (46), *The Trial* (63).

WELLMAN William

American. 1896-1975. As a young man he had a spell as pilot in the Lafayette Flying Squadron in World War I. He drew upon his experiences for *Men with Wings* (1938), a story of the pioneers of the air; *Lafayette Escadrille* (1958) with his son playing himself, and *Wings* (1929) one of the best flying films of any period, the spectacular dog-fights balanced with a tender love triangle. *Wings* was the first movie to win an Oscar and-

breathless globe-trotting film. A Mercury production, it is like quicksilver, although Welles resembles Neptune, filmed as ever from below to stress his power. Power is the sustaining motif of his work. *Touch of Evil* (1958) opens with a breathtaking tracking shot and the camera continues to move through a hot night of corruption in a Mexican border town. *Othello* (1952) was shot in different countries over three years, *Macbeth* (1948) was shot on one set in three weeks, but both have a unity of time and space with Welles's tragic stature at the centre of a barbaric world. Barbaric too, is the world of *The Lady from Shanghai* (1948) which ends with a shoot-out between Rita Hayworth and her crippled power-hungry husband Everett Sloane in a hall of mirrors, hitting images of each other before finding the flesh. 'It's true, I made a lot of mistakes,' she says in her dying breath. Welles made the mistake of going off to Mexico while RKO edited down *The Magnificent Ambersons* (1942) from 131

William Wellman's *Wings* (1929).

Wellman's name is most often associated with action pictures of this nature. He earned the nickname 'Wild Bill' because of his impatience with actors, his devil-may-care personality and his aerial past, but although there are plenty of he-man epics such as *Call of the Wild* (1935), *Beau Geste* (1939) and *Buffalo Bill* (1944), there is also *Wild Boys of the Road* (1933), a deeply-felt Depression story of young people who travel around the country hopping trains and trying to survive, *A Star is Born* (1937) with Janet Gaynor and Fredric March that says more about Hollywood than its two remakes, *Nothing Sacred* (1937), a hilarious Ben Hecht-scripted satire with Frederic March and Carole Lombard taken at a cracking pace, *Roxie Hart* (1942), a cynical 20's spoof with Ginger Rogers and *Magic Town* (1947), a CAPRAesque comedy about how a small town, polled as representing the norm in America, becomes abnormal. He directed five movies with Barbara Stanwyck, not bad for someone with a reputation for working mainly with men. However, Robert Mitchum emerged as a star in the semi-documentary, *The Story of G.I. Joe* (1945) and James Cagney found stardom in one of the first of the Warners gangster cycle, *Public Enemy* (1931) which includes the anthology scene of him shoving half a grapefruit into Mae Clark's kisser. **Also:** *The Light That Failed* (39), *The Ox-Bow Incident* (43), *Yellow Sky* (48), *Battleground* (49), *Across the Wide Missouri* (51), *Westward the Women* (51), *Island in the Sky* (53), *The High and the Mighty* (53), *Darby's Rangers* (58).

WENDERS Wim

German. Born 1945. 'The Yanks have colonized our subconscious,' says one of the German friends in *Kings of the Road* (1976). Wenders is more aware than most contemporary German directors of the American cultural influence on post-war German youth. His films do not condemn this, nor do they wholly embrace it, but accept that American imperialism filled a gap for a people emerging from years of Nazi rule. He was brought up on the music and movies of the occupiers. He was diverted from becoming a Catholic priest by the discovery of Rock 'n roll and pinball machines. His isolated and emotionally stunted characters are resensitized by juke-boxes, pinballs and hitting the road. Wenders

takes the word 'movie' more literally than most. His people are 'movies' who move from town to town, city to city. In the tradition of the novels of Kerouac and films such as *Easy Rider* the characters never stay anywhere for very long. In *Summer in the City: Dedicated to the Kinks* (1970), his first feature after leaving the Munich Film School, a newly-released prisoner goes from one gloomy town to the next trying in vain to contact his old friends. An almost wordless German journalist, numbed by recent assignments, journeys down the East coast of America with a nine-year-old girl in *Alice in the Cities* (1974). *Wrong Movement* (1975), based on Goethe's Wilhelm Meister, has a writer travelling through modern Germany in search of his identity and the *Kings of the Road* are two itinerant cinema projector mechanics. These leisurely-paced, odd odysseys, superbly photographed by Robbie Muller, reach metaphysical dimensions although the tedium and angst are rather thickly spread. However, the flashy camerawork of *The American Friend* (1977) works against the Patricia Highsmith story through which Wenders's heroes Sam FULLER, Nicholas RAY (whom he filmed in his last days in *Lightning Over Water* 1980) and Dennis HOPPER distractingly wend their way in an attempt to create resonances the film lacks. *Hammett* (1982), shot against fine, atmospheric sets at COPPOLA's Zoetrope studios, frustrates Wenders forte for long takes and outdoor movements. **Also:** *The Goalkeeper's Fear of the Penalty* (71), *The State of Things* (82).

WERTMULLER Lina

Italian. Born 1932. Worked as a writer for travelling puppet shows. Wrote plays and directed on radio and TV. Assistant on FELLINI's 8½ (1963). In the early 70's, this Alien descended upon America and began to infiltrate art-houses with her pernicious works. She used her evil powers to take away the critical faculties of the average, intelligent moviegoer and these poor, demented, brainwashed creatures were seen lining up to see grotesque, leering, facetious, offensive, reactionary movies disguised as socialist parables with twee titles like *Swept Away by the Unusual Destiny in the Blue Sea of August* (1974) and *The End of the World in Our Usual Bed in a Nightful of Rain* (1977). **Also:** *The Lizards*

(63), *The Seduction of Mimi* (71), *Love and Anarchy* (72), *All Screwed Up* (73), *Seven Beauties* (75).

WEXLER Haskell

American. Born 1926. Excellent cinematographer of *In the Heat of the Night* (1967) and *American Graffiti* (1973) etc. Worked on many radical documentary films such as *Conversation with President Allende* (1971) and *Interviews with My Lai Veterans* (1971). *Medium Cool* (1969) is a semi-fictional feature shot during the chaotic Democratic Convention in Chicago in 1968. It tells, rather systematically, of the politicization of a TV news cameraman as he moves from one consciousness-raising assignment to another. The actual footage of the Convention comes across dynamically and there is one real moment when the director is hit by tear-gas.

WHALE James

British. 1889-1957. Worked in the English theatre as designer, actor and director. His staging of R.C. Sherriff's World War I drama, *Journey's End* in New York, led to an invitation to film it in Hollywood in 1930. After a shaky beginning, he triumphed with his third film, *Frankenstein* (1931). Bela Lugosi turned down the role of the monster and Whale chose a compatriot, Boris Karloff nee William Henry Pratt. (He preferred, on the whole, to work with English actors.) It is perhaps the 'Englishness' of the director and of Mary Shelley's Gothic novel that frees *Frankenstein* from

Boris Karloff as the monster in James Whale's *Frankenstein* (1931).

155

the Germanic expressionism usually associated with the genre. Although one of the most famous horror films ever made, it is full of self-mocking black humour and, at its centre, a touching, poetic pantomime from Karloff (with make-up devised by Jack Pierce). It was the start of Universal Studio's cycle of horror movies to which Whale was to contribute three more classic comedy-thrillers. *The Old Dark House* (1932), the one about a group of travellers stranded in a mountain retreat during a storm with Karloff as a sinister butler and Charles LAUGHTON (in his first American film) as one of the guests. Claude Rains, making his screen debut, disappears as *The Invisible Man* (1933), using only his mellifluous voice to build a character in this superlative adaptation from the H.G. Wells novel. The climax of his work in the genre was *The Bride of Frankenstein* (1935) in which parody, fantasy, wit and terror combine perfectly, with the brilliant cast, Elsa Lanchester as the startling bride and as Mary Shelley in the prologue, Karloff, Ernest Thesinger and Colin Clive camping it down. The very next year, Whale and his photographer, John Mescall moved smoothly and effectively from Frankenstein to Hammerstein with the best of the three screen versions of *Show Boat* (1936). In 1941, he retired from film-making to devote himself to painting. He died after a mysterious accident in his swimming pool. **Also:** *The Great Garrick* (37), *Port of Seven Seas* (38), *The Man in the Iron Mask* (39) *Green Hell* (40).

WHORF Richard
American. 1906-1966. As a screen actor, he starred in *Blues in the Night* (1941) and played producer Sam Harris in *Yankee Doodle Dandy* (1942). As a director, he failed to animate the drooping screenplay on the 'life' of Jerome Kern in *Till the Clouds Roll By* (1946) between the many excellent numbers staged by Robert Alton, George SIDNEY and Vincente MINNELLI. Two modest MGM musicals followed, *It Happened in Brooklyn* (1947) and *Luxury Liner* (1948). Became a producer and directed TV series such as *Rawhide* and *The Beverly Hillbillies*. **Also:** *Champagne for Caesar* (50).

WICKI Bernhard
Swiss. Born 1919. Acted in many films including ANTONIONI's *La Notte* (1961) and in his own satire,

The Miracle of Malachias (1961) as the gentle monk who wills the destruction of a gambling casino. He made his name with *The Bridge* (1959), one of the few interesting films made in Germany in the 50's. Made in a semi-documentary style, it movingly retells the true story of a group of teenage boys called up into the German army and killed in the last days of the war in 1945. **Also:** *The Longest Day* (62. Co–directed), *The Visit* (63), *Morituri* (65).

WIDERBERG Bo
Swedish. Born 1930. Novelist, playwright, short-story writer. Former film critic who attacked Ingmar BERGMAN for not dealing with contemporary issues, although most of his colour-supplement socialist films are set at the turn of the century, in 1912 and in the 30's. How picturesque poverty is in *Raven's End* (1963), and why are the workers striking in *Adalen 31* (1969) when they live in such sun-kissed, dappled, beauteous surroundings? And what's the point of striving for a better life if everything is viewed already with a Utopian eye in *Joe Hill* (70), about the Swedish immigrant American union-leader balladeer? Soft-focus photography, slow-motion, the slow movement from Mozart's piano concerto no. 21 in *Elvira Madigan* (1967), accompany the oozy romance between a nobleman and a tightrope walker who elope to spend a last summer together before committing suicide. **Also:** *Love 65* (65), *Thirty Times Your Money* (67), *Stubby* (74), *The Man on the Roof* (76), *Victoria* (79).

WIENE Robert
German. 1881-1938. Former actor and director in the Berlin theatre. His reputation is based entirely on *The Cabinet of Doctor Caligari* (1919), considered to be the first true example of Expressionism in the cinema and an influence on German films for the next decade. Caligari (Werner Krauss), a director of a lunatic asylum, hypnotises his servant (Conrad Veidt) to murder at night. The distorted sets and grotesquely angled photography, create an atmosphere of dream and madness, a style that became known as 'Caligarism'. The critic Siegfried Kracauer used it as the starting point for his book, 'From Caligari to Hitler' (1947) in which he analyses the German psyche through German films. Wiene made several mediocre attempts to repeat Cali-

gari's success. He lived in France from 1933.

WILCOX Fred M.
American. 1908-1964. Worked in publicity. Assistant to King VIDOR. Did an excellent three-handkerchief job on three Lassie movies, *Lassie Come Home* (1943), *The Courage of Lassie* (1946) and *Hills of Home* (1948), and the atmospheric children's fantasy, *The Secret Garden* (1949) which bursts into colour in the last reel. *The Forbidden Planet* (1956) has a reputation far beyond its quality, but it is a modest, amusing sci-fi story vaguely inspired by Shakespeare's 'The Tempest' featuring Robbie the Robot who predates Hal in *2001* and R2D2 and C-3PO in *Star Wars*. **Also:** *Three Daring Daughters* (1948), *Tennessee Champ* (1954), *I Passed for White* (1960).

WILCOX Herbert
British. 1892-1977. Producer and director. From the early 30's, he directed his wife, Anna Neagle, in a series of films in which she appeared as indomitable, historical heroines such as *Nurse Edith Cavell* (1939), the pilot Amy Johnson in *They Flew Alone* (1942), French Resistance worker, *Odette* (1950), Florence Nightingale in *The Lady with the Lamp* (1951) and Queen Victoria in *Victoria the Great* (1937) and *Sixty Glorious Years* (1938), all sentimental, stiff-upper-lip codswallop. He also paired his wife with insipid Michael Wilding in sugary, snobbish musical-comedies with fashionable London areas in the titles like *Spring in Park Lane* (1948) and *Maytime in Mayfair* (1949). In the late 50's, they tried to get 'with it' by catering to both parents and teenagers in excruciating films such as *The Lady is a Square* (1958) (Berkeley Square?). **Also:** *Nell Gwynn* (34), *No, No, Nanette* (40), *Piccadilly Incident* (46), *The Courtneys of Curzon Street* (47), *Trent's Last Case* (52), *King's Rhapsody* (55), *My Teenage Daughter* (56), *Those Dangerous Years* (57).

WILDE Cornel
American. Born 1915. An expressionless actor who directed a handful of naive, message-laden adventure films, produced, written and starring himself and his wife, Jean Wallace. **Titles:** *The Devil's Hairpin* (57), *The Naked Prey* (65), *Beach Red* (67), *No Blade of Grass* (70), *Shark's Treasure* (74).

WILDER Billy

American. Born 1906 in Vienna as Samuel Wilder. Former journalist in Vienna and Berlin. Scriptwriter on several films before leaving for France in 1933. In Paris, he wrote and co-directed, *Mauvaise Graine* (1933) starring Danielle Darrieux. In Hollywood from 1938 to 1941, he co-wrote (with Charles Brackett) films for Ernst LUBITSCH and Mitchell LEISEN. He wrote all his own films, first with Brackett and from 1957 with I.A.L. Diamond. An important emphasis is placed on the art of screenwriting and the structuring of the plots. His comedies derive from the satiric Viennese theatre of Johann Nestroy and Arthur Schnitzler, the witty elegancies of Lubitsch and the harsher screwball comedies of the 30's. His is the perfect mixture of sweet and sour. He is often seen mistakenly as a cynical, heartless and vulgar director. Many of his characters do have these traits such as the sensation-seeking reporter (Kirk Douglas) in *Ace in the Hole* (1951) the slick insurance agent in *Double Indemnity* (1944) and the weak, exploitative businessman in *The Apartment* (1960), both played by Fred MacMurray; Dean Martin's self-parodic, horny crooner in *Kiss Me, Stupid* (1964) and Walter Matthau's shyster lawyer in *The Fortune Cookie* (1966. *Meet Whiplash Willie* – GB), but Wilder's attitude is condemnatory. His tenderness is reserved for

Audrey Hepburn desperately trying to choose between contrasting brothers, Humphrey Bogart and William Holden in *Sabrina* (1954) or painfully smitten by middle-aged playboy Gary Cooper in *Love in the Afternoon* (1957); Marilyn Monroe innocently saving Tom Ewell from adultery in *Seven Year Itch* (1955) and poignantly telling Tony Curtis in drag how much she loves the Cary Grant-like millionaire (Tony Curtis in mufti) in *Some Like It Hot* (1959); and Shirley MacLaine rescued from suicide by nebbish Jack Lemmon in *The Apartment*. Being a romantic, a certain bitterness comes from the disappointment that life is not perfect, love is thwarted, people can be avaricious and cruel and that the world might not be improving. *Sunset Boulevard* (1950) is the glorious swan song of silent screen star, Norma Desmond (Gloria Swanson) dementedly thinking she is making a comeback. 'I'm still big, it's the pictures that got small.' *Fedora* (1978) is *Sunset Boulevard* revisited twenty years on, in which a Garboesque star remains mysteriously unchanged by the passing years in her meeting with the ageing William Holden, a survivor from the earlier film. Both films reflect a changing Hollywood and Wilder, who has suffered from the change, remains to record it. However, he has never been enclosed in the movie world. *A Foreign Affair* (1948) is set in a Berlin ravaged by war, *Stalag 17* (1953) in a p.o.w. camp, *One, Two, Three* (1961) returns to a Berlin divided by the wall. These sombre backgrounds give body to the astringent comedies played out in front of them. *Double Indemnity*, based on James M. Cain's novel, is written with acid humour, but is about murder and greed, and *Lost Weekend* (1945) is one of the first films to deal seriously with alcoholism. The films are compassionate, polished and, above all, extremely funny. Ginger Rogers pretending to be a twelve-year-old in *The Major and the Minor* (1942), Curtis and Lemmon as musicians in an all-girl band in *Some Like It Hot*, a highpoint in American post-war comedy, James Cagney's non-stop verbal machine-gun tour de force in *One, Two, Three* and other scenes too humorous to mention. There have been lapses and a falling off in films like *Irma La Douce* (1963) and *Buddy Buddy* (1981), but then 'Nobody's perfect'. **Also:** *Five Graves to Cairo* (43), *Witness for the Prosecution* (57), *The*

Private Life of Sherlock Holmes (69), *Avanti* (72), *Front Page* (74).

WILDER Gene

American. Born 1934. Real name Jerry Silberman. Curly-headed comic who has made hysteria hysterical. Both *The Adventures of Sherlock Holmes' Smarter Brother* (1975) and *The World's Greatest Lover* (1977) are school of Mel BROOKS, but they have a quirky humour all their own and are stylishly made, although they go too often for the cheap laugh.

WINNER Michael

British. Born 1935. Worked for the BBC. Made independent shorts. From 1957 to 1969 made instantly forgettable British family films, many of them starring brutish Oliver Reed. In America, he makes immediately detestable movies, many of them starring brutish Charles Bronson. **Titles:** *The Jokers* (66), *I'll Never Forget What's 's Name* (67), *Hannibal Brooks* (69), *The Games* (69), *Lawman* (70), *The Nightcomers* (71), *Chato's Land* (72), *Scorpio* (72), *The Stone Killer* (73), *Death Wish* (74), *The Big Sleep* (78), *Firepower* (79), *Death Wish II* (81), *The Wicked Lady* (82).

WISE Robert

American. Born 1914. Entered films as editor in 1933. Editor (with Mark ROBSON) on WELLES' *Citizen Kane* (1941) and *The Magnificent Ambersons* (1942). Like Robson, he started directing chillers for Val Lewton; the dreamlike *The Curse of the Cat People* (1944) and *The Body Snatcher* (1945) with Boris Karloff and Bela Lugosi. Without any consistency or imposing any discernible personality on his films, he continued to leap from genre to genre, from style to style, in a workmanlike manner. There is gritty realism in *The Set-Up* (1949), a downbeat boxing drama with a compelling, tragic performance from Robert Ryan, *I Want to Live* (1958) with Susan Hayward as the girl framed for murder who goes to the gas chamber, and *Odds Against Tomorrow* (1959), an over-emphatic heist movie shot in New York (therefore considered more realistic than films shot elsewhere). New York's Lower East Side is a studio set in *Somebody Up There Likes Me* (1956), almost a direct riposte to *The Set-Up*, celebrating professional boxing as part of the American Dream. *West Side Story* (1961) is an awkward mixture of realism, social comment, opera, ballet and show biz. The magnificent use of the unpolluted scenery around Saltzburg and Julie Andrews' hygienic performance innocuously helped to make *The Sound of Music* (1965) a chocolate box-office hit. After tripping lightly over the hills, Miss Andrews and Robert Wise fell flat on their faces with *Star!* (1968). From this old-hat biopic of Gertie Lawrence, he moved Wisely into the safer profits of sci-fi (*The Andromeda Strain* – 1971, *Star Trek* – 1979), disaster movie (*The Hindenburg* – 1975) and the occult (*Audrey Rose* – 1977). **Also:** *The Day the Earth Stood Still* (51), *Destination Gobi* (53), *The Desert Rats* (53), *So Big* (53), *Executive Suite* (54), *Helen of Troy* (55), *Tribute to a Bad Man* (56), *Until They Sail* (57), *Run Silent, Run Deep* (58), *Two for the Seasaw* (62), *The Haunting* (63), *The Sand Pebbles* (66).

WISEMAN Frederick
American. Born 1930. Trained as a lawyer. A leading exponent of Direct Cinema. Most of his documentaries are made for National Educational Television (NET). His method is to enter various institutions with his hand-held camera and shoot a vast amount of footage over a long period. He then edits it dispassionately, being careful not to give special weight to any particular scene in case it makes a subjective point. The films are shown without narration or music. The results are often fascinating eavesdroppings on institutions such as a mental home (*Titicut Follies* – 1967), *High School* (1968), *Hospital* (1970), the Army (*Basic Training* 1971), *Juvenile Court* (1973), *Welfare* (1975) and *Model* (1981), but which cry out for some editorial comment. **Also:** *Law and Order* (69), *Essene* (72), *Primate* (74), *Meat* (76), *Canal Zone* (77), *Sinai Fields Mission* (78).

WOOD Edward D.
American. 1924-1978. Has a cult following as the worst director of all time. So cheap are his films, he was known to smuggle a tape-recorder into screenings of other films to get his musical tracks. The spaceships in *Plan 9 from Outer Space* (1958) are represented by spinning hubcaps and paper plates. *Glen or Glenda* (1953) is a hilariously well-meaning film on transvestism presented as an educational documentary but interrupted, from time to time, by a ranting and raving Bela Lugosi. The theme was

particularly close to the director's heart as he himself was a transvestite who, as a soldier attacking Iwo Jima, wore a bra and women's underwear under his uniform. **Also:** *Jail Bait* (54), *Bride of the Monster* (55), *Revenge of the Dead* (59), *The Sinister Urge* (61), *Take it out in Trade* (70).

WOOD Sam
American. 1883-1949. Assistant to Cecil B. DE MILLE at Paramount. Directed over eighty movies from 1919 up to his death. His first films are fairly run-of-De-Mille, but he came into his own at MGM in the 30's. He injected an element of sentimentality into the Marx Brothers first two pictures for MGM, *A Night at the Opera* (1935) and *A Day at the Races* (1937), but they are full of hilarious set-pieces such as the famous ship's cabin scene in the former. His best film at MGM was the pedantophiliac weepie, *Goodbye Mr Chips* (1939), due mainly to Robert Donat's chalky school-masterly performance. His heavy, sticky-palmed hand is felt in *Our Town* (1940), the essential theatricality of Thornton Wilder's play hardly translating to the screen, *Kitty Foyle* (1940), obtaining an Oscar-winning performance from Ginger Rogers, and *King's Row* (1942), a sub-SIRKian melo starring an utterly inadequate Robert Cummings with Ronald Reagan in his second greatest role waking up after having his legs amputated and asking, 'Where's the rest of me?' The rest of Sam Wood's work consisted mainly of four movies with Gary Cooper: the baseball hagiopic on Lou Gehrig, *The Pride of the Yankees* (1942), *For Whom the Bell Tolls* (1943) a Wooden version of Hemingway, *Casanova Brown* (1944) a mouse of a comedy, and *Saratoga Trunk* (1946) a sluggish Edna Ferber adaptation. **Also:** *Raffles* (40), *The Devil and Miss Jones* (41), *Ivy* (47), *The Stratton Story* (49).

WYLER William
American. 1902-1981. Born in Alsace, then part of Germany. Studied in Switzerland and Paris. Went to New York as publicist for Universal Pictures at the age of eighteen. In Hollywood, he worked his way up from prop boy to director of dozens of short Westerns, each made in a few days. He soon graduated to more prestigious projects. From 1936 onwards, he made sturdy, tasteful,

smooth, respectable, quality entertainments that generally won Oscars. The days of his quickies were over and he worked painstakingly, earning the sobriquet of 'Ninety-Nine Take Wyler'. His reputation dates from his first encounter with cameraman Gregg Toland on *These Three* (1936), his first version of Lillian Hellman's 'The Children's Hour', less lesbianism. Toland's camerawork, especially his deep-focus photography, gave Wyler's films a definition they might not have had. Producer Sam Goldwyn also helped him to do his best work on *Dodsworth* (1936), an expert Sinclair Lewis adaptation with Walter Huston and *Wuthering Heights* (1939), written by acid humorists Ben Hecht and Charles MacArthur on a train journey, shot in a studio and starring Laurence OLIVIER and Merle Oberon, a good enough melodrama, but why the title? Other Goldwyn productions were *Dead End* (1937), a stagey social drama about crime in the slums of New York which introduced the Dead End Kids to the screen, *The Little Foxes* (1941), the lush Hellman drama with Bette Davis at her bitchy best and a fine supporting cast (he also directed Davis excellently in *Jezabel* – 1938 and *The Letter* – 1940) and, above all, *The Best Years of Our Lives* (1946), *the* returning veterans movie which was to inspire *The Deer Hunter* thirty-two years later. Its schematic, didactic plot follows the lives of three soldiers (Fredric March, Dana Andrews, Harold Russell) on their return to civilian life, each representing a different armed service and social class. Particularly memorable among a superb cast is Harold Russell who had lost both his hands in the war and used hooks with great dexterity. Wyler's meticulous style filled the canvases of *Friendly Persuasion* (1956), a gentle tale of a Quaker family forced to take up arms in the Civil War, *The Big Country* (1958), a vast anti-Western and *Ben Hur* (1959), the main credit of which should go to second-unit directors Andrew Marton and Yakima Canutt who staged the rousing (from sleep) sea–battle and chariot race. **Also:** *The Good Fairy* (35), *The Westerner* (40), *Mrs. Miniver* (42), *The Heiress* (49), *Detective Story* (51), *Carrie* (52), *Roman Holiday* (53), *The Desperate Hours* (55), *The Children's Hour* (62. *The Loudest Whisper* – GB), *The Collector* (65), *How to Steal a Million* (66), *Funny Girl* (68), *The Liberation of L.B. Jones* (70).

YATES Peter

British. Born 1929. Former motor–racing driver. Stage director and film-editor before directing his first film, *Summer Holiday* (1962), a clean-cut popsicle of a youth musical. After making *Robbery* (1967), a competently realized drama on the famous Great Train Robbery of 1963, he went to Hollywood to make *Bullitt* (1968), the one with the car chase to end all car chases. It didn't, it only began a spate of them. Other movies on wheels are *The Hot Rock* (1972), *Mother Jugs and Speed* (1976), two forced comedies, and *Breaking Away* (1979), an amusing and ingratiating comedy centred around a nineteen-year-old cyclist who creates an Italian persona as an escape from the small American town that inhibits him. The final bike race, however, is corny Disney fantasy. Away from cars, bikes and heists, Yates shows an adult side to his nature in two thrillers, *The Friends of Eddie Coyle* (1973), an intriguing cops and cons yarn with Robert Mitchum at his most seedy, and *The Janitor* (1981) an above-average HITCHCOCKian homage. Like Hitchcock, Yates has a fine sense of place as in the San Francisco of *Bullitt*, Bloomington, Indiana in *Breaking Away* or Boston, Mass. in *Eddie Coyle*. **Also:** *One Way Pendulum* (64), *John and Mary* (69), *Murphy's War* (71), *For Pete's Sake* (74), *The Deep* (77).

YORKIN Bud

American. Born 1926. TV director formerly an associate of producer-screenwriter, Norman Lear. Made two uncouth sitcoms, *Come Blow Your Horn* (1963) from Neil Simon's first hit play, and *Never Too Late* (1965) about a senior citizen couple who disover they are going to have a baby. Laughs, it isn't! *Divorce American Style* (1967) is a mild middle-class satire with a good cast;

Inspector Clouseau (1968), a clumsy Clouseauesque attempt to put Alan Arkin in Peter Sellers' boots, *Start the Revolution Without Me* (1969) is a good running joke that runs out and *The Thief Who Came to Dinner* (1973) is about . . . Who remembers?

YOUNG Terence

British. Born 1915. Screenwriter in the early 40's. From 1948, he made routine adventure yarns with bold men and pulchritudinous women which led up naturally to the first James Bond movie, *Dr. No* (1962) which set the flamboyant, tongue-in-the-cheek style for the seemingly endless series. He followed it with two other Sean Connery-Bonds, *From Russia with Love* (1963) and *Thunderball* (1965) before gadgetry took them over. **Also:** *That Lady* (55), *Storm over the Nile* (55), *Safari* (56), *Zarack* (56), *Action of the Tiger* (57), *Too Hot to Handle* (60), *The Amorous Adventures of Moll Flanders* (65), *Triple Cross* (66), *Wait Until Dark* (67), *Mayerling* (69), *Red Sun* (71), *The Valachi Papers* (72), *The Klansman* (74), *Bloodline* (79).

ZANUSSI Krzysztof

Polish. Born 1939. Studied physics and philosophy. Many of his ironic and forthright comedies take place in the scientific and/or academic community from which he makes wider philosophical and political statements. He has moved from his rather dry, polemical early films into becoming a brilliant stylist and a mordant commentator on Polish life. *Camouflage* (1977) is set at a summer camp for scientists but is really about more general bureaucratic pettiness and the crushing of idealism, *The Contract* (1980) is the marriage contract drawn up for the sake of the 'advancement' of a young couple and in *The Constant Factor* (1981), told in a brisk cutting style a young mountaineer refuses to collaborate

with the corrupt system and ends up as a window cleaner. **Also:** *The Structure of Crystals* (69), *Family Life* (71), *Behind the Wall* (71), *Illuminations* (73).

ZEFFIRELLI Franco

Italian. Born 1923. Studied architecture in Florence. Former stage actor and designer. Principally a director of opulently-mounted plays and operas around the world. His first two films are bustling, energetic, and colourful Shakespeare adaptations, *The Taming of the Shrew* (1967) with Taylor and Burton duelling raucously, and the touching youthfulness about the playing of *Romeo and Juliet* (1968), although the couple are inadequate in the tragic scenes. The rest of his work is 'kinda lousy' as Shakespeare might say. The flower-child rompings of *Brother Sun, Sister Moon* (1973), golden-haired gap-toothed moppet turning on the waterworks every minute in *The Champ* (1979), and the teen-girl mag adolescent couple feeling *Endless Love* (1981), are all bathed in yucky, romantic pretty-pretty photography.

ZETTERLING Mai

Swedish. Born 1925. Actress who made her name in Alf SJOBERG's *Frenzy* (1944) and had a mediocre film career. Directed documentaries for the BBC. Her first two features, *Loving Couples* (1964) and *Night Games* (1966) are wickedly sensuous Strindbergian dramas, handled with maturity and a sharp eye for decadent details. *The Girls* (1968) is a passionate, intelligent, contrived feminist morality tale about three actresses analysing their attitudes to 'Lysistrata'. **Also:** *Dokter Glas* (67), *Scrubbers* (82).

ZINNEMANN Fred

American. Born 1907 in Vienna. Studied music and law. Joined MGM in 1937 as a documentary film-maker. His best features are sincere, humanist, naturalistic, economical, black-and-white movies concerned with social problems. He is particularly sensitive to actors and Marlon BRANDO, Montgomery Clift, Pier Angeli, John Ericson, Rod Steiger, Julie Harris, Brandon de Wilde and Shirley Jones all made their screen debut's in a Zinnemann film. The aftermath of war is a central theme in four of his early movies. In an ingenious and taut thriller, *Act of Violence* (1948) sinister Robert Ryan tracks down respectable Van Heflin,

Gary Cooper and Grace Kelly as his bride in Zinnemann's *High Noon* (1952).

Germany, *A Man for All Seasons* (1967), however, is a handsomely mounted, well-acted historical drama that improves upon the play. **Also:** *Kid Glove Killer* (42), *The Seventh Cross* (44), *Little Mr. Jim* (46), *My Brother Talks to Horses* (46).

although Heflin turns out to be an ex-Nazi. Only the hard-boiled would find their eyes unmoist during *The Search* (1948) with Monty Clift (debut) as a G.I. caring for a war orphan in post-war Berlin; *The Men* (1950) with Marlon Brando's (debut) moving portrait of a paralysed war vet; and *Teresa* (1951) about a G.I. (John Ericson – debut) returning to New York with his Italian bride (Pier Angeli – debut). Steiger (debut) plays a sympathetic shrink. *High Noon* (1952) is the high-water mark of his career. 'Do not forsake me, oh my darling,' sings Tex Ritter as Gary Cooper, the town marshal faces a group of gunmen alone on his wedding day. The pulsating action takes place during the one-and-a-half hours running time of the film, and despite the intended analogy with McCarthyism, it is the classic (and much imitated) tale of the loner doing 'what a man has to do'. *A Member of the Wedding* (1953) is an excellent transposition (despite an unsuccessful 'opening out' section) of Carson McCullers' play about growing pains,

a rare case of using all the actors from the original stage production, including Julie Harris (debut), Brandon de Wilde (debut) and Ethel Waters. *From Here to Eternity* (1953), a low-key, forceful (for the 50's) film on the last day before Pearl Harbour, changed the images of Frank Sinatra (rescued from the doldrums) and Deborah Kerr (rescued from gentility). Apart from *Hatful of Rain* (1957), an over-fraught tale of a junkie, it was the last, small-scale, realist drama he made. With Zinnemann, it was the bigger, the worse. The Todd-A-*Oklahoma!* (1955) exposed 'the corn as high as an elephant's eye', but again his casting against type (Gloria Graham) triumphed. *The Nun's Story* (1959) treads too gently for too long, *The Sundowners* (1960) is too interested in the location photography in Australia, *The Day of the Jackal* (1973) is a slick, well-paced, international commercial product and *Julia* (1977) is a discursive, unconvincing (based on a Lillian Hellman memoir) mood piece which only comes alive in the central section in

160